INTERNATIONAL INVESTMENTS

Second Edition

Bruno Solnik

Hautes Études Commerciales—Institut Supérieur des Affaires

ADDISON-WESLEY PUBLISHING COMPANY

Reading, Massachusetts □ Menlo Park, California □ New York
Don Mills, Ontario □ Wokingham, England □ Amsterdam □ Bonn
Sydney □ Singapore □ Tokyo □ Madrid □ San Juan

Sponsoring Editor: Barbara Rifkind
Production Supervisor: Peggy J. Flanagan
Production Services: Ann Kilbride
Cover Designer: Jean Seal
Copy Editor: Carmen Wheatcroft
Manufacturing Supervisor: Roy Logan

ISBN 0-201-50778-1
1 2 3 4 5 6 7 8 9 0-MA-95949392

Preface

Back in 1974, I published an article in the *Financial Analysts Journal* entitled "Why not diversify internationally rather than domestically?" At the time, U.S. pension funds had never invested outside of the United States. The situation was not very different in most countries outside of the United States in which international investment by pension funds and other institutional investors was legally prohibited or regarded as exotic. Although European banks and private investors have long been international investors by cultural heritage as well as necessity (given the small size of each country), pension funds guidelines often limited or prohibited international investments. Because pension plans are large and sophisticated investors, their absence on the international scene was significant. Back in 1974, the world stock market capitalization stood below $1 trillion and the U.S. market share was close to 60%.

Since the publication of the first edition, the world stock market capitalization passed the $9 trillion mark and the U.S. stock market share has dropped to 30%. It is now common to see U.S. pension funds with 10 or 15% of their assets invested internationally. The value of foreign assets held by U.S. pension funds has been multiplied by a factor of one hundred in the past ten years to reach more than $70 billion by the end of 1989. A similar trend toward international investing can be seen in all countries and, notably, Japan and Europe. For example, ABP, the pension fund of Dutch civil servants and one of the largest in the world with total assets of more than $70 billion, decided in 1989 to move from a purely domestic strategy to invest 5% of its assets abroad.

The rapid pace of international investing is due to a change in mentality based on many factors. First, the benefits of international diversification in terms of risk and return have progressively been recognized; they are detailed in this book. This has led to a push toward guidelines and legislation more favorable to foreign investments. For example, many U.S. public pension funds have obtained, or tried to obtain, a modification of their investment constraints.

A second factor is the deregulation and internationalization of financial markets throughout the world. This integration of financial markets leads to reduced costs, easier access to information, and the development of a worldwide expertise by major financial institutions. In 1986 foreign organizations and banks were allowed to become members of the Tokyo and London stock exchanges. A similar step was taken in France in 1988 and in Spain in 1989. Computerized quotation and trading systems have been developed that will allow global round-the-world and round-the-clock trading. At the end of 1989, restrictions to capital flows had been removed within the countries of the European Community (EC); European-based investment management firms can freely market their products to residents of any EC member state. A complete integration of the European financial market is expected to take place by 1992. This total freedom of capital movement has shocked countries such as France, which is used to extensive capital and currency controls as well as fiscal inquisition. This internationalization of investment management has led to increased competition among money managers of all nationalities as well as a wave of alliances, mergers, and acquisition among financial institutions in order to extend their international management expertise and the geographic coverage of their client base. The trend is most visible in Europe, where banks and insurance companies have acquired brokers (at home or abroad) and engaged in alliances and takeover to access the global European market. It is also visible in the United States and Japan. For example, Sumitomo took a participation in Goldman Sachs. Wells Fargo and Nikko Securities, two leading money managers in the United States and Japan, merged their pension fund management activities in a joint company that manages over $130 billion of assets.

When I wrote the first edition of this book, I noted that international investment is not an easy achievement. In writing the second edition, given the events I've just described, international investment in the 1990's will be no easier. It requires a familiarity with foreign cultures, financial instruments, and markets. Financial traditions vary across the world and strongly influence the organization and functioning of markets. A global investor must obtain information from different sources and be able to interpret it. Regulations, dealing practices, taxes, and costs complicate the investment process. The multi-currency dimension must be dealt with. All these aspects must be taken into account in structuring an international investment approach. The purpose of this book is to provide concepts, techniques, and institutional information to assist the reader in this task.

Chapter 1 presents the international environment. It provides both a theoretical and an empirical analysis of the basic economic aspects of the international capital market. Chapter 2 presents the case for international investment, its pros and cons. The next nine chapters review the major investment vehicles, the instruments, the markets, as well as the concepts and the techniques used to analyze those investments. Chapter 3 deals with foreign exchange and its related markets; it focuses on exchange rate determination.

Chapter 4 describes the stock markets in the world, whereas Chapter 5 studies the concepts and techniques used in international equity investment and focuses on asset pricing in an efficient international market. In turn, Chapter 6 describes the world bond market, whereas Chapter 7 studies the concepts and techniques used in international bond portfolio management. Speculative investments such as futures and options are described in Chapters 8 and 9, which stress their use in global portfolio management. The specific issue of currency risk management is discussed in Chapter 10. A Frenchman could not avoid spending a chapter on gold: Chapter 11 studies real assets such as gold and all the various investments that are linked to gold. Chapter 12, the final chapter, is devoted to the practical implementation of a global investment strategy. It attempts to incorporate the various concepts introduced earlier into an integrated approach from conception to performance measurement.

A basic investment course is a useful prerequisite to this text. Some knowledge of international economics may also be of help in the early chapters. Some familiarity with discounting techniques and basic statistics (e.g., standard deviation, correlation) will make some of the chapters easier to read. However, this book is intended to be accessible to students and portfolio managers without recent training in portfolio theory. Concepts and theories are presented with a focus on their practical relevance rather than on their mathematical formulation. The more advanced sections are put in appendixes.

This book is the result of fifteen years of teaching international investment to students and executives on four continents. My interest in this topic started with my doctoral dissertation at the Massachusetts Institute of Technology, and I am grateful to my former teachers R. Merton, F. Modigliani, S. Myers, G. Pogue, and M. Scholes. I also owe a special debt to many colleagues at universities where I taught international investment: Stanford, Berkeley, École Polytechnique, Université de Genève, and Centre HEC-ISA (CESA) (recently renamed Group HEC). In times when international diversification was often regarded as an exotic idea, several organizations have supported me in spreading the *bonne parole*. Special thanks are due to N. de Rothschild (Banque Rothschild), D. Nichol (Ivory Sime), J. Twardowski (Frank Russell and Q Group), G. Stevenin (Rondeleux Oudart), K. Mathysen Gerst and P. Keller (Lombard Odier), H. P. Baljet (Lombard Odier-Kempen), F. Grauer (Wells Fargo), C. Nowakowski (Intersec), J. D. Nelson, L. R. Golz and D. Umstead (State Street Bank), F. s'Jacob and R. Van Maasdyck (LOIPM), and S. Fukabori (Kokusai). Few people have done more for the promotion of international investment than R. and S. Toigo, whose Institute for Fiduciary Education (IFE) organized numerous seminars on this issue throughout the world.

From my association with Lombard Odier, I discovered that no theory could ever reflect the complexity of international finance, but also that many ideas and techniques presented in this book could provide valuable assistance to investment management. Thierry Lombard provided constant stimulation for this book, and Patrick Odier contributed so much that he came close to becoming a coauthor.

R. Samuelson provided magnificent editing assistance equaled only by the typing work of G. Yonner and her staff.

My final words are for my wife, Catherine, who suffered through my sixth book (four in French and two in English). She has now enjoyed all the exciting aspects of the leading financial cities of the world and the top ten hotels of *Institutional Investor*'s list, with the exception of those located in Paris. She also shared numerous sleepless, interminable airplane hauls and middle-of-the-night phone calls from Hong Kong, Tokyo, or San Francisco. Let this book add to the long list of pleasures and suffering we happily share.

Paris   Bruno Solnik

Contents

3

Foreign Exchange   70

4

Equity: Markets and Instruments   99

5

Equity: Concepts and Techniques   125

6

7

8

12
Strategy, Organization, and Control   352

1

The Economics of the International Environment

International investment is rapidly growing throughout the world. U.S. investors are attracted by its risk diversification benefits as well as the better performance provided lately by many non-U.S. markets. As can be seen in Chapter 2, the performance of the U.S. stock market has been well below that of foreign stock markets for the past ten, twenty, or thirty years. The same applies to bond markets. For example, the U.S. stock market registered an average annual return of 9.9%, including the dividend yield, from 1970 to 1988. Over the same period, the Morgan Stanley Capital International EAFE index, which is a market-capitalization-weighted index of non-American stock indexes, had an average annual dollar return of 18.2%. This means that a typical U.S. portfolio yielded a total return of 445% from 1970 to the end of 1988. Over the same period a well-diversified non-American portfolio had a total return of 1,911%, a German stock portfolio had a total return of 1,407%, and a Japanese stock portfolio had a total return of 6,329%, all in U.S. dollar terms. Some emerging markets such as Hong Kong had an even higher performance.

International investment is not an easy achievement. Investing abroad may come as a cultural shock: There are marked differences in institutions, sources of information, trading procedures, reporting, and many financial traditions that often find their roots in the national cultures of each country. One of the objectives of this book is to make the reader sufficiently familiar with foreign markets and procedures. However, other impediments to international investment exist besides the technical and cultural knowledge required. These constraints are discussed in Chapter 2 and are detailed throughout the book; they include psychological barriers, legal restrictions, transaction costs, discriminatory taxation, political risks, exchange risks, etc. The existence of different numeraires throughout the world is the major constraint. Prices of foreign assets must be converted into the home currency using exchange rates.

Exchange rate uncertainty adds an important dimension to the economics of capital markets. Returns on foreign investments are directly affected by currency movements because they must be translated from foreign to domestic currencies. They are also indirectly influenced by the reaction of asset prices to exchange rate adjustments. Indeed, asset prices, interest rates, and foreign-exchange rates are interrelated in a complex manner.

The purpose of this chapter is to present the various building blocks of the international market structure. The first section reviews basic economic parity relations linking monetary variables such as foreign-exchange, interest, and inflation rates. This set of parity relations provides a most useful framework for investment analysis. The second section addresses the influence of monetary variables on equity and bond prices. The final section is devoted to asset pricing in international capital markets.

While theory is not the major objective of this book, a minimal familiarity with the major conceptual issues is required before getting to the practical aspects of international investment. It helps to understand how to structure investment analysis and management in the complex international setting. This global view of the investment structure is a prerequisite to the detailed study of the various investment vehicles presented later, and their integration in a disciplined and consistent international investment process.

INTERNATIONAL PARITY RELATIONS: INFLATION RATES, INTEREST RATES, AND EXCHANGE RATES

Short-term fluctuations in exchange rates seem to be generated by a large variety of economic events. Before presenting some of the basic models of exchange rate determination in Chapter 3 it may be useful to recall the well-known international parity conditions linking domestic and foreign monetary variables: inflation rates, interest rates, and foreign-exchange rates. These relations are the basis for a simple model of the international monetary environment, which is quite useful for analyzing the relationships among the various domestic and foreign monetary variables and their influences on asset prices. After presenting the model we shall discuss the empirical validity of the various building blocks, which rely on some key assumptions such as perfect trade and perfect certainty.

The variables that appear below are

The spot exchange rate, S. This is the rate of exchange of two currencies. It tells us the amount of foreign currency that one unit of domestic currency can buy. *Spot* means that we refer to the exchange rate for immediate delivery. For example, the French franc/U.S. dollar spot exchange rate might be $S = 8.00$ indicating that one U.S. dollar is worth eight French francs.

The forward exchange rate, F. This is the rate of exchange of two currencies set on one date for delivery at a future specified date. For example, the French franc/U.S. dollar forward exchange rate for delivery in one year is 8.2909 French francs per U.S. dollar. Spot and forward exchange markets are described in Chapter 3.

The interest rate, r. This is the rate of interest for a given time period. Interest rates are a function of the length of the time period and the denomination of the currency. Interest rates are usually quoted in the marketplace as an annualized rate. For example, the one year rate on U.S. Treasury bills might be $r_\$ = 10\%$ while the one year rate on French franc bills might be $r_{FF} = 14\%$. In this case the *interest rate differential* is equal to 4% ($r_{FF} - r_\$ = 4\%$).

The inflation rate, I. This is equal to the rate of consumer price increase over the period specified. The *inflation differential* is equal to the difference of inflation rates between two countries. For example, if the inflation in France is $I_{FF} = 12.87\%$, while it is $I_\$ = 8.91\%$ in the United States, then the inflation differential over the period is approximately 4%.

The theoretical parity relations of international finance[1] are

1. The *purchasing power parity* relation linking spot exchange rates and inflation.
2. The *international Fisher* relation linking interest rates and inflation.
3. The *foreign exchange expectation* relation linking forward exchange rates and expected spot exchange rates.
4. The *interest rate parity* relation linking spot exchange rates, forward exchange rates, and interest rates.

The Theory

Purchasing power parity

Purchasing power parity[2] (PPP) is a well-known relation in international finance. It states that spot exchange rates adjust perfectly to inflation differentials. If goods prices rise in one country relative to another, then the country's exchange rate must depreciate to maintain a similar real price for the goods in the two countries. This argument is obvious for internationally traded goods with no trade restrictions. Let's consider the following scenario: The French franc price of wheat rises by 12.87%, the French inflation rate, while the U.S. dollar price of wheat rises only by 8.91%, the U.S. inflation rate. If the French franc depreciation does not offset this 4% inflation differential, it will make French wheat less competitive in the international market and induce trade flows from the United States to France to take advantage of the price differential. If trade could take place instantaneously, at no cost, and with no impediments, one would expect the exchange rate to exactly offset any inflation differential. The purchasing power parity relation might be written as follows:

$$\frac{S^1}{S^0} = \frac{1 + I_F}{1 + I_D} \qquad (1.1)$$

where S^0 is the spot exchange rate at the start of the period (the foreign price of one unit of the domestic currency),

S^1 is the spot exchange rate at the end of the period,

I_F is the inflation rate, over the period, in the foreign country, e.g., France, and

I_D is the inflation rate, over the period, in the domestic country, e.g., the United States.

Using the figures given previously for our French/American illustration the end-of-period spot exchange rate should be equal to S^1, such that

$$\frac{S^1}{8.00} = \frac{1.1287}{1.0891} \text{ and}$$

$$S^1 = 8.00 \frac{1.1287}{1.0891} = 8.2909.$$

The purchasing power parity relation is often presented as the linear approximation stating that the exchange rate variation is equal to the inflation rate differential:

$$\frac{S^1}{S^0} - 1 = \frac{S^1 - S^0}{S^0} \simeq I_F - I_D.$$

This is only a first order approximation of the exact relation (Eq. 1.1). This purchasing power parity relation is of major importance in international port-folio management. If it holds, purchasing power parity (PPP) implies that the real return on an asset is identical for investors from any country. For example, consider an Italian asset with an annual rate of return equal to 20% in lira. Assume that the inflation rate is 10% in Italy, 2% in the USA and that purchasing power parity is verified so that the lira depreciated against the U.S. dollar by about 8%. With the linear approximation, the dollar rate of return on this Italian asset is roughly 12% (20% − 8% of lira depreciation). The real rate of return is approximately 10% for an Italian investor (20% − 10% of Italian inflation) as well as for an American investor (12% − 2% of U.S. inflation). Since investors should care about real returns, they all agree, whatever their national-ity, on the return and risk of a specific asset. Exchange rate movements have no influence since they only mirror inflation differentials and equalize real returns across countries.

International Fisher relation

A traditional domestic approach is to define a nominal interest rate, r, as the sum (or, rather, compounding) of the real interest rate, p, and expected inflation over the life of a bill, $E(I)$:

$$(1 + r) = (1 + p)(1 + E(I)). \tag{1.2}$$

The nominal interest rate is observed in the marketplace and is usually referred to as the interest rate, while the real interest rate is calculated from the observed interest rate and the forecasted inflation.

For example, let's suppose a nominal U.S. interest rate of 10% and an expected inflation rate of 8.91%. The real interest rate is then equal to 1% since:

$$1 + 0.10 = (1 + 0.01)(1 + 0.0891).$$

This relation is often presented using the linear approximation[3] stating that the interest rate is equal to a real interest rate plus expected inflation:

$$r \simeq p + E(I).$$

The economic theory proposed by Fisher (1930) is that fluctuations in interest rates are caused by revisions in inflationary expectations, since real interest rates are very stable over time.

Keynesians[4] provide a different explanation for fluctuations in nominal short-term interest rates. They claim that monetary shocks leave short-term inflation unaffected because of sticky goods prices, while real rates react immediately to liquidity conditions. For example, a sudden contraction in the money supply growth rate leads to an immediate increase of nominal interest rates: the real interest rate goes up because money becomes rare and expensive while short-term inflationary expectations are unchanged. Those expectations adjust only gradually to the slowdown in money supply growth.

The international counterpart of Eq. (1.2) is that the interest rate differential between two countries is linked to the difference in real interest rates and expected inflation:

$$\frac{1 + r_F}{1 + r_D} = \frac{1 + p_F}{1 + p_D} \times \frac{1 + E(I_F)}{1 + E(I_D)} \tag{1.3}$$

or the first-order linear approximation:

$$r_F - r_D \simeq p_F - p_D + E(I_F) - E(I_D).$$

The interest rate differential is the linear approximation of

$$\frac{r_F - r_D}{1 + r_D}.$$

The approximation will be poor for high levels of interest rates.

If real rates are equal in two countries, differences in nominal interest rates are caused by different inflationary expectations. This relation is often referred to as the international Fisher relation.

Note that our French/American illustration verifies the international Fisher relation if we expect a continuation of inflation at the same levels. The real rates are identical in the two countries and equal to 1%.

$$1 + r = (1 + p)(1 + E(I)).$$

In France

$$1 + 0.14 = (1 + 0.01)(1 + 0.1287)$$

and in the United States

$$1 + 0.10 = (1 + 0.01)(1 + 0.0891)$$

and

$$\frac{1 + r_{FF}}{1 + r_{\$}} = \frac{1 + 0.14}{1 + 0.10} = \frac{1 + E(I_F)}{1 + E(I_{\$})} = \frac{1 + 0.1287}{1 + 0.0891}.$$

This international Fisher relation has important implications for portfolio management. If real interest rates are stable and equal across countries as claimed by the relation, interest rate differentials across countries are basically caused by different expectations of national inflation rates. Differences in real interest rates would motivate capital flows between countries to take advantage of these differentials. The first two parity relations imply an equalization of real interest rates across countries.

Foreign exchange expectations

The foreign exchange expectation relation states that the forward exchange rate quoted at time zero for delivery at time one is equal to the expected value of the spot exchange rate at time one.

$$F = E(S^1). \tag{1.4}$$

This relation would certainly hold if the future values of exchange rates were known with certainty. If one were sure at time zero that the exchange rate would be worth S^1 at time one, then the current forward rate for delivery at time one would have to be S^1; otherwise a riskless arbitrage opportunity would exist.

Let's assume, for example, that we know for sure that the spot exchange rate will be 8.2909 FF/$ in a year, while the one-year forward rate is only 8 FF/$. One could then do the following arbitrage:

□ Buy dollars forward at eight francs per dollar and hold the contract until maturity.

□ At maturity simultaneously deliver the forward contract and take an offsetting position in the spot exchange rate market.

On the forward contract the arbitrager pays eight francs per dollar, but receives 8.2909 francs on the spot market leading to a profit of 0.2909 francs per dollar. If the expected spot exchange rate is certain, this is a riskless arbitrage that requires no invested capital on the forward commitment. Banks would keep doing this arbitrage until the buying pressure pushes the forward exchange rate to 8.2909 FF/$.

Of course this parity relation depends strongly on the certainty assumptions. However, it is sometimes claimed that the forward exchange rate should be an unbiased predictor of the future spot exchange rate in the presence of uncertainty, thereby leading to Eq. (1.4). Other researchers claim the existence of a risk premium appended to this relation.[5]

The foreign exchange expectation relation is often stated relative to the current spot exchange rate. If we subtract S^0 on both sides of Eq. (1.4) (remember that the current spot exchange rate is known with certainty) and divide by S^0, we get

$$\frac{F - S^0}{S^0} = E\left(\frac{S^1 - S^0}{S^0}\right).$$

The left-hand side is usually referred to as the forward discount or premium. It is the percentage deviation of the forward rate from the current spot rate. This relation states that the forward discount (or premium) is equal to the expected exchange rate movement and is equivalent to

$$\frac{F}{S_0} - 1 = \frac{E(S^1)}{S_0} - 1.$$

The practical relevance of this foreign exchange expectation relation is obvious. If verified, it means that there is, on the average, no reward for bearing foreign exchange uncertainty. If a risk premium were to be added to the relation, the symmetry of the exchange rate means that it will be paid by some investors (e.g., those selling forward Liras for dollars) and received by other investors (e.g., those buying forward Liras for dollars). A zero risk premium means that a forward hedge, i.e., the use of forward currency contracts to hedge the exchange risk of a portfolio of foreign assets, will be "costless" in terms of expected returns (except for commissions on the forward contracts).

Interest rate parity
The interest rate parity relation states that on free money markets, the interest rate differential must equal the forward discount or premium, i.e., the percentage difference between the forward exchange rate, F, and the spot exchange rate, S^0, both quoted at time zero. The exact mathematical relation is

$$\frac{F}{S^0} = \frac{1 + r_F}{1 + r_D}$$

(1.5)

or with the first-order linear approximation

$$\frac{F}{S^0} - 1 = \frac{F - S^0}{S^0} = \frac{r_{\text{F}} - r_{\text{D}}}{1 + r_{\text{D}}} \simeq r_{\text{F}} - r_{\text{D}}.$$

Again the linear approximation might be quite wrong when interest rates are high. This is not an economic theory, but a technical arbitrage condition that is demonstrated in Chapter 2. It must hold; otherwise, riskless arbitrage would take place to exploit this situation.

Note that this interest rate parity relation is verified in our simple example, where

$$\frac{F}{8.00} = \frac{1 + 0.14}{1 + 0.10}$$

and F is 8.2909 francs per dollar.

The four parity relations might be combined in several ways to link the four variables:

- The interest rate differential.
- The inflation differential.
- The forward discount or premium:

$$f = \left(\frac{F}{S^0} - 1 \right).$$

- The exchange rate movement:

$$s = \left(\frac{S^1}{S^0} - 1 \right).$$

For example, the interest rate parity relation combined with the foreign exchange expectation relation implies that the difference in interest rates is equal to the expected exchange rate movement.

The various parity relations are illustrated in Exhibit 1.1. They provide a very useful base to the relationship between exchange rates, inflation and interest rates. Using this simple framework as a starting point, an international investor can draw several practical implications:

- Interest rate differentials reflect expectations about currency movements. In other words, the expected return on default free bills should be equal across countries. This is true whether we measure return in a common currency or in real terms.
- Exchange risk reduces to inflation uncertainty. An investor caring about real returns would not be affected by exchange rate uncertainty.

EXHIBIT 1.1
International Parity Relations
Linear approximation

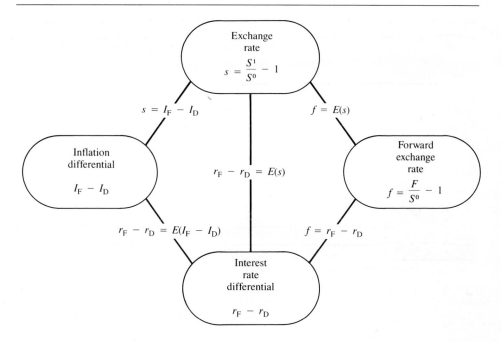

The Empirical Evidence

The economic theory presented above is a useful framework in which to analyze the international interplay of monetary variables. As a theory, it relies on restrictive assumptions about the perfection of trade and money markets. In the real world future inflation and exchange rates are uncertain, goods cannot be transferred instantaneously from one country to another, shipping costs are high, and import restrictions of various forms restrict international trade. While the stylized system of equilibrium presented above is a useful starting point for understanding the international financial environment, its empirical validity must be studied. The next step is to evaluate the extent to which each link holds true and examine the causes of deviation.

Purchasing power parity is a poor explanation for short-term exchange-rate movements. Regression of monthly or quarterly exchange-rate movements on inflation differentials yields a low explanatory power (R^2) for the recent period of floating exchange rates. Little exchange-rate volatility is explained by inflation. For example, Adler and Dumas found that inflation differentials explained less than 5% of monthly exchange rate movements in the 1970s. In other words 95% of currency movements were not caused by current inflation. Nonetheless, many believe that, while purchasing power parity may not hold for short periods (from one month to a year), it does hold over the long run. Unfortunately, it seems to take at least several years[6] before a deviation from purchasing power parity is corrected in the foreign exchange market. Several studies indicate that short-term movements in the real exchange rate, i.e., the exchange rate adjusted for the inflation differential, tend to follow a random pattern.[7]

why doesn't it hold true

There are several explanations for this phenomenon. First, the mere definition of an inflation rate is questionable. Investors throughout the world have different consumption preferences, and a common basket of consumption goods does not exist. In the short run, relative prices of different consumption goods vary extensively with specific influences on specific consumption baskets. As an illustration, the price of sake might double in Japan (thereby affecting the local price index), but the price rise should have little influence on the yen exchange rate, since few foreigners consume sake and it has little international trade. In the long run, consumption substitution will take place in Japan to reflect the higher price of sake and Japanese people may consume more beer or wine.

Second, transfer costs, import taxes and restrictions, as well as export subsidies, may prevent arbitrage in the goods markets to restore purchasing power parity. However, in the long run industries from countries with overvalued currencies will make direct investments in undervalued countries. For example, the U.S. dollar was vastly overvalued in terms of purchasing power parity in the early 1980s. This meant that the real price of U.S. goods was high compared to that of foreign countries. Because the U.S. dollar was strong, wages were lower in France than in the United States when converted into dollars. U.S. exports were not competitive because of their high prices, which were a result of the exchange rate; similarly, foreign imports to the U.S. were cheap. Because the situation persisted many U.S. companies built plants abroad to take advantage of this deviation from purchasing power parity. This behavior leads in time to a restoration of purchasing power parity.

Many factors other than inflation influence exchange rates. Because physical goods arbitrage is constrained, purchasing power parity plays only a small role in the short run, other variables have a major impact on the short-run behavior of exchange rates. The practical implications of these deviations from purchasing power parity are very important. The real return of one asset as measured by investors from different countries are different. For example, assume that the lira keeps a constant exchange rate with the dollar, despite the 8% inflation differential mentioned in the illustration above. Then the real return for an Italian investor is 10% while that of a U.S. investor is 18% (20% asset return in dollars minus 2% U.S. inflation rate). Furthermore, uncertainty about the real exchange rate adds uncertainty to the dollar return of a foreign investment.

The international Fisher relation is supported empirically when applied to the major currencies. Kane and Rosenthal studied the Eurocurrency market for six major currencies during the period from 1974 to 1979 and found support for

EXHIBIT 1.2
Real Interest Rates on Short-Term Instruments

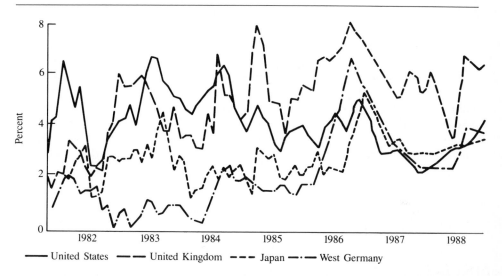

this model.[8] Studies on a more recent period (post-1979) seem to indicate that real interest rates are somewhat variable over time and differ across countries.[9] This is illustrated in Exhibit 1.2, which reproduces the real interest rate for three-month treasury bills or equivalent in four countries from 1982 to 1988. The calculation of a real interest rate is somewhat difficult, since it requires a measure of expected inflation. In Exhibit 1.2 expected inflation is simply replaced by the realized rate.

The foreign exchange expectation relation is usually tested by running a regression of the ex-post exchange rate movement on the interest rate differential at the start of the period. Exchange rate expectations are not directly observable, so the ex-post movements are used instead, assuming that the realized exchange rate movement is equal to its expectation plus a random unpredictable element. Again the explanatory power (R^2) is usually less than ten percent and often close to zero.

Two explanations have been advanced for this finding. First, exchange rates are so unpredictable that the statistical power of this test, using ex-post data for projections, is very poor. Second, Eq. (1.4) should include a risk-premium term because of the uncertainty in exchange rates, and risk premiums change over time. Some evidence of the existence of such a variable risk premium has been found.[10]

The current variability of exchange rates is very large compared to that of interest and inflation rates. So risk must be an important factor in the international Fisher and foreign exchange expectation relations. Any arbitrage strategy built to take advantage of real interest rate differentials or expected currency movements has a very uncertain outcome.

Without getting into sophisticated statistical methodologies, Exhibit 1.3 indicates the relationships between inflation rates, interest rates, and exchange rates from 1976 to 1988, when exchange rates were floating. Two pairs of countries and their exchange rates are analyzed: U.S. dollar/Japanese yen and deutsche mark/British pound. For each year, the figure indicates in percentages the inflation differential, the exchange rate movement, and the short-term interest rate differential. Differentials are calculated as the value for the first country minus that of the second one. For example, Exhibit 1.3 shows that in 1983 the United States had two percent more inflation than Japan and a higher short-term interest rate. The currency is calculated as the value of

EXHIBIT 1.3

Annual Comparison of Interest Rate Differentials, Inflation Differentials, and Exchange Rate Movements, 1976 to 1988

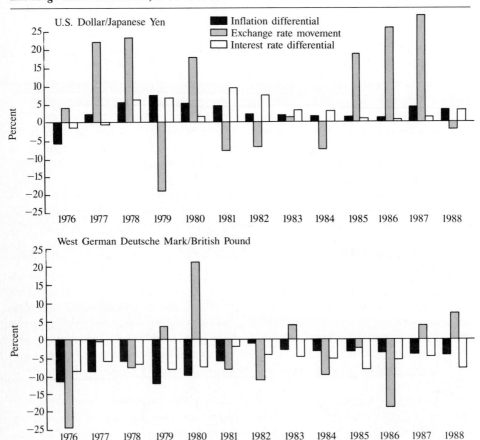

the second country's currency. For example, in Exhibit 1.3 we can track the
dollar value of the Japanese yen. In 1983 the yen appreciated by approximately
1.6% relative to the U.S. dollar. In theory, we would expect all three values to be
of the same sign and magnitude: For each year the three bars should be at the
same level, but they typically are not.

   While the interest rate and inflation differentials tend to be of the same
sign and magnitude, this is not the case for exchange rate movements. For many
years the exchange rate has moved in the opposite direction from interest
differentials (hence from the forward exchange rate discount, or premium.)
Note that this effect is not dollar-specific, since it also applies the deutsche
mark/pound exchange rate. For example Exhibit 1.3 shows that in 1985 the
dollar appreciated by more than twenty percent relative to the yen, while their
inflation and interest rates were fairly close.

   The various building blocks of the theory are more tenable over the long
run as can be seen in Exhibit 1.4. The means for inflation rate differentials,
interest rate differentials, and exchange rate movements are calculated for the
period from 1973 to 1988 and for a larger sample of currencies. Note that there
was more inflation in the United States than in Switzerland, West Germany, and
to some extent Japan, but less than in France or the United Kingdom. In
keeping with the theory, the dollar appreciated against the French franc and
British pound and depreciated against the deutsche mark, Swiss franc, and
Japanese yen. Yet, while the signs of the three variables are the same for each
country pair, their magnitude is sometimes quite different. This result also holds
true for non–dollar exchange-rates, e.g., deutsche mark/British pound. In
conclusion, the theory finds encouraging support over the long run, but little
support over the short run.

   These empirical findings are both perplexing and exciting. Exchange rates
are a matter of concern for all international investors because the evidence
shows that they do not simply neutralize inflation differentials in real terms.

EXHIBIT 1.4
Exchange Rate Movements, Inflation Rate Differentials, and Interest Rate Differentials
Average Annual Rates, 1973 to 1988

Countries	Exchange rate movement (%)	Inflation rate differential (%)	Interest rate differential (%)
U.S./Japan	6.23	0.96	2.70
U.S./West Germany	4.45	3.15	3.42
U.S./UK	−0.19	−4.03	−2.61
U.S./Switzerland	6.69	3.10	5.07
U.S./France	−0.68	−2.05	−2.46
West Germany/UK	−1.75	−6.92	−6.04

Furthermore, movements do not generally correct interest-rate differences between two currencies. Basically, one cannot rely on money markets to correctly assess and neutralize future exchange-rate movements. This gives economists a chance to improve significantly the performance of a portfolio by forecasting exchange rates correctly, a topic addressed in Chapter 3. Exchange rates add a dimension to international investment not encountered in the domestic situation, which makes it all the more important to gain an understanding of the influence of international monetary variables on equity and bond prices and develop international asset pricing models which explicitly incorporate exchange risk.

SECURITY PRICES AND MONETARY VARIABLES

Changes in inflation, interest rates, and exchange rates affect security prices. We will now briefly review the theory and empirical evidence for the relationship between security prices and monetary variables.[11]

Domestic Monetary Variables

Equity prices, inflation, and interest rates: The theory

Stocks are claims on cash flows generated by real assets. Traditional wisdom maintains that stocks provide a hedge against expected and unexpected inflation, but empirical studies consistently disproved this.[12]

The negative correlation between returns on equity investments and inflation has been justified by numerous ad hoc explanations, which will not be detailed here because they are unsatisfactory. However, two well-documented theories that rely on the monetary links between inflation and real economic activity have recently been proposed.[13] Both show that equity prices are good indicators of future changes in real economic activity. It appears that returns on stock markets satisfactorily forecast the real GNP growth rate, industrial production, corporate earnings, and employment.[14]

Fama (1981) proposes a money demand explanation for the negative correlation between returns on equity investments and inflation. Using a traditional version of the quantity theory of money demand, he claims that lower anticipated growth rates of real activity (hence positive real returns on equities) are associated with higher inflation. Lower activity implies a decrease in demand for real balances. With a fixed money supply this results in a relative increase in goods prices and therefore inflation.

Geske and Roll (1983) favor a money supply explanation. Their basic model holds that economic slowdowns lead to a reduction in tax revenues. With fixed expenditures this results in an increase in a country's budget deficit, which inflationary measures are expected to finance. In other words, a drop in stock prices signals a drop in economic activity, which leads to a revision of expected inflation. They further argue that because a government will borrow to finance a deficit the real interest rate may increase (assuming partial debt monetization). Therefore a fall in equity prices should go hand in hand with an increase in treasury bill rates because both expected inflation and real interest rates are seen as rising. This real-interest-rate effect is what people usually have in mind when they argue that high interest rates are bad for the economy. When interest rates rise well above inflation corporate sales and profit margins do not keep pace with the increase in financing costs. (The scenario is somewhat different where a rise in interest rates is simply a response to an increase in inflation, and therefore in sale prices and profit margins.)

Equity prices, inflation, and interest rates: The empirical evidence
While empirical studies on the U.S. capital market abound, few studies have been performed on other countries. The disruption of the international monetary system in 1971 and the subsequent unpegging of foreign-exchange rates have given rise to autonomous monetary policies and diverse domestic inflation rates. This means that different inflationary processes may be observed in different countries, which was theoretically not possible under the previous system of fixed exchange rates. Indeed, a single theoretical model need not apply to every country if it relies, as Geske and Roll's does, on the behavior of fiscal and monetary authorities.

In a test conducted from January 1971 to December 1989, monthly real equity returns were regressed against the level and changes in nominal interest rates for each country's stock market.[15] The results presented in Exhibit 1.5 show the consistently strong negative correlation between equity returns and changes in interest rates for every country studied. The correlations between interest rate changes and a country's stock market returns are large and significant for every country. In fact this seems to be the dominant monetary influence on all stock markets.

Separating inflationary expectations and real-rate effects is a difficult task, since there is no direct measure of real rates and expected inflation. A sophisticated econometric method proposed by Geske and Roll must be used.[16] The major finding is that the real-rate effect is significant, although often small, in most countries. It is greatest in countries that tend to demonetize their budget deficits, such as Japan, West Germany, and Switzerland. Demonetization means that governments finance unplanned deficits by borrowing on future taxes (or later surpluses), ultimately offsetting the increases in borrowing. The real-rate effect was weak in the 1970s for countries such as the United States and the United Kingdom, which increased their money supplies mostly to finance unplanned deficits. The change in U.S. monetary policy in the 1980s shows up in the data.

Some companies might be more interest-rate sensitive than others. A rise in expected inflation and interest rates affects a company's future cash flows. It will also increase its cost of financing and its required rate of return on equity. Banks might be more sensitive to interest rate movements. For example, their

EXHIBIT 1.5
The Relationships Between Monthly Real Stock Returns, Interest Rate, and Changes in Interest Rates, 1971 to 1989[a]: Regression Results

Country	Interest rate coefficient[b]	Change in interest rate coefficient[b]	R^2 (%)
Canada	− 2.5 (2.1)	− 24.1 (5.4)	11
France	− 1.3 (1.1)	− 8.1 (3.3)	6
West Germany	− 1.3 (0.9)	− 14.0 (2.8)	4
Japan	− 4.2 (2.7)	− 17.9 (2.2)	6
Netherlands	− 4.0 (2.7)	− 6.5 (1.6)	5
Switzerland	− 3.5 (2.4)	− 15.8 (3.7)	10
United Kingdom	− 1.8 (1.1)	− 24.2 (5.8)	15
United States	− 2.7 (2.5)	− 13.6 (4.1)	11

[a]All returns have been annualized (i.e., monthly rates of returns are multiplied by 1200) to be consistent with annualized interest rate quotations.
[b]Standard deviations of coefficient estimates appear in parentheses.

portfolios of existing fixed-interest loans drop in value if interest rates rise. This could lead to a severe drop in banks' stock prices. Banks might try to manage their interest rate exposure by adjusting their liabilities or using interest rate futures to hedge interest rate risk.

Bonds

Bond prices react negatively to a rise in interest rates; this is a technical (actuarial) relationship. An increase in inflationary expectations, or in the real interest rate, leads to an increase in interest rates and a drop in bond prices. There is a whole term structure of interest rates depending on the maturity of the bonds considered. A temporary rise in the short-term real interest rate might leave long-term interest rates and, therefore, bond prices unaffected. However, there is generally a negative relationship between bond prices and interest rates or inflation.

Exchange Rates

Let us now turn to the question of whether exchange rates affect domestic equity prices, and if so, in what way and to what extent.

From a practical standpoint, any investor should be concerned about the reaction of his domestic capital market to international monetary disturbances such as exchange rate movements. The international investor who uses domestic currency to value a portfolio measures total return as the sum of returns on the assets, in local currencies, plus any currency movements; the investor bears both market and exchange risk. Setting aside considerations of portfolio diversification, the reaction of asset prices to fluctuations in asset currencies is a matter of prime concern for international investors. A major question is whether stocks and bonds provide a hedge against exchange rate movements.

Let's consider an American investor holding shares of the French company Michelin and study various scenarios of the correlation of the price of Michelin stock with the French franc/U.S. dollar exchange rate. At time zero a share of Michelin is worth 3,000 francs, and one dollar is worth eight French francs (FF/$ = 8.00); this means that one franc is worth one-eighth, or 0.125, dollar ($/FF = 0.125). The dollar price of Michelin is $375 (3,000/8.00). Let's now assume a sudden depreciation of the French franc to 0.120 U.S. dollar ($/FF = 0.120 and FF/$ = 8.333). This means a 4% loss on the French currency for the U.S. investor. However, the price of Michelin shares may react in different fashions to this exchange rate movement:

□ A zero correlation between stock returns and exchange rate movements would mean no systematic reaction to exchange rate adjustments. The immediate rate of return on Michelin shares would tend to be zero for French investors (the French franc price of Michelin does not move) and −4% for U.S. investors because of the currency translation into U.S. dollars: one share of Michelin was worth $375 (3,000 × 0.125); it would now be worth $360 (3,000 × 0.12).

□ A positive correlation would mean that the local stock price benefits from a depreciation of the local currency. In other words the loss on the French currency would be partly offset by a French franc capital gain on the stock price. A perfect currency hedge would be attained if the French franc price of Michelin moved up to 3,125 francs. Then the return to a U.S. investor would be exactly zero since the final dollar price of Michelin would be unchanged at $375 (3,125 × 0.12).

□ A negative correlation would mean that the local stock price would be negatively affected by a depreciation of the local currency. For example, Michelin might drop to $2,950 with news of the franc depreciation (or go up, following a franc appreciation). The dollar return to a U.S. investor[17] would be −5.6%, since the dollar price of Michelin moved from $375 to $354 (2,950 × 0.12). In this case foreign asset prices would compound the currency effect and might be considered a negative hedge against currency movement.

Equity prices: The theory

To the extent that purchasing power parity holds, i.e., if exchange rates exactly adjust to inflation differentials, exchange rate movements simply mirror relative inflation and do not add another dimension to the analysis. They have no specific influence on the economy or equity prices beyond that of domestic inflation. But virtually all studies indicate that purchasing power parity does not hold, especially since the advent of floating exchange rates. This means that real exchange rate movements (deviations from purchasing power parity) are the relevant variable to study, and the actual effect of real exchange rate movements is large compared to inflation-induced variations. As such, real currency movements may have a significant influence on domestic economies and hence on stock markets.

It might be useful to look at an individual firm to examine the influence of a real exchange appreciation. Let's consider a strong real appreciation of the U.S. dollar relative to all currencies, including the French franc, as was the case from 1984 to 1985. Typically a U.S. tourist had great incentives to spend a vacation in France, since the dollar purchased much more in terms of accommodations and food. Conversely Michelin tires manufactured in France were highly price competitive when exported to the United States. The fifty percent real appreciation of the U.S. dollar in the early 1980s meant that Michelin could lower its U.S. selling price without reducing its French franc profit margin.[18] The effect of this real dollar appreciation is the opposite for the Goodyear tire company; it gives them incentives for establishing plants in countries, such as France, where they can benefit from lower costs. Note, however, that the importance of the exchange rate for an individual firm depends on the currency structure of its exports, imports, and financing. For example, a French firm importing U.S. typewriters and financed in U.S. dollars is badly hurt by the real dollar appreciation. An interesting analysis of the influence of a currency movement on the value of the firm is provided in Heckman.[19] She looks at the economic currency exposure of a corporation rather than its accounting exposure.

In the macroeconomic approach it is widely recognized that economic activity is a major determinant of stock market returns, so the influence of exchange rate movements on domestic economic activity may explain the relation between exchange rate movements and stock returns. Various economic theories have been proposed to explain the influence of real exchange rate movements on domestic economies.

The traditional approach[20] can be sketched as follows: A decline in a currency's real exchange rate tends to improve competitiveness, while the concomitant deterioration in the terms of trade increases the cost of imports, which creates additional domestic inflation and reduces real income and, hence, domestic demand and production. The initial reduction in real GNP caused by a deterioration in the terms of trade should eventually be offset by an improvement in international competitiveness and export demand until purchasing power parity is restored.

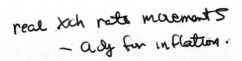

real xch rate movements
— adj for inflation.

A simple example may help to illustrate this phenomenon. Let's assume a sudden 10% depreciation of the French franc. Let's also assume that the French trade balance (French exports minus imports) is in deficit, which it has been in the early 1980s. The immediate effect of a 10% depreciation of the franc is to make current imports more expensive in terms of francs; if all imports were denominated in foreign currency, the cost of imports would immediately increase by 10%. This increase in cost has two major effects: First, the French trade balance deficit measured in francs widens. Although the franc value of exports increases somewhat because part of the export sales are contracted in foreign currency, the percentage of export denominated in foreign currency is usually smaller than that of import. Second, the rise in imported goods prices leads to an increase in the domestic price index and imports inflation. Both of these effects are bad for the French economy and, in a sense, the real wealth is reduced. However, this currency depreciation makes French firms more competitive; they can lower the price of their product by 10% in terms of foreign currency without lowering the French franc income. In the long run this should help increase foreign sales and stimulate the French economy. However, if the economy is slow to improve, this cycle of events threatens to become a vicious circle: The immediate economic and trade balance worsens leading to a further currency depreciation, which, in turn, may worsen domestic economic conditions and so on.

The stock market, which immediately discounts the overall influence on the economy of an exchange rate movement, may be positively or negatively affected depending on whether the short-term or long-term effect dominates. In late 1985 the U.S. dollar was at its highest point, well above its purchasing power parity value. The Group of Five leading industrialized nations (United States, Japan, United Kingdom, West Germany, and France) met in Washington, D.C., and made the surprise announcement that they would coordinate their intervention policies to lower the value of the dollar on the foreign exchange market. The reaction to this news was immediate; the dollar fell by five percent and the U.S. stock market rose by over one percent, anticipating that the dollar depreciation would have an overall positive effect on the U.S. economy. However, in many cases a currency depreciation is not followed by this type of stock market reaction.

A money demand model has also been proposed.[21] In this model real growth in the domestic economy leads to increased demand for the domestic currency through a traditional money demand equation. This increase in currency demand induces a rise in the relative value of the domestic currency. Because domestic stock prices are strongly influenced by real growth, this model justifies a positive association between real stock returns and domestic currency appreciation.

This book does not intend to get into the controversies surrounding various international economic theories. While the traditional trade approach suggests that a real exchange rate appreciation tends to reduce the competitiveness of the domestic economy and therefore reduce domestic activity, the money demand approach leads to the opposite effect, where an increase in domestic economic growth leads to a real currency appreciation.

Equity prices: The empirical evidence

The empirical evidence for the above theories is somewhat puzzling. All studies[22] point toward a very low correlation between stock returns and exchange rate movements. At the aggregate stock market level little correlation exists between stock market indexes and currency movements. For example, Exhibit 1.6 reports the sample correlation between monthly returns on equities and individual exchange rate fluctuations; each row gives the correlation coefficients between domestic stock market returns and the exchange rates of all currencies versus the domestic one. For example, 0.04 is the correlation coefficient between the U.S. market and the French franc/U.S. dollar rate; a positive coefficient means that the U.S. stock market tends to go up when the French franc appreciates (the U.S. dollar depreciates). Similarly, the U.S. stock market tends to go up when the deutsche mark appreciates. But in both cases the correlation is very weak. On the other hand, the French stock market tends to go down when the U.S. dollar appreciates (relative to the French franc), as is indicated by a correlation coefficient of −0.07, and tends to go up when the British pound appreciates (indicated by a positive correlation coefficient of 0.05). Different national monetary policies may explain differences among countries.

Exchange rate movements seem to have only a small systematic influence on stock prices, and the influence is weaker than expected. Similar conclusions have been reached in all studies. As Adler and Simon stress, foreign stock investments are poor hedges against currency movements. In other words, the dollar return on a French stock portfolio tends to follow movements in the dollar/franc exchange rate, since franc prices of French stock are affected little by exchange rate movements.

While the overall stock market shows little reaction to currency movements, the effect could be firm specific, depending on the amount of export and the cost structure. There has been little research on this topic so far, but preliminary evidence does not support the idea.[23] An extract from an article in *Fortune* magazine illustrates this point:

> "Though they welcomed the general prospect of a weaker dollar with a brief cheer —the Dow Jones industrial average rose more than 18 points the day after the Plaza Hotel[24] announcement—investors couldn't find much cause for excitement among individual U.S. stocks."
>
> *Source:* "Toppling the Dollar Could Cost A Lot," *Fortune*, October 28, 1985.

Bonds

Since bond prices are directly linked to long-term interest rates, the story for bonds is told by the relation between changes in long-term interest rates and exchange rates. Exhibit 1.7 shows the short-term (1983 to 1985) and long-term

EXHIBIT 1.6
Correlation Coefficients Between Stock Returns and Exchange Rates, 1973 to 1988

Stock Market	Currency							
	U.S. dollar	Japanese yen	West German deutsche mark	British pound	French franc	Canadian dollar	Dutch guilder	Swiss franc
U.S.		0.00	0.02	0.00	0.04	0.19	0.00	−0.05
Japan	−0.09		−0.09	−0.07	−0.08	−0.04	−0.09	−0.09
West Germany	0.03	0.03		0.05	0.02	0.04	0.03	0.02
UK	−0.06	−0.05	−0.09		−0.04	0.00	−0.03	−0.11
France	−0.07	0.00	−0.08	0.05		−0.02	−0.09	−0.05
Canada	−0.33	−0.07	−0.04	0.00	−0.03		−0.04	−0.04
Netherlands	0.19	0.11	−0.03	0.14	0.02	0.24		−0.01
Switzerland	0.11	0.05	0.10	0.17	0.15	0.17	0.16	

21

EXHIBIT 1.7
Correlation of Bond and Dollar Exchange Rates

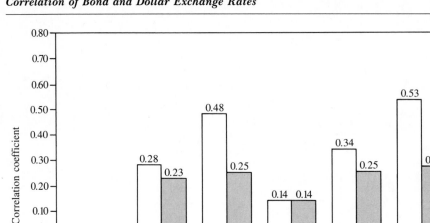

| | Short term, 1983–1985 | | Long term, 1971–1985 |

Source: K. Chollerton, P. Pieraerts, and B. Solnik, "Why Not Diversify into Foreign Currency Bonds?," *Journal of Portfolio Management*, Summer 1986.
[a]Relative to the deutsche mark for the United States.

(1971 to 1984) relationships between bond returns and the dollar exchange rate for the major currencies.

It is often claimed that a rise in national real interest rates leads to currency appreciation, but this mechanistic relationship does not seem to hold. Exhibit 1.7 may be interpreted as follows: The values of the U.S. dollar and U.S. interest rates tend to be positively related, leading to a negative correlation between U.S. bond returns and movements in the dollar. A rise in the U.S. real interest rate tends to be associated with a rise in the value of the dollar, which is consistent with the recent theory that a rise in domestic interest rates supports the home currency. On the other hand, nondollar bond prices are positively related to the value of their national currencies. For example the correlation of deutsche mark bond returns and the dollar value of the deutsche mark was 0.48 in the 1983 to 1985 period, implying that deutsche mark bond prices tend to go up when the deutsche mark goes up (relative to the U.S. dollar). This phenomenon is usually explained by the exchange rate policy followed by most countries. A fall in the domestic currency induces the monetary authorities to raise interest rates to defend the currency, and a strong domestic currency induces the authorities to ease the interest rate policy. Branson (1984),[25] calls this exchange rate policy reaction a "leaning-against-the-wind" policy where foreign monetary authorities use interest rates to stabilize the exchange rate of their home currency. For example, European governments adopted a monetary policy of high interest rates to slow the decline of their currencies relative to the U.S. dollar; rising interest rates lead to a decline of bond prices correlated to the decline of the local currency. These correlations depend on the monetary policy adopted by a government and show the key role played by the U.S. dollar on the international monetary scene.

Concluding Remarks

To summarize, the specific influence of international variables, such as exchange rates, is weak compared to that of domestic variables such as changes in inflationary expectations and interest rates. This may be comforting to domestic government policies in times of highly volatile exchange rates. It implies that either the effects of international monetary disturbances on domestic economic activity are weak and delayed, or markets expect governments to adopt economic and monetary countermeasures. Most of the apparent association between equity prices and currency movements seems to result from changes in domestic interest rates, which influence both variables, so that the specific influence of foreign variables is small when isolated from domestic monetary variables. The effect of foreign variables on major markets seems too small to justify extensive research by financial analysts, especially since exchange rate movements are so hard to predict.

It should be stressed that the negative correlation between returns on equity investments and interest rates, which has been consistently observed in the United States, also applies strongly to other major stock markets. Surprisingly, the same structural model seems to be at work in all countries; different coefficients depend on the country's fiscal–monetary policy mix. A more detailed study of domestic links between government policy and stock market behavior would be fruitful and rewarding for international investors.

It appears that stocks are a short-term negative hedge against inflation and climbing interest rates in all countries. Furthermore, they do not correct real exchange rate movements and are therefore a bad monetary hedge. Because real currency movements are unpredictable, foreign portfolios are subject to foreign exchange, as well as domestic monetary, risks.

INTERNATIONAL ASSET PRICING

A major question posed by the potential international investor is what determines asset pricing. The answer must first address the efficiency of international capital markets.

Efficient Markets

The notion of an efficient market is central to finance theory. In an efficient market any new information would be immediately and fully reflected in prices, and the adjustments in price would be so rapid that it would not pay to buy information that has already been available to other investors. Any new information will be immediately used by some privileged investors who will take positions to capitalize on this news, thereby making the asset price adjust (almost) instantaneously to this piece of information. For example, a new balance-of-payments statistic would immediately be used by foreign exchange traders to buy or sell a currency until the exchange rate reached a level considered consistent with the new information. Similarly, surprise information about a company such as a new contract or new forecasted income might be used by insiders to reap a profit until the stock price reached a level consistent with the news. Hundreds of thousands of financial analysts and professional investors throughout the world search for new information and make the world financial markets close to efficient.

In an efficient market the typical investor could consider an asset price to reflect its investment value at all times: An asset price would be equal to its true investment value, given the information available. Only news, i.e., unanticipated information, would cause a change in asset prices. In other words old data could not be used to forecast future changes in asset prices. Another implication is that it will be difficult to "beat" the market index.

Numerous studies on the efficiency of the major stock markets of the world have been performed.[26] The general conclusion is that the markets are very efficient, probably due to the intense competition among professional security analysts and managers in each national market. In addition, the number of foreign investors bringing their own techniques of financial analysis has increased, helping to make the national markets more efficient. Specific inefficiencies seldom exist for more than a few days and are often not meaningful enough to warrant speculation.

Each national market is quite efficient, making it difficult to consistently outperform the local index, but the question of international market efficiency remains unanswered. Could active asset allocation among countries consistently outperform the world market index? There is less competition among countries than within a single market. So far, there is little empirical evidence on the international efficiency of national markets. The fundamental issue of international market efficiency is often viewed in terms of international market integration or segmentation. An integrated world financial market would achieve international efficiency, in the sense that arbitrage across markets would take advantage of any new information throughout the world. For example, an international investor would not hesitate to move money from West Germany to France if the investor forecasted an election result in France that would improve the competitiveness of French firms against West German firms. Similarly a portfolio manager would arbitrage an Italian chemical stock against a U.S. chemical stock based on new information on their prospective earnings and market shares. In an efficient, integrated international market prices of all assets would be in line with their relative investment values.

It is sometimes claimed, however, that international markets are not integrated, but segmented. Although each national market might be efficient, numerous factors might prevent international capital flows from taking advantage of relative mispricing among countries:

Psychological barriers. Unfamiliarity with foreign markets, language, sources of information, etc., might curtail foreign investment.

Legal restrictions. Institutional investors are often constrained on their foreign investments. Also, some national markets regulate foreign investment flowing into or out of the market. Foreign ownership is often constrained to avoid loss of national control.

Transaction costs. The costs of foreign investment are high. Access to sources of information throughout the world is costly, as are international transaction costs, management fees, and custodial services.

Discriminatory taxation. Foreign investment might be more heavily taxed than domestic investment. Withholding taxes might lead to double taxation.

Political risks. The political risks of foreign investment might dampen the enthusiasm for international diversification. This political transfer risk might take the form of a prohibition on repatriation of profits and/or capital investment from a foreign country. While the risk is extremely small in the major markets, the associated potential loss is large.

Exchange risks. Foreign investments bear the risk of the local market and the foreign exchange rate. The issue of foreign exchange risk is addressed at some length in Chapter 2.

All these factors tend to reduce international capital flows and lead to somewhat segmented national markets. However, international integration requires only a sufficient flow of capital to make the world market efficient and to eliminate relative mispricing among countries. In many countries private and institutional investors are extensively invested abroad. All major corporations have truly multinational operations; their shares are often listed on several stock exchanges. Large corporations, as well as governments, borrow internationally and quickly take advantage of relative mispricing, thereby making the markets more efficient. The flow of foreign investment has been rapidly growing through the years, thus it does not seem that the international markets are fully segmented. The degree of international market efficiency is an empirical question that has not yet been answered.

Asset Pricing

Capital Asset Pricing Model

The value of an asset depends on its discounted anticipated cash flows adjusted for risk. For example, the value of a risk-free bill is equal to the repayment value of the bill discounted at the risk-free interest rate. There is a direct relationship between the price of an asset and its expected return and risk. Modern portfolio theory has proposed models of asset pricing in efficient markets. All of them attempt to determine what should be the expected return on an asset in an efficient market given the risk borne by the owner. Market equilibrium requires that the expected return be equal to the risk-free rate plus risk premia to reward the various sources of risk borne by the investor. The major challenge is to determine the relevant measures of risk as well as the size of the associated premia.[27] The Capital Asset Pricing Model (CAPM) is the first well-known model of market equilibrium. Since the reality of the international market is extremely complex, entailing a huge number of securities and sources of uncertainties, the objective of the model is to provide a simplified view of the world that captures the major aspects of reality. This simplification is required to allow the formation of operational concepts.

The traditional Capital Asset Pricing Model is built on fairly restrictive assumptions regarding investors' preferences. Many of these original assumptions can be somewhat relaxed, leading to more complex (and less operational) versions. The assumptions of the original CAPM may be recalled:

□ Investors care about risk and return. They are risk-averse and prefer less risk and more expected return.

□ A consensus opinion among all investors holds and everyone agrees about the expected return and risk of all assets.

□ Investors care about nominal returns, e.g., U.S. investors care about U.S. dollar returns.

□ There exists a risk-free interest rate with unlimited borrowing or lending capacity at this rate.

□ There are no transaction costs or taxes.

The conclusion of the CAPM is the *separation theorem*, which claims that everyone should hold the same portfolio of risky assets. This portfolio of risky assets must be the market portfolio, made up of all the assets traded. Investors adjust their risk preference by putting some of their money in the risk-free asset (more risk-oriented investors will borrow, instead of lend, at the risk-free rate). A direct byproduct is that the equilibrium expected return of an asset should be equal to the risk-free rate plus a risk premium proportional to the covariance of the asset return with the return on the market portfolio (the famous *beta*). The operational application of this theory is summarized in Chapter 5.

The simplifying assumptions of any theory, including the CAPM, are never verified exactly; the question is whether or not the conclusions are robust enough to be of practical use. As mentioned by Roll[28] a major problem of the CAPM is that it requires an exact identification of the market portfolio, including all assets, and it does not take into account the fact that investors in different countries have different currencies and consumption preferences. Also, a CAPM in real terms has to take exchange risk into account.[29] The CAPM could be applied to the real world only with the addition of two unreasonable assumptions:

☐ Investors throughout the world have identical consumption baskets.

☐ Real prices of consumption goods are identical in every country; in other words purchasing power parity holds exactly.

In this type of world, exchange rates would simply mirror inflation differentials between two countries. Exchange rate uncertainty would be pure money illusion; it would not matter whether one used francs or dollars or ten-dollar bills or five-dollar bills. The exchange rate would be purely a translation accounting device with no real importance.[30]

International asset pricing model

However, it has been shown before that deviations from purchasing power parity are the major source of exchange rate variation. Similarly, consumption preferences differ among countries. It follows that investors will want to hedge against foreign exchange uncertainties, which is sometimes referred to as real exchange risk or purchasing power risk. In equilibrium, the optimal investment strategy for each investor is a combination of two portfolios: a risky portfolio common to all investors, and a personalized hedge portfolio, used to reduce the purchasing power risks. This purchasing power hedge portfolio, which is different for each investor, constitutes the best protection against inflation. Since it may contain stocks and bonds that correlate with the consumption expenses of the investor, the world market portfolio of risky assets is not optimal anymore.[31] However, if there is no uncertainty about future inflation rates in any country, the purchasing power hedge portfolio reduces to the risk-free treasury bill in each currency. Then, by aggregation, the common portfolio of risky assets has to include the world market portfolio. The exchange risk associated with foreign investments may be hedged by selling forward foreign currency contracts when available. If currency hedging is fully available it can be shown that the world market portfolio hedged against currency risk is optimal for all investors and a simple risk pricing relation applies: The expected return on an asset that is hedged against currency risk should be equal to the domestic risk-free rate plus a risk premium proportional to the beta of the security with the world market portfolio (hedged against exchange risk). So the traditional CAPM pricing relation applies to securities hedged against currency risk. It should be stressed that the optimal currency hedge ratios need not be unitary and will generally be different for different currencies.

It has been repeatedly observed that the variability of inflation rates is small compared to that of exchange rates or asset returns. Therefore, this simple version of the international asset pricing model might be a good practical approximation in efficient markets. The numeraire used by any investor, including pension plans, should be denominated in real purchasing power terms. It is only because of the small variability in consumption prices relative to that of exchange rates and asset prices that using nominal dollars might be regarded as an acceptable approximation.

Market imperfections and segmentation

If currency hedging is not available either physically or legally, the simple pricing relation breaks down. Furthermore, official restrictions, fear of expropriation, discriminatory taxes, and higher investment costs will push domestic investors to underinvest in foreign assets compared to the world market portfolio. An investment is viewed as more risky and less profitable by a foreign investor than by a resident of the country where the asset is traded. For example, a German investor might perceive French stocks as more risky and more costly than does a French investor, and therefore underinvest in French shares relative to German shares. French investors might have a comparative advantage in buying French shares; they might have better and quicker access to company information as well as lower taxes. For example French investors benefit from an *avoir fiscal*, a tax credit for French taxes paid by the corporation. This tax advantage is not transferred to foreign residents. However, French shares are still a unique diversification vehicle with good potential return for German investors. Germans will invest in French shares, but their French counterparts will invest more.

The argument might sometimes go the other way. Before a French election whose results might negatively affect all French assets, French investors might want to diversify away the most liquid part of their wealth by investing in foreign capital markets. German investors might be willing to gamble for the higher French expected return, since only a small part of their total wealth is exposed to the French election–associated risk.

The argument for international comparative advantage in imperfect markets might be firm-specific; investors might prefer foreign companies that aren't found in other places of the world, e.g., the Club Meditérranée or Moët-Hennessy, and avoid companies that are deemed sensitive to national interests or in countries where foreign interests might get expropriated on short notice, e.g., armament companies.

If all these impediments to international investments are of significant magnitude, buying the market is not a reasonable first-cut strategy. However, it certainly does not mean that one should not have any foreign investments. The additional costs and risks of foreign investment may cause market segmentation and affect asset pricing.

International asset pricing under various forms of market segmentation, including differential taxes, has been studied, and more complex asset pricing relations have been found.[32] The risk premium has a more complex function than its role in the traditional Capital Asset Pricing Model. It generally depends on the form of market imperfection, the relative wealth of investors, and parameters of their utility. However, most forms of market imperfections and

constraints to foreign investments cannot be incorporated easily in an equilibrium asset-pricing framework. Hence their precise influence on the resulting
optimal portfolio holdings cannot be modeled.

Currency risk hedging

The issue of currency risk hedging is a source of controversy among practitioners. In a perfect world, with no inflation and following the assumptions described
above, everyone should hold a combination of his domestic (risk-free) bill and of
the same world market portfolio of equity hedged against currency risk. In the
theoretical derivations, we assume the existence of two types of assets: equity,
with a net supply equal to their market capitalization, and national bills (often
called bonds by various authors), with a zero net supply for each of them. As can
be seen in Chapter 3, a forward currency contract is equivalent to being short in
the foreign bill (borrowing in the foreign currency) and long in the domestic bill
(lending in the domestic currency). To make things simple, let's consider an
investor who is quite risk averse and therefore holds a combination of his
domestic (risk-free) bill and of the common risky portfolio made up of the world
market portfolio of equity and of positions in all national bills. Although the
weights of each national bill in this portfolio are complex functions, it is not
unreasonable to assume, for illustrative purposes, that they are negative. These
negative weights in the foreign bills correspond to selling forward currency
contracts except, of course, for the domestic bill position.

Black uses this result, derived by Solnik, Sercu and Adler and Dumas,[33] to
suggest that there exists a "universal hedging formula" that every investor
should use, independent of nationality and fairly easily estimated. Indeed,
everyone hedges the world market portfolio with national bills in the same way
since everyone holds the same risky portfolio. Similarly, the aggregate hedge
ratio[34] needs not be unity; and Black provides an historical estimate around 0.7.
Unfortunately, this "universal hedging formula" only gives the aggregate dollar
amount of foreign and domestic bills used to hedge as a proportion of the total
dollar value of the world market portfolio of equity. We have no indications on
how to achieve such an aggregate hedge using individual forward currency
contracts. We also know that these individual currency hedge ratios are complex
since they depend on parameters such as the covariance structure of assets and
currency. There are many ways to achieve a given *aggregate* hedge ratio, but only
one is optimal. Another problem is that the proportion of the foreign portfolio
optimally hedged with foreign currency contracts is nationality dependent.
Using Black's definition, the aggregate hedge ratio is universal (the same for
everyone) because it includes both *domestic* and foreign currencies. So we add to
foreign currency hedges some artificial domestic currency hedge that correspond
to no physical action or forward contract. Whereas the total demand for
domestic bills can always be split in two components, it does not change the fact
that the proportion of foreign forward currency contracts to be used to hedge
depends on nationalities.

More important, this nice result of a unique aggregate hedge ratio breaks down if, for theoretical or practical purposes, investors do not hold the world market portfolio. The simple fact that inflation differs across countries and varies randomly destroys the result that the hedged world market portfolio is efficient. This is not a trivial observation since interest and currency rates are clearly linked to inflation. For all kinds of additional reasons, investors tend to underweight foreign assets relative to the world market weights. For example, in 1989, American pension funds held only 15% of their holdings in foreign assets although they represent around 70% of the world market portfolio. Even if a U.S. pension fund puts its 15% of foreign assets in a rest-of-the-world index fund, there is no theoretical ground to suggest using the same hedge ratio that should be used if the fund was invested 70% in rest-of-the-world assets. Intuitively, the risk diversification benefits brought to the U.S. portfolio by the foreign assets are different in the two cases. The currency risk component may actually lower the total risk of a portfolio with only a small investment in foreign assets (say 5%) because it provides some diversification of the U.S. monetary policy risk. For example, Jorion[35] conducted an empirical study of optimal asset allocations for an American investor. He concluded that the importance of currency hedging depends on the proportion of foreign assets held in the portfolio and states that "this question of hedging may not matter so much if the amounts invested in the foreign assets are small, in which case overall portfolio volatility is not appreciably influenced by hedging. Hedging therefore brings no particular benefits in terms of risk reduction...." The difference should be even more pronounced if the portfolio of foreign assets is actively managed with country weights that markedly differ from the rest-of-the-world market index.

In the very simple theoretical world described above, simple aggregation results could be obtained from the fact that, at equilibrium, every investor held the same market portfolio with bills in zero net supply. International asset pricing theory cannot help us much to decide on an optimal hedging policy when investors strongly deviate from holding the world market portfolio. Hence currency hedging becomes an individual empirical decision function of the portfolio to be hedged and risk preferences matter.

Few tests of international market integration and asset pricing models have been performed so far.[36] The results are often inconclusive, partly because of the limited amount of historical data available on most capital markets. But the methodological problems are also serious. More recently, researchers have used the arbitrage pricing theory introduced by Ross to design tests of international asset pricing.[37] Given the problems involved in designing a general asset pricing model, this book will follow a more pragmatic approach.

SUMMARY

1. Exchange rates, interest rates, and inflation rates are linked internationally. However, the traditional economic relations are poorly supported by recent data.

2. Inflation does not explain short-term exchange rate movements well. Real exchange rate movements add a specific and important dimension to international investments.

3. In all countries, equity prices react fairly strongly to domestic monetary variables such as interest rates. The reaction to international monetary variables, such as exchange rates, is generally much weaker.

4. Bond prices tend to be strongly correlated to exchange rate movements because of the relationships between interest rates and exchange rates.

5. All major national capital markets of the world are regarded as efficient. However, we have as yet little evidence on the interefficiency of these markets, i.e., on whether international mispricing is arbitraged between markets. Transaction costs, political risks, legal restrictions on foreign investment, differential taxes, and exchange risks may limit international investment. International portfolio investment is, however, extensive and rapidly growing, which should lead to greater international market integration.

6. International asset pricing models have been developed assuming efficient markets. When exchange risk can be fully hedged, e.g., if there exist forward exchange contracts in all currencies, it is shown that the world market portfolio, (partly) hedged against currency risk, is optimal for all investors. A risk pricing relation in the CAPM spirit applies. Any form of market imperfection or the absence of exchange risk hedging possibilities will change this conclusion.

QUESTIONS AND PROBLEMS

1. The current Swiss franc/U.S. dollar spot exchange rate is 2 Swiss franc per dollar or SF/$ = 2. The expected inflation over the coming year is 2% in Switzerland and 5% in the United States. What is the expected value for the spot exchange rate, a year from now, according to purchasing power parity?

2. The spot exchange rate is SF/$ = 2.00. The one-year interest rate is equal to 4% in Switzerland and 8% in the United States. What should the current value of the forward exchange rate be?

3. Should nominal interest rates be equal across countries? Why?

4. Should real interest rates be equal across countries? Can a financial arbitrage take place in case of significant and persistent real interest rate differences between two countries?

5. Give some intuitive explanations for the negative relation between stock returns and changes in interest rates.

6. Consider two French firms which are listed on the Paris stock market:

> *Meca* manufactures engine parts in France which are exported and the prices are set and paid in dollars. Production costs are mostly domestic (the labor force) and considered to follow the French inflation rate.

> *Club* imports computers from the United States and sells them in France to compete with French products.

What will happen to the earnings of the two companies if there is a sudden depreciation of the French franc (say 20%)? What is the difference between the short-run effect and long-run adjustments? Would your findings be the same if the French franc depreciation was only a progressive adjustment to the U.S.-France inflation differential which reflected the higher French inflation rate?

7. Consider two Australian firms listed on the Sydney stock exchange:

> *Australia I*. Its stock return shows a consistent positive correlation with the value of the U.S. dollar. The stock price of Australia I (in Australian dollars) tends to go up when the U.S. dollar appreciates relative to the Australian dollar.

> *Australia II*. Its stock return shows a consistent negative correlation with the value of the U.S. dollar. The stock price of Australia II (in Australian dollars) tends to go down when the U.S. dollar appreciates relative to the Australian dollar.

An American investor wishes to buy Australian stocks but hesitates between Australia I and Australia II. She is afraid of a depreciation of the Australian dollar. Which of the two investments would offer some protection against a weak Australian dollar?

8. Refer to the statistics given in Exhibit 1.7. Back in 1985 a strong depreciation of the U.S. dollar was expected over the next two years. Were non-dollar bonds a good investment for American investors and why?

9. List reasons why an international extension of the capital asset pricing model is problematic. Why would the optimal portfolio differ from the world market portfolio, even if the markets are fully efficient?

NOTES

1. A derivation of these relations may be found in I. Giddy, "An Integrated Theory of Exchange Rate Equilibrium," *Journal of Financial and Quantitative Analysis*, December 1976; R. Roll and B. Solnik, "On Some International Parity Conditions," *Journal of Macroeconomics*, Summer 1979; and B. Solnik, "International Parity Condition and Exchange Risk: A Review," *Journal of Banking and Finance*, 2, 1978, pp. 281–293.

2. This theory was originally presented by G. Cassel in "The Present Situation on the Foreign Exchanges," *Economic Journal*, 1916, pp. 62–65. A review of purchasing power parity may be found in A. Shapiro, "What Does Purchasing Power Parity Mean?" *Journal of International Money and Finance*, December 1983.

3. The linear approximation ignores the cross-product term $p\,E(I)$ in the exact relation. This cross-product may be significant, especially in countries with high inflation rates. The same applies to all the parity relations. This theory was originally proposed by I. Fisher in *The Theory of Interest*, New York: Macmillan, 1930.

4. See R. Dornbusch, *Open Economy Macroeconomics*, New York: Basic, 1980.

5. See B. Solnik, "An Equilibrium Model of the International Capital Market," *Journal of Economic Theory*, 8, August 1974; R. Roll and B. Solnik, "A Pure Foreign Exchange Asset Pricing Model," *Journal of International Economics*, 7, May 1977; R. Stulz, "A Model of International Asset Pricing," *Journal of Financial Economics*, 9, December 1981; and M. Adler and B. Dumas, "International Portfolio Choice and Corporation Finance: A Synthesis," *Journal of Finance*, 38, June 1983.

6. See L. H. Officer, "The Purchasing Power Theory of Exchange Rates: A Review Article," *IMF Staff Papers*, March 1976; and I. B. Kravis, A. Heston, and L. Summers, *World Production and Income: International Comparisons of Real GDP*, Baltimore, MD: Johns Hopkins University Press, 1982.

7. See R. Roll, "Violations of Purchasing Power Parity and Their Implications for Efficient International Commodity Markets," in M. Sarnat and G. Szego (eds), *International Finance and Trade*, Cambridge, MA: Ballinger Pub., 1979.
This is usually referred to as "the efficient market version of purchasing power parity." This theory claims that the foreign exchange market immediately discounts the influence of the expected inflation rates, and that any future exchange rate movement is affected by future inflation, not past inflation rates. See also on this topic: R. Meese and K. Rogoff, "What Is Real? The Exchange Rate–Interest Rate Differential Relation over the Modern Floating-Rate Period," *Journal of Finance*, September 1988.

8. See E. Kane and L. Rosenthal, "International Interest Rates and Inflationary Expectations," *Journal of International Money and Finance*, April 1982. The Eurocurrency market is described in Chapter 3.

9. See F. S. Mishkin, "Are Real Interest Rates Equal Across Countries? An Empirical Investigation of International Parity Relations," *Journal of Finance*, December 1984.

10. See R. Roll and B. Solnik, "A Pure Foreign Exchange Asset Pricing Model," *Journal of International Economics*, 7, May 1977; E. Fama, "Forward and Spot Exchange Rates," *Journal of Monetary Economics*, November 1984; R. E. Cumby and M. Obstfeld, "A Note on Exchange Rates Expectations and Nominal Interest Rates Differentials," *Journal of Finance*, June 1981; and R. J. Hodrick and S. Srivastava, "An Investigation of Risk and Return in Forward Foreign Exchange," *Journal of International Money and Finance*, April 1984.

11. This section draws on B. Solnik, "Stock Prices and International Monetary Variables," *Financial Analysts Journal*, March 1984. Reprinted by permission.

12. See, for example, E. Fama and W. Schwert, "Asset Returns and Inflation," *Journal of Financial Economics*, November 1977.

13. See E. Fama, "Stock Returns, Real Activity, Inflation and Money," *American Economic Review*, September 1981; and R. Geske and R. Roll, "The Fiscal and Monetary Linkage Between Stock Returns and Inflation," *Journal of Finance*, March 1983.

14. Studies for other countries can be found in G. Mandelker and K. Tandon, "Common Stock Returns, Real Activity, Money and Inflation: Some International Evidence," *Journal of Finance*, March 1983; and A. de Freitas, "La Relation Entre Cours Boursiers, Monnaie et Activite Reelle," PhD Dissertation, CESA, 1981.

15. A detailed statistical analysis for the period 1970 to 1980 may be found in B. Solnik, "The Relationship Between Stock Prices and Inflationary Expectations," *Journal of Finance*, March 1983.

16. See Solnik, *op. cit.*

17. Generally the dollar rate of return on an asset, $r^{\$}$, is the franc rate of return of the asset, r^{FF}, plus the percentage movement in the exchange rate, $s^{\$FF}$ plus the product of these two terms:

$$r^{\$} = \left(r^{FF} + s^{\$FF} \right) + \left(r^{FF} s^{\$FF} \right).$$

18. The story is only partially true, since the real dollar appreciation rises the cost of some imported goods required to manufacture tires. Eighty percent of Michelin turnover is realized out of France, and thirty percent of the turnover comes from the United States.

19. C. R. Hekman, "Don't Blame Currency Values for Strategic Errors: Protecting Competitive Position by Correctly Assessing Foreign Exchange Exposure," *Midland Corporate Finance Journal*, Fall 1986, vol. 4, no. 3 and, "A Financial Model of Foreign Exchange Exposure," *Journal of International Business Studies*, Summer 1985.

20. See R. Dornbusch, *Open Economy Macroeconomics*, New York: Basic, 1980; F. Rivera-Batiz and L. Rivera-Batiz, *International Finance and Open Economy Macroeconomics*, New York: Macmillan, 1985.

21. See, for example, R. Lucas, "Interest Rates and Currency Prices in Two-Country World," *Journal of Monetary Economics*, November 1982.

22. See M. Adler and D. Simon, "Exchange Rate Surprises in International Portfolios," *Journal of Portfolio Management*, Winter 1986; and B. Solnik, "Capital Markets and International Monetary Variables," *Financial Analysts Journal*, March 1984.

23. See B. Solnik and A. de Freitas, "International Factors of Security Returns," in S. Khoury and A. Ghosh (eds), *Recent Developments in International Finance and Banking*, Lexington, MA: Lexington Books, 1988.

24. The Group of Five met in the Plaza Hotel, where they made the announcement referred to earlier.

25. W. H. Branson, "Exchange Rate Policy after a Decade of Floating," in J. Bilson and R. Marston (eds), *Exchange Rate Theory and Practice*, Chicago: University of Chicago Press, 1984.

26. The extensive evidence of the American market is summarized in textbooks such as H. Levy and M. Sarnat, *Portfolio and Investment Selection: Theory and Practice*, Englewood Cliffs, NJ: Prentice Hall International, 1984.

A good review of efficiency tests for European stock markets may be found in G. Hawawini, *European Equity Markets: Price Behavior and Efficiency*, Monograph 1984-4, Solomon Brothers Center, New York University, 1984. Evidence for other countries might be found in J. Ang and R. A. Pohlman, "A Note on the Price Behavior of Far Eastern Stocks," *Journal of International Business Studies*, Spring 1978; B. Lev and B. Vahalomi, "The Effect of Corporate Financial Statements on the Israeli Stock Exchange," *Management International Review*, 1933, vol. 2, no. 3.; R. R. Officer, "Seasonality in Australian Capital Markets," *Journal of Financial Economics*, March 1975; F. Roux and B. Gilbertson, "The Behavior of Share Prices on the Johannesburg Stock Exchange," *Journal of Business Finance and Accounting*, Summer 1978; K. Kato and J. Schallheim, "Seasonal and Size Anomalies in the Japanese Stock Market," *Journal of Financial and Quantitative Analysis*, June 1985; J. Jaffee and R. Westerfield, "Patterns in Japanese Common Stock Returns: Day of the Week and Turn of the Year Effects," *Journal of Financial and Quantitative Analysis*, June 1985; T. Berglund and E. Liljebom, "Market Serial Correlation on a Small Security Market: A Note," *Journal of Finance*, December 1988; P. T. Hietla,

"Asset Pricing in Partially Segmented Markets: Evidence from the Finnish Market," *Journal of Finance*, July 1989.

27. A description of the theory may be found in E. Elton and M. Gruber, *Security Evaluation and Portfolio Analysis*, Englewood Cliffs, NJ: Prentice Hall, 1984; H. Levy and M. Sarnat, *Portfolio Investment Selection*, Englewood Cliffs, NJ: Prentice Hall, 1984; and B. Jacquillat and B. Solnik, *Les Marches Financiers et la Gestion de Portefeuille*, Paris, Dunod, 1989.

28. See R. Roll, "A Critique of the Asset Pricing Theory's Test; on Past and Potential Testability of the Theory," *Journal of Financial Economics*, 4, March 1977.

29. See B. Solnik, "An Equilibrium Model of the International Capital Market," *Journal of Economic Theory*, July/August 1974; P. Sercu, "A Generalization of the International Asset Pricing Model," *Revue de l'Association Française de Finance*, June 1980; R. Stulz, "A Model of International Asset Pricing," *Journal of Financial Economics*, 9, December 1981; and an excellent review by M. Adler and B. Dumas, "International Portfolio Choice and Corporation Finance: A Synthesis," *Journal of Finance*, 38, June 1983.

30. Such a model has been developed in F. Grauer, R. Litzenberger, and R. Stehle, "Sharing Rules and Equilibrium in an International Capital Market under Uncertainty," *Journal of Financial Economics*, June 1976.

31. See B. Solnik, *op. cit.* or M. Adler and B. Dumas, *op. cit.* p. 944. The risky portfolio common to all investors is sometimes called the "logarithmic portfolio" since it is the portfolio that would be held by investors with a logarithmic utility function.

32. See F. Black, "International Capital Market Equilibrium with Investment Barriers," *Journal of Financial Economics*, 1, December 1974; V. R. Errunza and E. Losq, "International Asset Pricing under Mild Segmentation: Theory and Test," *Journal of Finance*, 40, March 1985; R. C. Stapleton and M. G. Subrahmanyam, "Market Imperfections, Capital Asset Equilibrium and Corporation Finance," *Journal of Finance*, 32, May 1977; R. Stulz "On the Effect of International Barriers to International Investment," *Journal of Finance*, 36, September 1981; M. G. Subrahmanyam, "On the Optimality of International Capital Market Integration," *Journal of Financial Economics*, 2, August 1975; I. Cooper and C. E. Kaplanis, "Costs to Crossborder Investment and International Equity Market Equilibrium," in E. Edwards, et al., (eds), *Recent Development in Corporate Finance*, NY: Cambridge University Press, 1986; V. Errunza and E. Losq, "Capital Flow Controls, International Asset Pricing and Investor's Welfare: A Multi-Country Framework," *Journal of Finance*, September 1989; C. Eun and S. Janakiramanan, "A Model of International Asset Pricing with a Constraint on the Foreign Equity Ownership," *Journal of Finance*, September 1986.

33. F. Black, "Universal Hedging: Optimizing Currency Risk and Reward in International Equity Portfolios," *Financial Analysts Journal*, July/August 1989; B. Solnik, *op. cit.*; P. Sercu, *op. cit.*; M. Adler and B. Dumas, *op. cit.* For a critique of Black's conclusions, see M. Adler and B. Prasad, "On Universal Currency Hedges," Columbia working paper, October 1989; M. Adler and B. Solnik, Letter to the Editor, "The Individuality of 'Universal' Hedging," *Financial Analysts Journal*, May/June 1990.

34. A definition of a hedge ratio is given in Chapter 8.

35. P. Jorion, "Asset Allocation with Hedged and Unhedged Foreign Stocks and Bonds," *The Journal of Portfolio Management*, Summer 1989.

36. See R. Stehle, "An Empirical Test of Alternative Hypothesis of National and International Pricing of Risky Assets," *Journal of Finance*, May 1977; P. Jorion and E. Schwartz, "Integration versus Segmentation in the Canadian Stock Market," *Journal of Finance*, July 1986; M. Gultekin, B. Gultekin, and A. Penati, "Capital Controls and International Market Segmentation: The Evidence from the Japanese and American Stock Markets," *Journal of Finance*, September 1989; S. Wheatley, "Some Tests of International Equity Integration," *Journal of Financial Economics*, September 1988.

   37. See D. C. Cho, C. Eun, and L. W. Senbet, "International Arbitrage Pricing Theory: An Empirical Investigation," *Journal of Finance*, June 1986; and P. Fontaine, *Arbitrage et Evaluation Internationale des Actifs*, Economica, Paris, 1984.

BIBLIOGRAPHY

Adler, M. and Dumas, B. "International Portfolio Choice and Corporation Finance: A Synthesis," *Journal of Finance*, 38, June 1983.

_____ and Prasad B. "On Universal Currency Hedges," Working Paper, Columbia University, October 1989.

_____ and Simon, D. "Exchange Rate Surprises in International Portfolios," *Journal of Portfolio Management*, Winter 1986.

Berglund, T. and Liljebom, E. "Market Serial Correlation on a Small Security Market: A Note," *Journal of Finance*, December 1988.

Black, F. "International Capital Market Equilibrium with Investment Barriers," *Journal of Financial Economics*, 1, December 1974.

_____ . "Universal Hedging: Optimizing Currency Risk and Reward in International Equity Portfolios," *Financial Analysts Journal*, July/August 1989.

Branson, W. H. "Exchange Rate Policy after a Decade of Floating," in Bilson, J. and Marston, R. (eds), *Exchange Rate Theory and Practice*, Chicago: University of Chicago Press, 1984.

Cassel, G. "The Present Situation on the Foreign Exchanges," *Economic Journal*, 1916, pp. 62–65.

Cho, D. C., Eun, C., and Senbet, L. W. "International Arbitrage Pricing Theory: An Empirical Investigation," *Journal of Finance*, June 1986.

Cooper, I. and Kaplanis, C. E. "Costs to Crossborder Investment and International Equity Market Equilibrium," in Edwards, E. et al. (eds), *Recent Development in Corporate Finance*, NY: Cambridge University Press, 1986.

Cumby, R. E. and Obstfeld, M. "A Note on Exchange Rates Expectations and Nominal Interest Rates Differentials," *Journal of Finance*, June 1981.

Dornbusch. *Open Economy Macroeconomics*, New York: Basic, 1980.

Elton, E. and Gruber, M. *Security Evaluation and Portfolio Analysis*, Englewood Cliffs, NJ: Prentice Hall, 1984.

Errunza, V. and Losq, E. "International Asset Pricing Under Mild Segmentation: Theory and Test," *Journal of Finance*, 40, March 1985.

_____ and _____ . "Capital Flow Controls, International Asset Pricing and Investor's Welfare: A Multi-Country Framework," *Journal of Finance*, September 1989.

Eun, C. and Janakiramanan S. "A Model of International Asset Pricing with a Constraint on the Foreign Equity Ownership," *Journal of Finance*, September 1986.

Fama, E. "Forward and Spot Exchange Rates," *Journal of Monetary Economics*, November 1984.

_____. "Stock Returns, Real Activity, Inflation and Money," *American Economic Review*, September 1981.

_____ and Schwert. "Asset Returns and Inflation," *Journal of Financial Economics*, November 1977.

Fontaine, P. *Arbitrage et Evaluation Internationale des Actifs*, Paris: Economica, 1984.

Geske, R. and Roll, R. "The Fiscal and Monetary Linkage Between Stock Returns and Inflation," *Journal of Finance*, March 1983.

Giddy, I. "An Integrated Theory of Exchange Rate Equilibrium," *Journal of Financial and Quantitative Analysis*, December 1976.

Grauer, F., Litzenberger, R., and Stehle, R. "Sharing Rules and Equilibrium in an International Capital Market Under Uncertainty," *Journal of Financial Economics*, June 1976.

Gultekin, M., Gultekin, B., and Penati, A. "Capital Controls and International Market Segmentation: The Evidence from the Japanese and American Stock Markets," *Journal of Finance*, September 1989.

Hawawini, G. *European Equity Markets*: *Price Behavior and Efficiency*, Monograph 1984-4, Solomon Brothers Center, New York University, 1984.

Heckman, C. R. "Don't Blame Currency Values for Strategic Errors: Protecting Competitive Position by Correctly Assessing Foreign Exchange Exposure," *Midland Corporate Finance Journal*, Fall 1986.

_____. "A Financial Model of Foreign Exchange Exposure," *Journal of International Business Studies*, Summer 1985.

Hietla, P. T. "Asset Pricing in Partially Segmented Markets: Evidence from the Finnish Market," *Journal of Finance*, July 1989.

Hodrick, R. J. and Srivastava, S. "An Investigation of Risk and Return in Forward Foreign Exchange," *Journal of International Money and Finance*, April 1984.

Jacquillat, B. and Solnik, B. *Les Marches Financiers et la Gestion de Portefeuille*, Dunod, 1989.

Jorion, P. "Asset Allocation with Hedged and Unhedged Foreign Stocks and Bonds," *Journal of Portfolio Management*, Summer 1989.

_____ and Schwartz, E. "Integration Versus Segmentation in the Canadian Stock Market," *Journal of Finance*, July 1986.

Kravis, I. B., Heston, A., and Summers, L. *World Production and Income*: *International Comparisons of Real GDP*, Baltimore, MD: Johns Hopkins University Press, 1982.

Levy, H. and Sarnat, M. *Portfolio Investment Selection*, Englewood Cliffs, NJ: Prentice Hall, 1984.

Lucas, R. "Interest Rates and Currency Prices in Two-Country World," *Journal of Monetary Economics*, November 1982.

Meese, R. and Rogoff, K. "What Is Real? The Exchange Rate-Interest Rate Differential Relation over the Modern Floating-Rate Period," *Journal of Finance*, September 1988.

Mishkin, F. S. "Are Real Interest Rates Equal Across Countries? An Empirical Investigation of International Parity Relations," *Journal of Finance*, December 1984.

Officer, L. H. "The Purchasing Power Theory of Exchange Rates: A Review Article," *IMF Staff Papers*, March 1976.

Roll, R. "Violations of Purchasing Power Parity and Their Implications for Efficient International Commodity Markets," in Sarnat, M. and Szego, G. (eds), *International Finance and Trade*, Cambridge, MA: Ballinger, 1979.

_____. "A Critique of the Asset Pricing Theory's Test: On Past and Potential Testability of the Theory," *Journal of Financial Economics*, 4, March 1977.

_____ and Solnik, B. "On Some International Parity Conditions," *Journal of Macroeconomics*, Summer 1979.

_____ and _____ "A Pure Foreign Exchange Asset Pricing Model," *Journal of International Economics*, 7, May 1977.

Sercu, P. "A Generalization of the International Asset Pricing Model," *Revue de l'Association Française de Finance*, June 1980.

Shapiro, A. "What Does Purchasing Power Parity Mean?," *Journal of International Money and Finance*, December 1983.

Solnik, B. "An Equilibrium Model of the International Capital Market," *Journal of Economic Theory*, 8, July/August 1974.

_____. "The Relationship Between Stock Prices and Inflationary Expectations," *Journal of Finance*, March 1983.

_____. "Capital Markets and International Monetary Variables," *Financial Analysts Journal*, March 1984.

_____. "The Validity of the Random Walk for European Stock Prices," *Journal of Finance*, December 1983.

_____. "An Equilibrium Model of the International Capital Market," *Journal of Economic Theory*, July 1974.

_____ and de Freitas, A. "International Factors of Security Returns," in S. Khoury and A. Ghosh (eds), *Recent Developments in International Finance and Banking*, Lexington, MA: Lexington Books, 1988.

Stapleton, R. C. and Subrahmanyam, M. G. "Market Imperfections, Capital Asset Equilibrium and Corporation Finance," *Journal of Finance*, 32, May 1977.

Stehle, R. "An Empirical Test of Alternative Hypothesis of National and International Pricing of Risky Assets," *Journal of Finance*, May 1977.

Stulz, R. "A Model of International Asset Pricing," *Journal of Financial Economics*, 9, December 1981.

_____. "On the Effect of International Barriers to International Investment," *Journal of Finance*, 36, September 1981.

_____. "The Pricing of Capital Assets in an International Setting: An Introduction," *Journal of International Business Studies*, Summer 1984.

Subrahmanyam, M. G. "On the Optimality of International Capital Market Integration," *Journal of Financial Economics*, 2, August 1975.

Wheatley, S. "Some Tests of International Equity Integration," *Journal of Financial Economics*, September 1988.

2

The Case for International Diversification

International portfolio investment has long been a tradition in Europe, but is a more recent practice in North America. However, there seems to be a trend toward international diversification, even among U.S. institutional investments such as corporate and public pension plans. U.S. pension assets invested abroad amounted to $70 billion in 1989 as opposed to only $3 billion in 1980. Pension assets are growing rapidly in foreign countries due to legal changes. By the end of 1985 pension assets reached more than $50 billion in the United Kingdom, The Netherlands, Japan, Canada, Switzerland, and other countries. The share of pension foreign investment is 10 to 30% in these countries as opposed to 5 to 15% in the United States. Many European institutional and private investors have more than 50% of their assets abroad. The trend toward global investment also includes U.S. private investors as illustrated in this quote from the U.S. magazine *MONEY*:

> Government economic policy makers and investors alike have taken on a global perspective rarely seen before. "We all should recognize that it is the world economy, not national economy, that is now dominant," says Donaldson Lufkin & Jenrette chief strategist Eric Miller. Investors have become more willing than ever to send their money across national boundaries in search of the best return. Last year, foreign investors poured $81 billion into U.S. stock and bond markets, and Americans invested some $2 billion in more than 45 mutual funds that buy foreign stocks and bonds."
>
> *Source:* "New Strategies for a New Era," *Money*, June 1986.

Indeed, the mere size of foreign markets justifies international diversification even for U.S. investors. At the end of 1989 the world stock market capitalization was over 10 trillion U.S. dollars. The U.S. stock markets accounted for one third of the world market size; the Far Eastern markets accounted for about half, and European markets for about twenty percent.[1] The breakdown is similar for the world bond market. The world market capitalization of publicly issued bonds was estimated by Salomon Brothers to be over ten trillion U.S. dollars at the end of 1989. U.S. dollar bonds accounted for roughly 50% of the world bond market; yen bonds accounted for approximately 20%, and bonds denominated in European currencies accounted for over 25%.

In a fully efficient, integrated, international capital market, buying the world market portfolio would be the natural strategy. However, we have seen that the case for an integrated international capital market has not yet been fully built; furthermore numerous constraints may give a competitive advantage to domestic investors. If buying the market is not the obvious strategy for all investors, the case for international diversification has to be established empirically. Since foreign-exchange risk hedging may not be available, we assume in this chapter that exchange risk is fully borne by international investors; this tends to penalize foreign investments in terms of risk.

Even then the basic arguments in favor of international diversification are that foreign investments offer additional profit potentials while reducing the total risk of the portfolio. In other words, international diversification helps to improve the risk-adjusted performance of a domestic portfolio.

Domestic securities tend to move up and down together because they are similarly affected by domestic conditions such as money supply announcement, movements in interest rates, budget deficit, and national growth. This creates a strong positive correlation between all national securities traded in the same market. The correlation applies equally to stocks and bonds; bond prices on a national market are very strongly correlated. Investors have searched for methods to spread their risks and diversify away the national market risk. Foreign capital markets, in their variety, provide good potential for diversification beyond domestic instruments and markets.

This chapter presents the major arguments in favor of international investment. Our case has been supported by extensive empirical evidence provided by academicians as well as practitioners. The strong advantages have to be weighed against some of the impediments to foreign investment, which are discussed in the last section.

Before discussing the increased profit opportunities offered by international investment we will present the well-established case of international risk reduction.

RISK DIVERSIFICATION

The argument often heard in favor of international investment is that it lowers risk without sacrificing expected return. A prerequisite for this argument is that the various capital markets of the world have somewhat independent price behavior. If the Paris Bourse and London Stock Exchange moved in parallel with the U.S. market, diversification opportunities would not exist.

Market Correlation

An impression of the relative independence of the world stock markets may be obtained by looking at the performance of major stock markets from 1975 to 1988 as plotted in Exhibit 2.1. Each reader, however, may have his or her own interpretation of this graph; so that Exhibit 2.2 is more reliable in evaluating market independence.[2] The correlations between various stock and bond markets are systematically monitored by major international money managers, and they arrive at the same conclusions regardless of the period of time analyzed. Although the correlation coefficients between markets vary over time,[3] they are always far from unity. For the portfolio manager this means there is ample room for successful risk diversification.

For example, Exhibit 2.2 indicates that the correlation between the German and U.S. stock markets is 0.34. The square of this correlation coefficient, usually called R^2, indicates the percentage of common variance between the two markets. Here only 10% ($R^2 = 0.34^2$) of stock price movements are common to the German and U.S. markets.[4] Note that on the average the common variance between the U.S. and other markets is less than 20% (average R of 0.4). The correlation with Canada is, of course, quite strong (0.70), because the two economies are closely linked. Other groups of countries are also highly correlated, indicating strong regional links. The deutsche mark block, for instance, is readily apparent. West Germany, Switzerland, The Netherlands, and Belgium tend to have high correlations because their currencies and economies are interrelated. Conversely, Hong Kong and Singapore show little correlation with European markets.

The last two rows and columns in the exhibit give the correlation of each national market with two international indexes. The world index is a market capitalization–weighted index of all the major stock markets of the world. The Europe, Australia, and Far East (EAFE) index is the non-American world index and is made up of stock markets from those parts of the world. Both indexes are computed in U.S. dollar terms by Morgan Stanley Capital International. The correlation of the U.S. market with the EAFE index is only 0.48. Therefore, the overall common variance between U.S. and non-U.S. stock indexes is 23% ($R^2 = 0.48^2 = 23\%$). This implies that any well-diversified portfolio of non-U.S. stocks provides an attractive risk-diversification vehicle for a domestic U.S. portfolio. The same holds true for any other domestic portfolio.

The correlation of the U.S. stock market with the world index is much larger ($R^2 = 0.85^2 = 72\%$) than it is for the EAFE index. But this should not be surprising, since the U.S. market accounts for half of the world market.

After the United States, the most "international" market, in terms of correlation with the world index, is the Dutch stock market; much of the Dutch

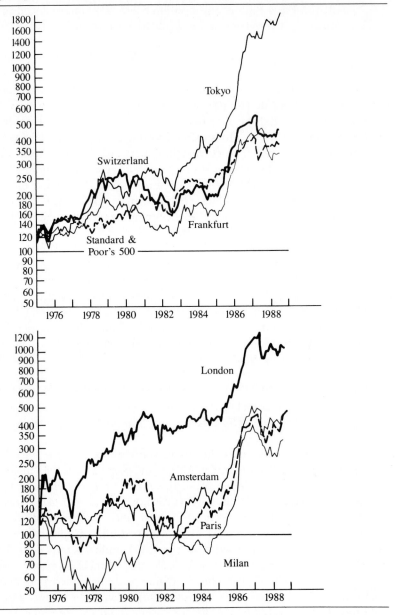

Source: Lombard, Odier and Cie, *International Financial Markets*, February 1989. Reprinted by permission.

market capitalization is accounted for by truly multinational firms with international ownership, including Royal Dutch-Shell, Unilever, Philips, and AKZO.

In general we find that all stocks within a given market tend to move up and down together, whereas stocks in different national markets as a rule do not. This provides opportunities for the expert international investor to time the markets by buying those markets that he or she expects to go up and neglecting the bearish ones. It also allows naive investors to spread risk, since some foreign markets are likely to go up when others go down. Actually, this reasoning is simply a variation on the traditional domestic diversification argument, except that it is extended to a larger universe of fairly independent markets.

The degree of independence of a stock market is directly linked to the independence of a nation's economy and government policies. To some extent, common world factors affect expected cash flows of all firms, and therefore, their stock prices. However, purely national or regional factors seem to play an important role in asset prices, leading to sizable differences in the degrees of independence between markets. It is clear that constraints and regulations imposed by national governments, technological specialization, independent fiscal and monetary policies, and cultural and sociological differences all contribute to the degree of a capital market's independence. On the other hand, when there are closer economic and government policies, as between the Benelux countries or the members of the European Economic Community, one observes more commonality in capital market behavior. In any case, the covariation between markets is still far from unity, leaving ample opportunities for risk diversification.

Two assets considered in Exhibit 2.2 are gold mining shares and gold ingots. Their correlations with all of the stock markets in the world are very weak and sometimes negative. The risk protection property of gold assets is discussed in Chapter 11.

Similar conclusions may be reached for bonds, as seen in Exhibit 2.3. U.S. dollar bonds are poorly correlated with other bond markets both in the short run (1983 to 1985) and over a long period (1971 to 1985). Again, the co-movement of the foreign bond markets with the U.S. dollar bond market is less than 10% in all cases (correlation less than 0.33). It appears that the markets' correlations were quite low in the early 1980s compared to the long-term figure.

Finally, the correlation of foreign bonds with the U.S. stock market also is weak (Exhibit 2.4). This is not surprising given the independence between U.S. and foreign national economic and monetary policies. The correlation of the U.S. bond and stock markets indicates the well-known reaction of stock prices to movements in domestic interest rates. However, the correlation is very weak, and sometimes negative, in the case of foreign bond markets. Clearly, foreign monetary and budgetary policies have little impact on U.S. economic growth and on U.S. share prices. Foreign bonds offer great diversification potential to a stock portfolio manager. Again, this is not surprising, since bonds are primarily

EXHIBIT 2.2
Correlation Matrix: Stock Markets, 1971 to 1988
Monthly returns in U.S. dollars

	West Germany	Belgium	Denmark	France	Italy
West Germany	1.00	0.64	0.41	0.58	0.37
Belgium	0.64	1.00	0.45	0.64	0.42
Denmark	0.41	0.45	1.00	0.35	0.29
France	0.58	0.64	0.35	1.00	0.44
Italy	0.37	0.42	0.29	0.44	1.00
Norway	0.38	0.53	0.31	0.46	0.26
Netherlands	0.67	0.65	0.46	0.58	0.37
United Kingdom	0.41	0.50	0.35	0.52	0.36
Sweden	0.40	0.43	0.31	0.33	0.31
Switzerland	0.70	0.64	0.44	0.60	0.37
Spain	0.33	0.39	0.27	0.35	0.35
Australia	0.28	0.31	0.24	0.37	0.26
Japan	0.40	0.46	0.38	0.41	0.38
Hong Kong	0.24	0.31	0.26	0.25	0.19
Singapore	0.24	0.32	0.32	0.26	0.17
Canada	0.31	0.37	0.31	0.44	0.27
United States	0.34	0.41	0.32	0.43	0.23
Gold Mines	0.14	0.25	0.05	0.24	0.17
Gold	0.16	0.24	0.11	0.22	0.18
World Index	0.54	0.60	0.46	0.61	0.44
EAFE Index	0.61	0.63	0.45	0.62	0.53

	Spain	Australia	Japan	Hong Kong	Singapore
West Germany	0.33	0.28	0.40	0.24	0.24
Belgium	0.39	0.31	0.46	0.31	0.32
Denmark	0.27	0.24	0.38	0.26	0.32
France	0.35	0.37	0.41	0.25	0.26
Italy	0.35	0.26	0.38	0.19	0.17
Norway	0.25	0.40	0.16	0.27	0.31
Netherlands	0.36	0.39	0.43	0.40	0.40
United Kingdom	0.30	0.44	0.34	0.35	0.50
Sweden	0.30	0.36	0.30	0.25	0.31
Switzerland	0.32	0.37	0.39	0.31	0.35
Spain	1.00	0.31	0.34	0.22	0.14
Australia	0.31	1.00	0.27	0.34	0.41
Japan	0.34	0.27	1.00	0.29	0.33
Hong Kong	0.22	0.34	0.29	1.00	0.46
Singapore	0.14	0.41	0.33	0.46	1.00
Canada	0.25	0.57	0.27	0.27	0.39
United States	0.23	0.49	0.28	0.28	0.45
Gold Mines	0.04	0.22	0.13	−0.01	0.07
	0.13	0.28	0.18	0.12	0.04
World Index	0.39	0.57	0.63	0.35	0.51
EAFE Index	0.44	0.47	0.80	0.31	0.46

Norway	Netherlands	United Kingdom	Sweden	Switzerland
0.38	0.67	0.41	0.40	0.70
0.53	0.65	0.50	0.43	0.64
0.31	0.46	0.35	0.31	0.44
0.46	0.58	0.52	0.33	0.60
0.26	0.37	0.36	0.31	0.37
1.00	0.53	0.40	0.39	0.44
0.53	1.00	0.63	0.46	0.70
0.40	0.63	1.00	0.41	0.53
0.39	0.46	0.41	1.00	0.46
0.44	0.70	0.53	0.46	1.00
0.25	0.36	0.30	0.30	0.32
0.40	0.39	0.44	0.36	0.37
0.16	0.43	0.34	0.30	0.39
0.27	0.40	0.35	0.25	0.31
0.31	0.40	0.50	0.31	0.35
0.42	0.56	0.53	0.35	0.47
0.43	0.58	0.50	0.38	0.46
0.27	0.21	0.12	0.12	0.25
0.24	0.20	0.08	0.12	0.22
0.50	0.74	0.68	0.48	0.61
0.41	0.69	0.70	0.45	0.60

Canada	United States	Gold Mines	Gold	World Index	EAFE Index
0.31	0.34	0.14	0.16	0.54	0.61
0.37	0.41	0.25	0.24	0.60	0.63
0.31	0.32	0.05	0.11	0.46	0.45
0.44	0.43	0.24	0.22	0.61	0.62
0.27	0.23	0.17	0.18	0.44	0.53
0.42	0.43	0.27	0.24	0.50	0.41
0.56	0.58	0.21	0.20	0.74	0.69
0.53	0.50	0.12	0.08	0.68	0.70
0.35	0.38	0.12	0.12	0.48	0.45
0.47	0.46	0.25	0.22	0.61	0.60
0.25	0.23	0.04	0.13	0.39	0.44
0.57	0.49	0.22	0.28	0.57	0.47
0.27	0.28	0.13	0.18	0.63	0.80
0.27	0.28	−0.01	0.12	0.35	0.31
0.39	0.45	0.07	0.04	0.51	0.46
1.00	0.70	0.27	0.22	0.71	0.49
0.70	1.00	0.12	−0.03	0.85	0.48
0.27	0.12	2.00	0.57	0.21	0.19
0.22	−0.03	0.57	1.00	0.14	0.21
0.71	0.85	0.21	0.14	1.00	0.85
0.49	0.48	0.19	0.21	0.85	1.00

EXHIBIT 2.3
Correlation of U.S. and Nondollar Government Bond Index (in U.S. Dollars)
Monthly returns

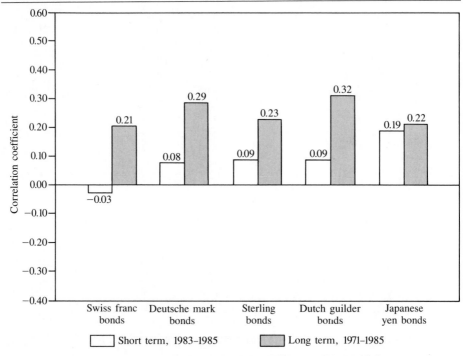

Source: K. Chollerton, P. Pieraerts, and B. Solnik, "Why Invest in Foreign Currency Bonds?," *Journal of Portfolio Management*, Summer 1986. Reprinted by permission.

affected by different factors than stocks: namely, interest rates, credit worthiness, and monetary liquidity.

Some investigators have attempted to find leads or lags between markets. However, no evidence of a systematic delayed reaction of one national market to another has ever been found. The existence of such simple market inefficiencies is, indeed, unlikely, since it would be so easy to exploit them to make an abnormal profit. Also, no systematic trend toward a growing synchronization of stock markets has been found. This may be explained by the growing competition between national economies and the recent importance of monetary factors on the behavior of security prices. National monetary policies do not appear to be well coordinated across the world. To be sure, correlation coefficients are not constant. In some periods, all stock markets are affected by the same worldwide factors. This was the case with the oil shock of 1974 or the international crash of October 1987 or the Gulf crisis of 1990. In other periods, all markets tend to move independently and even in opposite directions. Altogether we cannot discern an obvious and permanent trend toward a greater synchronization of

EXHIBIT 2.4
Correlation of Government Bond Indexes and Standard and Poor's 500 (in U.S. Dollars)
Monthly returns

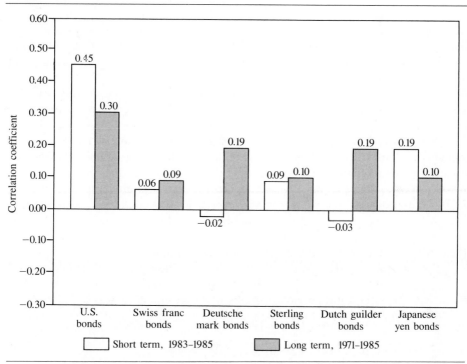

Source: K. Chollerton, P. Pieraerts, and B. Solnik, "Why Invest in Foreign Currency Bonds?," *Journal of Portfolio Management*, Summer 1986. Reprinted by permission.

capital markets. For example, we list below the correlation between the U.S. stock market and the EAFE index for successive periods of two years. This coefficient seems to vary randomly around an average value of 0.5

1970 1971	1972 1973	1974 1975	1976 1977	1978 1979	1980 1981	1982 1983	1984 1985	1986 1987	1988 1989
0.56	0.57	0.67	0.42	0.17	0.53	0.43	0.48	0.53	0.36

To summarize, all capital markets move together to some extent, but their relatively high degree of independence leaves ample room for risk diversification on both foreign stock and foreign bond markets.

Portfolio Volatility

One argument against foreign investment by U.S. investors is that foreign markets are more volatile than the U.S. domestic market, especially if currency risk is taken into consideration. Supporting evidence of this volatility is found in

Exhibit 2.5, which shows the recent performance of various market indexes. The average annual total return for a U.S. investor investing in each market is given in column 1. Columns 2, 3, and 4 segment this return into capital gains, yield, and the influence of exchange rate movements. The total risk of the market, measured by the standard deviation[5] of U.S. dollar monthly rates of return, is given in column 5, and the risk measured in local currency is given in column 6. The final column shows the standard deviation of the exchange rate of the local currency relative to the U.S. dollar.

The objective of a risk diversification policy is to reduce the total risk of a portfolio. Of course one hopes simultaneously to achieve high expected returns, as discussed in the next section. The total risk of most stock markets is larger than that of the U.S. market when the dollar is used as the base currency, even though the domestic risk of many markets is less than that of the U.S. market. Because of the exchange risk component, the same conclusion holds true for a Swiss, German, or Japanese investor if returns are computed in Swiss francs, deutsche marks, or yens, respectively. Nevertheless, the addition of more risky foreign assets to a purely domestic portfolio still reduces its total risk as long as the foreign assets correlation with the domestic market is not large. This can be demonstrated mathematically in the following example.

Assume that the domestic and foreign assets have standard deviations (σ) of $\sigma_d = 10\%$ and $\sigma_f = 12\%$, respectively, with a correlation of $R = 0.3$. The variance (σ^2) of the total portfolio equally invested in both assets σ_p^2, is given by

$$\sigma_p^2 = 0.5^2 \left[\sigma_d^2 + \sigma_f^2 + (2R\sigma_d\sigma_f) \right]$$

$$\sigma_p^2 = 0.5^2 \left[100 + 144 + (2 \times 0.3 \times 120) \right] = 79.$$

Hence, the standard deviation σ_p is given by $\sqrt{79}$ or 8.88%, which is significantly less than that of the domestic asset. Since one can diversify in several foreign markets, the total risk of the portfolio could be further reduced.

Column 6 in Exhibit 2.5 shows that the volatility of stock markets measured in their domestic currency is comparable to that of U.S. markets. Hong Kong's, however, is much more volatile, as are some of the smaller markets (Singapore, Italy, Norway). Also note that the London Stock Exchange has known a period of volatile stock prices.

Half of the market capitalization–weighted world stock index is U.S. securities, yet the index also includes some highly volatile markets such as Hong Kong. Nevertheless, the total risk of this internationally diversified index ($\sigma = 14.45\%$) is considerably less than that of a well-diversified U.S. portfolio (16.21%).

A similar conclusion holds for bond markets. For several years Salomon Brothers, Intersec, Lombard Odier, and others have computed monthly or daily bond indexes for the major domestic and European markets. They generally find that the world-weighted bond index, in U.S. dollars, is less volatile than the U.S. government bond index. For example, Salomon Brothers found a standard deviation of monthly dollar returns (interest plus price movement) equal to

EXHIBIT 2.5
Risk and Return for U.S. Dollar Investors, 1971 to 1988
Percent per year

	(1) Annual return	(2) Capital gain	(3) Dividend interest income	(4) Exchange gain	(5) Total risk	(6) Domestic risk	(7) Exchange risk
Stocks							
West Germany	14.34%	5.22%	4.63%	4.50%	20.67%	17.48%	12.09%
Belgium	20.89%	7.97%	10.95%	1.96%	21.28%	17.71%	12.03%
Denmark	15.78%	10.39%	4.82%	0.57%	18.93%	17.05%	11.10%
France	14.17%	8.92%	5.85%	−0.60%	25.90%	22.63%	11.22%
Italy	8.71%	10.25%	3.05%	−4.59%	27.20%	25.84%	9.83%
Norway	12.79%	8.23%	4.02%	0.54%	29.13%	27.75%	9.59%
Netherlands	16.47%	6.19%	6.52%	3.75%	19.37%	18.07%	11.57%
United Kingdom	14.54%	10.57%	5.83%	−1.87%	27.86%	25.04%	10.61%
Sweden	18.92%	15.36%	4.68%	−1.12%	21.49%	19.95%	10.28%
Switzerland	12.88%	3.57%	2.86%	6.44%	20.44%	16.63%	14.20%
Spain	10.06%	5.11%	7.95%	−3.00%	23.09%	20.33%	10.10%
Australia	10.80%	7.69%	4.83%	−1.72%	28.65%	24.94%	10.28%
Japan	26.16%	16.74%	2.23%	7.19%	21.16%	16.85%	11.51%
Hong Kong	23.37%	15.86%	4.85%	2.66%	40.54%	42.51%	6.07%
Singapore	10.52%	10.66%	2.73%	−2.88%	32.87%	32.72%	5.77%
Canada	10.95%	7.80%	4.18%	−1.04%	20.56%	18.82%	4.39%
United States	9.93%	5.26%	4.67%	0.00%	16.21%	16.21%	0.00%
Bonds							
West Germany	11.06%	−1.30%	7.99%	4.37%	16.61%	9.01%	12.09%
France	10.34%	−0.85%	11.77%	−0.58%	15.62%	9.14%	11.22%
Netherlands	10.79%	−1.29%	8.51%	3.57%	16.30%	9.01%	11.57%
United Kingdom	8.73%	−1.42%	11.92%	−1.78%	15.33%	9.10%	10.61%
Switzerland	9.88%	−1.29%	4.90%	6.27%	18.04%	8.96%	14.20%
Japan	13.18%	−1.20%	7.93%	6.45%	16.23%	9.18%	11.51%
Canada	7.99%	−1.58%	10.58%	−1.01%	10.72%	9.11%	4.39%
United States	8.17%	−1.37%	9.54%	0.00%	9.12%	9.12%	0.00%
Cash							
West Germany	10.27%	0.00%	5.94%	4.34%	12.04%	0.75%	12.09%
France	11.22%	0.00%	11.80%	−0.58%	11.31%	1.30%	11.22%
Netherlands	10.50%	0.00%	6.94%	3.56%	11.66%	0.81%	11.57%
United Kingdom	10.39%	0.00%	12.19%	−1.80%	10.74%	0.92%	10.61%
Switzerland	10.61%	0.00%	4.29%	6.31%	14.27%	0.74%	14.20%
Japan	13.44%	0.00%	6.98%	6.46%	11.53%	0.71%	11.51%
Canada	8.97%	0.00%	9.99%	−1.02%	4.48%	0.96%	4.39%
United States	9.66%	0.00%	9.66%	0.00%	0.99%	0.99%	0.00%
Gold and Gold-Related Vehicles							
Gold Mines	17.23%	7.53%	9.70%	0.00%	48.82%	48.82%	0.00%
Gold Bullion	14.17%	14.17%	0.00%	0.00%	26.42%	26.42%	0.00%
International Stock Indexes							
World (in U.S.$)	13.91%	9.45%	4.47%	0.00%	14.45%	13.10%	0.00%
EAFE (in U.S.$)	18.20%	14.19%	4.02%	0.00%	17.49%	14.50%	0.00%

These calculations are based on monthly index values and coupons obtained from Morgan Stanley Capital International (stocks) and Lombard Odier (bonds, cash).

EXHIBIT 2.6
International Diversification

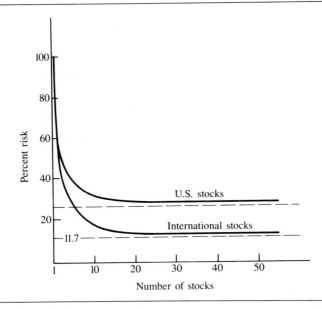

Source: B. Solnik, "Why Not Diversify Internationally Rather Than Domestically," *Financial Analysts Journal,*
July 1974. Reprinted by permission

3.48% for the U.S. government bond index and 3.18% for the world bond index
over a six-year period from January 1978 to December 1983.

Although the evidence is compelling at the market index level, it is not
clear that the same diversification payoffs can be obtained by a practicing
portfolio manager who selects only a few issues in a few markets. For example,
is it true that a portfolio diversified across fifty foreign and domestic securities is
less risky than a portfolio made up of fifty domestic securities? The answer again
is affirmative.

Exhibit 2.6 shows the total risk of domestic and internationally diversified
portfolios as a function of the number of securities held. Let us first consider the
top curve (U.S. stocks). In this exhibit 100% represents the typical risk of a
single U.S. security. When more U.S. stocks are added to the portfolio (all
securities are randomly selected), its total risk (standard deviation or variance)
is quickly reduced. Beyond forty or fifty stocks the addition of more domestic
securities provides little reduction in risk. That is why the top curve reaches an
asymptote corresponding to the U.S. market risk, which represents roughly 30%
of the typical risk of a single security. Adding foreign stocks to a purely domestic
portfolio reduces risk much faster, as can be seen on the bottom curve (international stocks). Indeed, with as few as forty securities equally spread among the
major stock markets (U.S. and European) the risk for a U.S. investor is less than

half that of a purely domestic portfolio of comparable size. The same finding has been attained for real or simulated portfolios over various time periods, including the recent era of volatile exchange rates, and in all cases international diversification provided a better and quicker reduction in risk, even for a portfolio with a limited number of securities.

Currency Risk

Another argument against international diversification is that currency risks (i.e., exchange risks) more than offset the reduction in security risks achieved by international diversification. Indeed, currency fluctuations affect both the total return and volatility of any foreign currency–denominated investment. From time to time, in fact, its impact on the investment return may exceed that of capital gain or income, especially over short periods of time. But currency fluctuation has never been the major component of total return on a diversified portfolio over a long period of time. This stems from the fact that the depreciation of one currency is often offset by the appreciation of another.[6] Since exchange rates are so difficult to forecast, we will focus on the contribution of exchange rate uncertainties to the total risk of the portfolio rather than to expected returns. Empirical studies[7] indicate that currency risk, as measured by the standard deviation of the exchange rate movement, is smaller than the risk of the corresponding stock market. This is shown by a comparison of the last two columns of Exhibit 2.5. On the other hand, currency risk is often larger than the risk (in local currency) of the corresponding bond market. It would seem then, that foreign investors stand to lose more, at least in the short run, on currency than on bond price movements. Does this mean that currency risk is so large that investors should avoid foreign investment? Not at all, and for several reasons.

First, market risks and currency risks are not additive. This would only be true if the two were perfectly correlated. In fact, there is only a weak, and sometimes negative, correlation between currency and market movements. If σ_D is the market risk in the domestic currency, σ_F the exchange rate volatility, σ the total risk in U.S. dollars, and R the correlation coefficient between the two risks, we have

$$\sigma^2 = \sigma_D^2 + \sigma_F^2 + 2R\sigma_D\sigma_F \text{ implying that } \sigma \leq \sigma_D + \sigma_F, \text{ since } R < 1.$$

To illustrate this point, Exhibit 2.5 shows the risk of each market measured in both U.S. dollars and domestic currency. The difference between the two is the contribution of currency risk to the total risk. Worldwide, exchange risk broadly amounts to 15% of the total stock market risk. For example, the French stock market has a risk of 22.63% when measured in local currency and a risk of 25.90% when measured in U.S. dollars. The contribution of currency risk is equal to the difference, 3.27%; this is far below the standard deviation of the

French franc/U.S. dollar exchange rate, which is equal to 11.22%. Equity investment risk is actually reduced for some markets such as Hong Kong. By contrast, exchange risk amounts to roughly 50% of the risk involved in foreign bonds, and, of course, is the major source of risk for short-term investments.

Chapter 1 features a discussion of the theoretical relationship between asset prices and exchange rates. A question often raised in this regard is: What is the appropriate numeraire to measure returns? Should a pension fund be concerned about real returns, adjusted for inflation, rather than nominal dollar returns? If so, the appropriate measure of currency risk should be in terms of purchasing power and its effect on the real returns for a domestic investor.

Second, the exchange risk of an investment may be hedged for major currencies by selling futures or forward currency contracts, buying put currency options, or even borrowing foreign currency to finance the investment.[8] Naturally, the cost of hedging should be weighed against the risk it eliminates.

Third, the contribution of currency risk should be measured for the total portfolio rather than for individual markets or securities, since part of that risk gets diversified away by the cocktail of currencies represented in the portfolio.

As can be seen in Exhibit 2.5, the currency component accounts for less than 20% of the total risk of the EAFE stock index. With no currency movements, the risk of this index would have been 14.50%, compared to 17.49% with the exchange rate movements. Given the large share of the U.S. market in the world portfolio, the currency contribution to the total risk of the world stock market portfolio is rather weak. As stressed by Jorion,[9] the contribution of currency risk to the total risk of a portfolio that includes only a small proportion of foreign assets (say, 5%) is insignificant. The contribution of currency risk is larger if one holds the world market portfolio and, hence, a large share of foreign assets. Then the question of the optimal currency hedging policy, already discussed in Chapter 1, becomes more relevant.

RISK-ADJUSTED RETURN

We have devoted so much attention to the risk reduction benefits of international investment because risk diversification is the most established and frequently invoked argument in favor of foreign investment, and justifies foreign investment even to the naive investor. However, it is not the sole motive for international investment. Indeed, mere risk reduction could more easily be achieved by simply investing part of one's assets in domestic risk-free bills. For that matter, the risk level of a domestic portfolio can be carefully modulated by changing its bill–bond–equity mix. Unfortunately, while the inclusion of risk-free bills lowers the portfolio risk, it also lowers expected return. In the traditional framework of the Capital Asset Pricing Model (CAPM), the expected return on a security is equal to the risk-free rate plus a risk premium. In an efficient market, reducing the risk level of a portfolio by adding less-risky investments implies reducing its expected return. International diversification, however, implies no reduction in return. It lowers risk by eliminating nonsystematic volatility without sacrificing expected return. Before presenting some empirical evidence on the risk-return characteristics of international investment, let us examine why this apparent free lunch exists.

To some extent the strictly domestic (noninternational) investor is like a U.S. investor who ignores all industrial sectors except chemicals on the New York Stock Exchange. By restricting oneself only to the equity of chemical firms, the investor incurs unnecessary risk. If stocks in other industries have the same expected return, the investor would be better off diversifying into those U.S. sectors, whether they be energy, high technology, banking, or something else. By so doing, the risks are considerably reduced without sacrificing return. The same argument holds for a domestic investor investing in foreign capital markets even when he or she does not expect a better performance in the foreign markets. One buys stocks abroad because the low correlation between national markets implies that it is likely that other markets will go up when the domestic stock market falls. Of course, during any given period it is possible that the foreign portfolio segment will underperform the domestic segment, but on average, the risk of loss is reduced.

The second argument in favor of international investment is that more profitable investments are possible in an enlarged universe. Higher returns may arise from faster-growing economies and firms located around the world or simply from currency gains.

Long-Term Performance

International money managers can rightfully call attention to the excellent track records of international portfolios since the sixties or the seventies. This is illustrated in Exhibit 2.5, which shows that the Morgan Stanley Capital International EAFE stock index markedly outperformed the U.S. stock index (18.20% per year versus 9.93%) between 1971 and 1988. The average annual total performance of the world stock index[10] in U.S. dollars was 13.91% compared to 9.93% for the U.S. index, and the volatility was much smaller (14.45% versus 16.21%).

A similar conclusion is reached for bonds or a combination of stocks and bonds, as seen in the next section. Focusing on bonds, Barnett and Rosenberg (1983) have run a computer simulation on portfolios of bond indexes for the period 1973 to 1983, from a U.S. investor viewpoint.[11] They started with a portfolio fully invested in U.S. bonds and then replaced them with a mix of foreign bonds from seven markets weighted in proportion to their size. They increased the proportion of foreign bonds in increments of 10% until the portfolio was made up of only foreign bonds. Then they measured the risk and return on the various portfolios they created and came up with the following

EXHIBIT 2.7
Risk / Return Trade-Off of an Internationally Diversified Bond Portfolio, January 1973 to March 1983

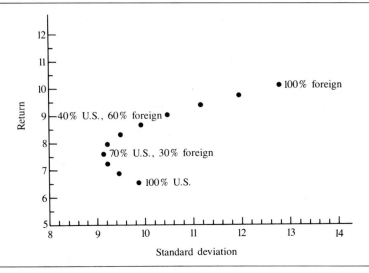

Source: G. Barnett and M. Rosenberg, "International Diversification in Bonds," *Prudential International Fixed Income Investment Strategy*, Second Quarter 1983. Reprinted by permission.

conclusions:

- As the U.S. bond content was reduced, portfolio return rose. This reflects the fact that foreign bonds outperformed U.S. bonds over the ten-year period.

- As the U.S. bond content was reduced from 100 to 70%, the volatility portfolio for a U.S. investor was actually reduced. This reflects the fact that returns on U.S. and foreign bonds were not highly correlated. At a 70% U.S. bond content, portfolio risk was minimized, as can be seen in Exhibit 2.7.

- As Exhibit 2.7 indicates, a U.S. investor could have committed up to 60% of his or her funds to foreign bonds without raising the level of risk above the level associated with holding only U.S. bonds. At the same time the total annual return would have been enhanced by a significant amount.

A similar study[12] has been conducted by Chollerton, Pieraerts, and Solnik (1986) over the 1971 to 1984 period with similar conclusions. In a well-documented study[13] of the total performance of the world capital markets using annual data from 1960 to 1984, Ibbotson, Siegel, and Love (1985) also found a superior performance for non-U.S. investments as shown in Exhibit 2.8.

This better performance is largely the result of higher growth rates in many foreign economies, especially in Asia. From 1960 to 1985 the real gross domestic product grew at an average annual rate of 3.4% in the United States compared

EXHIBIT 2.8
World Capital Market Total Annual Returns, 1960 to 1984

	Compound return	*Standard deviation*
Equities		
United States	8.81	16.89
Foreign		
Europe	7.83	15.58
Asia	15.14	30.74
Other	8.14	20.88
Foreign Total	9.84	16.07
Equities Total	9.08	15.28
Bonds		
United States		
Corporate	5.35	9.63
Government	5.91	6.43
United States Total	5.70	7.16
Foreign		
Corporate Domestic	8.35	7.26
Government Domestic	5.79	7.41
Crossborder	7.51	5.76
Foreign Total	6.80	6.88
Bonds Total	6.36	5.50
Cash Equivalents		
United States	6.49	3.22
Foreign	6.50	7.10
Cash Total	6.38	2.92

Source: Data from R. Ibbotson, L. Siegel, and K. Love, "World Wealth: Market Values and Returns," *Journal of Portfolio Management*, Fall 1985.

to over 4% in the other industrial countries. Over the same period the annual real growth rate was 7.5% in Japan and 8.7% in Korea. Such differences in growth rates are likely to persist, as evidenced in forecasts by the World Bank or the Organization for Economic Cooperation and Development (OECD). Some emerging economies offer attractive investment opportunities.[14] The local risks (volatility, liquidity, political) are higher, but the expected profit is large. Among the fast-growing economies with emerging stock markets, portfolio investors should seriously consider Hong Kong, Singapore, Thailand, Malaysia, Korea, Spain, India, and now the markets of Eastern Europe and of the People's Republic of China.

Economic flexibility is also an important factor in investment performance, which may explain differences between past and future performances among these countries. Wage and employment rigidity is bad for the national economy. In countries such as France, Canada, and the United Kingdom, companies have a difficult time adjusting to slowing activity; on the other hand, they do not take full advantage of growth opportunities, since they are reluctant to hire new employees whom they cannot fire if the activity slows. The degree of socialization of the economy is also an important issue. Some international money managers like to correlate the prospects of an economy and its stock market with the so-called lawyer intensity. They claim that stock market growth is negatively related to the time and costs lost in legal procedures, and recall that in 1983 there were 2.67 lawyers per 1,000 persons in the United States, 1.0 lawyer per 1,000 persons in the United Kingdom, 0.57 lawyer per 1,000 persons in West Germany, and only 0.1 lawyer per 1,000 persons in Japan.[15]

It should be stressed that there is no guarantee that the past will necessarily repeat itself. Indeed, over any given period one national market is bound to outperform the others, and if one had perfect foresight, the best strategy would be to invest solely in the top-performing market or even in the top-performing security in that market. But because of the great uncertainty of forecasts, it is always better to spread risk in the fund by diversifying internationally across markets with comparable expected return. This ensures a favorable risk-return trade-off, or in the jargon of theory, higher risk-adjusted expected returns. If managers believe that they have some relative forecasting ability, they will engage in active investment strategies that reap the benefits of international risk diversification while focusing on preferred markets. For example, an American investor may concentrate on U.S. and Japanese stocks if he or she is bullish on those markets, and avoid France for political or currency reasons.

Optimal International Asset Allocation

Solnik and Noetzlin (1982)[16] compared the performance of passive and active strategies for U.S. investors over the period 1970 to 1980. Their approach was to examine the expost efficient frontier (with no short-selling constraints on any investments) using a mean-variance Markowitz optimization. The risk and return curve for expost optimal investment strategies is given in Exhibit 2.9. The right-hand curve is the optimal set of strategies when investments are restricted to stock markets. The left-hand curve is the optimal set of strategies for all stock and bond market indexes. All computations are performed from a U.S. dollar investor viewpoint.[17] The set of optimal strategies represents the portfolio of market indexes that would have maximized the dollar performance for different levels of risk (standard deviation). Also shown in the same exhibit are some selected market indexes, especially the market capitalization–weighted indexes combining stocks and bonds. These indexes were calculated from the database of domestic market indexes using annually published market capitalizations. Monthly returns are used in the estimation process, but the weights of

EXHIBIT 2.9
Efficient Frontiers, December 1970 to December 1980

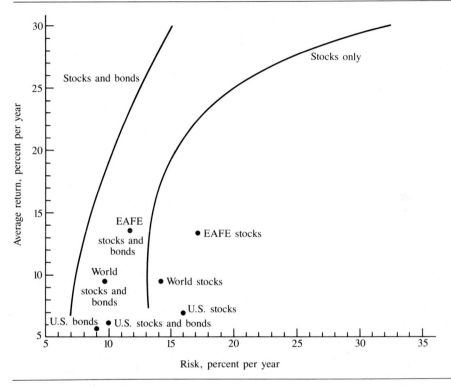

Source: B. Solnik and B. Noetzlin, "Optimal International Asset Allocation," *Journal of Portfolio Management,* Fall 1982. Reprinted by permission.

the strategies are set at the start of the period and stay fixed throughout the period. No short selling is allowed.

What follows are some of the conclusions reached by Solnik and Noetzlin (1982) on the risk-adjusted performance of optimal strategies.

> *Advantage of an international diversification.* Spreading investments over all major foreign markets reduces risk while enhancing return. Thus a passive diversification along the lines of the Morgan Stanley Capital International world stock index has less risk than a purely domestic U.S. portfolio (14% instead of 16%) and provides a return more than 50% higher, even though U.S. stocks make up more than half of this index.

> *Advantages of a balanced portfolio (stocks and bonds).* International diversification over both stock and bond markets results in substantially lower risk in spite of the volatility of bonds. As Exhibit 2.9 shows, the world stock-and-bond

index posted the same performance as the world stock-only index with much less volatility (10% instead of 14%). This same conclusion applies to optimal strategies as well (see Exhibit 2.9). Efficient portfolios made up of only stocks display 50 to 100% higher risk for the same level of return than efficient portfolios made up of stocks and bonds.

While there is no guarantee that higher risk-adjusted performance will always hold, the results strongly favor a global management approach that includes both stocks and bonds.[18]

Advantages of an optimal asset allocation. Modern financial market theory claims that the market portfolio must be efficient in a risk-return sense. In other words, the world market portfolio must be on the efficient frontier, as represented in Exhibit 2.9. It is therefore impossible to beat the market, whence the idea of the index fund approach. Internationally, market portfolios seem far from efficient,[19] at least judging from historical data. This implies that there is plenty of room for an asset allocation strategy different from market capitalization weights. Note that the asset allocation strategies applied here are passive in the sense that the market weights are set at the start of the period and remain unchanged thereafter.

As illustrated in columns 3 and 4 in Exhibit 2.10, optimal asset allocation makes it feasible to double or even triple the returns of a passive index fund and still retain the same level of risk. This exhibit indicates the return on efficient portfolios with a risk equal to that of selected market indexes.

There is, of course, no way of knowing in advance what these optimal asset allocations will be. Therefore, all we can conclude is that the opportunities for increased risk-adjusted returns are sizable, and that the performance gap between optimal international asset allocations and a simple index fund is potentially quite wide. Whether or not any money manager has sufficient expertise to realize most, or even part, of this performance differential is yet another question.

EXHIBIT 2.10
Compound Annual Return Comparisons of International Efficient-Frontier Portfolios Featuring Risk Levels Equal to the S + P 500 and World Indexes

	Return on Efficient Portfolios of Equal Risk (percent)			
Index	*(1)* *Risk*	*(2)* *Return*	*(3)* *Stocks only*	*(4)* *Stocks and bonds*
U.S. Stocks	16.0	6.8	20.3	30.8
World Stocks	14.2	9.4	16.7	28.0
World Stocks and Bonds	9.7	9.4	—	17.3

Other studies on optimal international asset allocation by Grauer and Hakansson (1987), Levy and Lerman (1988), or Jorion (1989) reach similar conclusions.[20]

CONSTRAINTS AND MISCONCEPTIONS

The relative size of foreign capital markets would justify extensive foreign investment by investors of any nationality. Empirical studies build a strong case for international diversification. However, international investment, although rapidly growing, is still not widespread in several countries, and certainly far from what it should be according to the world market portfolio weights. This conservative behavior may be explained by the prevalence of misconceptions and constraints. Although some barriers to foreign investment exist, they are usually exaggerated. We will now address the often-mentioned barriers to foreign investment.

Familiarity with Foreign Markets

A major impediment to foreign investment is cultural differences. Investors are often unfamiliar with foreign cultures and markets. They feel uneasy about the way business is done in other countries: the trading procedures, the way reports are presented, different languages, different time zones, etc. Because of these familiarity and communication problems, institutional investors often prefer to do their foreign trades through domestic brokers. Basically a lot of investors, especially Americans, feel more comfortable staying at home with local markets, even though this is a myopic and nonprofitable attitude. Foreign markets are perceived as more risky simply because they are unfamiliar.

It is clearly worth the effort to break this psychological barrier and invest some time in understanding foreign markets and business cultures. U.S. corporations have understood the benefits of direct foreign investment for a long time and possess truly multinational operations. It is interesting to find numerous private corporations that are very international on their corporation side but very parochial on their pension plan. Again the argument is not that one should go international because overseas is better than home, but rather that international investment is part of a global strategy of improving the risk-return trade-off.

Regulations

In many countries regulations limit foreign investment. At some times and in some countries investors are prohibited to invest abroad for capital control purposes. Investors in some European countries have had to use a special "financial" exchange rate to invest abroad, called the *dollar premium* in the

United Kingdom, the *devise titre* in France, and the *financial franc* in Belgium. These regulations applied to domestic investors wishing to buy foreign shares; they do not apply to foreigners investing on the domestic market. Institutional investors in most countries are often constrained on the proportion of foreign assets they can hold in their portfolios. However, there has been a slow but general worldwide relaxation of these constraints. This is certainly the case in the European Common Market, and Japan and North America are following the trend toward deregulation. The "prudent man" rule for U.S. pension plans allows for more extensive international diversification, and the proportion of foreign assets in U.S. pension plans is rapidly increasing, although it has not yet reached the level of UK or Dutch pension funds. Private pension funds have led the way toward international investment (several U.S. funds have over 15% of their assets in foreign investments), and public funds follow the lead when their legislatures pass a prudent man management rule.

Market Efficiency

A first issue in market efficiency is that of liquidity. Some markets are very small and others have a large volume for many issues traded. As mentioned previously non-American markets are similar, in terms of size and trading volume, to the U.S. stock and bond markets. U.S. institutions can easily find a few hundred foreign issues with good liquidity.

Of course, some issues on the major markets, as well as some of the smaller national markets, trade on little volume. Large institutional investors may wish to be careful and invest only a small part of their portfolios in these small-capitalization, less-liquid shares. Indeed, it may be difficult to get out of some national markets on a large scale. An excellent performance on a local index may not be transformed into a realized performance on a specific portfolio because of the share price drop when liquidating the portfolio. This has been the experience in Spain and Italy and suggests that one may improve liquidity by investing in a passive index portfolio of the local stock market, which, by definition, has the same performance as the market, whatever the liquidity problems, rather than by picking a few attractive stocks.

Another liquidity risk is the imposition of capital controls on foreign portfolio investments. Such a capital control prevents the sale of a portfolio of foreign assets and the repatriation of proceeds. This has never happened on any of the major capital markets of the world; the cost of such a political decision would be very high for any government as it would reduce its borrowing capacity on the international capital market. However, such capital controls may be imposed in an extreme financial crisis, and international money managers carefully monitor a few, high-risk countries.

Another issue in market efficiency is price manipulation. If foreign markets were too inefficient a manager would probably not run the risk of investing in these markets to benefit the domestic speculators. As mentioned in Chapter 1, a number of studies have established that all major stock markets are nearly efficient in the usual sense. Stock prices seem close to following a random walk, and systematic inefficiencies are hard to detect and never exist for long.

Risk Perception

Any unknown is perceived as risky; foreign capital markets are perceived as very risky by investors who are not familiar with them. But this is not a rational financial approach.

The true measure of the market risk borne by a portfolio is international market risk, and international diversification allows the elimination of all unnecessary national risks. Foreign assets might look more volatile than domestic assets, but their inclusion in a domestic portfolio will reduce, not increase, the total risk of the portfolio because of the low correlation between the various national markets. Remember that a good diversification asset is one with high volatility and low correlation with the portfolio. This phenomenon, amply demonstrated previously, runs against the intuition of some investors. But again, the net result of international diversification is the reduction of the magnitude of potential losses in any given time period. It should be stressed that a diversification of risk is not a complete insurance; diversification reduces risk but does not eliminate it. A good diversification eliminates all unnecessary risks while keeping profit opportunities intact, which is not the case with a fully hedged or insured program. The purpose is not to eliminate risk but to get rid of unnecessary risks while trying to maximize the performance. Some international investors focus solely on performance and build undiversified international portfolios; this might lead to a more risky portfolio with large potential losses. In all cases, risk should be closely monitored.

A major cause for the higher volatility of foreign assets is currency risk. As mentioned previously currency risk cannot be overstated:

- □ Currency risk gets partly diversified away in a well-diversified portfolio.
- □ Currency options and futures contracts may be used to fully or partly hedge currency risk if so desired.
- □ Currency risk may be desired by investors. Foreign currencies sometimes provide attractive profit opportunities to domestic investors. They also allow diversification of domestic monetary risks. As mentioned in Chapter 1, all private investors and pension sponsors should worry about the real purchasing power of their assets, not their nominal performance. Since foreign goods represent a sizable part of any consumption basket, foreign currency assets allow one to hedge the local price variation of these foreign consumption goods. Equally important is the fact that one major factor of domestic risk is monetary policy uncertainty. This domestic monetary risk cannot be diversified away locally, since domestic stock and bond prices react in the same direction to news on monetary policy. On the other hand,

a loose monetary policy will generally lead to a depreciation of the domestic currency and good performance of foreign assets because of the currency component.

Costs

Costs of international investments tend to be higher than those of domestic investments. This effect is more pronounced for investors in countries where all costs tend to be very low (e.g., the United States and France). This cost has several components which are detailed in the Appendix.

Conclusions

Altogether, foreign investment may not seem more costly for a resident from a high-cost country such as Switzerland or The Netherlands, but it is clearly more expensive for a U.S. resident. For a U.S. investor, a ballpark estimate of the increase in total costs (management fee, commissions, custody) is on the order of 0.5 to 0.75% for stocks and 0.25% for bonds. The difference would be less for a passively managed fund. These figures are still small compared to the return-risk advantage of foreign investment, as presented in the first part of this chapter. However, they could explain why one would desire to overweigh the domestic component of the portfolio compared to the world market portfolio weights. Information and transaction costs, differential taxes, and sometimes political or transfer risk give a comparative advantage to the domestic investor on the home market. This does not imply that foreign investment should be avoided altogether.

We have seen that international diversification reduces domestic market risk and therefore improves risk-adjusted performance, even for a passive international portfolio. An active international market, currency, or security selection strategy can further improve performance.

Although European investors, and even U.S. corporations, find foreign investment routine, psychological and cultural barriers still inhibit many U.S. money managers from following suit. The issue is not whether or not foreign markets can outperform the U.S. market, but whether or not so effective a means of diversification should remain untapped. Since the benefits of foreign diversification can be achieved with only a few securities, there is no need to invest in politically risky markets or illiquid issues. The advantages of international diversification seem to exceed the costs and difficulties associated with investment in foreign markets.

SUMMARY

1. Non-American capital markets account for more than half of the world market capitalization. The mere size of foreign markets justifies extensive international investment for the U.S. investor.

2. Markets across the world display only limited correlation. When one national market goes down, another is likely to go up simultaneously. Their relative independence leaves ample room for risk diversification on foreign stock and bond markets.

3. Although foreign securities may sometimes look more volatile, especially because of exchange risk, their addition to a purely domestic portfolio reduces the total risk of the portfolio. This is caused by the less-than-perfect correlation between foreign securities and the domestic market. The same risk reduction appears both for market indexes and for small portfolios made up of only a few securities.

4. Currency risk can be hedged to reduce the total risk of a foreign portfolio. Anyway, currency risk gets partly diversified away in portfolios including assets from several countries. Currency risk is the major source of risk for cash investments; it is a significant part of the total risk of a foreign bond portfolio but only a small part of the total risk of a stock portfolio.

5. In the past U.S. investors would have improved the portfolio risk-adjusted performance by diversifying a portfolio internationally. In other words, international (U.S. plus foreign) portfolios yielded both a higher return and a lower volatility than purely domestic U.S. portfolios. Foreign bonds allow diversification of U.S. monetary policy risk without sacrificing returns.

6. Higher growth rates in foreign economies explain part of their superior performance. Differences in real growth rates are likely to persist over time.

7. Several misconceptions and constraints may explain why foreign portfolio investment is still not widespread in some countries such as the United States. Some of these constraints are probably overstated; they should be carefully investigated and possibly relaxed so that the risk and return benefits of international diversification can be realized.

QUESTIONS AND PROBLEMS

1. The estimated volatility of a domestic asset is 15% (annualized standard deviation of returns). A foreign asset has a volatility of 18% and a correlation of 0.5. What is the volatility of a portfolio invested for 80% in the domestic asset and 20% in the foreign asset?

2. The best diversification vehicle is an asset with high volatility (σ) and low correlation with the portfolio. What do you think of this statement?

3. Using the long-term risk and return figures in Exhibit 2.8, explain the motivations for diversifying a U.S. dollar bond portfolio into foreign currency bonds.

4. Try to find some reasons why

□ stock and bond markets should be strongly correlated and

□ stock and bond markets should be weakly correlated.

5. It is often claimed that financial markets are increasingly integrated world-wide. Advance some reasons for this trend.

NOTES

1. The national breakdown of the world market size is detailed in Chapters 4 and 6. In 1986 the U.S. market shares dropped significantly because of the large drop in the value of the U.S. dollar relative to all other currencies.

2. A correlation coefficient between two random variable lies between -1.0 and $+1.0$. A coefficient of $+1.0$ means that the two markets go up and down in exact phase, while a coefficient of -1.0 means that they are exactly countercyclical. By way of illustration, two industry indexes on the same national stock market typically have a correlation of approximately 0.8.

3. Tests of the stability of correlation coefficients and their implications may be found in P. Jorion, "International Portfolio Diversification with Estimation Risk," *Journal of Business*, July 1985; R. Maldonado and A. Saunders, "International Portfolio Diversification and the Intertemporal Stability of International Stock Market Relationships," *Financial Management*, Autumn 1981, pp. 54–63; J. Watson, "The Stationarity of Inter-Country Correlation Coefficients: A Note," *Journal of Business, Finance and Accounting*, Spring 1980; and I. Shaked, "International Equity Markets and the Investment Horizon," *Journal of Portfolio Management*, Winter 1985.
   Original studies on international correlation coefficients may be found in H. Levy and M. Sarnat, "International Diversification of Investment Portfolios," *American Economic Review*, September 1970; and D. R. Lessard, "International Portfolio Diversification: A Multivariate Analysis for a Group of Latin-American Countries," *Journal of Finance*, June 1973. See also H. Levy and M. Sarnat, *Portfolio and Investment Selection: Theory and Practice*, Englewood Cliffs, NJ: Prentice Hall International, 1984; and C. Eun and B. Resnick, "Estimating the Correlation Structure of International Share Prices," *Journal of Finance*, December 1984.

4. An R^2 of 10% may be interpreted as follows: Ten percent of the German stock price movements are the result of influences of the U.S. stock market. In other words 90% of the price movements (or variance) are independent.

5. The standard deviation of returns is the simplest statistical measure of the volatility of a market or an asset. It is traditionally used to indicate the risk of an asset. The square of the standard deviation is referred to as the variance.

6. For a discussion of the relationships between currency movements and asset prices see Chapter 1.

7. See, for example, B. Solnik and B. Noetzlin, "Optimal International Asset Allocation," *Journal of Portfolio Management*, Fall 1982.

8. The strategies are discussed in Chapter 12. Empirical evidence is provided by J. Madura and W. Kieff, "A Hedge Strategy for International Portfolios," *Journal of Portfolio Management*, Fall 1985; and K. Chollerton, P. Pieraerts, and B. Solnik, "Why Invest in Foreign Currency Bonds?," *Journal of Portfolio Management*, Summer 1986.

9. See P. Jorion, "Asset Allocation with Hedged and Unhedged Foreign Stocks and Bond," *The Journal of Portfolio Management*, Summer 1989.

10. The total performance includes capital and currency gains as well as dividends. All returns are measured before taxes. Part of the withholding taxes on dividends might be lost. If all withholding taxes were unrecovered by the U.S. investor the annual return on the world stock index would be lowered by less than 0.30%. Because coupons are a larger component of the total return on bonds, the withholding tax effect might be larger on bonds. However, withholding taxes have been removed on most bond markets. For a discussion of withholding taxes see Chapters 4 and 6.

11. See G. Barnett and M. Rosenberg, "International Diversification in Bonds," *Prudential International Fixed Income Investment Strategy*, Second Quarter 1983.

12. See K. Chollerton, P. Pieraerts, and B. Solnik, "Why Not Diversify into Foreign Currency Bonds?", *Journal of Portfolio Management*, Summer 1986.

13. See R. Ibbotson, L. Siegel, and K. Love, "World Wealth: Market Values and Returns," *Journal of Portfolio Management*, Fall 1985; and I. Allan, "Return and Risk in International Capital Markets," *Columbia Journal of World Business*, Summer 1982.

14. See, for example, V. Errunza, "Emerging Markets: A New Opportunity for Improving Global Portfolio Performance," *Financial Analysts Journal*, September/October 1983.

15. See *Forbes*, January 1984.

16. See B. Solnik and B. Noetzlin, "Optimal International Asset Allocation," *Journal of Portfolio Management*, Fall 1982.

17. In theory investors care about purchasing power risks, not nominal dollar risks. As pointed out in Chapter 1, goods price level (CPI) fluctuations are very small compared to exchange rate fluctuations (or other asset prices fluctuations); using the nominal dollar as a numeraire may be regarded as a viable practical approximation. This point was already made by M. Adler and B. Dumas, "International Portfolio Choice and Corporation Finance: A Synthesis," *Journal of Finance*, June 1983.

18. A strong case in favor of foreign currency bonds has already been made by H. Hana, "Why Americans Should Have Diversified," *Euromoney*, March 1980; H. Klein Haneveld, "Investing Internationally: The Role of Foreign Currency Bonds in US-Dollar Based Portfolios," Morgan Guaranty Trust Company of New York, 1981; M. Adler, "Global Fixed Income Portfolio Management," *Financial Analysts Journal*, September/October 1983; and P. Jorion, "Why Buy International Bonds?," *Investment Management Review*, September/October 1987.

19. This single observation cannot be considered a formal and complete test of the international asset pricing theory introduced in Chapter 1.

20. See R. Grauer and N. Hakansson, "Gains from International Diversification: 1968–1985," *Journal of Finance*, July 1987; H. Levy, and Z. Lerman, "The Benefits of International Diversification of Bonds," *Financial Analysis Journal*, September/October 1988; and P. Jorion, "Asset Allocation with Hedged and Unhedged Foreign Stocks and Bonds," *The Journal of Portfolio Management*, Summer 1989.

BIBLIOGRAPHY

Adler, M. and Dumas, B. "International Portfolio Choice and Corporation Finance: A Synthesis," *Journal of Finance*, June 1983.

Barnett, G. and Rosenberg, M. "International Diversification in Bonds," *Prudential International Fixed Income Investment Strategy*, Second Quarter 1983.

Chollerton, K., Pieraerts, P., and Solnik, B. "Why Invest into Foreign Currency Bonds?," *Journal of Portfolio Management*, Summer 1986.

Eun, C. and Resnick, B. "Estimating the Correlation Structure of International Share Prices," *Journal of Finance*, December 1984.

Grauer, R. and Hakansson, N. "Gains from International Diversification: 1968–1985," *Journal of Finance*, July 1987.

Hanna, J. "Why Americans Should Have Diversified," *Euromoney*, March 1980.

Ibbotson, R., Siegel, L., and Love, K. "World Wealth: Market Values and Returns," *Journal of Portfolio Management*, Fall 1985.

Jorion, P. "Asset Allocation with Hedged and Unhedged Foreign Stocks and Bonds," *The Journal of Portfolio Management*, Summer 1989.

Jorion, P. "International Portfolio Diversification with Estimation Risk," *Journal of Business*, July 1985.

Lessard, D. R. "International Portfolio Diversification: A Multivariate Analysis for a Group of Latin-American Countries," *Journal of Finance*, June 1973.

Levy, H. and Lerman, Z. "The Benefits of International Diversification of Bonds," *Financial Analysts Journal*, September/October 1988.

Levy, H. and Sarnat, M. "International Diversification of Investment Portfolios," *American Economic Review*, September 1970.

―――――, *Portfolio and Investment Selection: Theory and Practice*, Englewood Cliffs, NJ: Prentice Hall International, 1984.

Madura, J. "International Portfolio Construction," *Journal of Business Research*, 13, 1985.

Maldonado, R. and Saunders, A. "International Portfolio Diversification and the Intertemporal Stability of International Stock Market Relationships," *Financial Management*, Autumn 1981, pp. 54–63.

Rhee, S. G. and Chang, R. P. (eds), *Pacific-Basin Capital Market Research*, North-Holland, Amsterdam, 1990.

Roll, R. "The International Crash of October 1987," *Financial Analysts Journal*, September/October 1988.

Solnik, B. "Crise Boursière et Théorie Moderne," *Lettre de l'AFFI*, March 1988.

Solnik, B. "Why Not Diversify Internationally Rather Than Domestically?," *Financial Analysts Journal*, July 1974.

Solnik, B. and Noetzlin, B. "Optimal International Asset Allocation," *Journal of Portfolio Management*, Fall 1982.

Tapley, M. (ed), *International Portfolio Management*, Euromoney Publications, London 1986.

Vertin, J. (ed), *International Equity Investing*, Homewood, IL: Dow Jones-Irwin, 1984.

Chapter 2: Appendix
Costs in International Investment

COMMISSIONS

It is difficult to calculate the average commission on a typical trade given the many ways a commission is charged (bid–ask spread, variable schedule, negotiable commissions). However, brokerage commissions on stocks tend to be low in the United States (typically 0.18% for large transactions) and higher in foreign countries (ranging from 0.30% to above one percent). In some countries commissions are fixed and a stamp tax applies. However, the deregulation of capital markets is lowering these commissions. For example, they became negotiable for large trades in France in 1985, and "the big bang" in London drastically reduced the commissions charged in 1986. The commissions are detailed in Chapter 4.

It is even more difficult to quote a so-called average commission for bonds. On most of the major bond markets (including the Eurobond market) prices are quoted net, so that the commissions have to be inferred from the bid–ask spread, which depends on the volume of transactions on a specific bond. In general commissions on bonds tend to be very low on all markets.

MARKET IMPACT

Because of poor liquidity, a given transaction may have an impact on the market price. Several U.S. studies have estimated the market price impact of a typical stock trade as a function of its size. Such studies do not exist on other markets, so we cannot get estimates of the differential cost in foreign markets. The only suggestion is that the lower the liquidity (turnover) in the market for the shares, the higher the market impact.

CUSTODY COSTS

International custody costs tend to be higher for international investment because here one engages in a two-level custodial arrangement; a money manager generally acquires a master custodian with a network of subcustodians in every country. Higher costs are also incurred because of the necessity of a multi-currency system of accounting, reporting, and cash flow collection.

Some countries have a very inexpensive and efficient centralized custodial system with a single clearinghouse (see Chapter 12), and local costs tend to be less than in the United States. However, the need for the international network may raise the annual cost to more than 0.10% of assets.

WITHHOLDING TAXES

Withholding taxes have been progressively eliminated on bonds. Coupon hopping is a technique to avoid the taxes where they exist. In many markets, regulated institutional investors (e.g., insurance companies, which in many countries such as Japan, France, and Switzerland cannot treat unrealized capital gains as profit) have a demand for income, so they may want to buy bonds before the coupon date and sell them shortly after the coupon is paid. A foreign investor wanting to avoid withholding tax on the coupon can sell the bond before the coupon date and repurchase it a day later at little or no cost.[1] This is more difficult on stock markets where the institutional demand for coupon hopping is weaker, transaction costs are higher, and the gain is less, since the yield is lower on equity than on bonds.

Withholding taxes exist on most stock markets (see Chapters 4 and 6). This tax can usually be reclaimed after several months; this time lag creates an opportunity cost. In very few cases part of the tax is completely lost according to the tax treaty between the two countries. A taxable investor may claim this amount as a tax credit in his home country, but this is not possible for a nontaxable investor (such as pension plans). However, the withholding tax (generally 15%) applies only to the dividend yield. For a yield of 4%, a total loss of withholding tax on common stocks would imply a 0.60% reduction in performance.

MANAGEMENT FEE

Fees charged by international money managers tend to be higher than those charged by domestic management. This is justified by the higher costs borne by the money managers in terms of

- international database subscription,
- data collection,
- research,
- international accounting system, and
- communication costs (international telephone, computer links, and travel).

Management fees for foreign portfolios typically run 0.10% to 0.30% higher than fees on similar domestic portfolios. Some investors believe that they can limit costs by simply buying foreign firms listed on their domestic markets[2] (called American Depository Receipts, or ADRs, in the United States). While this may be a practical alternative for the private investor, it is a questionable strategy for larger investors. A growing number of companies have multiple listings, but they tend to be large multinational firms that provide less foreign diversification benefits than a typical foreign firm. Also, the foreign share price of a company (e.g., the U.S. dollar ADR price of a French firm) is determined by its domestic market price adjusted by the exchange rate. When a large order to buy an ADR is received, brokers will generally arbitrage between the prices in New York and the local market. This means that, on most ADRs, the execution will be made at a high price compared to the domestic price (adjusted for the exchange rate). The commission seems low, but the market impact on the price tends to be very high. It is usually in the best interest of a large customer to deal on the primary market, where there is the largest transaction volume for the shares.[3]

NOTES

1. In most countries only the payment of the interest coupon is treated as income for tax purposes, so only the bondholder of record on the date of coupon payment is liable for income tax. Accrued interest is added to the bond price and treated as capital gain.

2. Multiple listings of equity shares are discussed in Chapter 4. *Euromoney* regularly publishes a list of companies listed on several markets. The May 1986 issue had a detailed list.

3. The domestic market is usually where the largest transacting volume takes place. However, there are a few exceptions. Several Dutch, Swiss, and British companies have a very large stock transaction volume on American markets. South African gold mining shares are heavily traded in London.

3

Foreign Exchange

The international investor is faced with a complex task. The financial markets throughout the world are quite different from each other, and information on them is sometimes difficult to obtain. Trading in different time zones and languages further complicates the task. But the most important aspect of international investment is the use of multi-currencies. An American investing in France must do so in French francs; therefore, the performance (and risk) of the investment will partly depend on changes in the French franc/U.S. dollar exchange rate. Because of the importance of exchange rates in international investment, we will continue our discussion of the economics behind the foreign-exchange market in this chapter.

A FEW HISTORICAL COMMENTS

Each country uses a different currency. This means that an exchange rate (i.e., a spot exchange rate) must be set for trade in goods and assets to occur between countries. The traditional method has been to use a common standard for assessing the value of each currency. Over the centuries a variety of physical commodities have served as the international standard, including small sea shells, salt, and metals such as bronze and silver. The best-known, and most-recent, standard is gold. Silver played an important role until the middle of the nineteenth century, when gold was found in Transvaal and California. During the era of the gold standard, gold was the international means of payment and each currency was assessed according to its gold value. At the time, one could exchange French francs for British pounds in exact proportion to their gold value. For example, if one ounce of gold bullion was worth ten francs in France and two pounds in the United Kingdom, the exchange rate was five French francs per British pound, or 0.2 British pounds per French franc. The domestic

70

purchasing power of a currency, i.e., its *gold content*, was set by the domestic monetary authorities, who thereby controlled the exchange rate.

Adjustments in exchange rates occurred only rarely, when a government was forced to reduce the gold content of its currency. To maintain equilibrium in the system, gold bullion was used to settle international transactions. The balance of all monetary flows in and out of a country was usually referred to as the *balance of payments*. The balance of payments accounted for all monetary flows over a given time period. These flows were either linked to trade (payments of imports and exports) or to capital flows (borrowing and lending abroad). A deficit in the balance of payments resulted in a gold outflow and a reduction in the domestic reserves; this was equivalent to a reduction in the domestic money supply, since the gold stock of a country was its real money supply. Gold made up all the international reserves of a country.

In order to soften the impact of balance-of-payments deficits or surpluses on the domestic economy, hard currencies were introduced to increase international reserves. These currencies—the U.S. dollar, followed by the British pound and deutsche mark—were freely convertible into gold. This system, called the Bretton-Woods system, or gold exchange standard, also allowed exchange rates to fluctuate in a wide band around fixed parities. It further allowed for infrequent de(re)valuation of the fixed parities. The gold exchange standard lasted for about twenty years after World War II.

But in the early 1970s international trade and financial transactions grew to the point where this direct link of currencies to a gold standard with fixed parities exploded. The international monetary system progressively evolved toward a system of floating exchange rates. Under the current system the price of each currency is freely determined by market forces. Exchange rate parities are not fixed by governments, but fluctuate according to supply and demand. The important dates in the evolution of the international monetary system since World War II are given in Exhibit 3.1.

In this world of flexible exchange rates, some governments have linked their currency to others. Sometimes the link is rigid. For example, fourteen African countries that are former French colonies tie their currencies to the French franc. The franc used by these countries is exactly equal to two French centimes. Many currencies are linked tightly or loosely to the U.S. dollar. Others are linked to a basket of currencies such as the Special Drawing Right (SDR).[1] However, the most important linkage affecting major investment currencies is the original system put into place by the European Economic Community known as the European Monetary System (EMS), often called the Snake. As of August 1990, this system comprised the currencies of the following countries:

- Belgium
- Denmark
- France
- West Germany

EXHIBIT 3.1
Important Dates in the International Monetary System Since 1940

1944	Creation at Bretton Woods of a fixed exchange rate system based on gold and the dollar (gold exchange standard). The International Monetary Fund (IMF) and the World Bank are also created.
1950	U.S. balance of payments is in deficit and remains so for many years.
1958	The Common Market, or European Economic Community, is created. European countries restore the convertibility of their currencies into dollars and gold for nonresidents.
1960	A rush on gold causes the creation of the London gold pool by major central banks to hold the price of gold down.
1963	The United States levies the interest equalization tax on foreign borrowing by U.S. residents.
1967	A world monetary crisis follows the devaluation of the British pound.
1968	A new run on gold forces governments to adopt a two-tier gold market. Central banks trade at the official price, but a market is established for other investors where the price fluctuates freely. The United States imposes mandatory control on direct foreign investment.
1969	The deutsche mark floats for a few weeks and then is revalued.
1970	Special Drawing Rights are created at the IMF to supplement gold and the dollar as international reserves.
1971	The United States runs an international trade deficit for the first time this century and a massive balance-of-payments deficit. Because of the conversion of dollars by other nations, the gold stock of the United States falls below $10 billion. On August 15, the convertibility of the U.S. dollar into gold is suspended and the dollar floats. On December 17, a new international monetary system is prepared at the Smithsonian Institution. The dollar is devalued and new central rates are set with a wide fluctuation margin (2.25%) on either side. Dollar convertibility into gold is not reinstated.
1972	The Common Market countries plus the United Kingdom and Denmark join a European Monetary Union. The two latter countries quickly leave the system.
1973	International monetary pressures are high and remain so until 1975. Many currencies float while the dollar drops. The European Monetary Union (less Italy) floats against the dollar.
1976	A new international monetary system is agreed on in Jamaica. Currencies are allowed to float and reference to the price of gold is abandoned.
1979	A new European Monetary System is created where parities between European currencies are maintained with narrow margins. The European Snake is allowed to float against all other currencies, particularly, the U.S. dollar.
1985	The U.S. dollar hits a high of 3.45 deutsche marks while the United States runs a current account deficit of $30 billion per quarter.
1985	The Group of Five (France, West Germany, Japan, the United Kingdom, and the United States) announces the coordination of national policies to push the dollar down. Following this announcement in September, the dollar drops and hits a low of 1.65 deutsche marks in November 1987.
1990	East Germany merges with West Germany and its currency is replaced by the deutsche mark. The Soviet Union takes the first step toward full convertibility of the ruble by opening a foreign currency market. A wave of liberalization and reforms in Eastern Europe leads to the opening of the economies and financial markets of many countries of this region.

□ Ireland

□ Italy

□ Luxembourg

□ Netherlands

□ Spain

□ United Kingdom

Although the United Kingdom had been part of the European Economic Community, its currency only joined the EMS at the end of 1990. The British refusal to join the EMS had been a matter of intense controversy in Europe. The European integration of 1992 should lead to a closer monetary cooperation with a tightening of the EMS and the development of more formal European monetary institutions.

The European system may be characterized as a joint float. The currencies float freely relative to the U.S. dollar and other currencies, but maintain a narrow range of exchange rate flexibility among themselves. In other words, a central exchange rate is set for the eight currencies, and the individual rates are allowed to fluctuate only within a narrow band around this central rate. Changes are occasionally made in the central rates by the European monetary authorities when there is too much tension in the system. A by-product of this system is the European Currency Unit (ECU), which is used in the accounting of the European Monetary System. The ECU is a composite currency, i.e., the weighted average of the European Economic Community currencies. Each currency's share in the basket of currencies is weighted broadly, in line with the respective country's growth, national product, and foreign trade. The weights are periodically adjusted. Recently, the ECU has been used in private transactions, and several bonds denominated in the ECU have been issued. The exchange rate arrangements as of the end of 1989 are given in Exhibit 3.2.

The current international monetary system may be characterized as a system of floating exchange rates with constraints. The forces of supply and demand continually move the prices of major currencies but the exchange rates are also constrained by certain institutional agreements like the EMS, which are only infrequently adjusted.

FOREIGN EXCHANGE QUOTATIONS

Basic Principles

All currencies are quoted against the U.S. dollar. For example, the value of the French franc is quoted as 8.00 French francs per U.S. dollar. In other words, one dollar can be exchanged in the foreign-exchange market for 8.00 francs. Conversely, the value of one French franc in terms of U.S. dollars is given by the reciprocal of 8.00, which is 0.125 dollars. We will define FF/$ as the number of

EXHIBIT 3.2
Exchange Rate Arrangements

		Currency Pegged to		
U.S. dollar	French franc	Other currency	SDR	Other composite
Afghanistan	Benin	Bhutan	Burundi	Algeria
Antigua and	Burkina Faso	(Indian	Iran, I. R. of	Austria
Barbuda	Cameroon	Rupee)	Libya	Bangladesh
Bahamas, The	C. African Rep.	Kiribati	Myanmar	Botswana
Barbados	Chad	(Australian	Rwanda	Cape Verde
Belize		Dollar)		
Djibouti	Comoros	Lesotho	Seychelles	Cyprus
Dominica	Congo	(South	Zambia	Fiji
El Salvador	Côte d'Ivoire	African		Finland
Ethiopia	Equatorial	Rand)		Hungary
Grenada	Guinea	Swaziland		Iceland
Guatemala	Gabon	(South		
Guyana	Mali	African		Israel
Haiti	Niger	Rand)		Jordan
Honduras	Senegal	Tonga		Kenya
Iraq	Togo	(Australian		Kuwait
		Dollar)		Malawi
Liberia				
Nicaragua				Malaysia
Oman				Malta
Panama				Mauritius
Peru				Nepal
				Norway
St. Kitts and				
Nevis				Papua New
St. Lucia				Guinea
St. Vincent				Poland
Sudan				Sao Tome and
				Principe
Suriname				
Syrian Arab Rep.				Solomon
Trinidad and				Islands
Tobago				Somalia
Uganda				Sweden
				Tanzania
Viet Nam				
Yemen Arab				Thailand
Rep.				Vanuatu
Yemen, P.D.				Western Samoa
Rep.				Zimbabwe

Source: International Monetary Fund, *International Financial Statistics*, December 1989.
Reprinted with permission of the International Monetary Fund.

Flexibility Limited in Terms of a Single Currency or Group of currencies			More Flexible	
Single currency	Cooperative arrangements	Adjusted according to a set of indicators	Other managed floating	Independently floating
Bahrain	Belgium	Brazil	Argentina	Australia
Quatar	Denmark	Chile	China, P. R.	Bolivia
Saudi Arabia	France	Colombia	Costa Rica	Canada
United Arab Emirates	Germany	Madagascar	Dominican Rep.	Gambia, The
	Ireland	Portugal	Ecuador	Ghana
	Italy		Egypt	Japan
	Luxembourg		Greece	Lebanon
	Netherlands		Guinea	Maldives
	Spain		Guinea-Bissau	New Zealand
			India	Nigeria
			Indonesia	Paraguay
			Jamaica	Philippines
			Korea	South Africa
			Lao P. D. Rep	United Kingdom
			Mauritania	United States
			Mexico	Uruguay
			Morocco	Venezuela
			Mozambique	Zaïre
			Pakistan	
			Singapore	
			Sri Lanka	
			Tunisia	
			Turkey	
			Yugoslavia	

French francs per dollar, and \$/FF as the number of dollars per French franc:

FF/\$ = 8.00 and

\$/FF = 0.125.

Similarly, the deutsche mark (DM) may be quoted as 2.5 deutsche marks per dollar, so that one deutsche mark is worth forty cents. From the quotation of two currencies against the U.S. dollar, one can derive the cross exchange between the two currencies:

FF/\$ = 8.00 and

DM/\$ = 2.50 implies that

FF/DM = 3.20.

In this example, one deutsche mark is worth 3.20 French francs, or one French franc is worth 0.3125 deutsche marks.

Foreign-exchange quotations are difficult to follow for someone who does not trade in currency frequently. This is because a single number is usually quoted without any indication of the role played by each currency. Foreign-exchange quotations are therefore confusing if one is not familiar with the usual direction of quotation. For example, the French franc/U.S. dollar may be quoted either in terms of francs per dollars or in terms of dollars per francs.

Quotations are generally made in terms of the amount of local currency required to purchase one unit of foreign currency. For example, the French quote the deutsche mark exchange rate as 3.20 FF/DM while the Germans quote 0.3125 DM/FF. Because of the leading role played by the British pound up to the twentieth century, London quotations are the reverse of continental quotations. In other words, London bankers quote the amount of foreign currency required to purchase one pound. The Americans decided to adopt the British convention in the early 1980s. In New York the pound exchange rate is still quoted as the number of dollars required to purchase one pound, given the historical dominance of the pound sterling. As a result, the dollar/French franc exchange is quoted in exactly the same way in Paris and in New York.

Depending on the direction of quotation, an increase in the exchange rate may mean an appreciation or a depreciation of the currency. If the French franc rate moves from 8.00 to 9.10, the French franc depreciated, or, equivalently, the U.S. dollar appreciated relative to the franc.

Organization of the Market

The foreign-exchange market is a worldwide interbank market. Only the major banks, and specialized brokers who act as middle men for some local markets, are admitted to this club, which is linked by telephone and telex. The market is organized like an international over-the-counter market. A customer wanting to buy a specified amount of a currency will call several banks to get the best price. The foreign-exchange dealer does not quote a single price, but two. The *bid* price is the exchange rate at which the dealer is willing to buy a currency, and the *ask* (or offer) price is the exchange rate at which the dealer is willing to sell a currency. An example may help the reader to understand how a transaction is initiated and completed.

A U.S. portfolio manager wants to buy $1 million-worth of French bonds. The manager calls several banks to get their French franc quotation without indicating whether a sale or purchase of francs is desired. Bank A gives the following quotation:

FF/$ = 8.0000–8.0025.

In other words, Bank A is willing to buy a dollar for 8.0000 French francs or sell a dollar for 8.0025 French francs. To make the quotation faster, only the last digits, called the *points*, are quoted. The above quotation would usually be given as

FF/$ = 8.0000–25

or even

FF/$ = 000–25.

Traders who follow the market immediately understand the missing figures. Because these are net prices there is no commission, so the spread between the bid and ask price is a form of remuneration for the dealer who makes a firm quotation without knowing whether the customer wants to buy or sell.

Returning to the example, let's assume that the portfolio manager gets the following quotations from three different banks:

	Bank A	Bank B	Bank C
FF/$ =	8.0000–25	7.9985–20	7.9995–30

The manager will immediately choose Bank A and indicate that he or she will buy 8 million French francs for $1 million. Both parties indicate where each sum should be transferred. The portfolio manager indicates that the French francs should be transferred to an account with the Société Générale, the manager's business bank in Paris, while Bank A indicates that it will receive the dollars at its account with Morgan Guaranty in New York. Telexes are exchanged to confirm the oral agreement. The settlement of the transaction takes place simultaneously in Paris and in New York two days later.

Most currencies are quoted against the U.S. dollar, so that cross rates must be calculated from dollar quotations. For example, the FF/DM rate is calculated using the DM/$ and FF/$ rates. This usually implies a larger bid-ask spread on cross exchange rates.

Below are the quotations given by Bank A:

FF/$ = 8.0000–25

DM/$ = 2.5000–20.

The FF/DM quotation is obtained as follows:

□ The FF/DM bid price is the price at which Bank A is willing to buy deutsche marks against French francs, i.e., the number of francs it is willing to pay for one deutsche mark. This transaction (buy deutsche marks–sell French francs) is equivalent to selling French francs to buy dollars (at a bid rate of 8.0000) and then reselling those dollars to buy deutsche marks (at an ask rate of 2.5020). Mathematically, the transaction is as follows:

$$\text{bid FF/DM} = \frac{8.0000}{2.5020} = 3.1974.$$

□ The FF/DM ask price is the price at which Bank A is willing to sell deutsche marks for French francs, i.e., the number of francs it wants to get for selling one deutsche mark. This transaction (sell deutsche marks–buy French francs) is equivalent to buying French francs with dollars (at an ask rate of 8.0025) and simultaneously purchasing these dollars against deutsche marks (at a bid rate of 2.5000). This may be expressed as follows:

$$\text{ask FF/DM} = \frac{8.0025}{2.5000} = 3.2010.$$

The resulting quotation by the bank is

FF/DM = 3.1974–3.2010.

Arbitrage aligns exchange rate quotations throughout the world. The quotation for the DM/$ rate must be the same, at a given instant, in Frankfurt and in New York. If quotations deviated by more than the spread, a simple phone call would allow one to make enormous profits. There are enough professionals in the world watching continuous quote fluctuations to rule out such riskless profit opportunities.

Quotations are directly available on-line from many financial institutions that have their own computer services. International database services such as Reuter and Telerate provide continuous quotations for several banks that are revised constantly. Portfolio managers armed with this information on market prices can rapidly arbitrage or hedge their portfolios of foreign assets.

So far we have only discussed the interbank market, which is a large wholesale market for currencies. A normal transaction amounts to $1 million or more. A U.S. customer wanting to buy French bonds for $10,000 will not be charged these interbank rates. The bank used by the money manager adds a commission to the exchange rate. The commission is usually a function of the size of the transaction. For small transactions (a few thousand dollars) the commission is often very large (sometimes up to 0.5%), while the commission is nominal for large transactions (above $1 million). In other words, a customer must pay a larger spread than the interbank quotation. When the quote is

FF/$ = 8.0000–25

the small-transaction customer may receive only 7.9800 francs for each dollar purchased. This means that a commission of two French centimes per U.S. dollar is charged for the transaction, or 0.25%.

It should be stressed that the interbank spread and commissions are very small for the major investment and trade currencies (U.S. dollar, deutsche mark, British pound, Swiss franc, French franc, and Japanese yen). Transaction costs increase for less-traded currencies such as the Swedish krona or Singapore dollar.

SATELLITE MARKETS

Forward Market

Spot exchange rates are quoted for immediate currency transactions, although in practice, the settlement takes place forty-eight hours later. Spot transactions are extensively used to settle commercial purchases of goods, as well as for investments.

Foreign-exchange dealers also quote forward exchange rates in the inter-bank market. These are rates contracted today, but with delivery and settlement in the future, usually thirty or ninety days hence. For example, a bank may quote the one-month FF/$ exchange rate as 8.0200–50. This means that the bank is willing to commit itself today to buy dollars in one month for 8.0200 French francs or to sell them for 8.0250 French francs. In a forward, or futures, contract (described in detail in Chapter 8) a commitment is irrevocably made on the transaction date, but delivery, i.e., the exchange of currency, takes place later, on a date set in the contract. The origins of the forward currency market may be traced back to the Middle Ages, when merchants from all over Europe met at major trade fairs where they made forward contracts for the next fair.

Forward exchange rates are often quoted as a *premium*, or *discount*, of the exchange rate. There is a premium when the forward exchange rate is higher than the spot rate, and a discount otherwise. If the one-month forward exchange rate is FF/$ = 8.0200 and the spot rate is FF/$ = 8.0000, the dollar quotes with a premium of 0.02 franc or two centimes. Conversely, when a trader announces that a currency quotes at a premium, the premium should be added to the spot exchange rate to obtain the value of the forward exchange rate. If a currency quotes at a discount, the discount should be subtracted from the spot exchange rate to obtain the value of the forward rate.

The forward discount or premium is often calculated as an annualized percentage deviation from the spot rate as given by the following formula:

$$\text{Annualized forward premium (discount)} = \left(\frac{\text{Forward rate} - \text{Spot rate}}{\text{Spot rate}} \right)\left(\frac{12}{\text{No. months forward}} \right)100\%.$$

EXHIBIT 3.3
Foreign Exchange Quotations

DOLLAR SPOT—FORWARD AGAINST DOLLAR			
July 14	Close	Three months	% p.a.
UK†	1.4810-1.4820	1.30-1.25c pm	3.44
Ireland†	1.3745-1.3755	1.25-0.80 pm	2.99
Canada	1.3760-1.3770	0.58-0.63dis	−1.76
NethInd.	2.4565-2.4575	0.61-0.56 pm	0.95
Belgium	44.85-44.96	3-6 dis	−0.40
Denmark	8.14½-8.15	4.00-4.60dis	−2.10
W. Ger.	2.1790-2.1800	1.18-1.13 pm	2.11
Portugal	150-150¼	250-550dis	−10.65
Spain	138.85-138.95	250-350 dis	−8.60
Italy	1495¾-1496¼	17-20½ dis	−4.99
Norway	7.63¾-7.64¼	14.25-14.75ds	−7.57
France	7.0075-7.0125	1.05-1.20dis	−0.64
Sweden	7.14¼-7.14¾	5.60-6.00dis	−3.24
Japan	160-160½	0.85-0.80 pm	2.04
Austria	15.34-15.34½	7-5 pm	1.56
Switz.	1.7785-1.7795	0.84-0.79 pm	1.82

† UK and Ireland are quoted in US currency. Forward premiums and discounts apply to the US dollar and not to the individual currency. Belgian rate is for convertible francs. Financial franc 45.15-45.25.

Source: Financial Times, July 15, 1986. Reprinted by permission.

The percentage premium (discount) is annualized by multiplying by twelve and dividing by the length of the forward contract in months.

$$\text{Annualized forward premium} = \left(\frac{8.02-8.00}{8.00}\right)\left(\frac{12}{1}\right)100\% = 3.0\%.$$

The interbank quotations are often done in the form of an annualized premium (discount) for reasons that will become obvious in the next section. However, forward rates quoted to customers are usually outright (e.g., FF/$ = 8.0200–50).

Exhibit 3.3 gives the spot and forward dollar exchange rates as found in the *Financial Times*. For example, the spot DM/$ exchange rate on July 14, 1986, was DM/$ = 2.1790–2.1800. At the same time, the deutsche mark for delivery three months later quoted at a premium of 1.18–1.13 pfenig (one pfenig is one-hundredth of one deutsch mark). In other words, the dollar quoted at a discount, since a deutsche mark premium as indicated in the exhibit is a dollar discount. The forward DM/$ is therefore quoted outright as DM/$ = 2.1672 − 2.1687, where the forward bid is obtained by subtracting the bid premium/ discount of 0.0118 deutsche marks from the spot bid of 2.1790. The annual percentage premium is equal to 2.11% per annum; this is obtained by taking the middle premium of 1.15 pfenig and dividing it by the middle spot rate of 2.1795.

$$\text{Annualized three-month forward premium} = \left(\frac{0.0115}{2.1795}\right)\left(\frac{12}{3}\right)100 = 2.11\%.$$

Euro-Currency Market

The interbank forward exchange market is closely linked to the *Euro-currency* market. The Euro-currency market is often called the *Euro-dollar* market, although several other currencies are traded. This is the interbank market for short-term borrowing and lending. It is an offshore market and therefore beyond the purview of domestic regulations. This market started during the cold war between the Soviet Union and the United States, when the Soviets feared that the U.S. dollars they owned as reserve currencies might be frozen by U.S. authorities. Typically these U.S. dollar reserves were invested with the Federal Reserve Bank. To avoid any problems the Banque Commerciale de l'Europe du Nord and the Narodny Bank, which are the Soviet banks in Paris and London, were asked to remove these dollars and lend them to a European bank. This started a market between European-based banks in short-term dollar deposits. Soon the European branches of U.S. banks joined the active market. Other currencies started being traded on the Euro-currency market such as the British pound, deutsche mark, Swiss franc, French franc, Japanese yen, Dutch guilder, and Canadian dollar, and now the Euro-currency market is enormous.

One should be careful to distinguish between the Euro-currency market and the *Eurobond* market. The Eurobond market, which is described in Chapter 6, is a traditional bond market where a syndicate of underwriters is assembled and in a few weeks floats a bond for a specific company. By contrast, the Euro-currency market is an interbank market closely linked to the foreign-exchange market. Bank credits are extended to corporations on the basis of these Euro-currency interest rates plus a spread reflecting the credit risk borne by the bank in its lending to a "risky" corporation. On the same telecommunication network, banks quote spot currencies as well as term currencies, i.e., interest rates with maturities from one day to one year. If a foreign-exchange trading room is asked for its quotation on the three-month deutsche mark, it will give the interest rate quotation on a three-month Euro-deutsche mark in the form of a bid-ask spread. For example, a quotation of $4\frac{1}{2}$–$4\frac{5}{8}$ indicates that the bank stands ready to borrow deutsche marks for ninety days at $4\frac{1}{2}$% or to lend deutsche marks at $4\frac{5}{8}$%. As with foreign-exchange, Euro-currency quotations can change at any instant to reflect changes in the market. When a trader gives a quotation, it means that the bank is ready to borrow from, or lend to, any institution of good standing at these rates. The minimum amount is usually $1 million. Maximums are set by the borrowing bank to limit the risks. A corporation or investor wanting to invest in this market will receive the bid rate minus a commission. For example, a customer might be able to lend at $4\frac{7}{16}$% if the bank charges a commission of $\frac{1}{16}$%. Similarly, a customer wanting to borrow will be charged the ask rate plus a commission. This commission may be large because it includes a risk premium. A good-quality corporate customer might borrow at $5\frac{1}{8}$%, i.e., $4\frac{5}{8}$% plus a commission of $\frac{1}{2}$% over the interbank market rate.

EXHIBIT 3.4
Euro-currency Quotations

EURO-CURRENCY INTEREST RATES

July 14	Short term	7 Days notice	1 Month	Three Months	Six Months	One Year
Sterling.......	$9\frac{5}{8}$ $9\frac{7}{8}$	$9\frac{13}{16}$-$9\frac{15}{16}$	10-$10\frac{1}{16}$	10-$10\frac{1}{8}$	10·$10\frac{1}{8}$	$9\frac{15}{16}$-$10\frac{1}{16}$
U.S. Dollar...	$6\frac{1}{2}$-$6\frac{5}{8}$	$6\frac{9}{16}$-$6\frac{11}{16}$	$6\frac{9}{16}$-$6\frac{11}{16}$	$6\frac{9}{16}$-$6\frac{11}{16}$	$6\frac{9}{16}$-$6\frac{11}{16}$	$6\frac{5}{8}$-$6\frac{3}{4}$
Can Dollar...	$8\frac{1}{4}$-$8\frac{1}{2}$	$8\frac{1}{4}$-$8\frac{1}{2}$	$8\frac{1}{8}$-$8\frac{3}{8}$	$8\frac{1}{8}$-$8\frac{3}{8}$	$8\frac{3}{8}$-$8\frac{5}{8}$	$8\frac{1}{2}$-$8\frac{3}{4}$
D Guilder ...	$5\frac{5}{8}$-$5\frac{7}{8}$	$5\frac{5}{8}$-$5\frac{7}{8}$	$5\frac{3}{4}$-$5\frac{7}{8}$	$5\frac{9}{16}$-$5\frac{11}{16}$	$5\frac{7}{16}$-$5\frac{9}{16}$	$5\frac{3}{8}$-$5\frac{1}{2}$
Sw. Franc....	$2\frac{3}{4}$-3	$2\frac{3}{8}$-$2\frac{5}{8}$	$4\frac{15}{16}$-$5\frac{1}{16}$	$4\frac{15}{16}$-$5\frac{1}{16}$	$4\frac{15}{16}$-$5\frac{1}{16}$	$4\frac{7}{8}$-5
Deutschmrk	$4\frac{7}{16}$-$4\frac{9}{16}$	$4\frac{1}{2}$-$4\frac{5}{8}$	$4\frac{7}{16}$-$4\frac{9}{16}$	$4\frac{1}{2}$-$4\frac{5}{8}$	$4\frac{9}{16}$-$4\frac{11}{16}$	$4\frac{5}{8}$-$4\frac{3}{4}$
Fr. Franc	$7\frac{1}{8}$-$7\frac{1}{4}$	$7\frac{1}{8}$-$7\frac{1}{4}$	$7\frac{1}{8}$-$7\frac{1}{4}$	$7\frac{3}{16}$-$7\frac{5}{16}$	$7\frac{1}{4}$-$7\frac{3}{8}$	$7\frac{1}{4}$-$7\frac{3}{8}$
Italian Lire..	9-$10\frac{1}{2}$	$10\frac{1}{4}$-$11\frac{1}{4}$	$10\frac{3}{4}$-$11\frac{1}{2}$	11-$11\frac{1}{2}$	$11\frac{1}{8}$-$11\frac{1}{2}$	$10\frac{7}{8}$-$11\frac{3}{8}$
B.Fr.(Fin)......	$7\frac{1}{8}$-$7\frac{3}{8}$	$7\frac{1}{8}$-$7\frac{3}{8}$	$7\frac{1}{8}$-$7\frac{3}{8}$	$7\frac{1}{8}$-$7\frac{3}{8}$	7-$7\frac{1}{4}$	7-$7\frac{1}{4}$
B.Fr.(Con) ...	7-$7\frac{1}{2}$	7-$7\frac{1}{2}$	7-$7\frac{1}{2}$	$6\frac{7}{8}$-$7\frac{3}{8}$	$6\frac{7}{8}$-$7\frac{3}{8}$	$6\frac{7}{8}$-$7\frac{3}{8}$
Yen.............	$4\frac{3}{8}$-$4\frac{1}{2}$	$4\frac{5}{8}$-$4\frac{11}{16}$	$4\frac{11}{16}$-$4\frac{3}{4}$	$4\frac{5}{8}$-$4\frac{11}{16}$	$4\frac{9}{16}$-$4\frac{5}{8}$	$4\frac{5}{8}$-$4\frac{11}{16}$
D. Krone	$8\frac{3}{4}$-$9\frac{1}{4}$	9-$9\frac{1}{2}$	$8\frac{3}{4}$-$9\frac{1}{4}$	$8\frac{3}{4}$-$9\frac{1}{4}$	$9\frac{1}{4}$-$9\frac{3}{4}$	$9\frac{1}{2}$-10
Asian $ (Sng)	$6\frac{5}{8}$-$6\frac{3}{4}$	$6\frac{5}{8}$-$6\frac{3}{4}$	$6\frac{9}{16}$-$6\frac{11}{16}$	$6\frac{9}{16}$-$6\frac{11}{16}$	$6\frac{9}{16}$-$6\frac{11}{16}$	$6\frac{5}{8}$-$6\frac{3}{4}$

Long-term Eurodollars: Two years 7-$7\frac{1}{4}$ per cent; three years $7\frac{1}{2}$-$7\frac{3}{4}$ per cent; four years $7\frac{3}{4}$-8 per cent; five years 8-$8\frac{1}{4}$ per cent nominal. Short-term rates are call for US Dollars and Japanese Yen; others, two days' notice.

Source: Financial Times, July 15, 1986. Reprinted by permission.

Exhibit 3.4 gives some Euro-currency interest rate quotations. These short-term investments are often called *fiduciary deposits* because of the legal form they take. They are not tradeable.

As we can see, the Euro-currency market functions like the foreign exchange market, into which it is thoroughly integrated. The default risks are larger, so banks exert better control over term transactions (Euro-currency) than spot transactions (foreign exchange). On the other hand, access to the club of this huge and extremely rapid market is reserved to institutions of top quality. This is necessary to ensure that vast amounts of money are reliably transacted over the telephone between institutions located throughout the world and functioning under different regulations.

The forward exchange market and the Euro-currency market are so closely tied to one another that only one of the two markets needs to exist.

Exchange Rate and Interest Rate Markets

Spot exchange rates, forward exchange rates, and interest rates are technically linked for all currencies that are part of the free international market. The relation known as interest rate parity has been introduced earlier and states that the forward discount or premium is equal to the interest rate differential between two currencies. In other words, the forward exchange rate is equal to the spot exchange rate adjusted by the interest rate differential. The interest rate parity relation derives from the fact that arbitrage exists. If it did not, riskless arbitrage would occur. The example below illustrates how the arbitrage is done.

EXHIBIT 3.5
Currency Speculation

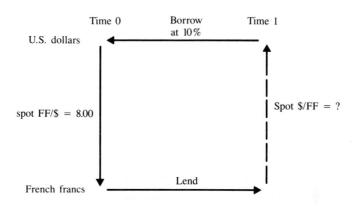

Assume the following data exists for French francs and U.S. dollars.

Spot exchange rate	FF/$ = 8.00
One-year forward rate	FF/$ = 8.08
One-year interest rates	
French franc	14%
U.S. dollar	10%

To take advantage of the interest rate differential, a speculator could borrow dollars (at 10%), convert them immediately into French francs (at a rate of FF/$ = 8.00) and invest the francs (at 14%). This action is summarized in Exhibit 3.5. The speculator makes a profit of 4% on the borrowing/lending position but runs the risk of a large depreciation of the French franc.

In Exhibit 3.5, borrowing dollars means bringing money from the future to the present, while lending means the reverse. At time one, the speculator must convert French francs into U.S. dollars at an unknown rate to honor the claim in dollars.

This position may be transformed into a covered (riskless) interest rate arbitrage by buying simultaneously a forward exchange rate contract to repatriate in one year the French francs into U.S. dollars at a known forward exchange rate of FF/$ = 8.08. In the process described in Exhibit 3.6, the investor still benefits on the interest rate differential (a gain of 4%) but loses on the repatriation of French francs into dollars on the forward contract. In one year,

EXHIBIT 3.6
Covered Interest Rate Arbitrage

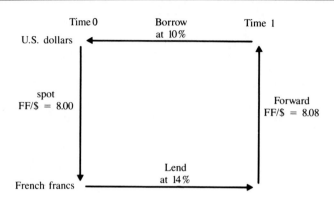

the exchange rate loss will be equal to

$$\frac{8.00 - 8.08}{8.00} = -1\%.$$

Per dollar borrowed, the net gain on the position is 3%. This gain is certain at time zero, since all interest rates and exchange rates are fixed at that time.

No capital is invested in the position, which is a pure swap with simultaneous borrowing and lending. If such rates were quoted in reality, banks would arbitrage to exploit this riskless profit opportunity. Enormous swaps could occur since no capital needs to be invested. To prevent this obviously riskless arbitrage, the forward discount must exactly equal the interest rate differential. More exactly, the various rates must adjust so that interest rate parity holds. Note that if the forward discount were larger than the interest rate differential, the arbitrage would simply go the other way. Arbitrageurs would borrow French francs and swap them for U.S. dollars.

The exact mathematical relationship is slightly more complicated because one must buy a forward contract covering both the principal and the accrued interest in order to achieve a perfect arbitrage. In the previous example, for every dollar borrowed, the forward hedge should cover eight francs plus the interest rate of 14% i.e., 8.00(1.14) = 9.12. The exact mathematical formula is given by

$$\frac{\text{Forward rate}}{\text{Spot rate}} = \frac{1 + \text{currency } B \text{ interest rate}}{1 + \text{currency } A \text{ interest rate}} = \frac{1 + r_B}{1 + r_A}. \tag{3.1}$$

where r_A is the interest rate of currency A and r_B is the interest rate of currency B and the exchange rates are quoted as the price of one unit of currency A in terms of units of currency B.

The forward premium (discount) is equal to

$$\frac{\text{Forward rate} - \text{Spot rate}}{\text{Spot rate}} = \frac{r_B - r_A}{1 + r_A}. \tag{3.2}$$

If one returns to the previous example, where exchange rates are quoted as the price of one U.S. dollar (currency A) in terms of French francs (currency B), arbitrage ensures that

$$F(1 + r_\$) = S(1 + r_{FF})$$

where S and F are the spot and forward exchange rates (French franc price of one U.S. dollar) and r_{FF} and $r_\$$ are the interest rates in French francs and U.S. dollars. This relation implies that

$$\frac{F - S}{S} = \frac{r_{FF} - r_\$}{1 + r_\$}.$$

If the spot exchange rate is FF/\$ = 8.00, and the dollar and franc interest rates are 10% and 14%, the forward exchange rate must equal

$$F = S\frac{1 + r_{FF}}{1 + r_\$} = 8.00\frac{1.14}{1.10} = 8.2909.$$

The calculation of forward exchange rates is often confusing if one does not frequently trade in the currencies involved. In Eq. (3.1), it is easy to confuse the role played by the two currencies depending on the direction of quotation. Here, one should remember that a currency with a high interest rate is considered weak, while a currency with a low interest rate is considered strong. A currency with a high interest rate should trade with a forward discount reflecting the expectation that it will depreciate. A currency with a low interest rate should trade with a forward premium reflecting the expectation that it will appreciate. To cite an example, the French franc trades with a forward discount relative to the U.S. dollar, while the U.S. dollar trades with a forward premium relative to the French franc.

A similar arbitrage relation holds for maturities of less than a year, provided the right interest rates are used. Annual interest must be converted into rates over the investment period. For a contract with n months maturity, the quoted interest rate must be divided by twelve and multiplied by n. As an illustration, assume that the data given below hold.

Spot exchange rate	FF/\$ = 8.00
Three-month interest rates	
French franc	13%
U.S. dollar	10%

The three-month forward exchange rate is equal to

$$\begin{array}{c} \text{Forward} \\ \text{exchange} \\ \text{rate} \end{array} = \begin{array}{c} \text{Spot} \\ \text{exchange} \\ \text{rate} \end{array} \frac{1 + r_{\text{FF}}}{1 + r_{\$}}$$

$$= 8.00 \frac{1 + \left(13\frac{3}{12}\%\right)}{1 + \left(10\frac{3}{12}\%\right)} = 8.00 \frac{1 + 3.25\%}{1 + 2.50\%} = 8.0585.$$

The forward exchange rates and interest rates on July 14, 1986, given in Exhibits 3.3 and 3.4 broadly verify the relationship. For example, the three-month interest rate on dollars is $6\frac{9}{16}$–$6\frac{11}{16}$ while the interest rate on deutsche marks is $4\frac{1}{2}$–$4\frac{5}{8}$. The forward premium of 2.11% is indeed consistent with the interest rate differential. Of course the bid-ask spreads define a band for the value of the premium, and it is easy to verify that the premium (discount) lies within that band. The interest rate parity relation only holds at a given point in time; one has to compare interest rates and exchange rates quoted at the same point in time.[2]

It is clear that forward exchange rates and interest rates are direct substitutes, and one need trade in only one of the two investments. Because the market for interest rates is very large for purposes other than forward exchange transactions, it must exist anyway. This means that forward exchange contracts are not traded on the interbank market. Forward exchange rates are simply calculated by applying interest rate differentials to spot exchange rates. If a bank needs to hedge a forward contract written to a customer, it will engage in a swap as described in Exhibit 3.6. The bid and ask forward exchange rates are calculated using the bid-ask quotations on spot exchange rates and interest rates. For currencies that are not available on the Euro-currency market, the bank calculates an implicit forward exchange rate by engaging in a swap on the domestic interest rate markets.

Long-term forward exchange rates are based on swaps between bonds denominated in two different currencies. The pricing formula is somewhat more complex, as shown in Chapter 7.

Euro-Note Market

A market for international short-term notes became quite active in 1984. This market is a complement to the traditional international system of interbank time deposits and bank credits described previously. Euro-notes take several forms, such as banker's acceptance, Euro-commercial papers, and certificates of deposit. They are often issued with numerous option clauses, and the techniques used by banks placing these notes are somewhat complex and will not be detailed here.[3] Bankers usually call the techniques Note Issuance Facilities

(NIF). Altogether the volume for the various forms of Euro-notes, commercial papers, and banker's acceptance has reached more than 100 billion U.S. dollars in 1989. Euro-notes replace the traditional short-term credits granted by pools of international banks. They witnessed the evolution towards a greater "securitization" of credit markets. This means that traditional bank credits are progressively replaced by negotiable securities which provide 1) greater liquidity to the lending party and 2) give direct access to other, nonbank investors. The secondary market is not yet very liquid, but it offers a welcome extension to the Euro-currency market. The interest rates on these facilities are closely linked to the interest rates quoted on the Euro-currency market.

EXCHANGE RATE DETERMINATION

Exchange rate forecasting is novel to traditional portfolio investors. Rather than examining companies or industrial sectors, financial analysts must study the relative social, political, and economic situation of several countries. Two methods are actively used to forecast exchange rates: Economic analysis is the usual approach for assessing the fair value, present and future, of foreign exchange rates. However, it is often argued that technical analysis may better explain short-run exchange rate fluctuations. This brings us back to the traditional segmentation of financial analysts into fundamentalists and technicians. Both methods employ quantitative models that make extensive use of computers as well as qualitative (or judgmental) analysis.[4]

Our objective is not to detail the various methods, but to pursue the reader's initiation into the international finance scene. This section features a brief presentation of these forecasting methods and an evaluation of their performance.

The Forecasting Methods

The forward rate It is important to determine what our naive forecast would be in the absence of any specific model or information. In other words assuming efficient foreign-exchange markets, what is the exchange rate prediction implicit in market quotations? As discussed previously, the forward exchange rate (or spot exchange rate plus the interest rate differential) is the rational, expected value of the future spot exchange rate in a risk-neutral world. Therefore, if the spot French franc is quoted at 8.00 francs per dollar on January first and the one-year interest rates are 14% for the French franc and 10% for the U.S. dollar, the implied market prediction for the FF/$ rate on December 31 would be

$$8.00 \frac{1.14}{1.10} = 8.2909.$$

If this forward exchange rate did not reflect all information available to the market, arbitrageurs would buy (or sell) currency forward and arbitrage away profit opportunities. Note that the international money market does in fact meet most of the technical criteria of an efficient market,[5] at least for the major currencies. A huge volume of quick and almost-costless transactions are performed by numerous informed and competent traders. The only restriction on the market might be central-bank intervention. On the other hand, central banks may simply be regarded as transactors like any others, though having somewhat different motives. The main upshot of this scenario is that investors should average the same returns on their deposit in every currency; the reason being that short-term interest rate differentials are expected to offset exchange rate movements.

In a risk-averse world forward exchange rates deviate from the pure expectation value by a risk premium.[6] Since the direction and magnitude of this bias is unpredictable and volatile over time, the best market estimate of future spot exchange rates is still the forward rate.

As mentioned in the previous chapters, several studies have shown that forward exchange rates are poor indicators of future spot rates. This does not necessarily mean that a better forecasting model can be found. It may be the case that unanticipated news has a frequent and strong influence on spot rates, making them inherently volatile and unpredictable. The various approaches to foreign-exchange forecasting and methods used to judge the performance of these forecasting techniques against forward rates are worth reviewing now.

Economic models The best-known model for exchange rate determination is the purchasing power parity (PPP) relation described in Chapter 1. If purchasing power parity held true forecasting exchange rates would boil down to forecasting relative inflation in the two countries. Unfortunately purchasing power parity has been poorly verified,[7] especially in the short run (up to a few years). Since investors care about the short-term behavior of asset prices and exchange rates, more complex, and hopefully better-performing, economic models must be employed.

The body of literature on exchange rate determination[8] is enormous, and a detailed discussion of this subject is well beyond the scope of this book. To follow the press articles on exchange rate determination or the material prepared by forecasters, it is sufficient to recall that the theories currently used can be classified into two major groups.

> *The balance-of-payments approach.* This approach focuses on the relationship between balance-of-payments flows and the exchange rates. The balance of payments tracks all financial flows crossing the borders of a country. There are two major components of a balance of payments: the current account and the capital account. The current account records all flows linked to foreign trade and services (the trade balance is the major component of the current account); the capital account records all foreign borrowing and

lending flows. The overall balance of payments of a country must be equilibrated at every moment to avoid default. Therefore, a trade deficit has to be compensated by a surplus in the capital account. It is necessary, however, to draw the line between flows that are autonomous and caused by current economic conditions, and those that are created to compensate a potential imbalance. For example, the drop in oil prices in 1985 and 1986 led to a Mexican trade balance deficit; the value of the oil that Mexico exports suddenly dropped without a corresponding reduction in imports. This deficit forced the Mexican government to borrow abroad to offset the imbalance; it also led to a depreciation of the peso.

The balance-of-payments approach focuses on the relationship between international flows and exchange rate movements. For example, consider the trade flows elasticities in response to a movement in exchange rate: How will imports and exports react to an exchange rate adjustment and vice versa? The answers have to be built on often-complex models of the economy.

The asset market approach. Many economists reject the view that the short-term behavior of exchange rates is determined in flow markets. Exchange rates are asset prices traded in an efficient financial market. Indeed, an exchange rate is the relative price of two currencies and therefore is determined by the willingness to hold each currency. Like other asset prices, the exchange rate is determined by expectations about the future, not current trade flows.

A parallel with other asset prices may illustrate the approach. Let's consider the stock price of a winery traded on the Bordeaux stock exchange. A frost in late spring results in a poor harvest, in terms of both quantity and quality. After the harvest the wine is finally sold, and the income is much less than the previous year. On the day of the final sale, there is no reason for the stock price to be influenced by this flow. First, the poor income has already been discounted for several months in the winery stock price. Second, the stock price is affected by future, in addition to current, prospects. The stock price is based on expectations of future earnings, and the major cause for a change in stock price is a revision of these expectations.

A similar reasoning applies to exchange rates: Contemporaneous international flows should have little effect on exchange rates to the extent they have already been expected. Only news about future economic prospects will affect exchange rates. Since economic expectations are potentially volatile and influenced by many variables, especially variables of a political nature, the short-run behavior of exchange rates is volatile.

The opposition of the traditional balance-of-payments approach and of the asset market approach may be illustrated as follows. In the balance-of-payments approach (more complex models are used by many balance-of-payments specialists) domestic real growth tends to be bad for the domestic currency: Higher domestic growth leads to a boost in imports necessary for the higher production; exports do not increase, since foreign activity is unchanged. The net result is a trade balance deficit that leads to a depreciation of the domestic currency. By contrast, proponents of the asset market approach contend that prospects for higher domestic growth lead to capital inflows caused by foreign investments attracted by the higher returns. This results in increased demand for the home currency and a stronger currency, not a weaker one. This scenario took place in the United States in the period 1983 to 1984 accompanied by rapid economic growth, a widening trade balance deficit, and an appreciating dollar.

Advisory services and institutional investors that have developed foreign-exchange forecasting tools may use a subjective approach, an econometric model, or both. One set of models attempts to deduce theoretical values for current exchange rates. If the values deviate from going market rates the models assume the deviation will be quickly corrected by the market. Another set of models assumes that current exchange rates are correctly priced, or in equilibrium, and attempts to forecast rates in the future based on the present and predicted values of other variables.

Econometric models, which are statistical estimations of the economic theories, make it feasible to take complex correlations between variables explicitly into account. Parameters for the models are drawn from historical data. Then current and expected values for causative variables are entered into the model, producing forecasts for exchange rates. Econometric models clearly suffer from two drawbacks. First, most of them rely on predictions for certain key variables (money supply, interest rates) that are not easy to forecast. Second, the structural correlation estimated by the parameters of the equation can change over time, so that even if all causative variables are correctly forecast the model can still yield poor exchange rate predictions. In periods when structural changes are rapid compared with the amount of time-series data required to estimate parameters, econometric models are of little help.[9] In these instances subjective analysis is generally more reliable.

Many econometric forecasts rely on a single equation founded on PPP and equated to an expression containing variables for interest rates, trade balances, and money supply. Other models rely on sets of 10 to 900 simultaneous equations, which no doubt provide a more satisfactory description of international correlations than simplistic single-equation models. But at the same time, complex models cannot be revised frequently. Moreover, it is costly to simulate each scenario.

Several banks and advisory services make their models available worldwide on time-sharing systems. Using terminals with simple telephone modems, subscribers may input their own forecasts for the causative variables and even change parameters in the model equations. In fact it is not uncommon to see portfolio managers use home or hotel telephones to connect portable terminals to any one of several wire services that provide information ranging from up-to-date economic forecasts, to quoted prices, to investment management packages. In periodic reports, econometric forecasts are generally combined with more subjective discussions of the international scene.

Technical analysis Technical analysis[10] of exchange rates bases predictions solely on price information. The analysis is technical in the sense that it does not rely on fundamental analysis of the underlying economic determinants of exchange rates, but only on extrapolations of past price trends. Technical analysis looks for the repetition of specific price patterns. Once the start of such patterns has been detected, it automatically suggests what the short-run behavior of an exchange rate will be.

   Technical analysis has long been applied to commodity and stock markets. Its application to the foreign-exchange market is a recent phenomenon, but has attracted a wide and rapidly growing audience. One difference that sets apart the currency market from other markets is that trading-volume data are not available for currencies, so price history is the only source of information. As for economic analysis, technical analysts often use quantitative computer models or subjective analysis based on the study of charts (*chartism*).

   Computer models attempt to detect both major trends and critical, or turning, points. They are usually very simple and rely on *moving averages, filters,* or *momentum*. With all computer models the objective is to detect when a sustainable trend has begun.

☐ In moving-average models, buy and sell signals are usually triggered when a short-run moving average (SRMA) of past rates crosses a long-run moving average (LMRA). The aim of a moving average is to smooth erratic daily swings of exchange rates in order to signal major trends. An LRMA will always lag an SRMA because it gives a smaller weight to recent movements of exchange rates than an SRMA does. If a currency is moving downward, its SRMA will be below its LRMA. When it starts rising again, as in Exhibit 3.7A, it soon crosses its LRMA, generating a buy signal. The converse holds true for sell signals.

EXHIBIT 3.7
Computer Methods in Technical Analysis

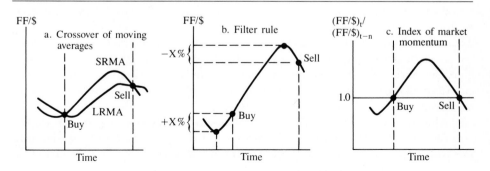

☐ Filter methods generate buy signals when an exchange rate rises X percent (the filter) above its most recent trough, and sell signals when it falls X percent below the previous peak. Again the idea is to smooth (filter) daily fluctuations in order to detect lasting trends (see Exhibit 3.7B).

☐ Momentum models determine the strength of a currency by examining the change in velocity of currency movements. If an exchange rate climbs at increasing speed, a buy signal is issued.

In a sense these models monitor the derivative (slope) of a time series graph. Signals are generated when the slope varies significantly.

Note that there is a good deal of discretionary judgment inherent in these models. Signals are sensitive to alterations in the filters used, the period lengths used to compute moving averages, and the methods used to compute rates of change in momentum models. Recently, more sophisticated statistical models have evolved, some of which are direct applications of statistical models developed for other disciplines such as physics and seismology. Among them are wave- and cycle-models, or ARIMA estimations à la Box-Jenkins. Some powerful quantitative methods have recently been applied to forecast the short-term behavior of foreign-exchange rates such as the multivariate vector autoregressive methods, the multivariate spectral methods, ARCH models and the nonlinear autoregressive methods.

Chartism technical analysis relies on the interpretation of exchange rate charts. Analysts usually attempt to detect recurrent price formations on bar charts that plot daily price ranges as vertical bars. They also use line charts connecting daily closing prices, or point-and-figure charts, which take into account a series of price movements in the same direction.

Numerous price patterns are considered significant by chartists. Each pattern is representative of a typical market situation, the outcome of which is usually predictable, thereby giving clear sell or buy signals. The various patterns are interpreted as logical sequences in various market phases (accumulation, resistance, breakaway, reaction). Colorful terminology is generally used to describe the various patterns, including flag, pennant, head and shoulder, and camel.

Obviously chartism is more an art than a science. Its main tenant is that market participants tend to behave in the same way over time when confronted with a similar market environment. This repetition of response is ascribed partly to emotional factors, and partly to the regulatory and other constraints imposed on major market participants such as multinational companies' treasurers, bankers, and central bankers. In other words, guidelines, regulations, and central-bank intervention help cause repeated and predictable currency market patterns.

Charts are sometimes used to time purchases and sales of currencies when large actors such as central banks intervene in the market. With the development of graphic software on microcomputers, many more people now engage in technical analysis. One should be aware that technical models such as moving averages are constantly calculated by thousands of investors. As a result, those who use this method rarely beat the market because so many others use similar models.

The Use and Performance of Forecasts

Technical analysts closely follow the market and forecast the very near future. Detecting a pattern is beneficial if the market continues to follow that pattern faithfully. But no pattern can be expected to last for more than a few days, possibly weeks; market inefficiencies are just too quickly corrected. Indeed, if a technical analyst persuades enough clients to act on his or her recommendations, prices will move rapidly to a level that rules out additional profits. The more publicity a successful analyst gets, the faster the market corrects the inefficiencies he or she reports. As a result, all systematic black-box models must be continually modified to counter this self-correcting process.

A client must react very quickly to a technical recommendation. Unfortunately there are often time lags between the moment a technical service issues a recommendation, the time it takes to reach the money manager, and the moment it is finally implemented. For this reason immediate transmission via telex or computer terminal of buy and sell signals is essential in order to make a profit.

The corporate treasurer who manages a complex international position with daily cash flows and adjustments in his or her foreign-exchange exposure can respond readily to technical analysis recommendations. This is not the case for portfolio managers; they cannot continually adjust their long-term asset allocation on the basis of technical signals on currencies. In practice, therefore, technical foreign-exchange models are used mainly by money managers for timing their investment sales and purchases, or for hedging decisions. Transaction costs on equity are just too high to make an active trading strategy based on short-term currency forecasts worthwhile.

By contrast, long-term economic forecasts for currencies and interest rates are a basic component of the international asset allocation decision. In fact, currency analysis is one of several economic analyses of the international environment that a manager must undertake. Briefly, economic models of exchange rates are commonly used for long-term asset allocation, whereas technical models are more helpful for timing transactions.

One question that remains for the user of foreign-exchange forecasts is: How does one measure the performance of these forecasts, and what is their track record?

All methods compare a particular forecast to the forward exchange rate, which is both the implied market forecast and the price at which an investor may contract to try and make a profit based on his or her specific forecast. In order to study the performance of a given forecasting model over a specific time period, one must collect the values for the following series:

- Forecasts formulated in t for time $t + n$ ($\hat{S}_t$);
- Forward rates quoted in t for time $t + n$ (F_t); and
- Spot rates realized in t (S_t) and $t + n$ (S_{t+n}).

With this set of data in hand, several methods may be used to evaluate the performance of a forecast relative to the forward rate.

A common statistical approach is to compare the forecast errors of the two models (the forecasting model versus the forward rate). The percentage forecast errors (E and e) for each forecast are computed as

$$E^n_{t+n} = \frac{S_{t+n} - \hat{S}_t}{S_{t+n}} \quad \text{and}$$

$$e^n_{t+n} = \frac{S_{t+n} - F_t}{S_{t+n}}.$$

Average forecasting accuracy is usually measured by the mean squared error (MSE). The error is squared because a positive error is no better than a negative one; the MSE averages the squared errors over all forecasts. A forecasting model is more accurate than the forward rate if it has a smaller MSE.

This commonly used statistical measure of forecasting accuracy does not satisfy some managers. For them, the important contribution of a forecast is the generation of correct buy and sell signals even if the magnitude of the expected move is inaccurate. In other words, they want to know the number of times the forecast turns out to be on the correct side of the forward exchange rate. The fraction P = correct forecast/total forecasts estimates the probability of making correct forecasts during a given period. If the model has no forecasting ability, P is close to 0.5. If it is unusually accurate, P should be larger than 0.5, and its statistical significance may be measured.

A final method for evaluating forecasting performance is to assume that the money manager systematically buys forward contracts if the forecast is above the forward rate and sells them if the forecast is below the forward rate. The expost financial return on this strategy is then computed, and the forecasting ability is judged on the basis of the manager's return on the capital invested.

Euromoney has provided an annual performance review since August 1979 of major foreign-exchange advisory services using the three methods mentioned previously.[11] While results vary every year, there is no doubt that exchange rate forecasting is very difficult. In some years, advisory services have consistently underperformed the forward exchange rate. As one might expect, the reward for active exchange rate forecasting strategies is potentially large, but so are the risks. Technical models seem to have a slightly better track record, at least in the short run. But those models are quite difficult for the international portfolio manager to use systematically because the transaction costs are so high.

An illustration of the rather poor performance of forecasters is given in the summary of the 1984 *Euromoney* survey. The average return is very poor (4.5%), and no single service was able to beat the treasury bill rate over 1983.

> "*Euromoney*'s sixth annual survey of foreign exchange forecasters finds that technical services were once again profitable. But their performance declined in terms of return on capital at risk, from 10.8% in 1982 to 4.5% in 1983. In addition, their percentage of correct signals was only 44.9%, worse than the toss of a coin."
>
> *Source: Euromoney*, August 1984.

SUMMARY

1. The international monetary system has evolved toward a system of floating exchange rates constrained by some institutional agreements such as the European Monetary System.

2. The foreign-exchange market is an international interbank market. Transactions take place by telephone throughout the world.

3. The markets for forward exchange and Euro-currency interest rates are directly linked to the foreign-exchange markets.

4. Forward exchange rates are rates quoted for future delivery. These rates are often quoted as a premium or discount from the spot exchange rate. This premium or discount is equal to the interest rate differential for the two currencies.

5. Foreign exchange forecasting is a difficult exercise and no theory of exchange rate determination can claim to be consistently successful.

6. Forecasters resort to economic analysis or technical analysis methods. Technical analysis focuses on the short-run behavior of exchange rates, while the economic approach is, by nature, better designed for long-run forecasts.

7. Different measures of forecasting ability can be used. The track record of forecasters shows the difficulty of the task and suggests that the foreign-exchange market is quite efficient.

QUESTIONS AND PROBLEMS

1. Briefly describe the current international monetary system.

2. You visit the foreign-exchange trading room of a major bank. A trader asks for quotations of the French franc to various correspondents, and hears the following quote:

- □ From Bank A 7.9610–50
- □ From Bank B 620–55.

What do they mean?

3. The French franc is quoted as FF/$ = 7.9610–50 and the deutsche mark is quoted as DM/$ = 2.4100–40. What is the implicit FF/DM quotation?

4. The spot FF/$ is equal to 7.9630. The one-year interest rates on the Euro-currency market are 13% in French francs and 9% in U.S. dollars. What is the one-year forward exchange rate? The one-month interest rates are 12% in French francs and 8% in U.S. dollars. What is the one-month forward exchange rate?

5. The bid-ask rates are as follows:

> DM/$ 2.4100–40
>
> One-year Euro-DM $4\frac{1}{2}-\frac{5}{8}$
>
> One-year Euro-$ $9\frac{1}{8}-\frac{1}{4}$.

What is the quotation for the one-year DM/$ forward exchange rate?

6. Is foreign-exchange rate forecasting consistent with market efficiency? What would be the expected exchange rate movement in an efficient market? (Assume that you know the interest rates and inflation rates.)

7. A foreign-exchange forecasting service projects a strong appreciation of the deutsche mark against the French franc. How would you capitalize on this forecast?

NOTES

1. The SDR is a basket of currencies. The composition of the basket of currencies has changed over time, but the dollar value of the SDR is calculated daily based on the country weights and the market exchange rate for each currency. Beginning January 1, 1986, the SDR valuation basket consists of the currencies of the five members having the largest exports of goods and services during the period 1980 to 1984, i.e., the U.S. dollar, deutsche mark, French franc, Japanese yen, and pound sterling. The weights for the five currencies (U.S. dollar, 42%; deutsche mark, 19%; Japanese yen, 15%; French franc and pound sterling, 12% each) broadly reflect the relative importance of these currencies in international trade and finance.

2. Tests of the interest rate parity relation may be found in J. Frenkel and R. Levich, "Transaction Costs and Interest Arbitrage: Tranquil Versus Turbulent Periods," *Journal of Political Economy*, 85, December 1977. This relationship is usually found to hold within transaction costs.

3. A description may be found in J. O. Grabbe, *International Financial Markets*, New York: Elsevier, 1986. The evolution of the international is detailed in the quarterly magazine *Trends in Financial Markets*, Organization of Economic Cooperation and Development and *Euromoney*.

4. A review of forecasting models may be found in A. Shapiro, *Multinational Financial Management*, Newton, MA: Allyn, 1986.

5. Tests of the efficiency of the foreign-exchange markets have been provided by B. Cornell and K. Dietrich, "The Efficiency of the Foreign Exchange Market Under Floating Rates," *Review of Economics and Statistics*, February 1978; J. Westerfield, "Empirical Properties of Foreign Exchange Rates Under Fixed and Floating Regimes," *Journal of Monetary Economics*, Spring 1977; A. Farber, R. Roll, and B. Solnik, "An Empirical Study of Exchange Risk Under Fixed and Flexible Exchange," *Journal of Monetary Economics*, Spring 1977; R. Levich, "On the Efficiency of Markets for Foreign Exchange," in R. Dornbusch and J. A. Frenkel (eds), *International Economic Policy: Theory and Evidence*, Baltimore, MD: Johns Hopkins University Press, 1979, and J. A. Frenkel, "Flexible Exchange Rates, Prices and the Role of 'News': Lessons from the Seventies," *Journal of Political Economy*, 80, September 1981, pp. 665–705.

6. See Chapter 1 and M. Adler and B. Dumas, "International Portfolio Choice and Corporation Finance: A Survey," *Journal of Finance*, June 1983 and R. J. Hodrick, "International Asset Pricing with Time-Varying Risk Premium," *Journal of International Economics*, November 1981.

7. References are given in Chapter 1.

8. See, for example, J. A. Frenkel and H. G. Johnson (eds), *The Economics of Exchange Rates—Selected Studies*, Reading, MA: Addison-Wesley, 1978; R. Dornbusch and J. A. Frankel, *International Economic Policy: Theory and Evidence*, Baltimore, MD: Johns Hopkins University Press, 1979; R. Dornbusch, *Open Economy Macroeconomics*, New York: Basic, 1980; and F. Rivera-Batiz and L. Rivera-Batiz, *International Finance and Open Economy Macroeconomics*, Woodbridge, IL: McMillan Pubns., 1985.

9. The failure of econometric models to satisfactorily depict the behavior of the exchange rates is illustrated in G. Haache and J. Townsend, "Exchange Rates and Monetary Policy Modelling: Sterling's Effective Exchange Rate, 1972–1980," *Oxford Economic Papers*, 33, 1981; R. Meese and K. Rogoff, "Empirical Exchange Rate Models of the Seventies: Are They Fit to Survive?," *International Finance Discussion Papers*, 184, June 1981; R. Meese, and K. Rogoff, "What Is Real? The Exchange Rate-Interest Rate Differential Relation over the Modern Floating-Rate Period," *Journal of Finance*, September 1988; and J. Huizinga, "An Empirical Investigation of the Long Run Behavior of Real Exchange Rates," in K. Brunner and A. Meltzer (eds), Carnegie-Rochester Series on Public Policy, 27, North Holland, Amsterdam, 1987.

10. For a general description of technical analysis, see S. Levine (ed), *Financial Analyst's Handbook*, Homewood, IL: Dow Jones-Irwin, 1975; and M. Rosenberg, "Is Technical Analysis Right for Currency Forecasting?," *Euromoney*, June 1981.

11. See also R. Levich, "Evaluating the Performance of the Forecasters," in R. Ensor (ed), *The Management of Foreign Exchange Risk*, Euromoney Publications, London 1982; the article was also reprinted in D. Lessard (ed), *International Financial Management*, New York: Wiley, 1985.

BIBLIOGRAPHY

Adler, M., and Dumas, B. "International Portfolio Choice and Corporation Finance: A Survey," *Journal of Finance*, June 1983.

Chrystal, K. A. "A Guide to Foreign Exchange Markets," *Federal Reserve Bank of Saint Louis Review*, March 1986.

Coninx, R. *Foreign Exchange Dealer's Handbook*, Homewood, IL: Dow Jones-Irwin, 1986.

Cornell, B. and Dietrich, K. "The Efficiency of the Foreign Exchange Market Under Floating Rates," *Review of Economics and Statistics*, February 1978.

Dornbusch, R. *Open Economy Macroeconomics*, New York: Basic, 1980.

Farber, A., Roll, R., and Solnik, B. "An Empirical Study of Exchange Risk Under Fixed and Flexible Exchange," *Journal of Monetary Economics*, Spring 1977.

Frenkel, J. A. "Flexible Exchange Rates, Prices and the Role of 'News': Lessons from the Seventies," *Journal of Political Economy*, 80, September 1981, pp. 665–705.

Frenkel, J. A. and Johnson, H. G. (eds), *The Economics of Exchange Rates—Selected Studies*, Reading, MA: Addison-Wesley, 1978.

Frenkel, J. and Levich, R. "Transaction Costs and Interest Arbitrage: Tranquil Versus Turbulent Periods," *Journal of Political Economy*, 85, December 1977.

Grabbe, J. O. *International Financial Markets*, New York: Elsevier, 1986.

Haache, G. and Townsend, J. "Exchange Rates and Monetary Policy Modelling: Sterling's Effective Exchange Rate, 1972–1980," *Oxford Economic Papers*, 33, 1981.

Hodrick, R. J. "International Asset Pricing with Time-Varying Risk Premium," *Journal of International Economics*, November 1981.

Lessard, D. (ed), *International Financial Management*, New York: Wiley, 1985.

Levich, R. "Evaluating the Performance of the Forecasters," in Ensor, R. (ed), *The Management of Foreign Exchange Risk*, Euromoney Publications, London, 1982.

Levich, R. "On The Efficiency of Markets for Foreign Exchange," in Dornbusch, R. and Frenkel, J. A. (eds), *International Economic Policy: Theory and Evidence*, Baltimore, MD: Johns Hopkins University Press, 1979.

Levine, S. (ed), *Financial Analyst's Handbook*, Homewood, IL: Dow Jones-Irwin, 1975.

Meese, R. and Rogoff, K. "Empirical Exchange Rate Models of the Seventies: Are They Fit to Survive?," *International Finance Discussion Papers*, 184, June 1981.

Meese, R. and Rogoff, K. "What Is Real? The Exchange Rate-Interest Rate Differential Relation over the Modern Floating-Rate Period," *Journal of Finance*, September 1988.

Riehl, H. and Rodriguez, R. *Foreign Exchange and Money Markets*, New York: McGraw Hill, 1983.

Rivera-Batiz, F. and Rivera-Batiz, L. *International Finance and Open Economy Macroeconomics*, Woodbridge, IL: McMillan Pubns., 1985.

Rosenberg, M. "Is Technical Analysis Right for Currency Forecasting?," *Euromoney*, June 1981.

Shapiro, A. *Multinational Financial Management*, Newton, MA: Allyn, 1986.

Westerfield, J. "Empirical Properties of Foreign Exchange Rates Under Fixed and Floating Regimes," *Journal of Monetary Economics*, Spring 1977.

4

Equity: Markets and Instruments

The financial specialist is often struck by the differences among stock market organizations across the world. Traditionally, national stock markets have not only different legal and physical organizations, but also different transaction and accounting methods. The international investor must have a minimum familiarity with these technical differences because they influence the price, commission, speed, and accounting of every transaction.

This chapter begins with a statistical overview of the activity of the major stock exchanges of the world. It then highlights some important differences among the markets.

SOME STATISTICS

Market Size

The American stock exchanges are the largest exchanges in the world. Since 1970 U.S. stocks represented between 35 and 60% of world market capitalization. The market values of the major stock exchanges are given in Exhibit 4.1. Japan has the largest market outside of the United States, with capitalization larger than that of all the European markets combined.

It is worth noting that the U.S. capital market is very large compared to the U.S. economy. The U.S. stock market capitalization represents roughly 50% of the U.S. gross national product. The corresponding figure for France is only 20%. This difference between the United States and France has several explanations. Most American firms prefer to go public, whereas in France, as well as in the rest of Europe, tradition calls for maintaining private ownership as much as possible. In many European countries corporations are undercapitalized and rely

EXHIBIT 4.1
Comparative Market Sizes (in billions of U.S. dollars)

Area or country	1988	1986	1984	1982	1980	1978	1976	1974	1972
Europe	1860	1338	489	408	457	362	239	198	303
United Kingdom	718	440	219	182	190	118	65	38	140
West Germany	241	246	78	69	71	83	54	45	43
Switzerland	148	132	43	41	46	41	22	13	17
France	224	150	40	29	53	45	28	26	31
Netherlands	86	73	31	22	25	22	17	11	14
Sweden	89	49	19	17	12	10	10	8	8
Italy	135	141	23	20	25	10	9	12	14
Spain	87	42	12	10	16	15	18	31	22
Belgium	58	36	12	8	10	12	9	8	9
Other Countries	74	29	12	9	9	6	6	5	4
Europe as Percent of United States	69	61	31	31	37	44	28	39	35
Europe as Percent of World	24	24	17	18	20	22	17	22	21
Pacific Area	4104	1910	722	496	479	378	217	141	195
Japan	3840	1746	617	410	357	327	179	116	152
Australia	134	78	52	41	60	27	20	18	26
Singapore	43	33	27	24	24	11	6	3	8
Hong Kong	74	53	26	21	38	13	12	4	10
Pacific as Percent of United States	152	87	45	38	39	46	25	28	23
Pacific as Percent of World	47	34	25	21	21	23	16	16	14
North America	2702	2369	1709	1413	1353	884	908	554	921
United States	2481	2203	1593	1308	1240	817	856	510	864
Canada	221	166	116	105	113	67	52	44	57
United States as Percent of World	29	39	54	56	54	50	62	57	61
Canada as Percent of World	3	3	4	5	5	4	4	5	4
World	8680	5642	2945	2317	2289	1625	1371	892	1423

Source: Morgan Stanley Capital International.

heavily on bank financing. West Germany, where banks assist corporations extensively, thereby reducing the need for outside equity capital, is a typical example. In Europe, banks tend to provide corporations with all financial services. They assist them in their commercial needs as well as in their long-term debt and equity financing.

It is common for European banks to own shares of their clients. By contrast U.S. commercial banks are prohibited by law (Glass–Stegall Act) to participate in their clients' equity. This forces American companies, especially small- and medium-size ones, to go public and raise capital in the marketplace, thereby increasing the public stock market capitalization. In other countries, many large firms are nationalized and therefore not listed on the capital markets. In France, for example, a large part of steel, arms-manufacturing, oil, chemical, electronic, automobile, banking, insurance, and transportation industries is owned by the government.

The size of the world stock market grew steadily in the seventies and eighties and passed the $10 trillion mark in 1989. It has multiplied by ten since the end of 1974. Currency movements induce changes in the total size and geographical breakdown of the world market. A drop in the value of the dollar reduces the market share of U.S. stocks; the dollar value of non-U.S. stocks increases by the amount of the dollar depreciation, assuming that the stocks' values in domestic currency does not change, while the dollar value of U.S. stocks stays constant. For example, the share of the U.S. market dropped from 55% in mid-1985 to 45% in mid-1986 because of a dramatic drop in the dollar value. The structure of the world financial market has undergone a dramatic change in the past decades. As we can see in Exhibit 4.1, the share of American markets has decreased from two-thirds of the world market capitalization in 1972 to only one-third by 1988. While the share of European markets remained constant, at around 20 to 25%, the importance of Asia grew dramatically and its share of the world market tripled. Japan accounts for roughly 40% of the world market capitalization. This figure is somewhat inflated by the practice of cross-holding of stocks among publicly traded Japanese companies and financial institutions. McDonald (1989) conducted a detailed study of this affect (called "Mochiai") and reported that the weight of Japan in the world market portfolio at the end of 1988 should be revised from 44% to 39%.

The eighties have seen the emergence end rapid growth of stock markets in many developing countries. In Africa, stock markets have opened in countries such as Egypt, Morocco, or the Ivory Coast, but with limited growth. The growth has been somewhat faster in Latin America, especially in Brazil or Mexico. However the most spectacular change has been witnessed in Asia. Stock markets have rapidly grown in several countries, such as India, Indonesia, Malaysia, Thailand, Korea, and Taiwan (R.O.C.). Many of these markets were closed to foreign investors but are progressively opening up. In March 1989, the market capitalization of Taiwan, Korea, and Thailand was respectively 107, 161, and 10 billions of U.S. dollars. The total represents around three percent of the world stock market capitalization. In addition, the transaction volume on some of these markets is very large in regard to their size, which leads to a large volatility in prices. Some of these markets can only be accessed by foreign investors through country funds specifically set up for foreigners. These country funds tend to sell at a premium relative to their net asset value because foreign investors have no other alternative to invest in the country. The premium is volatile and often judged excessive. All these emerging countries are liberalizing their economies and quickly opening up their financial markets to foreign investment. A wave of liberalization and reforms took place in Eastern Europe in the early nineties. Stock markets have opened in other countries, like Hungary, that are moving away from communism. Some investors conjecture that this region will see a rapid development of their capital markets, mostly through foreign investment, in order to finance its economic growth.

Transaction Volume

Another measure of the bourse activity is transaction volume. Once again New York and Tokyo have the largest share turnover, as revealed in Exhibit 4.2.

EXHIBIT 4.2
Turnover on Major Stock Exchanges

Stock Exchange[a]	Total Value of Share Turnover (billions of U.S. dollars)								
	1988	*1986*	*1984*	*1982*	*1980*	*1978*	*1976*	*1974*	*1972*
United States (NYSE)	1356	1374	756	751	381	200	164	99	160
Japan (First Section)	2181	954	267	213	157	148	76	42	68
United Kingdom	166	133	48	43	36	20	13	15	25
West Germany	174	136	30	33	15	17	10	5	7
Canada	68	57	25	29	29	11	7	6	8
France	69	56	10	12	14	11	6	5	8
Netherlands	30	30	12	10	5	5	3	2	3
Sweden	19	20	9	10	2	0.4	0.5	0.5	0.3
Australia	38	27	11	9	10	1.2	0.8	0.8	1
Hong Kong	26	15	6	5	19	6	3	2	8
Singapore	6	5	7	9	4	1.5	0.5	0.5	1
Italy	31	45	4	4	8	2	2	3	3
Belgium	11	7	3	3	2	1.2	1.4	1.2	1.1
Spain	28	16	3	1.5	2	1.4	3	4	2
Denmark	5	1.9	0.2	0.2	0.1	0.1	0.1	0.1	0.1
Austria	1	0.5	0.1	0.1	0.1	0.1	0.1	0.1	0.1
Total	4211	2877	1190	1134	683	425	290	186	295

Source: Morgan Stanley Capital International. Reprinted with permission.

[a]Figures for Switzerland are not available.

Depending on market activity, these figures can vary widely from one year to the next, but in general most major markets enjoy a similar degree of liquidity in terms of transaction volume. In fact, annual turnover as a percentage of market capitalization varies significantly over time. For example, the U.S. annual turnover as a percentage of market capitalization varied from 30 to 70% from 1977 to 1987; the same statistic ranged from 20 to 80% for France. Therefore, comparison of national market liquidity based on this variable could lead to different conclusions if different years were observed. During any given year Japan, Hong Kong, France, West Germany, the United States, or some other country may turn out to be the most active market in proportion to its size.

Another informative statistic is the degree of concentration found in the major markets. It is important for the investor to know whether a national market is made up of myriad small firms or concentrated in a few large firms. Institutional investors are reluctant to invest in small firms for fear that they offer poor liquidity. Also, it is easier for the investor to track the performance of an index fund (i.e., national market capitalization weighted) if it is dominated by a few large issues. On the other hand a market dominated by a few large firms provides fewer opportunities for risk diversification and active portfolio strategies.

As shown in Exhibit 4.3, the American stock exchange is a diverse market where the top ten firms represent less than 15% of the total market capitalization. In the United States, IBM represents less than 13% of the capitalization of the New York Stock Exchange. At the other end of the spectrum the top ten Dutch multinational firms account for more than 70% of the Amsterdam Stock Exchange. Only five Dutch companies make up more than 60% of the Dutch market capitalization. It should be stressed that a large number of Japanese and European firms are on the list of the fifty largest international companies using market capitalization as a ranking criterion. As indicated in Chapter 5, non-American companies make up the majority of the top fifty industrial or banking corporations when sales (or assets) are used as a ranking criterion. These observations suggest that there exist a large number of American, Japanese, and European companies offering sufficient market capitalization and liquidity even to the largest institutional investors.

MAJOR DIFFERENCES AMONG MARKETS

Financial paper has long been traded in Europe, whereas trading in company shares is relatively recent. The Amsterdam Bourse is usually considered the oldest stock market. The first common stock was publicly traded in the Netherlands on the famous East Indies Trading Company (Verenigde Oost-Indische Compagnie) in the early seventeenth century.[1] In Paris, a stock market was started on a bridge, while in London it originated in a tavern; churches and open-air markets were also used as stock markets on the continent. For example, the Amsterdam Bourse spent some time in the Oude-Kerk (Old

EXHIBIT 4.3
The Ten Largest Market Capitalizations and Their Share of National Stock Markets

Country	Millions of dollars	Percent of total	Country	Millions of dollars	Percent of total
Japan			**United States**		
NTT	185354	4.9	IBM	68363	2.5
Industrial Bank of Japan	74684	2.0	Exxon Corp.	60676	2.3
Sumitomo Bank	72901	1.9	General Electric	43189	1.6
Daiichi Kangyo Bank	69544	1.8	American Tel & Tel	37176	1.4
Fuji Bank	67668	1.8	Philip Morris Cos	29519	1.1
Mitsubishi Bank	62109	1.6	Merck & Co.	26879	1.0
Tokyo Electric Power	57702	1.5	Du Pont de Nemours	26488	1.0
Toyota Motor Corp.	53753	1.4	Ford Motor	26169	1.0
Sanwa Bank	50666	1.3	General Motors	25949	1.0
Nomura Securities	47843	1.3	Amoco Corp.	22479	0.8
Total Top Ten	742224	19.5	Total Top Ten	366887	13.7
Total Stock Market	$3774 billion		Total Stock Market	$2685 billion	
United Kingdom			**Germany**		
British Telecom	27023	3.5	Daimler-Benz	15392	6.3
British Petroleum	25670	3.4	Allianz	14790	6.1
Shell T & T	22871	3.0	Siemens	13952	5.7
Glaxo Holdings	17411	2.3	Deutsche Bank	11134	4.6
Bat Industries	13877	1.8	Bayer	10241	4.2
Imperial Chemical	13704	1.8	BASF	9201	3.8
British Gas	13121	1.7	Hoechst	9081	3.7
Hanson	12383	1.6	RWE	6376	2.6
General Electric	10592	1.4	Veba	6325	2.6
BTR	10359	1.4	Volkswagen	5471	2.3
Total Top Ten	167011	21.9	Total Top Ten	101963	41.9
Total Stock Market	$762 billion		Total Stock Market	$243 billion	
France			**Canada**		
Aquitaine (ELF) Snea	7947	3.3	BCE	8901	3.8
LYMH	7414	3.1	Imperial Oil	7603	3.3
Peugeot	6696	2.8	Seagram Co.	7062	3.0
Compagnie du Midi	5983	2.5	Canadian Pac Ltd.	6153	2.6
BSN-Gervais Danone	5698	2.4	Alcan Aluminium	4890	2.1
Saint-Gobain	5426	2.3	Toronto-Dominion Bank	4820	2.1
Suez (Cie Financiere)	5190	2.2	Royal Bank of Canada	4414	1.9
Cie Generale Electricite	4927	2.1	Shell Canada	4373	1.9
Societe Generale	4574	1.9	Texaco Canada	4133	1.8
Generale Eaux	4548	1.9	Northern Telecom	3916	1.7
Total Top Ten	58403	24.5	Total Top Ten	56265	24.2
Total Stock Market	$240 billion		Total Stock Market	$233 billion	
Switzerland			**Italy**		
Nestle	14276	9.7	Assicurazioni Generali	16537	12.4
Ciba-Geigy	9465	6.4	Fiat	13952	10.5
Hoffmann-La Roche	8611	5.8	Stet	4483	3.4
Schweiz Bankgesell, UBS	8076	5.5	Ras	4039	3.0
Sandoz	8034	5.4	Montedison	3838	2.9
Schweiz Bankverein SBS	6569	4.5	La Fondiaria	3737	2.8
CS Holding	6012	4.1	Sip	3534	2.7
Zurich Versicherung	4724	3.2	Olivetti	3440	2.6
Schweiz Ruckversicherung	3201	2.2	Mediobanca	3216	2.4
Winterthur	3126	2.1	Banca Commerciale	3196	2.4
Total Top Ten	72094	48.9	Total Top Ten	59972	45.1
Total Stock Market	$148 billion		Total Stock Market	$133 billion	

EXHIBIT 4.3   (CONTINUED)

Country	Millions of dollars	Percent of total	Country	Millions of dollars	Percent of total
Australia			**Sweden**		
Broken Hill Proprietary	8167	6.6	Volvo	5786	5.9
Westpac	4074	3.3	Skanska	4849	4.9
BTR Nylex	3900	3.2	Asea	4638	4.7
Elders IXL	3875	3.1	Stora Kopparberg	3860	3.9
National Australia	3790	3.1	Electrolux	3674	3.7
CRA	3744	3.0	Skandinav, Enskilda Bank	3566	3.6
Coles Myer	3342	2.7	Sca sv Cellulosa	3318	3.4
Western Mining	3304	2.7	Ericsson (LM)	2721	2.8
Anz Group Holdings	3179	2.6	Sandvik	2709	2.8
News Corp.	2601	2.1	Procordia	2708	2.8
Total Top Ten	39976	32.4	Total Top Ten	37829	38.5
Total Stock Market	$123 billion		Total Stock Market	$98 billion	
Netherlands			**Spain**		
Royal Dutch Petroleum	34838	36.9	Telefonica de Espana	7624	8.3
Unilever	10165	10.8	Banco Bilbao Vizcay	7319	8.0
Philips	4913	5.2	Banco Santander	5830	6.4
Nationale-Nederland	4138	4.4	Endesa	4326	4.7
Akzo	2929	3.1	Banco Espanol de Credito	4221	4.6
Algemene Bank Nederland	2388	2.5	Banco Central	4212	4.6
Amro Bank	2240	2.4	Banco Hispano Americano	2877	3.1
Elsevier	2140	2.3	Iberduero	2284	2.5
DSM	2006	2.1	Banco Popular Espanola	2215	2.4
Dordtsche Petroleum	1995	2.1	Valenciana Portland	2032	2.2
Total Top Ten	67752	71.8	Total Top Ten	42940	46.8
Total Stock Market	$94 billion		Total Stock Market	$92 billion	
Hong Kong			**Belgium**		
Hong Kong Telecom	7676	8.8	Petrofina	7258	12.0
Hong Kong Shanghai Bank	4654	5.4	Societe Gen de Belgique	5061	8.4
Swire Pacific	4355	5.0	Tractebel	3545	5.9
Hutchison Whampoa	4349	5.0	Intercom	2904	4.8
Hong Kong Land	3622	4.2	Solvay	2902	4.8
Cathay Pacific Airways	3443	4.0	Ebes	2213	3.7
Cheung Kong	3262	3.8	Royale Belge	2158	3.6
Sun Hung Kai Properties	2730	3.1	Generale Banque	2101	3.5
Hang Seng Bank	2705	3.1	Groupe Bruxelles Lambert	2056	3.4
China Light & Power	2612	3.0	AG Financiere	1607	2.7
Total Top Ten	39408	45.4	Total Top Ten	31805	52.8
Total Stock Market	$87 billion		Total Stock Market	$60 billion	
Singapore / Malaysia					
Singapore Airlines	4271	8.4			
OCBC Oversea Chinese Bk	2532	5.0			
Sime Darby	2035	4.0			
Development Bk Singapore	1954	3.8			
United Overseas Bank	1306	2.6			
City Developments	1026	2.0			
Harrisons M. Plantations	896	1.8			
Fraser & Neave	880	1.7			
Singapore Press Holdings	851	1.7			
Malayan Banking	798	1.6			
Total Top Ten	16549	32.6			
Total Stock Market	$51 billion				

Source: Morgan Stanley Capital International Perspective, Geneva, Switzerland, May 1989. Reprinted with permission.

Church) and later in the Nieuwe-Kerk (New Church). Most of these European exchanges became recognized as separate markets and were regulated around 1800. Stock exchanges in the United States and Japan are more recent creations.

Historical and cultural differences explain most of the significant differences in stock trading practices around the world. Rather than engage in a detailed analysis of each national market, we will try to bring out the major oppositions in terms of market structures and trading procedures.

Differences in Market Structure

Each stock exchange has its own unique characteristics and legal organization, but broadly speaking all exchanges are one of three market structure types:

- □ the public bourse,
- □ the private bourse, and
- □ the banker bourse.

We will briefly describe the major characteristics of these three structures and highlight specific aspects of the major representative markets where it is appropriate. To be sure, some national markets display characteristics of more than one of these structures.

The public bourses The public bourse market structure has its origin in the legislative work of Napoléon I, the French emperor. He designed the bourse to be a public institution where brokers are appointed by the government and enjoy a monopoly over all transactions. Brokerage firms are, of course, private, and new brokers are proposed to the state for nomination by the broker's association. Stock exchanges organized under the authority of the state are found in the historical sphere of influence of Napoléon I: Belgium, Spain, Italy, Greece, and some Latin American countries.

The Paris Bourse was a good example of a capitalistic market that is under the authority of the government. Until 1989, commissions were set by the Ministry of Finance, but a certain amount of regulatory authority was delegated to the association of brokers. The advantage to the brokers of this highly regulated market is that they have a monopoly. Their number is fixed and all transactions must legally go through them. So even if a private deal is arranged by two banks the transaction must be registered by a broker and a minimum commission must be paid. On the other hand, the commissions for small trades are low compared to those of other stock markets. As in most countries, stock brokers may engage in portfolio management activities. Bonds as well as stocks are traded on the bourse. Deregulation is progressively affecting all public bourses. The French brokers are losing their monopoly, and their capital is now fully open to domestic and foreign financial institutions. Fixed commissions have been abolished. A similar "big bang" is taking place in Spain, Italy, and Belgium, meaning that banks are becoming brokers.

The private bourses Private stock exchange corporations are founded by independent members for the purpose of securities trading. Several private stock exchanges may compete within the same country, as in the United States, Japan, and Canada. In other countries, such as the United Kingdom, one leading exchange has emerged through either attrition or absorption of its competitors. Although these bourses are private, they are not free of public regulation. But the mix of self-regulation and government supervision is oriented more toward self-regulation than in the public bourses.

Private exchanges often require members to perform all of their transactions on the floor of the exchange. Commissions are either set by the exchange or imposed by the public authority. They are fully or partly negotiable in many countries. Canada, Australia, South Africa, Japan, and the Far East operate major private bourses that are organized according to the Anglo-American model.

The bankers bourses In some countries, banks are the major, or even the only, securities traders. In West Germany the Banking Act grants a brokerage monopoly to banks. Bankers bourses are found in the German sphere of influence: Austria, Switzerland, Scandinavia, and the Netherlands. (Amsterdam is to some extent a hybrid private and bankers bourse, where nonbank members are active participants. All members must deal through the exchange.)

Bankers bourses may be either private or semipublic organizations, but their chief function is to provide a convenient place for banks to meet. Many regional bankers bourses, in fact, have been founded by local chambers of commerce and are not even incorporated. Sometimes trading takes place directly between banks without involving the official bourse at all. Government regulation is imposed both on the bourse itself and directly on the banks.

Differences in Trading Procedures

Apart from legal structure numerous other differences are found in the operation of national stock markets. The most important differences are in the trading procedures.

Cash versus futures markets In most markets stock are traded on a cash basis, and transactions must be settled within a couple of days. In some countries, such as West Germany and Japan, forward and futures trading was explicitly forbidden, so that only cash markets can exist.

To allow more leveraged investment, margin trading is available on many cash markets such as those of United States, Canada, Japan (for domestic investors), and Switzerland. In margin trading the investor borrows money (or shares) from a broker to finance a transaction. The following example illustrates how a margin purchase works:

An investor buys 100 shares of XYZ at $100 per share. He does not have much cash, so he borrows $10,000 from his broker to make the purchase. The broker holds the shares as collateral. But this collateral, or guarantee, can drop in value if there is a decline in stock prices. If XYZ's price drops to $80, the stock loses $20 per share in value or $2000. Margin deposits of 30% (of stock value) are therefore required to guarantee that an investor will cover potential losses. The margin deposit must be increased immediately to match any decline in stock value and reconstitute the guarantee. Moreover, interest charges must be paid on the money borrowed.

Margin trading is very costly compared to trading on an organized futures market because private contracts must be arranged for each deal. This is still a cash market transaction and delivery of the shares takes place immediately; however, a third party steps in to lend money (shares) to the buyer (seller) to honor a cash transaction commitment.

In contrast, futures or forward stock markets provide an organized exchange for levered stock investment. Some of these forward stock markets, such as those in Rio de Janeiro and the Far East, have sprung up quite recently as competitors to old cash stock markets. But the major forward stock markets, for example, those in London and Paris, are old, established markets.

The Paris Bourse may serve as an illustration of how forward markets function. All major stocks are traded on a forward market (marché à terme or règlement mensuel). To simplify the clearing operations all transactions are settled at the end of the month on the settlement day, that is, on a periodic settlement system. Of course, a deposit is required to guarantee a position, as on most forward markets. Moreover, the transaction price is fixed at the time of the transaction and remains at this value even if the market price has changed substantially by the settlement time.

Settling all accounts once a month greatly simplifies the security clearing system. But it also opens the door to short-term speculation and to frequent misconceptions on the part of foreign investors who are unfamiliar with the technique. For example, American institutions sometimes credit their newly purchased French shares immediately in their portfolio accounting even though the cash outflow occurs at the end of the month. This leads to an overvaluation of the account.

If an investor insists on being paid cash for a sale, the broker will advance him the transaction proceeds minus a fee corresponding to an interest charge up to the settlement date. On the Paris Bourse both infrequently traded smaller issues and bonds are negotiated on a cash basis.

The British system is quite similar to the French system except that the account period is shorter. All deals are settled fortnightly, although accounts can run as long as three weeks because of public holidays. Gilts (government bonds) are traded on a cash basis. Other stock markets in both the Far East (Singapore) and Europe (Switzerland) offer the option of a more remote settlement day.

A large variety of contracts are now traded on futures commodity markets (as distinguished from traditional stock exchanges). Futures contracts in stock indexes are a good example of the innovations introduced by these commodity markets and are discussed in Chapter 8.

Fixed versus continuous quotation American investors are accustomed to a *continuous* market, where transactions take place all day and where large *market-makers* assure market liquidity at virtually any point in time. In some markets, the market maker has a monopoly for a given security, as is the case for the *specialist* on the New York Stock Exchange. In most other markets, the market makers, who might be called *dealers* or *jobbers*, compete with one another. The market maker quotes both a *bid* price (the price at which he is willing to buy the security) and an *ask* price (the price at which he is willing to sell the security). The client will turn to the market maker who provides the best quote. Of course, market makers adjust their quotes continuously to reflect supply and demand for the security as well as their own inventory. In other countries, however, an asset is traded only once or a few times per day and its price is determined through a competitive auction system. This is known as a *call* or *fixing* market, where a single price applies to all transactions.

The mechanisms used to arrive at a transaction are diverse and influenced by historical and cultural factors. Their description would require an entire book.[2] It is important, though, that foreign investors understand the difference between the two extremes, namely, a fixing (or call) market and a continuous market.

The increased volume of transaction as well as computerization has pushed most exchanges to move toward a continuous market. However, many markets in Europe, Asia and South America still retain some traditional procedures inherited from the times of fixed quotations. The Paris Bourse and the criée (call) system it retained until the early 1990s is a good example of a fixing market. Brokers assemble when the name of a major stock company (e.g., Club Meditérannée) is called out. The bourse clerk's job is to determine the equilibrium price that allows demand to equal supply. This is done through an open auction system (the *criée*). The clerk calls out an initial price for the Club and writes it on the board. Then brokers begin shouting how many shares they are willing to buy or sell at this price. The actual transactions are settled among the brokers themselves. If there is still a net demand for the Club at the price on the board, the bourse clerk quotes a higher price, all previous transactions are cancelled, and the shouting starts again. The process converges more or less rapidly to an equilibrium price, which is the official opening price and applies to all transactions negotiated during that auction. The largest volume of trading occurs during the opening criée, but other trades may take place in the following hour, again on a competitive auction basis.

Stocks with smaller volume have their prices fixed in an auction system but without a criée. Orders are submitted to a clerk, who enters them in a book and then determines the price at which the maximum volume of transactions will occur. Again the result is a single market price for all executed orders. This criée is being progressively replaced by an electronic order-matching system, as discussed in the next section.

In Frankfurt, all stocks trade according to a call auction system that begins at noon. Orders are accumulated before the opening of the market and crossed at a price that maximizes the volume of trading. Stocks with a large trading volume are also traded in a continuous market with market makers, but the opening and closing prices are determined by a call auction.

In Tokyo, a call auction system, called *itayose*, is used to establish prices at the start of the morning and afternoon sessions. During the sessions, a continuous auction is used to treat new orders. This auction system, called *zaraba*, is still an order-matching method and does not require the intervention of a market maker.

On the New York Stock Exchange, the opening price is determined through a call auction.

Computerization   Trading on a floor where participants noisily meet is progressively being replaced by computerized trading. Computerization allows a more efficient handling of orders, especially when there is a large number of small orders. The increase in the volume of trading pushed the need for computerized systems from the back to the front office. This includes price quotation, order routing, and automatic order matching. Trading hours have to be extended to accommodate investors from different time zones. While a single call auction provides an excellent liquidity at one point in time, it makes trading at other times difficult. Hence the market making function is being progressively developed on all call auction markets such as Paris, Tokyo, or Frankfurt to allow the possibility of trading throughout the day.

Floor trading is still very important on the New York Stock Exchange. However, computerized order routing and trading is increasing with the DOT (Designated Order Turnaround) and Super DOT systems. The National Association of Security Dealers (NASD) has developed an electronic trading system known as NASDAQ. London adopted a NASDAQ-type system called SEAQ, which now allows the electronic execution of small orders. The Computer Assisted Trading System (CATS) developed by the Toronto Stock exchange allows the automated execution of orders entered by traders in their office. It is a system well adapted to auction markets without market makers, and CATS has been adopted by many foreign markets (Paris, Tokyo, Madrid, etc.). The CATS system eliminates the need for a floor where participants meet. Therefore, these electronic trading systems have been strongly resisted by floor members, especially in Toronto and Tokyo. The human problem slows down the implementation of such systems. These systems initially were used to take care of small orders or of stocks with limited trading volume. Their use is now extended to all stocks and also to sizeable trades. However, it is likely that large blocks will still be traded over the phone rather than through an automated matching system.

Another implication of the computerization of the stock exchanges is that many of the national peculiarities of each market structure are progressively disappearing. Some of the market mechanisms described earlier will soon be only of interest to historians. This is welcome news for most international investors.

Internationalization The development of global investment calls for an increase in international trading. This need can be fulfilled in several ways.

To service international investors, American, British, Japanese, and other securities firms have developed an international network of offices. The required staff and investment makes this strategy very expensive. International financial centers have removed constraints to foreign securities firms; they have opened their doors to remain competitive with New York or London.

Some stock markets believe that they can safeguard their share of global trading by establishing links with other markets. This trend was most apparent among futures and options markets but also affected stock markets. For example, The American Stock Exchange and the Toronto Stock Exchange inaugurated in 1985 an automated trading link for a few of the major companies listed on their markets. The results were disappointing, and the agreement was dropped in 1988. The volume on most of these linkages was small, partly due to legal and technical problems, and to the advantage of the largest, more liquid market. The European stock markets are studying various linkage alternatives.

These linkages seem to be superseded by around-the-clock electronic trading. The NASDAQ system is being made available to investors in the UK and Singapore. The International Stock Exchange in London and the NASD have agreed not to compete by avoiding electronic quotes and trading for the same stocks. Some markets believe that they need not join a cooperative agreement with other national markets but that they should simply make their own automated trading system available worldwide on a 24-hour basis. With modern telecommunications, it is relatively easy to connect a screen on a computer system anywhere in the world. To be attractive, such a system requires more than the computer software; it also requires round-the-clock market makers and sufficient liquidity to attract active participation by international investors. Efficient clearing and settlement procedures are also needed. Global electronic trading may also be offered by vendors of trading information such as Reuters or others.

It is too early to tell which type of global trading system or linkages will emerge, but it is certainly a major challenge to the profession and its future.

SOME PRACTICAL ASPECTS

Dual Listings

Some companies are listed on several stock markets around the world.[3] Multinational firms such as Royal Dutch-Shell or Ciba-Geigy are traded on more than a dozen markets. The procedure for admitting foreign stocks to a local market varies. In some markets the regulations are quite lax. For example, as of 1986 the Quebec Securities Act allowed a foreign company to list in Montréal simply by meeting the same regulatory requirements as those in its own jurisdiction. In other markets foreign companies must abide by the rules of the local exchange. For instance, foreign companies wanting to be listed on U.S. stock exchanges must satisfy the requirements of both the exchange and the U.S. Securities and Exchange Commission. While this SEC regulation offers some protection to the U.S. public, it imposes substantial dual-listing costs on foreign companies, which have to produce frequent reports in English.

In countries such as the United States and France trading takes place in special shares of the foreign company. American investors deal in American depository receipts (ADRs). Under this arrangement foreign shares are deposited with a U.S. bank that, in turn, issues ADRs in the name of the foreign company. To avoid unusual share prices ADRs may represent a combination of several foreign shares. For example, Japanese shares are often priced at only a few yen per share. They are therefore combined into lots of 100 or more so that their value is more like that of a typical U.S. share price.

Multiple listing implies that the share values of a company are linked on several exchanges. One company should sell at the same share price all over the world, once adjustments for exchange rate and transactions costs have been made. Arbitrage among markets ensures that this is so.

An important question is: What is the dominant force affecting the stock price of a multiple-listed company? In a dominant satellite market relationship[4] the home market is the dominant force, and the price in the foreign market (the satellite) simply adjusts to the home market price. This is clearly the case for many dual-listed stocks where only a very small proportion of capitalization is traded abroad. However, the answer is less obvious for a few British, Dutch, and Swiss companies that have a very active market in other countries (especially the United States). Since stock trading takes place at different times around the world, American stocks listed on the Paris Bourse are traded before the opening of the American markets. Their French price reflects the previous close in New

York and the current exchange rate, but also anticipation about today's new price based on new information that surfaced during the night.

A domestic investor wanting to buy foreign shares has several alternatives. First, the investor can check whether or not the foreign firm is listed on the domestic market. If it is, these shares can most conveniently be bought domestically. The advantage of ADRs for an American investor is simply their convenience; they are traded just like domestic securities. Another alternative is to check on whether or not certain local institutions make a market in the foreign stock. For example, U.S. and British brokers maintain an active over-the-counter market for numerous foreign issues. The third alternative is to buy the shares abroad, directly on the company's primary market. Whereas the small investor may find it more convenient to trade ADRs, the large investor may find the primary market of overseas companies to be more liquid. In all cases, price levels, transaction costs, taxes, and administrative costs should be major determinants of which market the investor chooses.

Foreign companies have a variety of reasons for being listed on several national stock markets at once, despite the costs involved.[5] Multiple listing gives them more access to foreign ownership, allowing a better diversification of their capital and access to a larger amount of funds than is available from smaller domestic equity markets.[6] Diversified ownership in turn reduces the risk of a domestic takeover. Also, foreign listing raises the profile of a firm in foreign markets, which enables it to raise financing more easily on both the national and international bond markets. Finally, greater visibility of a company's name abroad is good advertising for its product brands. The only danger of foreign listing may be the increased volatility of the firm's stock in response to domestic economic news. Bad political and economic news in the Scandinavian countries, for example, has frequently been followed by an immediate reflux of shares from abroad, dramatically driving domestic share prices down in these illiquid stock markets. Scandinavian shareholders display less volatile behavior than foreign investors for two reasons: They are not as shaken by bad domestic news, and controls and regulations give them few attractive investment alternatives.

Tax Aspects

Foreign investments may be taxed in two locations:

1. the investor's country,
2. the investment's country.

Taxes are applied in any of three areas:

1. transactions,
2. capital gains,
3. income (dividends, etc.).

Some countries impose a tax on transactions. This tax is sometimes proportional to the amount transacted, as in Switzerland, where there is a federal stamp of 0.09%. In countries where brokers charge commissions rather than trade on net prices, the tax is proportional to the commission charged. Many European countries, for example, levy a value-added tax on the commission. Other countries charge a fixed tax per transaction. Although transaction taxes are generally small, institutional investors sometimes avoid certain markets altogether simply to reduce their tax liability.

Capital gains are normally taxed where the investor resides, no matter what the national origin of the investment is. In other words, domestic and international investments are taxed the same way.

Income on foreign stocks is paid from the legal entity of one country to a resident of another country. This often poses a conflict of jurisdiction, since both countries may want to impose a tax on that income. The international convention on taxing income is to make certain that taxes are paid by the investor in at least one country. That is why withholding taxes are levied on dividend payments. Since many investors are also taxed on income received in their country of residence, double taxation can result from this practice, but is avoided through a network of international tax treaties. An investor receives a dividend net of withholding tax plus a tax credit from the foreign tax government. The investor's country of residence imposes its tax on the gross foreign dividends, but the amount of this tax is reduced by the withholding tax credit. In other words, the foreign tax credit is applied against the home taxes.

To a tax-free investor, such as a pension fund, this tax credit is worthless, since the investor does not pay taxes at home. In this case, the investor can reclaim the tax withheld in the foreign country. Reclaiming a withholding tax is often a lengthy process requiring at least a few months and even up to a couple of years to actually recover the money. In a few countries part of the withholding tax is kept by the country of origin. Tax rules change frequently; Exhibit 4.4 indicates the major withholding tax rates that were in effect in 1987. Note that some investors such as public funds can obtain complete exemption from withholding taxes. Also, withholding-tax treatment is quite different for bonds. No withholding tax is applied to Eurobonds, and many countries have removed withholding taxes on domestic bonds purchased by nonresidents (see Chapter 6).

To illustrate these fiscal aspects, let's consider an American investor who buys 100 shares of Heineken listed in Amsterdam for 170 guilders. She goes through an American broker, and the current exchange rate is one guilder = 0.3 U.S. dollar. Her total cost is $5100, or $51 per share of Heineken (170 guilders × 0.3 $/gldr). Three months later, a gross dividend of 6 guilders is paid and our American decides to sell the Heineken shares. Each share is now worth 160 guilders and the current exchange rate is $/gldr = 0.4, since the guilder has sharply risen against the dollar. The same exchange rate applied in the dividend payment date. Here is the cashflow she received in U.S. dollars:

Dividend Payment Minus Withholding Tax (\$ / gldr. = 0.4)

	Net dividend	Tax credit
In guilders per share	5.1	0.9
In dollars per share	2.04	0.36
Net in dollars	204	36

Sale of Heineken Shares (\$ / gldr. = 0.4)

In guilders per share	160
In dollars per share	64
Net in dollars	6400

Our investor has made a capital gain of \$1300 (\$6400 − \$5100) that will be taxed in the United States at the U.S. capital-gain tax rate. She will also declare a total gross dividend of \$240 as income, which will be taxed at her income tax rate. However, she can deduct from her income tax a tax credit of \$36 thanks to the United States–Netherlands tax treaty.

Commissions

Commissions vary among markets, as discussed in Chapter 2. They are fully negotiable in the United States, while they are often fixed by the government or the stock exchange in other countries. There is a definite trend toward deregulation, and France, the United Kingdom, and other countries have moved toward negotiated rates. The dealers bid-ask spread should also be taken into account. Commissions are quite different among countries as shown in Exhibit 4.5. On call (fixing) markets such as Paris's, the buyer and the seller get the same price, so there is no bid-ask spread to take into account. Exhibit 4.5 indicates the range of fixed commissions depending on the size of trade, as well as the trade size at which the lower rate applies. It also indicates the typical range of commissions in countries with negotiable rates and transaction taxes, often called stamp taxes.

Stock Market Indexes

Stock market indexes allow one to measure the average performance of a national market. One or several market indexes may track a national market at any given time.

EXHIBIT 4.4
Dividend Taxation, 1987

Company's Domicile

Shareholder's Domicile[a]	Australia	Austria	Belgium	Canada	Denmark	France	W. Germany	Hong Kong	Italy	Japan	Luxembourg	Mexico	Netherlands	Norway	Singapore	Spain	Sweden	Switzerland	U.K.	U.S.
Australia		20	15	15	15	15	15	0	15	15	15	55	15	15	0	18	15	15	15	15
		C	C	C	C	C	C	—	C	C	C	C	C	C	—	C	C	C	C	C
Austria	30		15	15	10	15	25	0	15	20	15	55	15	15	0	15	10	5	15	15
	D		C	C	C	C	C	—	C	C	C	D	C	C	—	C	C	C	C	C
Belgium	15	15		15	15	15	15	0	15	15	15	55	15	15	0	15	15	15	0	15
	D,C	D,C		D,C	D,C	D,C	D,C	—	D,C	D,C	D,C	D,C	D,C	D,C	—	D,C	D,C	D,C	—	D,C
Canada	15	15	15		15	15	15	0	15	15	15	55	15	15	0	15	15	15	15	15
	C	C	C		C	C	C	—	C	C	C	C	C	C	—	C	C	C	C	C
Denmark	15	10	15	15		0	15	0	15	15	15	55	15	15	0	15	15	0	15	15
	C	C	C	C		—	C	—	C	C	C	C	C	C	—	C	C	—	C	C
France	15	15	15	15	0		15	0	15	15	15	55	15	15	0	15	0	5	15	15
	C	C	C	C	—		C	—	C	C	C	D	C	C	—	C	—	C	C	C
West Germany	15	20	15	15	15	0		0	32.4	15	15	55	15	15	0	15	15	15	0	15
	C	C	C	C	C	—		—	C	C	C	C	C	C	—	C	C	C	—	C
Hong Kong	30	20	25	25	30	25	25		32.4	20	15	55	25	25	0	18	30	35	0	30
	—	—	—	—	—	—	—		—	—	—	—	—	—	—	—	—	—	—	—
Italy	15	15	15	15	15	15	25	0		15	15	55	0	25	0	15	15	15	0	15
	C	C	C	C	C	C	C	—		C	C	C	—	C	—	C	C	C	—	C for 8
Japan	15	20	15	15	15	15	15	0	15		15	55	15	15	0	15	15	15	15	15
	C	C	C	C	C	C	C	—	C		C	C	C	C	—	C	C	C	C	C
Luxembourg	30	15	15	25	15	15	15	0	15	20		55	15	25	0	18	15	35	15	15
	C	C	C	C	C	C	C	—	C	C		C	C	C	—	C	C	C	C	C
Mexico	30	20	25	25	30	25	25	0	32.4	20	15		25	25	0	18	30	35	0	30
	C	C	C	C	C	C	C	—	C	C	C		C	C	—	C	C	C	—	C
Netherlands	15	15	15	15	15	15	15	0	32.4	15	15	55		15	0	15	15	15	15	15
	C	C	C	C	C	C	D	—	D	C	C	C		C	—	C	C	C	C	C
Norway	15	15	15	15	15	15	15	0	32.4	15	15	55	15		0	15	15	5	15	15
	C	C	C	C	C	C	C	—	C	C	C	C	C		—	C	C	D	C	C
Singapore	15	20	15	15	15	15	15	0	10	15	15	55	15	0		18	15	15	15	30
	C	D	C	C	C	C	C	—	C	C	D	D	C	—		D	C	C	C	D
Spain	30	15	15	15	15	15	15	0	15	15	15	55	15	15	0		15	15	15	30
	C	C	C	C	C	C	C	—	C	C	C	C	C	C	—		C	C	C	C
Sweden	15	10	15	15	15	15	15	0	15	15	15	55	15	15	0	15		5	15	15
	C	C	C	C	C	C	C	—	C	C	C	C	C	C	—	C		C	C	C
Switzerland	15	5	15	15	0	15	15	0	15	15	15	55	15	5	0	15	5		15	15
	C	C	C	C	—	C	C	—	C	C	D	D	C	D	—	C	C		C	D
United Kingdom	15	15	15	15	15	15	15	0	15	15	15	55	15	15	0	15	15	5		15
	C	C	C	C	C	C	C	—	C	C	C	C	C	C	—	C	C	C		C
United States	15	10	15	15	15	15	15	0	15	15	7.5	55	15	15	0	18	15	15	15	
	C	C	C	C	C	C	C	—	C	C	C	C	C	C	—	C	C	C	C	

Source: Morgan Stanley Capital International, 1987. Reprinted with permission.

[a] Top number indicates the effective rate of dividend withholding tax. Bottom letter describes the treatment of the foreign withholding tax in the shareholder's country of residence. D = deduction for foreign tax paid; i.e., the shareholder's country of residence imposes its tax on net foreign dividends; C = credit for foreign tax paid; i.e., the shareholder's country of residence imposes its tax on gross foreign dividends, but the amount of this tax is reduced by the amount of the foreign dividend withholding tax.

EXHIBIT 4.5
Estimates of Commissions and Costs, January 1990

Market	Commission Structure			Transaction Taxes (percent)
	Highest rate, (percent)	Lowest rate, (percent)	Trade size for lower rate (local currency)	
United States	Negotiable (typically: 0.3–1.3)			None
Canada	Negotiable (typically: 0.3–2.0)			None
Japan	1.25	0.15	¥1 billion	0.30 (sell only)
Hong Kong	0.75	0.75		0.355
Singapore	1.0	0.5	S$1 million	0.35 (buy only)
Australia	Negotiable (typically: 0.5–0.75)			0.30
United Kingdom	Negotiable (typically: 0.2–0.5)			0.5 (buy only)
W. Germany	0.5	0.5		0.08
Switzerland	1.1	Negotiable (0.2)	SF 500,000	0.09
France	Negotiable (typically: 0.2–0.65)			0.15–0.30
Italy	0.7	0.7		0.1125
Sweden	0.5	0.25	SEK 1 million	1.0

International stock indexes Morgan Stanley Capital International (MSCI) publishes national market value–weighted indexes on 22 countries based on approximately 1500 stocks. They also publish several regional indexes. The major ones are:

- World (approximately 1500 stocks)
- Europe (approximately 600 stocks)
- Europe, Australia, and the Far East (EAFE, approximately 1000 stocks).

These indexes are used widely by international money managers for asset allocation decisions and performance measurements. They cover about 60% of the each market capitalization, which means that 40% of the market is not represented. Hence more broadly based indexes can have significant differences in performance. These indexes have been available since 1970. Morgan Stanley Capital International also publishes related information on their sample of stocks, including financial ratios such as price earnings, price to book value ratios, and yield.

Since 1987 the Financial Times has published the FT-Actuaries world indexes in association with Goldman Sachs and Wood MacKenzie. Twenty-four national indexes are provided as well as numerous industrial and regional indexes. The most important regional indexes are the World index, the Europe index, the Pacific Basin index, and the Europe and Pacific index. The FT-Actuaries indexes have a wider coverage than the MSCI indexes since they are based on a sample of around 2400 stocks and cover more than 70% of each market capitalization.

In 1987 Salomon Brothers and Frank Russell also launched the Salomon/Russel Global Equity indexes.

Other international indexes are available. Union de Banques Suisses (UBS) calculates regional and world indexes based on the major national indexes most commonly used in each market. These daily indexes are market value–weighted averages of the national indexes presented in Exhibit 4.6. First Boston has also started to develop national and international indexes published regularly in *Euromoney*.

Domestic stock indexes Domestic investors prefer indexes that are calculated and published locally. Exhibit 4.6 gives a list of the most commonly used stock indexes for the major stock markets. Most of these indexes are broadly based and market value weighted. In other words, each company is assigned an index weight proportional to its market capitalization. Market value–weighted indexes are true market portfolio indexes in the sense that when the index portfolio is held by an investor, it truly represents movements in the market. This is not true of equal-weighted indexes such as the U.S. Dow Jones or the Japanese Nikkei/Dow Jones. The Dow Jones Industrial Average (DJIA) simply adds up the stock price of thirty corporations. In other words, each company is assigned an index weight proportional to its market price. Not only is the DJIA narrowly based, but its weighted method is artificial; IBM was removed from the index a few years ago because its price was so high compared to the other twenty-nine corporations. All stock indexes published do not include dividends.

Local indexes are widely used by domestic investors. Private international investors often prefer these indexes over the international indexes such as MSCI or FT for several reasons:

- In most cases the local indexes have been used for several decades.
- Local indexes represent a broader coverage of securities.
- Local indexes are calculated immediately and are available at the same time as stock market quotations on all electronic price services.
- Local indexes are available every morning in all the newspapers throughout the world.
- The risk of error in prices and capital adjustment is minimized in local indexes by the fact that all calculations are done locally with excellent information available on the spot.

EXHIBIT 4.6
Major National Stock Indexes

Locality	Exchange	Index[a]
United States	New York Stock Exchange	Standard and Poor's Composite (500)
	New York Stock Exchange	Dow Jones Industrial (30)
	New York Stock Exchange	NYSE Composite (about 1500)
	American Stock Exchange	AMEX index
	Over the counter	NASDAQ index (3000)
Canada	Toronto	TSE 300
	Montréal	Montréal Industrial
Japan	Tokyo	Nikkei/Dow Jones Average (225)
	Tokyo	Tokyo Stock Exchange (TSE) (1000), TOPIX
Hong Kong	Hong Kong	Hang Seng
Singapore	Singapore	Straits Times
Australia	Sydney	All Ordinaries
South Africa	Johannesburg	Composite Stock Index
Belgium	Brussels	Stock Index
France	Paris	Agefi
	Paris	Société des Bourses Francaises (SBF and CAC)
West Germany	Frankfurt	Commerzbank
	Frankfurt	F.A.Z., DAX
Italy	Milan	M.I.N.
Netherlands	Amsterdam	ANP-CBS General
Sweden	Stockholm	Affaersvaerlden
Switzerland	Zurich	Swiss Bank Corporation
	Zurich	Crédit Suisse, Swiss Index
United Kingdom	London	Financial Times Ordinary (30)
	London	Financial Times Stock Exchange (100)
	London	Financial Times all shares (750)

[a]The approximate number of securities in the index is given in parentheses for the three leading markets (United States, Japan, and the United Kingdom).

Pension funds, on the other hand, prefer to use the MSCI, FT, or other international indexes for the following reasons:

□ The pension funds do not need up-to-the-minute indexes.

□ The indexes on all stock markets are available in a central location, whereas local indexes must be drawn from several locations.

□ All MSCI or FT indexes are calculated in a single consistent manner, allowing for direct comparisons between markets.

□ They provide global indexes (world, EAFE), which are what international money managers need to measure overall performance.

The choice of index is important. In any given year the difference in performance between two indexes for the same stock market can be significant by as much as several points.

This is illustrated in Exhibit 4.7, where we plot two widely used market value–weighted Dutch stock indexes from 1979 to 1986. The solid line is the Morgan Stanley Capital International index and the dotted line is the ANP-CBS index. To allow for comparisons, both indexes are set at 100 on December 31, 1978, and the graph uses a logarithmic scale.

Marked divergences appear over the years. In 1979 the MSCI index went up by 8%, while the ANP-CBS index went down by 5%. Conversely, in 1985 the ANP-CBS index went up by 40%, and the MSC index, only by 18%. The two indexes show a similar performance over the total 1979 to 1986 period, but this is not typical of other countries.

SUMMARY

1. The world market size is over eight trillion U.S. dollars. North American markets make up roughly 30% of the world market capitalization; Tokyo and New York are the largest national markets. European countries tend to be under-represented compared to the relative size of their economies. European companies tend to rely more on banks for debt and equity financing and have less need for external equity financing. Other companies are not listed on the stock exchanges because they are owned by the state. Emerging countries, especially in Asia, have contributed to the rapid growth in world stock market capitalization in the eighties; Eastern Europe could provide further growth in the nineties.

2. The degree of stock market concentration varies greatly among countries. However, an extensive number of companies with large market capitalization and good liquidity are available in Europe, Japan, and North America.

3. Stock market structures differ considerably among countries. The different organizations and trading procedures are inherited from tradition and culture.

EXHIBIT 4.7
Comparative Performance Indicated by Two Dutch Stock Indexes

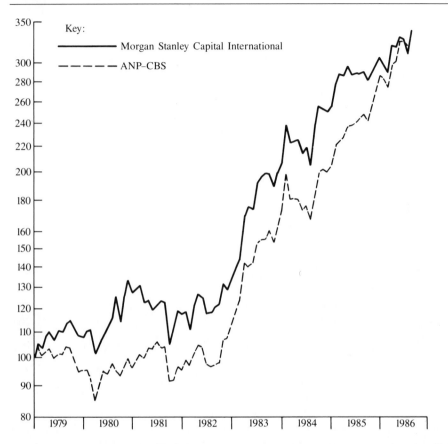

Source: Lombard Odier and Cie. Reprinted with permission.

The various stock exchanges (or bourses) may be classified into three categories: public exchanges, private exchanges, and bankers exchanges.

4. Among the many differences in trading procedures the major one is the opposition between call and continuous markets. In a call market purchase and sell orders are confronted at a given point in time and the equilibrium price is determined. In a continuous market dealers make a market by quoting bid and ask prices at which they stand ready to buy or sell shares.

5. Several companies are now listed on foreign stock markets. The shares of dual-listed foreign companies in the United States are called ADRs. Although these shares are more easily available to local investors, it is often cheaper to buy them directly on their home market.

6. Capital gain and income taxes are levied by the investor's country of residence. However, the foreign country where the dividend is paid often imposes a withholding tax on the dividend paid. The tax rate is generally equal to 15%. International tax treaties allow investors to claim this foreign withholding tax as a tax credit against income taxes paid at home. Tax-free investors such as pension funds have no use for tax credits, so they must file a claim for a refund of the tax in the foreign country.

7. Commissions vary across markets. The commission is either negotiable or follows a fixed schedule as a function of the size of the transaction.

8. Stock market indexes are readily available to measure the performance of each market.

QUESTIONS AND PROBLEMS

1. Describe the trend in stock market growth using Exhibits 4.1 and 4.2.

2. Compare the figures given in Exhibit 4.1 with the gross national product of the following nations (in billions of U.S. dollars):

France	864	Switzerland	169	Japan	2329
West Germany	1112	United Kingdom	652	Canada	413
Netherlands	211	Australia	194	United States	4429

3. A French investor buys one hundred shares of IBM on January 1 on the New York Stock Exchange at $120. The franc/dollar exchange rate is FF/$ = 7.00. Over the year, the investor has received a gross dividend of $4 per share; the net dividend per share received is equal to $3.4 because of a 15% withholding tax levied by the United States. The exchange rate at the time of dividend payments is FF/$ = 7.1. By December 31, the investor resells the IBM shares at $140 but the exchange rate has dropped suddenly to FF/$ = 6.8. Ignoring commissions, what is the rate of return on the investment (in dollars and in French francs), gross and net of taxes? Our French investor is taxed at 50% on income and 15% on capital gains; the U.S. withholding tax can be used as a tax credit in France.

4. Collect statistics on the major stock market indexes used in your own country and compare their performance over a few years.

5. Some Dutch and Swiss companies with multiple listing are famous for having a very large transaction volume on foreign stock markets. Why? Newly privatized British firms such as British Telecom have a very large trading volume in New York. Advance some reasons.

NOTES

1. A good historical review of the development of stock exchanges can be found in M. Tapley (ed), "Historical Introduction," in *International Portfolio Management*, Euromoney Publications, 1986; and the *Columbia Journal of World Business*, Summer 1982. A detailed description of each market can be found in I. George and I. Giddy (eds), *International Finance Handbook*, New York: Wiley, 1983; or Institut d'Etudes Bancaires et Financières, *Les Bourses de Valeurs dans le Monde*, Dunod, 1975.

2. A good analysis of the microstructure of equity markets is found in K. J. Cohen, S. F. Maier, R. A. Schwartz, and D. K. Whitcomb, *The Microstructure of Securities Markets*, Englewood Cliffs, NJ: Prentice Hall, 1986.

3. Euromoney periodically provides a list of companies with multiple listing in its annual equity market review.

4. A theorical analysis of dual-listed securities may be found in K. D. Garbade and W. L. Silber, "Dominant and Satellite Markets: A Study of Dually Traded Securities," *The Review of Economics and Statistics*, August 1979.

5. Foreign listing costs tend to be very high. Besides all the direct costs of introducing the stock on another market, the company must conform to the local regulations and prepare various reports to shareholders in the prescribed format and language.

6. For a discussion of this topic, see in A. Stonehill and Dullum, *Internationalizing Cost of Capital*, New York: Wiley, 1982.

BIBLIOGRAPHY

"Annual Equity Market Review," *Euromoney*, May 1986.

Caires, B. de (ed), *The GT Guide to World Equity Markets 1987*, London, Euromoney Publications, 1987.

Cooper, I. and Kaplanis, C. E. "Costs to Crossborder Investment and International Equity Market Equilibrium," in Edwards et al. (eds), *Recent Advances in Corporate Finance*, New York: Cambridge University Press, 1986.

Eiteman, D. K. "International Capital Markets," in N. Roussekis (ed), *International Banking: Principals and Practices*, Praeger, 1983.

Garbade, K. D. and Silber, W. L. "Dominant and Satellite Markets: A Study of Dually Traded Securities," *The Review of Economics and Statistics*, August 1979.

George, I. and Giddy, I. (eds), *International Finance Handbook*, New York: Wiley, 1983.

Haller, A. and Stoll, H. "Market Structure and Transaction Costs: Implied Spreads in the German Stock Market," *Journal of Banking and Finance*, September 1989.

Institut d'Etudes Bancaires et Financières, *Les Bourses de Valeurs dans le Monde*, Dunod, 1975.

Kemp, L. J. *A Guide to World Money and Capital Markets*, New York: McGraw Hill, 1982.

McDonald, J. "The Mochiai Effect: Japanese Corporate Cross-holdings," *The Journal of Portfolio Management*, Fall 1989.

Rhee, S. G. and Chang, R. P. (eds), *Pacific-Basin Capital Market Research*, North Holland, Amsterdam, 1990.

Roll, R. "The International Crash of October 1987," *Financial Analysts Journal*, September/October 1988.

Schwartz, R. *Equity Markets*, New York, Harper & Row, 1988.

Solnik, B. and Bousquet, L. "Day-of-the-Week Effect on the Paris Bourse," *Journal of Banking and Finance*, January 1990.

Stonehill, A. and Dullum, K. *Internationalizing Cost of Capital*, New York: Wiley, 1982.

Takagi, S. "The Japanese Equity Market: Past and Present," *Journal of Banking and Finance*, September 1989.

Tapley, M. (ed), *International Portfolio Management*, Euromoney Publications, 1986.

Vertin, J. (ed), *International Equity Investing*, Homewood, IL: Dow Jones-Irwin, 1984.

5

Equity: Concepts and Techniques

Investing in foreign stocks poses at least two types of problems:

- First, the portfolio manager must gain a sufficient familiarity with the operations, trading mechanisms, costs, and constraints of foreign markets. We addressed this issue in Chapter 4.
- Second, the portfolio manager's investment approach must be global, that is, his or her method for analyzing and selecting stocks should be part of an optimal worldwide investment strategy. The technical aspects of this analysis are discussed below, and Chapter 12 is devoted to designing a global international asset allocation strategy.

The greatest challenge faced by an international money manager is dealing with the sheer complexity of the international capital markets. Among the many factors the manager must take into account are the following:

- the large variety of instruments that currently exist, including stocks, bonds, treasury bills, and futures;
- the large number of national markets and currencies that are found worldwide;
- the many sectors there are from which to choose, ranging from industrial to geographic sectors; and finally
- the range of objectives sought by the investors the manager serves.

In order for our approach to international investment to be effective, these aspects must be incorporated into both the operational design and performance controls of our investment strategy. Analyzing a particular investment is a technical undertaking, but it is only a first step. The next step is to analyze each investment in terms of a tractable number of parameters so we need to 1) identify the major factors influencing international security price behavior and 2) determine the sensitivity of each security to these factors. Only then can we directly compare the alternatives and thereby reach our overall investment objectives.

The purpose of this chapter is to present some methods used to reduce the complexity of a detailed analysis of a company stock to a limited number of parameters. These parameters are then used to structure a global portfolio consistent with a desired strategy as outlined in Chapter 12. We will review the common problems of international financial analysis, then identify the major factors influencing stock price behavior. From this foundation, we will discuss the applicable theoretical framework.

FINANCIAL ANALYSIS AND VALUATION

Approaching International Analysis

There is nothing unique to financial analysis in an international context. American analysts must already take foreign variables into account in valuating domestic U.S. firms. After all, product markets in which many domestic industrial companies compete are international.

Large domestic firms tend to export extensively and head a network of foreign subsidiaries. These companies must be analyzed as international firms, not purely domestic ones. In many sectors the competition is fully international. Exhibit 5.1 indicates the fifty largest industrial corporations ranked by sales. Most of the world's major car manufacturers appear on this list (they all belong on the top 100 list); the same holds true for other industrial sectors such as petroleum, chemicals, and electronics. Twenty-one European and ten Japanese corporations appear on this list versus only seventeen U.S. corporations. General Motors ranks first, but Royal Dutch-Shell would be first if ranked by assets. A similar ranking of banks according to different criteria is published yearly by *Fortune* and *Euromoney*. The 1990 ranking of banks by *Fortune* based on total assets is given in Exhibit 5.2. There are only three U.S. banks among the top fifty institutions. Japan and Europe have twenty two banks each represented in the top fifty.

The methods and data required to analyze U.S.-, French-, or Italian-type manufacturers are quite similar, and for this reason are not covered in detail here. In brief, research on a company should produce two pieces of information:

Expected return. The expected return on an investment can be measured by a rate of return over some time period, by a potential price appreciation, or by some other quantified form of buy-or-sell recommendation.

EXHIBIT 5.1
The World's Largest Industrial Corporations

Corporation	Nationality	Sales $ billions
1. General Motors	U.S.	127.0
2. Ford motor	U.S.	96.9
3. Exxon	U.S.	86.7
4. Royal Dutch-Shell	Britain/Netherlands	85.5
5. I.B.M.	U.S.	63.4
6. Toyota Motor	Japan	60.4
7. General Electric	U.S.	55.3
8. Mobil	U.S.	51.0
9. Hitachi	Japan	50.9
10. British Petroleum	Britain	49.5
11. IRI	Italy	49.1
12. Matsushita Electric Ind.	Japan	43.1
13. Daimler-Benz	Germany	40.6
14. Philip Morris	U.S.	39.1
15. Fiat	Italy	36.7
16. Chrysler	U.S.	36.2
17. Nissan Motor	Japan	36.1
18. Unilever	Britain/Netherlands	35.2
19. E. I. Du Pont de Demours	U.S.	35.2
20. Samsung	South Korea	35.2
21. Volkswagen	Germany	34.7
22. Siemens	Germany	32.7
23. Texaco	U.S.	32.4
24. Toshiba	Japan	29.5
25. Chevron	U.S.	29.4
26. Nestlé	Switzerland	29.4
27. Renault	France	27.5
28. ENI	Italy	27.1
29. Philips	Netherlands	27.0
30. Honda Motor	Japan	26.5
31. BASF	Germany	25.3
32. NEC	Japan	24.6
33. Hoechst	Germany	24.4
34. Amoco	U.S.	24.2
35. Peugeot	France	24.1
36. BAT Industries	Britain	23.5
37. ELF Aquitaine	France	23.5
38. Bayer	Germany	23.0
39. CGE (Cie Générale d'Electricité)	France	22.6
40. Imperial Chemical	Britain	21.9
41. Procter and Gamble	U.S.	21.7
42. Mitsubishi Electric	Japan	21.2
43. ASEA Brown Boveri	Switzerland	21.2
44. Nippon Steel	Japan	20.8
45. Boeing	U.S.	20.3
46. Occidental Petroleum	U.S.	20.1
47. Daewoo	South Korea	20.0
48. United Technology	U.S.	19.8
49. Fujitsu	Japan	18.7
50. Eastman Kodak	U.S.	18.5

Source: Fortune International, July 30, 1990.

EXHIBIT 5.2
The World's Largest Banks

Bank	Nationality	Assets $ millions
1. Dai-Ichi Kangyo Bank	Japan	413,214
2. Sumitomo Bank	Japan	407,227
3. Fuji Bank	Japan	397,629
4. Mitsubishi Bank	Japan	380,857
5. Sanwa Bank	Japan	373,404
6. Industrial Bank of Japan	Japan	292,154
7. Norinchukin Bank	Japan	244,902
8. Crédit Agricole	France	242,578
9. Tokai Bank	Japan	238,783
10. Banque Nationale de Paris	France	232,024
11. Citicorp	U.S.	230,643
12. Bank of Tokyo	Japan	222,382
13. Mitsubishi Trust & Banking	Japan	221,727
14. Mitsui Bank	Japan	220,363
15. Crédit Lyonnais	France	211,237
16. Sumitomo Trust & Banking	Japan	207,582
17. Barclays Bank	Britain	206,036
18. Deutsche Bank	W. Germany	203,601
19. Long-Term Credit Bank of Japan	Japan	196,628
20. Mitsui Trust & Banking	Japan	191,573
21. National Westminster Bank	Britain	187,587
22. Taiyo Kobe Bank	Japan	181,773
23. Bank of China	China	181,543
24. Société Générale	France	176,213
25. Daiwa Bank	Japan	162,031
26. Yasuda Trust & Banking	Japan	160,171
27. Groupe Des Caisse D'Épargne	France	151,021
28. Dresdner Bank	W. Germany	147,723
29. Cie Financière de Paribas	France	139,003
30. Hong Kong & Shanghai Banking	Hong Kong	132,928
31. Toyo Trust & Banking	Japan	124,616
32. Nippon Credit Bank	Japan	123,645
33. Union Bank of Switzerland	Switzerland	114,260
34. Commerzbank	W. Germany	113,379
35. Deutsche Genossenschaftsbank	W. Germany	110,639
36. Kyowa Bank	Japan	110,168
37. Istituto Bancario San Paolo di Torino	Italy	107,700
38. Chase Manhattan Corp.	U.S.	107,369
39. Swiss Bank Corp.	Switzerland	105,465
40. Westdeutsche Landesbank	W. Germany	105,021
41. Banca Nazionale Del Lavoro	Italy	104,524
42. Bayerische Vereinbank	W. Germany	102,758
43. Saitama Bank	Japan	102,688
44. Midland Bank	Britain	100,872
45. BankAmerica Corp.	U.S.	98,764
46. Royal Bank of Canada	Canada	97,657
47. Amsterdam-Rotterdam Bank	Netherlands	94,168
48. Lloyds Bank	Britain	92,901
49. Shoko Chukin Bank	Japan	91,776
50. Bayerische Landesbank	W. Germany	91,301

Source: Fortune International, July 30, 1990.

Risk sensitivity. Risk sensitivity measures how much a company's value responds to certain key factors such as economic activity, energy costs, interest rates, currency volatility, and general market conditions. Risk analysis enables a manager or investment policy committee to simulate the performance of an investment in different scenarios. It also helps them to design more diversified portfolios.

The overall purpose of our analysis is to find securities with superior expected returns, given current (or foreseeable) domestic and international risks.

Quantifying the analysis facilitates a consistent global approach to international investment. This is all the more desirable when the parameters that must be considered are numerous and their interrelationships, complex.

Although qualitative analysis is easier to conduct in some institutions than others, it must be very carefully structured so that it is consistent for every security. For a qualitative method to be effective it must offer the same investment guidance as mathematically derived factor sensitivity coefficients (described below).

A major challenge faced by all investment organizations is structuring their international research efforts. Their choice of method depends on what they believe are the major factors influencing stock returns. The objective of security analysis is to detect relative misvaluation, i.e., investments that are preferable to other comparable investments. That is why sectoral analysis is so important. Securities that are part of the same world market sector, such as the dollar Eurobond market, French common stocks, or high-technology companies across the world, are by definition influenced by similar factors. In an homogeneous sector research should detect securities that are under- (or over-) priced relative to the others. Currently, investment organizations use one of two major approaches to international research, depending on their vision of the world:

1. If a portfolio manager believes that all securities in a national stock market are primarily influenced by domestic factors, his or her research effort should be structured on a country-by-country basis. The most important investment decision in this approach is how to allocate assets among countries. Thereafter, securities are given a relative valuation within each national market.

2. If a portfolio manager believes that the value of companies worldwide is primarily affected by international industrial factors, his or her research effort should be structured according to industrial sectors. This means that companies are valued relative to others within the same industrial sector, e.g., the chemical industry. Naturally, the financial analysts who use this approach are specialists in particular industrial sectors. Unfortunately, this approach has major drawbacks. As shown later in this chapter, the stock return of most companies is primarily influenced by domestic factors, not industrial factors. Also, there are a number of practical impediments to conducting a comparative analysis of companies located in different countries, as we shall soon discover.

The Technical Problems

A firm is typically valued in two steps. First, the company's financial statements are studied along with its overall market and growth potential. On the basis of this analysis a forecast is made of the company's future earnings. Next, an assessment is made of how the stock market will value these forecasts. In other words, the first level of analysis is specific to the company and its product market, and the second level is general, focusing on the relative valuation of the company within the stock market. The traditional measures for these two forms of analyses are, respectively, expected earnings per share (EPS) and the price-earnings (PE) ratio. Recently these two measures of a firm's performance have been replaced by a more quantitative approach that is based on projecting dividend streams (rather than earnings) and that requires the dividend discount model (DDM). But no matter how the financial analysis is done, problems arise at both levels of valuation.

Information The information on foreign firms is often difficult to obtain; and once obtained, it is often difficult to interpret and analyze using domestic methods. It is no wonder then that comparisons of similar figures for foreign firms is often misleading.

In the United States, companies publish their quarterly earnings, which are publicly available within just a couple of weeks. The 10-K reports are particularly useful for trend analysis and intercompany comparisons. Moreover, these reports are available on computerized databases. In contrast, certain European or Far Eastern firms only publish their earnings once a year. French companies follow this pattern and don't actually publish their earnings until six months[1] after the end of their fiscal year. As a result, French earnings estimates are outdated before they become public. To remedy this lack of information, international corporations with large foreign ownership have begun announcing quarterly or semiannual earnings estimates. The format and reliability of these announcements vary from firm to firm, but overall they help investors to get better-quality financial information faster. Like American firms, British firms publish detailed financial information frequently. Similarly, Japanese firms have begun publishing American-style financial statements, though not as frequently as American firms.

Other problems arise from the language and presentation of the financial reports. Many reports are only available in a company's local language. Whereas multinational firms tend to publish both in their local language and in English, many smaller but nevertheless attractive foreign firms do not. In general, financial reports vary widely from country to country in format, degree of detail, and reliability of the information disclosed. For this reason, additional information must often be obtained directly from the company.

Fortunately, as international investment has grown brokers, banks, and information services have started to provide even more financial data to meet investors' needs. In fact, today many large international brokerage houses and banks provide analysts' guides covering companies from a large number of countries. The guides include information ranging from summary balance sheet and income statement information to growth forecasts, expected returns on equity investments, and risk measures such as betas, which are discussed below. The reports are usually available in both the domestic language and English. Similarly, data services such as Extel, DAFSA, and Moody's are extending their international coverage of companies and currently feature summary financial information on an increasing number of foreign corporations.

Despite these developments, to get the most timely information possible financial analysts must actually visit foreign corporations. This, of course, is a time-consuming and expensive process. Moreover, the information obtained is often not homogeneous across companies and countries.

Comparative analysis Another technical problem is trying to compare financial statements from different countries. Different countries employ different accounting principles, and even where the same accounting methods are used, cultural, institutional, political, and tax differences can make between-country comparisons of accounting numbers hazardous and misleading.

For example, the treatment of depreciation and extraordinary items varies greatly among countries, so much so, in fact, that an analyst would probably have to double the net income of Swedish, West German, or Japanese firms in order to make a meaningful comparison with the corresponding figures for British or American firms. This disparity is partly the result of different national tax incentives and the creation of "secret" reserves in certain countries. German and Swiss firms, for example, are known to stretch the definition of a liability, that is, they tend to overestimate contingent liabilities and future uncertainties when compared to U.S. firms.

West German firms create hidden reserves often equal to 100 percent of fixed assets to economize on taxes. Their inventories tend to be understated for tax purposes and are not revalued when prices go up. Mergers and takeovers are reported in the balance sheet based on the book value, not the actual transactions price, so underestimating the value of equity. West German reports to stockholders have to be those produced for tax purpose. Since corporations use accounting techniques to reduce taxable earnings, the reported earnings understate the true economic earnings compared to a similar American or English company. Similarly, Sweden has a very favorable tax system for corporations. Tax incentives such as accelerated depreciation, inventory write-off, and various other provisions cause Swedish firms to report what are considered distorted net income figures by the standards of the U.S. generally accepted accounting principles (GAAP).

Comparing Japanese and American earnings figures or accounting ratios is virtually meaningless.[2] As a result, most large Japanese companies now publish secondary financial statements in English that conform to the U.S. GAAP and are audited by major U.S. accounting firms. But even when we examine these statements we find that financial ratios differ markedly between the two

EXHIBIT 5.3
Major Differences in Accounting Practices Among Countries

- □ Publication of consolidated statements
- □ Publication of accounts corrected for fiscal distortion
- □ Inflation accounting
- □ Currency adjustments
- □ Treatment of extraordinary expenses
- □ Existence of "hidden" reserves
- □ Depreciation rules
- □ Inventory valuation
- □ Stability of accounting principles used

countries. For example, financial leverage is high in Japan compared to the United States, and coverage ratios are poor. But this does not mean that Japanese firms are more risky than their U.S. counterparts, only that the relationship between banks and their client corporations is different from that in the United States.[3]

An overview of national accounting principles has been described by Choi and Mueller.[4] It appears that the most important differences arise in nine main areas as shown in Exhibit 5.3.

Stock market valuation Stock markets in different countries value different attributes. Thus the same earnings forecast can lead to a different stock price valuation depending on the nationality of the corporation. For example, the average price-earnings ratio varies greatly among countries as shown in Exhibit 5.4. Indeed, we find that comparable firms in the same industry but different countries can have markedly different PE ratios. For example, U.S. and U.K. corporations tend to have much lower PE ratios than French or Japanese firms. Therefore, the cheapest companies are not necessarily the most attractive. All this indicates is that there are national differences in earnings accounting and stock market perception rather than mispricing of comparable firms.

Japanese and German firms tend to sell well above their accounting book values if their ratios of stock-price to book-value are compared to those of Dutch or Italian firms. But this does not mean that German equity should be arbitraged against Dutch equity. Rather, it means that the two markets react differently.

Investors often rely on a dividend discount model for estimating the expected return on a stock investment. The value of an asset is determined by the stream of cash flows it generates for the investor. In a DDM the stock market price is set equal to the stream of forecasted dividends.

$$P = \frac{D_1}{1+r} + \frac{D_2}{(1+r)^2} + \frac{D_3}{(1+r)^3} + \cdots . \tag{5.1}$$

EXHIBIT 5.4
Stock Market Valuation

P / BV	P / CE	P / E	Yield	Index
				International Indexes (in U.S. dollars)
2.53	8.1	18.8	2.3	World Index
3.02	9.6	26.0	1.6	Europe, Australia, Far East (EAFE) Index
1.80	6.4	13.0	3.6	Europe Index
				National Indexes (in U.S. dollars)
1.87	11.9	13.3	3.8	Hong Kong
2.56	6.3	33.4	1.6	Norway
1.91	7.7	11.5	4.4	United Kingdom
1.96	12.8	23.6	1.4	Singapore/Malaysia
1.57	7.4	11.3	4.7	Australia
1.68	7.0	12.0	3.2	Canada
1.94	6.9	12.1	3.6	United States of America
1.10	6.5	10.2	5.6	New Zealand
2.49	9.1	15.6	1.9	Sweden
1.38	5.0	10.7	4.3	Netherlands
1.92	5.9	13.2	2.7	France
4.97	18.4	56.9	0.5	Japan
2.00	6.3	14.2	3.9	Belgium
1.24	4.6	15.8	3.6	Spain
1.50	8.3	14.2	2.2	Finland
1.59	9.8	18.1	2.0	Denmark
1.65	5.3	28.1	2.4	Austria
1.77	3.7	15.3	2.6	Italy
1.51	7.8	15.4	2.3	Switzerland
1.91	4.8	15.8	3.6	Germany

Source: Morgan Stanley Capital International, February 1989.

P/BV = price to book-value ratio; P/CE = price to cash-earnings (earnings + depreciation) ratio; P/E = price-earnings ratio; Yield = gross dividend yield.

Financial analysts take great care in forecasting future earnings and hence dividends. A typical DDM approach is to decompose the future in three phases. In the near future (e.g., the next two years), earnings are forecasted individually. In the second phase (e.g., years two to five), a general growth rate of the company's earnings is estimated. In the final stage the growth rate in earnings is supposed to revert to the average rate of all firms in the market. Application of Eq. (5.1) where the expected dividends (D_t) and the current stock market price (P) are known, allows the derivation of the expected return (r) on an investment in the company's stock.

These models readily permit the direct comparison of corporations traded on the same stock market (after adjusting for risk). But to make an international comparison of expected returns requires an accurate forecast of currency movements as well. The presence of so many differences among countries explains why most international money managers value corporations relative to their domestic markets, before even attempting to value them globally in relation to their direct product market competitors. The logic behind this country-specific approach is amply supported by the study of the major factors influencing stock returns discussed below.

Country Analysis

Asset allocation is a major decision in international portfolio management. The choice of instruments, markets, and currencies often has more impact on portfolio performance than the selection of specific securities within each market. An active allocation strategy requires the study and forecast of changes in at least three macroeconomic variables: currencies, interest rates, and stock markets.

The latter two variables affect the performance of bond and stock portfolios. Currency not only is one of the many variables indirectly affecting asset prices, but directly affects the domestic performance of all foreign assets through the translation of foreign currency into the domestic one. The issue of currency forecasting was addressed in Chapter 3, where we stressed that it is difficult. It is not easier to forecast the relative performance of national stock markets. In each country economists try to monitor a large number of economic, social, and political variables such as

- ◻ anticipated real growth,
- ◻ monetary policy,
- ◻ wage and employment rigidities,
- ◻ competitiveness,
- ◻ social and political situations,
- ◻ fiscal policy (including fiscal incentives for investments), and
- ◻ economic sensitivity to energy costs.

Real economic growth is probably the major influence on a national stock market.[5] Of course stock markets react to anticipated growth. If the past gives any indication of the future, Exhibit 5.5 indicates marked differences in real growth among countries. This figure shows the cumulative growth rate of the growth domestic product (GDP) of the United States, the major industrial countries,[6] and selected Asian countries. While the United States had a cumulative real growth rate close to 100% from 1963 to 1984, this is below the average of industrial countries and well below that of most Asian countries. The

EXHIBIT 5.5
Cumulative Percentage Change in Real GDP

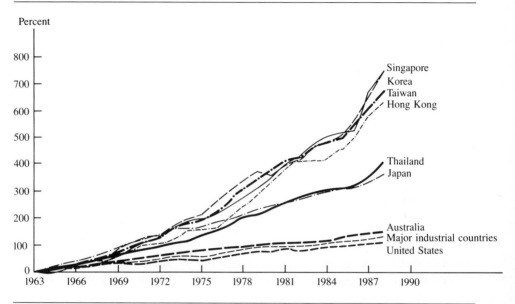

Source: State Street Bank.

economic growth of Japan, Hong Kong, and Singapore explains their excellent long-term performance. The volatility of economic growth in developing countries explains the greater volatility of their stock markets.

INTERNATIONAL FACTORS IN SECURITY RETURNS

To structure a portfolio properly a manager must have a clear understanding of the main factors influencing the return on a security. The first step is to determine whether the price of an individual security is primarily affected by international or purely domestic factors.

Domestic versus International Factors

Lessard (1976) and Solnik (1976)[7] researched the relative importance of industry, domestic, and international factors. They concluded that there existed an international influence on stock returns, but that domestic effects were much stronger. International industry effects appeared weak compared to national effects. These studies used old data (prior to 1973) from a time when most exchange rates were fixed. Since 1973 and the advent of flexible exchange rates, currency movements make a significant contribution to the total return of a foreign portfolio, and their influence on stock return must be further studied. Recent studies by Solnik (1984) and Adler and Simon (1986)[8] suggest a weak correlation between stock market indexes and currency movements, but this does not rule out the existence of a selective exchange rate influence on specific firms, depending on the activity of the firm.

A simple approach to determining the relative importance of each factor is to separately correlate each individual stock with

- □ the world stock index,
- □ the appropriate (international) industrial sector index,
- □ the currency movement, and
- □ the appropriate national market index.

The first three factors may be regarded as international, and the last one as domestic.

This approach was taken in a study by Solnik and de Freitas.[9] The R^2 is a measure of correlation that tells us which of the four factors is most important in explaining the return of a particular stock. The average R^2 for all companies from a given country are reported in the first four columns of Exhibit 5.6. The behavior of the domestic market is by far the most important factor affecting individual stock returns; on the average, this factor explains 42% of the return on individual securities. The world and industrial factors explain 18 and 23% of the return, whereas the influence of currency movements on the local stock prices is almost insignificant. Note that the various correlations do not add up; the four factors are correlated with each other. In fact, most of the influence of the world factor is common to that of the domestic factor. This is revealed by running a multiple regression including all four factors. The average R^2 of this joint regression is given in the last column of Exhibit 5.6. The simple regression of stock returns on the domestic market index return has an average R^2 of 0.42; the value rises to 0.46 when the three international factors are added in the regression. This is a rather small improvement in R^2. However, the story differs among countries; the increase in R^2 is fairly large for companies in the United States (from 0.35 to 0.55) and in France (from 0.45 to 0.60). A detailed analysis of the results indicates that the marginal contribution of the international industrial factor is generally positive and significant. The contribution of the currency movement is generally very weak but positive, and appears to be country specific but not company specific. A local currency appreciation tends to be good for the local stock market.

Factor analysis was also used in this study to extract common factors from the sample of companies and correlate them with the four sets of indexes. The previous conclusions were confirmed: The influence of the domestic market is dominant, although weaker industrial factors are significant. The influence of exchange rates is very weak and usually positive. There is little evidence of firm-specific currency influence. Note that this last result indicates that stocks

EXHIBIT 5.6
Relative Importance of World, Industrial, Currency, and Domestic Factors in Explaining Return of a Stock

	Average R^2 of Regression on Factors				
	Single-Factor Tests				Joint Test
Locality	World	Industrial	Currency	Domestic	All Four Factors
Switzerland	0.18	0.17	0.00	0.38	0.39
West Germany	0.08	0.10	0.00	0.41	0.42
Australia	0.24	0.26	0.01	0.72	0.72
Belgium	0.07	0.08	0.00	0.42	0.43
Canada	0.27	0.24	0.07	0.45	0.48
Spain	0.22	0.03	0.00	0.45	0.45
United States	0.26	0.47	0.01	0.35	0.55
France	0.13	0.08	0.01	0.45	0.60
United Kingdom	0.20	0.17	0.01	0.53	0.55
Hong Kong	0.06	0.25	0.17	0.79	0.81
Italy	0.05	0.03	0.00	0.35	0.35
Japan	0.09	0.16	0.01	0.26	0.33
Norway	0.17	0.28	0.00	0.84	0.85
Netherlands	0.12	0.07	0.01	0.34	0.31
Singapore	0.16	0.15	0.02	0.32	0.33
Sweden	0.19	0.06	0.01	0.42	0.43
All Countries	0.18	0.23	0.01	0.42	0.46

tend to be poor hedges against currency movements. When translated into the investor's home currency, all stock prices of a given foreign market tend to go up and down with the exchange rate.

Grinold, Rudd, and Stefek[10] used a slightly different methodology to study the relative importance of country and industry factors in stock returns over the period 1983 to 1988. They also conclude that country factors are more important than industry factors. However, some industry factors are more "global" than others. For example, they found that the oil industry factor is highly significant, which is not the case of the factor for consumer goods.

The Valuation of Multinational Firms: Domestic or International?

Some companies conduct a large percentage of their activities abroad. The largest companies in Switzerland (Nestle and Ciba-Geigy) and in the Netherlands (Royal Dutch-Shell, Philips, and Unilever), for example, derive most of their profits from foreign sales and operations. Many of the largest corporations in the world, including quite a few American ones, derive over 50% of their earnings and sales from abroad.[11]

The extent of foreign operations for many multinational firms (MNFs) raises the following question: Can a portfolio of MNF stocks achieve true international diversification? In other words, do MNF stock prices behave like diversified international stocks, thereby offering a good substitute to direct foreign portfolio investment?

This issue is most relevant to an American money manager who may invest in the large universe of United States-based MNFs. Ideally the manager would want to monitor his or her exposure in specific countries by buying or selling the shares of U.S. companies with important activities in these countries. This would avoid the difficulties and costs involved in investing directly in foreign capital markets. Furthermore, better information is available on U.S. companies than on many of the exotic firms quoted in distant stock markets.

Few studies have focused on MNF stock price behavior, but the conclusions reached by Senschack and Beedles[12] are a good summary of the current evidence. They state that "the evidence seems to support strongly the behavior guide to investors that positioning in U.S. multinational firms does *not* provide all the benefits available from direct investment in foreign securities." Specifically, they found that the total risk of a portfolio of U.S. MNFs is no smaller than that of a portfolio of U.S. stocks with predominantly domestic activities. Indeed, MNFs do not even provide additional diversification benefits to a portfolio of purely domestic firms.

Similarly, Jacquillat and Solnik examined firms from nine countries and found that MNF stock prices behave very much like those of purely domestic firms (Exhibit 5.7). Their approach was to formulate a multifactor model where each factor represented a national market index. Their results show that MNF stock prices are more strongly affected by the domestic market index than by foreign factors in most cases. This is especially true for U.S. and British firms, where the addition of foreign factors to the (domestic) market model does not significantly improve its explanatory power (R^2). This is less true for French, Swiss, Belgian, and Dutch companies. But even in these countries, the impact of foreign factors is much less than that of the domestic factor, despite the fact that many of their firms are more active abroad than domestically.[13]

The impact of national control and management policy, as well as government constraints on a firm's performance, may explain why multinationals are not a good substitute for international portfolio diversification. Government influence on the prices of the major stock market on which the firm is traded may also be a factor.

The dominance of the national factor is compounded by the currency translation which is common to all securities of a local market. From a domestic viewpoint all stocks of a foreign market tend to have a fairly similar price behavior because of both the local market factor and the exchange rate movement when translated into the domestic currency. Note that a similar

EXHIBIT 5.7
Average Betas of Portfolios of Domestic MNFs with Selected National Indexes

Nationalities of MNF	National Index										Single index beta	Single index R^2 adjusted
	United States	Netherlands	Belgium	West Germany	Italy	Sweden	France	Switzerland	United Kingdom	R^2 adjusted		
American MNF	<u>0.94</u>	0.12	−0.05	−0.01	−0.04	0.04	0.02	−0.01	−0.07	0.31	1.02	0.29
Dutch MNF	0.31	<u>0.76</u>	0.09	0.16	−0.02	−0.28	0.25	−0.21	−0.06	0.63	0.98	0.50
Belgian MNF	−0.27	0.07	<u>1.04</u>	0.06	0.03	0.19	0.06	0.08	0.07	0.58	1.03	0.45
German MNF	0.24	0.03	−0.21	<u>1.18</u>	−0.02	−0.01	0.10	−0.15	−0.11	0.74	1.18	0.65
Italian MNF	−0.10	0.06	0.10	0.01	<u>0.83</u>	0.11	−0.19	−0.16	0.20	0.51	0.91	0.47
Swedish MNF	0.06	−0.15	−0.02	0.08	<u>−0.10</u>	<u>0.96</u>	0.01	0.15	0.02	0.50	0.92	0.42
French MNF	−0.10	0.14	0.33	0.18	0.02	−0.16	<u>0.95</u>	−0.22	0.03	0.62	1.08	0.45
Swiss MNF	−0.12	−0.23	−0.04	−0.09	−0.02	0.16	−0.11	<u>1.74</u>	0.16	0.75	1.39	0.52
British MNF	−0.10	−0.11	0.30	0.09	−0.04	−0.13	−0.09	0.07	<u>0.84</u>	0.49	1.06	0.44

Source: B. Jacquillat and B. Solnik, "Multinationals Are Poor Tools for International Diversification," Journal of Portfolio Management, Winter 1978.

conclusion holds for bonds. The return on all bonds issued in a given currency are mostly affected by movements in that currency's interest rate and the exchange rate. Differences in bond price behavior between securities issued in the same currency are, however, minor compared to the national factor. These conclusions do not rule out international asset pricing; they suggest that investment analysis ought to be structured on a geographic top-down approach.

RISK AND RETURN: AN INTERNATIONAL CAPITAL ASSET PRICING MODEL

Asset Pricing

Forecasting the expected return on a security is not sufficient. Returns on very risky assets should be higher than returns on less risky security: A risk premium should compensate the risk-averse investor for the extra risk borne. For example, an investment in Daimler-Benz shares should only be considered if the expected return is at least higher than the interest rate on a short-term Euro-deutsche mark deposit. Risk-averse investors would take into account the possibility of incurring a sizable loss on their shares of Daimler-Benz if their forecast is proven wrong.

To determine if a security is under (or over) valued in the market we must decide if the expected return is too large (or small) given the risks incurred. This means that we need a theory to tell us what the normal (or required) expected return should be on a security given its risks, and what that relevant measure of risk is.

The traditional Capital Asset Pricing Model (CAPM) proposes a simple and operational theory of asset pricing in a domestic framework. This model, introduced in Chapter 1, relies, as does any theory, on simplifying assumptions. Its practical implications for active portfolio management are discussed in the appendix. The major conclusions of the model are the following:

□ The relevant measure of risk is the covariance of the return on the asset with the return on the market portfolio, which is often called beta.[14]

□ The risk premium, i.e., the difference between the expected return on the asset and the risk-free interest rate, is proportional to this beta.

The total risk of a security can be broken down into two parts: its *market risk*, which is proportional to the risk of the market portfolio, and its *specific risk*, which is uncorrelated with the market risk. In a diversified portfolio all specific risks of individual securities are diversified away and only the market risk proportional to the beta of the portfolio remains. The CAPM makes the commonsensible claim that only the market risk (β) should be compensated by a risk premium in an efficient market, and not the specific risks, which can be easily eliminated by diversification.

The theoretical framework of the CAPM can be readily extended to the international situation.[15] Subject to very restrictive assumptions, this model makes the claim that the risk that is priced in the market is measured by the international beta of a security, that is, the beta relative to the world market portfolio hedged against exchange risk.

The question is: How can this theory be reconciled with our empirical observation that the domestic market factor is the major source of influence on the return of a security? To answer this question, we now introduce a simple multi-country model or top-down approach.

A Multi-Country Model

The model According to the simple, descriptive, multi-country model each security is influenced by its domestic market factor, which in turn is influenced by the single world market factor. In other words, a security is indirectly sensitive to the world market factor through its national market factor.[16] National market risk may be dissected into a risk caused by the world factor and a risk specific to the country.

The sensitivity a country displays to this world factor is the result of many influences, including its degree of international trade and investment, domestic monetary and economic policy, regulation and controls of international trade, and capital flows. Thus the world beta of a security (β_{iw}) is the product of its domestic beta (β_i) and the sensitivity of the domestic country factor to the world market factor (β_{cw}). This is illustrated in Exhibit 5.8.

The theoretical implication of this world CAPM is that each security's expected return is proportional to its world beta (β_{iw}) and its domestic beta (β_i), which is consistent with the domestic versions of the traditional CAPM.

The model's practical use Although this theoretical framework is useful for structuring the investment process, most money managers do not regard the world capital market as fully efficient. Therefore, this model of international security returns leads to a multi-country or top-down approach to the international investment process of trying to exploit inefficiencies within a coherent framework. The first step in the top-down approach requires economists and analysts to attempt to forecast national market returns and currency movements. These forecasts lead to international asset allocation with an under (or over) weighting of some markets relative to the world index. In the second step, individual companies are valued within the context of their national market. Superior performance can come from two sources: country selection and individual selection within a national market.

A good forecast of the domestic factor is very important because it affects the return of all stocks of the country through their domestic betas. The returns are compounded by currency movements, which affect all the local stocks from a foreign investor's viewpoint.

Beta coefficients have to be estimated, which is no simple task. The simplest method used by large investment institutions is to employ a simple regression model over past data. Many data services, brokers, and banks make these beta

EXHIBIT 5.8
A Multi-Country Model

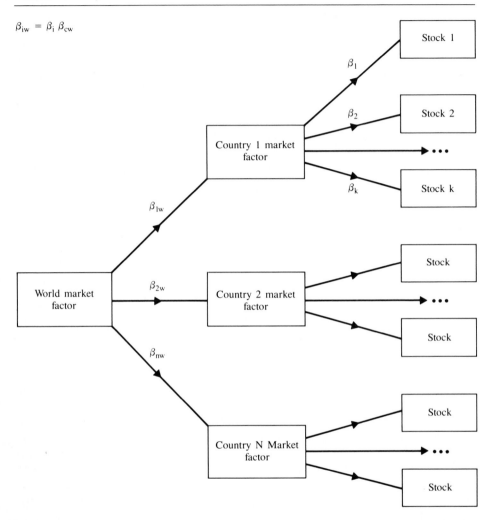

$$\beta_{iw} = \beta_i \, \beta_{cw}$$

estimates available in frequent publications or on time-sharing systems across the world; but one must often refer to several institutions to get betas from different countries. Institutions with a large in-house historical database have an obvious advantage in being able to compute betas directly for all the stocks under their management.

A second method of determining betas is to adjust the regression estimates to factor in certain statistical properties of the estimation, as well as other information on the company studied.

Both methods are based on the notion that risk estimates are stable over time, so that past data give indications on what the beta for the next period will be. Again, we use past data only to the extent that they help us to estimate the future betas, since money managers are only interested in the future stock sensitivity to domestic and international factors.

To summarize, a financial analyst should compute both the expected return and risk of stocks relative to his or her domestic market. This allows a list of stocks with abnormally high expected returns given their risk level to be drawn. From this list, the manager can select securities to achieve the desired international asset allocation among markets, which is based on general forecasts of markets, interest rates, and currencies. If the manager is bullish on a particular national stock market, he or she should select stocks with high betas for that market. On the other hand, if the manager is bullish in the currency but quite uncertain about the market itself, he or she should select only low-beta stocks in that market.

RISK AND RETURN: AN INTERNATIONAL ARBITRAGE PRICING THEORY

The Problems with CAPM

The multi-country model approach has several drawbacks. A world Capital Asset Pricing Model is hard to defend on theoretical grounds in the presence of real exchange risk and market imperfections (see Chapter 1). Furthermore, all the criticisms of the practical use of the domestic CAPM are even more valid for the international version. Roll[17] showed that if the market portfolio was not identified exactly, the practical use of the CAPM was difficult. Yet internationally the mere definition of a world market portfolio is close to impossible. Ideally, it includes the whole range of instruments, stocks, bonds, short-term deposits in foreign currencies, gold, etc.; yet the market size of many instruments is not known precisely. Also, restrictions on investment, limited negotiability, differential taxes, and high transaction costs make the design of a complete world market equilibrium model a hopeless operational task.

Even if all equities were priced consistently with their international betas (a doubtful hypothesis), a portfolio manager who actively trades individual stocks still needs information on the reaction of each security price to all the important factors.

A single world factor model plainly fails to accurately describe international stock price behavior. The multi-country model presented previously is better, since the national market factor picks both the real and monetary influences on all stocks traded in the same market and currency. Also, we have seen that this domestic factor was the dominant influence in stock price behavior. Although a security is mostly influenced by the domestic factor, it seems unlikely that all domestic influences, whether real or monetary, can be summarized in a single domestic factor identical for every firm. As we already discussed, each security reacts somewhat differently to currency movements or is influenced by factors specific to its industry.

In short, the simple multi-country model is a good practical step toward describing the true complexity of international stock price behavior, but it needs refinement. The next step requires the introduction of arbitrage pricing theory (APT).

Arbitrage Pricing Theory

The great advantage of the APT is that it can be applied to a subset of investments, so that we do not need to consider every single world asset as we did in the asset pricing model. It starts with a descriptive model, where the return on a security is determined by a number of common factors plus a term specific to the security, and leads to a theory of what returns should be in an efficient market.

The descriptive model The multifactor model, where R is the rate of return on the security and a is a constant term, $\delta_1, \delta_2, \ldots,$ may be written mathematically as

$$R = a + \beta_1\delta_1 + \beta_2\delta_2 + \cdots + \beta_k\delta_k + \varepsilon \tag{5.2}$$

where $\delta_1 \cdots \delta_k$ are the k factors common to all securities, and ε (epsilon) is a random term specific to this security, and therefore independant of all δs (deltas) and other εs (random-factor epsilons). The ε is the source of idiosyncratic or diversifiable risk, and $\beta_1 \cdots \beta_k$ represent the sensitivity of this security to each factor. The betas vary among securities. Some stocks may be highly sensitive to certain factors and much less sensitive to others.

The theory Arbitrage ensures that only the βs should be priced, so that $E(R)$, the expected return on a security, is a linear function of these betas:

$$E(R) = R_0 + \beta_1 RP_1 + \beta_2 RP_2 + \cdots + \beta_k RP_k. \tag{5.3}$$

where RP_i is the risk premium associated to factor i and R_0 is the risk-free rate.

According to the CAPM, we need to identify all securities in the world in order to construct the world market portfolio and derive the theoretical pricing relation. This is not necessary for the APT because it focuses on the relative pricing of the securities under study, the common factors being exogenous.

The next question is what the factors that determine the return on a security are. The answer is that they must be estimated from the data; they are not specified by the theory. Generally, three sets of factors are selected by financial analysts:

- ☐ The first set of factors is international in nature and may be linked to a real variable such as economic growth, a monetary variable such as inflation or changes in interest rate, or energy costs such as the price of oil.

☐ The second set of factors is purely domestic, reflecting the deviation of a nation from the world economy path. It could range from a single domestic market factor that affects all national firms traded on the local market, to a more detailed set of domestic factors such as deviation from world real growth, inflation, or domestic real currency variation.

☐ A third set of factors is common to companies within the same industry regardless of the country they're in. These are known as industrywide factors.

Remember that the various factors are not necessarily orthogonal (statistically independent). Furthermore, the evidence indicates (see Exhibit 5.6) that domestic factors are the most important influence in explaining stock price behavior. International APT models are still being developed and refined, but are nevertheless attractive to investment managers because they provide more rigorous tools for determining economic, monetary, financial, and industrial factors. Rather than using market indexes or subindexes, this approach attempts to get at the major underlying influences on asset prices.

The model's practical use In order to illustrate the APT approach we will propose a very simple four-factor model.[18] In this model each company stock price is affected by only four factors, and three of them vary among companies according to their nationality and industrial sector. A description of the proposed factors is given below:

1. *World economic activity.* World economic activity affects all companies in the world but to different degrees. U.S. corporations would probably be more sensitive to this factor than other corporations simply because of the large size of the U.S. economy compared to the rest of the world. This factor would explain why all stock prices in the world tend to be positively correlated.

2. *Domestic real growth.* Domestic real growth relative to world real growth would be a country-specific factor.

3. *Currency movements.* A firm would have a positive or negative beta with respect to this country-specific factor depending on both its import–export structure and the currency denomination of its financing.

4. *Industrywide conditions.* This last factor would be industry-specific across national boundaries.

The next step is for financial analysts to provide estimates for the model's sensitivity coefficients, β_s. With the β_s in place, we can project expected returns on securities. Where markets are not efficient, we would expect to find securities with an expected return that is larger than the equilibrium value given by the theory. These are the securities we should add to our portfolio.

The structuring of the portfolio also depends on specific forecasts for each factor. For example, let's assume that a manager believes in the following scenarios: worldwide slowdown in real growth and inflation, and better relative economic performance of Japan. He or she will then invest in companies that are less sensitive to changes in real growth, most favorably influenced by the reduction in inflation, and directly affected by the better performance of the Japanese economy.

Although this chapter deals with equity, the risk and return analysis is equally valid for other investment media. The global approach to international investment strategies is discussed in Chapter 12.

SUMMARY

1. Faced with the complexities of international money management, an investor must analyze each particular investment in a systematic fashion. The end result should be reflected in a tractable number of parameters that can be used to structure the portfolio in a global approach. Basically an investor needs indications of the expected return on the asset as well as of the sensitivity of the asset price to the various sources of uncertainties, i.e., the major factors affecting an asset price behavior.

2. Financial analysis techniques are well known, but their application in comparing corporation values among countries poses numerous problems.

3. A majority of the largest industrial corporations and financial institutions are non-American. The analysis of any large company must be international to account for its worldwide market and competition. However, the available information on companies varies widely among countries. In many countries good quality information is scarce and published after long delays. Differences in accounting principles make international comparisons of companies in the same industrial sector very difficult when based on accounting data. Also, different stock markets value firms' attributes differently. For example, a leverage ratio may be regarded as too high by U.S. standards and reasonable by Japanese or German standards. A high price-earnings ratio in one country may be regarded as low in another country. While relative valuation within a specific national market is useful, international value comparison is a very difficult exercise.

4. An empirical study of the major factors affecting stock price behavior indicates the dominance of domestic factors over foreign factors. Currency factors are very weak, and international industrial factors are significant, although dominated by the national market influence. The importance of national factors suggests that international investment analysis should be primarily structured along a top-down geographic approach.

5. Portfolio selection decisions should be structured around a risk and return analysis. Managers should select both a risk level and securities with superior return for that risk level. A model of the world capital market is required to determine: (1) what the appropriate measures of risk are and (2) what the normal return for a given risk level is.

6. Two models of international asset pricing have been proposed in this chapter. The international arbitrage pricing theory (APT) provides a fruitful approach to equity analysis and investment.

QUESTIONS AND PROBLEMS

1. Explain why a corporation can have a stock market price well above its accounting book value.

2. The accounting and fiscal standards of many countries allow their corporations to build extraordinary reserves (or "hidden" reserves) in anticipation of foreseen or unpredictable expenses. How would this practice affect the book value of a corporation and its ratio of market price to book value?

3. In the past twenty years the best-performing stock markets have been found in countries with the highest economic growth rate. Should current growth rate guide you in picking stock markets if the world capital market is efficient?

4. Exhibits 5.6 and 5.7 indicate that the influence of the domestic market is dominant. Does this imply that foreign factors have no influence?

5. You are an American pension fund who cares about dollar return. Here are your forecasts for the coming year and the betas of stocks calculated relative to their domestic index.

Country	Expected Return (percent)	Beta
United States		
Current risk-free rate	8	
Stock market	10	1
Company A	13	1.2
Company B	9	0.9
Company C	11	1.5
France		
Current risk-free rate	10	
Stock market	11	1
Company D	12	0.8
Company E	12	2
Company F	11	1.1
Franc (against $)	− 5	
Japan		
Current risk-free rate	6	
Stock market	14	1
Company G	16	1.25
Company H	18	1.1
Company I	12	0.9
Yen (against $)	+5	

If you believe in the multi-country approach, how would you structure your portfolio? What risk considerations would you take into account?

NOTES

1. A study by the French Analysts Federation shows that corporations publish their annual reports with a lag after the end of the fiscal year that varies from country to country. The average lags follow: the United States, 6 weeks; the Netherlands, 10 weeks; Japan, 12 weeks; the United Kingdom, 14 weeks; West Germany, 16 weeks; and France, 24 weeks.

2. See, for example, F. D. Choi, H. Hino, S. Min, S. Nam, H. Ujiie, and A. Stonehill, "Analyzing Foreign Financial Statements: The Use and Misuse of International Ratio Analysis," *Journal of International Business Studies*, Summer 1983.

3. Other explanations for differences in debt ratios among countries are provided in J. Rutherford, "An International Perspective on the Capital Structure Puzzle," *Midland Corporate Finance Journal*, Fall 1985; and W. C. Kester, "Capital and Ownership Structure: A Comparison of U.S. and Japanese Manufacturing Corporations," *Financial Management*, Spring 1986.

4. See F. D. Choi and G. G. Mueller, *International Accounting*, Englewood Cliffs, NJ: Prentice Hall, 1984. Other comparative studies of accounting practices can be found in M. K. Oldham, *Accounting Systems and Practices in Europe*, UK: Gower Pub. Co., 1981; and C. Nobes and R. Parker (eds), *Comparative International Accounting*, R. D. Irwin, 1981. Also, international accounting and auditing firms provide up-to-date information on reporting practices in most countries.

5. See references in Chapter 1.

6. This is the average over all major industrial countries as defined by the Organization for Economic Coordination and Development.

7. See D. Lessard, "World, Country and Industry Relationships in Equity Returns," *Financial Analysts Journal*, January/February 1976; and B. Solnik, "L'Internationalisation des Places Financières," *COB-Université*, 1976.

8. See M. Adler and D. Simon, "Exchange Risk Surprises in International Portfolios," *Journal of Portfolio Management*, Winter 1986; and B. Solnik, "Stock Prices and Monetary Variables: The International Evidence," *Financial Analyst Journal*, March/April 1984.

9. See B. Solnik and A. de Freitas, "International Factors of Stock Price Behaviour," in S. Khoury and A. Ghosh (eds), *Recent Developments in International Finance and Banking*, Lexington, MA: Lexington Books, 1988. They used monthly observations on a sample of 279 firms from eighteen countries over the period December 1971 to December 1984. The country, industrial, and world indexes come from Morgan Stanley Capital International. The currency movement is that of the local currency relative to the U.S. dollar (U.S. dollar price of one unit of local currency). The deutsche mark replaced the U.S. dollar as the reference currency for tests on U.S. companies.

10. See R. Grinold, A. Rudd, and D. Stefek, "Global Factors: Fact or Fiction," *Journal of Portfolio Management*, Fall 1989.

11. The ratio of foreign to total sales, earnings, and assets of major corporations is periodically reported by *Business International*. While this information is publicly available for U.S. corporations, it is much harder to obtain for European and Asian corporations. Another interesting reference is J. Stopford and J. H. Dunning, *"World Directory of*

Multinational Enterprises: *Company Performance and Global Trends*," Woodbridge, IL: McMillan Pubns., 1983.

12. See A. Senschack and W. Beedles, "Is International Diversification Desirable?," *Journal of Portfolio Management*, Winter 1980. On this topic see also B. Jacquillat and B. Solnik, "Multinationals are Poor Tools for International Diversification," *Journal of Portfolio Management*, Winter 1978; and T. Agmon and D. Lessard, "Investor Recognition of Corporate International Diversification," *Journal of Finance*, September 1977.

13. A. Rugman reports that measures of foreign activities such as sales assets, net income, and number of employees are highly correlated (correlation of more than 0.8). Letter to the editor, *Financial Analysts Journal*, March/April 1976.

14. The famous beta, β, is equal to the covariance of the return on the asset with the return on the market portfolio divided by (or normalized by) the variance of the market portfolio return. This is also equal to the slope of a regression of the asset return on the market portfolio return.

15. See the discussion and references in Chapter 1, and in M. Adler and B. Dumas, "International Portfolio Choice and Corporation Finance: A Synthesis," *Journal of Finance*, June 1983.

This asset pricing theory applies equally to all securities, bonds, as well as common stocks. In this chapter we only consider the application to common stocks.

16. See B. Solnik, "The International Pricing of Risk: An Empirical Investigation of the Work Capital Structure," *Journal of Finance*, May 1974; and W. Sharpe, *Investments*, Englewood Cliffs, NJ: Prentice Hall, 3rd ed, 1987.

17. See R. Roll, "A Critique of the Asset Pricing Theory's Tests," *Journal of Financial Economics*, March 1987.

18. Chen, Roll, and Ross have identified four factors for the U.S. equity market as growth rate in industrial production, unexpected inflation, twists in the yield curve (the difference between long- and short-term interest rates), and changes in the attitude toward risk as proxied by changes in the pricing of default risk implicit in the difference between yields on Aaa and Baa rated corporate bonds. See N. Chen, R. Roll, and S. Ross, "Economic Forces and the Stock Market," *Journal of Business*, September 1986.

An interesting estimation of economic factors influencing Euro-currency interest rates can be found in A. Anckonie, "An Examination of the Linkage between Eurocurrency Deposit Rates and Fundamental Economic Variables Using the Arbitrage Pricing Theory," *Economic Aziendale*, December 1984. Again, the APT approach could be applied to any investment media and any subset of securities.

19. See W. Sharpe, *Investments*, Englewood Cliffs, NJ: Prentice Hall, 3rd ed, 1987.

BIBLIOGRAPHY

M. Adler and B. Dumas, "International Portfolio Choice and Corporation Finance: A Synthesis," *Journal of Finance*, June 1983.

M. Adler and D. Simon, "Exchange Risk Surprises in International Portfolios," *Journal of Portfolio Management*, Winter 1986.

T. Agmon and D. Lessard, "Investor Recognition of Corporate International Diversification," *Journal of Finance*, September 1977.

A. Anckonie, "An Examination of the Linkage Between Eurocurrency Deposit Rates and Fundamental Economic Variables Using the Arbitrage Pricing Theory," *Economic Aziendale*, December 1984.

N. Chen, R. Roll, and S. Ross, "Economic Forces and the Stock Market," *Journal of Business*, September 1986.

F. D. Choi, H. Hino, S. Min, S. Nam, H. Ujiie, and A. Stonehill, "Analyzing Foreign Financial Statements: The Use and Misuse of International Ratio Analysis," *Journal of International Business Studies*, Summer 1983.

F. D. Choi and G. G. Mueller, *International Accounting*, Englewood Cliffs, NJ: Prentice Hall, 1984.

R. Grinold, A. Rudd, and D. Stefek, "Global Factors: Fact or Fiction," *Journal of Portfolio Management*, Fall 1989.

M. Hagigi, "Industry Versus Country Risk in International Investments of U.S. Pension Funds," *Financial Analysts Journal*, September/October 1988.

B. Jacquillat and B. Solnik, "Multinationals Are Poor Tools for International Diversification," *Journal of Portfolio Management*, Winter 1978.

D. Lessard, "World, Country and Industry Relationships in Equity Returns," *Financial Analysts Journal*, January/February 1976.

C. Nobes and R. Parker, *Comparative International Accounting*, R. D. Irwin (ed), 1981.

M. K. Oldham, *Accounting Systems and Practices in Europe*, UK: Gower Pub. Co., 1981.

R. Roll, "A Critique of the Asset Pricing Theory's Tests," *Journal of Financial Economics*, March 1987.

A. Rugman, letter to the editor, *Financial Analysts Journal*, March/April 1976.

A. Senschack and W. Beedles, "Is International Diversification Desirable?," *Journal of Portfolio Management*, Winter 1980.

W. Sharpe, *Investments*, Englewood Cliffs, NJ: Prentice Hall, 3rd ed, 1987.

B. Solnik, "L'Internationalisation des Places Financières," *COB-Université*, 1976.

B. Solnik, "The International Pricing of Risk: An Empirical Investigation of the Work Capital Structure," *Journal of Finance*, May 1974.

B. Solnik, "Stock Prices and Monetary Variables: The International Evidence," *Financial Analyst Journal*, March/April 1984.

B. Solnik and A. de Freitas, "International Factors of Stock Price Behaviour."

J. Stopford and J. H. Dunning, *World Directory of Multinational Enterprises*: Company Performance and Global Trends, Woodbridge, IL: McMillan Pubns., 1983.

Chapter 5: Appendix
Investment Analysis and Asset Pricing
Theory: Practical Application

The financial analysis of common stocks focuses on analyzing stock price behavior and estimating expected return. Understanding stock price behavior implies determining the factor(s) that influence daily stock price movements. The traditional domestic approach, which relies on a single-factor model (or market model), proceeds in two steps:

- First, a descriptive model of stock price returns (price variations and income received) is postulated and then tested over real data (the market, or factor, model).

- Second, an equilibrium (efficient market) theory[19] is applied to determine the theoretical relative values of securities in an efficient market (the Capital Asset Pricing Model, or CAPM).

Numerous descriptive models are consistent with the CAPM, but the simplest single factor is most often used.

A Descriptive Model

A single-factor model may be written as follows:

$$R = \beta\delta + a + \varepsilon \tag{5.A1}$$

where

R is the rate of return on equity i over a given time interval (day, week, or month).

δ is the return (or percentage variation) of a factor common to all stocks. (In the usual market models, δ is the return on the market portfolio.)

$a + \varepsilon$ is the return on security i not explained by the common factor.

ε is a random component with zero mean that is independent of δ.

β is the beta, or sensitivity of a stock return to the common factor. It means that ceteris paribus, the stock price goes up by beta% when the factor return is 1%.

A *defensive stock* will have a small beta, and an *aggressive stock* will have a large beta. The traditional approach is to use the market return, R_m (on a market index), as the common factor. The coefficient beta associated with that market return is very important in structuring a portfolio because it determines how vulnerable the portfolio is to market movements.

An Equilibrium Theory

Under certain restrictive assumptions, the CAPM theory asserts that coefficient a should equal the risk-free rate R_0 for every security. In other words, the expected return on a security should equal the risk-free rate plus a risk premium, which is proportional to β:

$$E(R) = R_0 + \beta[E(R_m) - R_0] = R_0 + \beta \times RP \tag{5.A2}$$

where $E(R)$ refers to the expected rate of return on the security, R_0 corresponds to the risk free rate, and RP to the risk premium and only β and $E(R)$ vary across securities.

The efficient market approach described in Eq. (5.A2) provides a useful starting point, but many managers do not believe that the market is so efficient that they cannot spot securities with superior performance. Their aim, in fact, is to find securities with a risk-adjusted return higher than what is called for in theory.

They would therefore add an α factor to Eq. (5.A2) as shown in Eq. (5.A3) below

$$E(R) = \alpha + R_0 + \beta \times RP. \tag{5.A3}$$

In this equation, superior expected performance implies that there are securities with positive alphas. In fully developed capital markets, thousands of analysts compete to obtain the best-possible information so that they can identify securities with positive alphas. Purchasing these securities pushes their stock prices upward to the point where they are no longer attractive. By definition, a truly efficient market is so competitive that prices reflect all new relevant information almost instantaneously.

Investment Management in a Semiefficient Market

The general consensus is that national markets are quite efficient, but that superior analysts can temporarily identify securities with either positive or negative alphas. This means that stock markets are efficient enough to warrant using the CAPM as a reference model with which to measure deviations from true efficiency.

The basic goal of modern active portfolio management is to simultaneously diversify away all unnecessary risks and profit by virtue of superior forecasting ability. This approach is illustrated in Exhibit 5.9.

A passive investor can easily achieve the level of return described by Eq. (5.A2) simply by investing part of his or her portfolio in a market index fund and

EXHIBIT 5.9
Market Line

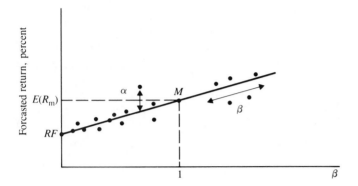

part in liquid risk-free assets (e.g., treasury bills). The investor picks the desired risk level by investing more or less in each of the two investments. This automatically moves one along the market line R_0M shown in Exhibit 5.9. For example, a β of 0.5 can be achieved by putting half of the money in treasury bills and the other half in the market index fund. Thus, the CAPM model is not just a theoretical pricing relation: It also describes the minimum risk-adjusted return that any investor can achieve with readily available investment vehicles.

An active investor, on the other hand, attempts to time the market, i.e., he or she moves up and down the market line according to expectations about the market relative to the risk-free rate. If the investor is bullish on a stock market $[E(R_m) \gg R_F]$, he or she will build a high-beta portfolio. If the investor is bearish, he or she will build a low-beta portfolio. In both cases, we assume the portfolio is well diversified and invested in securities with positive alphas. Active management is thus a combination of market timing (β) and astute security selection (α).

6

Bonds: Markets
and Instruments

Debt certificates have been traded internationally for several centuries. Kings and emperors borrowed heavily to finance their wars. Bankers from neutral countries assisted in arranging the necessary financing, and thereby created a market in the debentures. The Rothschilds, for example, became famous for supporting the British war effort against Napoléon I through their European family network. As a matter of fact, organized trading in domestic and foreign debentures took place well before the start of any domestic common stock market.

Although debt financing has always been international in nature, there is still no unified international bond market. Instead, the international bond market is divided into three broad market groups: *domestic bonds*, *foreign bonds*, and *Eurobonds*.

- Domestic bonds are issued locally by a domestic borrower and are usually denominated in the local currency.

- Foreign bonds are issued on a local market by a foreign borrower and are usually denominated in the local currency. Foreign bond issues and trading are under the supervision of local market authorities.

- Eurobonds are underwritten by a multinational syndicate of banks and placed mainly in countries other than the one in whose currency the bond is denominated. These bonds are not traded on a specific national bond market.

Foreign bonds issued on national markets have existed for a long time. They often have colorful names such as Yankee bonds (in the United States), samuraï bonds (in Japan), and bulldog bonds (in the United Kingdom).

Because many non-American firms have financing needs in U.S. dollars, there has for some years been an incentive to issue bonds in New York. But to do so the bonds must satisfy the disclosure requirements of the U.S. Securities and Exchange Commission. This can be a costly process for non-English-speaking corporations that use different accounting standards. In 1963 the United States imposed an Interest Equalization Tax (IET) on foreign securities[1] held by U.S. investors. The tax forced non-U.S. corporations to pay a higher interest rate in order to attract U.S. investors. A few years later the Federal Reserve Board restricted both U.S. lending to foreigners and the financing of foreign direct investment by U.S. corporations. These measures simultaneously made the U.S. bond market less attractive to foreign borrowers and created a need for offshore financing of U.S. corporate foreign activities. This led to the development of the Eurobond market in the early 1960s. The repeal of the IET in 1974, as well as various other measures taken to attract foreign issuers and borrowers to the U.S. domestic market, did not slow the growth of this new market.

In 1984 the United States rescinded the interest withholding tax on the earnings of foreign investors. Foreign investors could then directly purchase bonds on the U.S. market with the same fiscal treatment as on the Eurobond market. Some analysts expected that most of the U.S. dollar Eurobond market would move back to New York. This did not happen, and the Eurobond market continued to grow at a rapid pace; investors preferred the protection of anonymity offered by the Eurobond market and feared a change in U.S. regulations. More important, the Eurobond market came to be recognized by borrowers and investors alike as the most efficient, least costly, and most innovative market.

Bond investment is both technical and difficult. This stems from the vast diversity of markets, instruments, and currencies offered. Terminology and techniques vary from one market to the next, as do trading methods and costs. For example, U.S. yields are computed on an annual basis on the Eurobond market, but on a semiannual basis on the U.S. market. Accrued interest is not included in the bond market price, except in the United Kingdom. And the Japanese use a simple-interest method to calculate yield-to-maturity rather than the usual compound-interest method. Moreover, instruments vary in these markets from straight bonds and floating rate notes denominated in various currencies to bonds with numerous, and often exotic, option clauses.

This chapter first presents some statistics on the various markets. It then outlines the major differences among the markets and ends with a brief description of the Eurobond market.

SOME STATISTICS

Bond Markets in the World

The world bond market is growing rapidly. It is comprised of both the domestic bond markets and the international market, which includes foreign bonds and Eurobonds. The size of the world bond market was estimated around $10 trillion at the end of 1989. The figure is even larger if we include private placements, in

EXHIBIT 6.1

Size of Major Bond Markets at Year End, 1988

Nominal value outstanding, billions of U.S. dollars equivalent[a]

Bond market	Total publicly issued	As percent of public issues in all markets	Central government	Central government agency & government guarantee	State & local government	Corporation (including convertibles)	Other domestic publicly issued	International Bonds Foreign bonds	International Bonds Euro-bonds	Private placement and unclassified
U.S. dollar	$4,517.00	46.3%	$1,425.8	$1,116.9	$759.6	$715.8	$26.5	$59.9	$412.5	$496.2
Japanese yen	2,161.0	22.1	1,227.5	152.6	55.2	184.0	433.3	38.0	70.4	335.0
Deutsche mark	753.5	7.7	195.1	32.4	20.4	1.3	397.6	106.7		297.5[b]
Italian lira	534.3	5.5	414.9	22.2	—	5.1	87.4	1.9	2.8	—
UK sterling	344.4	3.5	247.6	—	0.2	23.0	—	6.5	67.1	—
French franc	332.4	3.4	101.8	152.5	3.0	63.1	—	3.2	8.8	—
Canadian dollar	245.3	2.5	94.6	—	79.3	37.0	0.9	0.8	32.7	—
Belgian franc	187.8	1.9	109.6	43.9	—	5.4	22.9	5.6	0.4	—
Danish krone	159.7	1.6	43.6	—	—	—	112.0	—	4.1	—
Swedish krona	157.0	1.6	65.0	—	2.2	9.7	79.9	—	0.2	—
Swiss franc	156.3	1.6	6.8	—	9.1	29.7	33.8	76.9	—	47.3
Dutch guilder	133.5	1.4	80.3	—	3.2	33.4	—	9.5	7.1	86.2[c]
Australian dollar	81.6	0.8	30.8	18.0	—	3.3	—	—	29.5	—
Total	$9,763.8[d]	100.0%	$4,043.4	$1,538.5	$932.2	$1,110.8	$1,194.3	$944.6[d]		$1,262.2[c]
Sector as Percent of Public Issues in All Markets		41.4%	15.8%	9.5%	11.4%	12.2%	9.7%		

Source: "How Big Is the World Bond Market? 1989 Update," *International Bond Market Analysis*, Salomon Brothers, Inc., June 1989. Reprinted with permission.
[a]Exchange rates prevailing as of December 31, 1988, are as follows: ¥125.85/US$, DM1.7803/US$, Lit1,305.8/US$, £0.5526/US$, Ffr6.059/US$, C$1.1927/US$, Bfr37.345/US$, Dkr6.874/US$, Skr6.157/US$, Sfr1.504/US$, Dfl1.9995/US$, A$1.1689/US$, and ECU0.861/US$.
[b]Includes straight, convertible and floating-rate debt.
[c]In addition, there exists an unspecifiable amount of privately placed issues of the private sector.
[d]In addition, $39.3 billion ECU-denominated Eurobonds were outstanding at year-end 1988.

which bonds are placed directly among the clients of the underwriting bank and are not offered publicly. The world market capitalization of bonds is therefore equivalent to that of equity. Bonds denominated in dollars currently represent roughly half the value of all outstanding bonds. Yen bonds represent roughly 20% of the world bond markets, and European currencies, 30%. A detailed analysis of the size of major bond markets is given in Exhibit 6.1. Note that the relative share of each currency market depends not only on new issues and repaid bonds, but also on exchange rate movements. For example, the U.S. dollar dropped by more than 40% against most currencies from 1985 to 1986, which substantially reduced the worldwide U.S. dollar bond market share.

As shown in Exhibit 6.1, government bonds represent a large share, approximately two-thirds, of all bonds issued in the world. The share is especially large for UK sterling, French franc, and Japanese yen bonds, and quite small for Swiss franc and deutsche mark bonds.

The market value of international bonds (Eurobonds and foreign bonds) represents approximately 10% of all outstanding bonds publicly issued, although the percentage is probably larger if private placements are included. The share of international bonds in terms of new issues (rather than total market size) is much larger for two reasons: This market has grown rapidly only recently, and Eurobonds tend to be issued with short maturities. As a result, despite the smaller market capitalization, the pace of new issues is very rapid in the Eurobond market.

We now turn to a more detailed analysis of the international market.

The International Bond Market (European and Foreign)

Exhibits 6.2, 6.3, and 6.4 give some background statistics on new issues in the international bond market. The growth of the international bond market in the 1980s, especially Eurobonds, has been remarkable.

Currency breakdown As of 1989 the U.S. dollar was the major currency of denomination in the market, followed by the Swiss franc and the yen. The deutsche mark was the fourth major currency. The importance of the Swiss franc as an investment currency is surprising given the small size of the country. Several factors explain this phenomenon. First, Switzerland has a history of stability and a strong currency. Second, Swiss banks have long specialized in international investment and are probably the largest investors in the international bond markets. Third, Switzerland is a large net exporter of capital. But note that their historical expertise in international financial intermediation has not prevented the Swiss Central Bank (Banque Nationale Suisse) from regulating the use of its currency on international capital markets. In fact, the Swiss Central Bank does not allow the Swiss franc to be used for Eurobond issues. Therefore, foreign borrowers must issue bonds on the foreign Swiss market. But fortunately, the regulations and administrative procedures for issuing foreign

EXHIBIT 6.2
New Issues on the International Bond Market
Summary data by type of market and type of instrument (billions of U.S. dollars)

Market	1981	1982	1983	1984	1985	1986	1987	1988
Eurobonds	31.3	50.3	50.1	83.7	136.7	187.0	140.5	177.2
Foreign Bonds	25.8	25.2	27.0	27.8	31.0	39.4	40.2	47.7
Total	52.8	75.5	77.1	111.5	167.7	226.4	180.7	224.9
Instruments								
Fixed Rate	n.a.	57.6	57.6	65.4	92.5	147.2	117.0	159.2
Floating Rate and CDs	n.a.	15.3	13.8	38.2	58.4	50.7	13.0	23.1
Convertible	n.a.	2.6	5.7	7.8	11.4	22.3	43.3	42.0
Other	–	–	–	–	5.4	6.2	7.4	0.6

Source: Data adapted from *Financial Market Trends*, Organization for Economic Cooperation and Development, various issues, Quarterly Report of Bank of England.

n.a. = not available.

Swiss bonds are simple and straightforward, making access easy for foreign borrowers.

Until 1984 Japan prevented the use of the yen for Eurobond issues except by foreign governments and supranationals such as the World Bank. As in Switzerland, the foreign yen (samuraï) bond market is relatively active. In 1984 the Japanese government relaxed its regulation of international financial activities and the yen Eurobond market began opening up, under the supervision of Japanese authorities, to private borrowers. Since then, the share of the Japanese yen in the international bond market has begun to increase.

It is perhaps surprising that a central bank can prevent its currency from being used in the Eurobond market, which is by definition an offshore market. This control is imposed through national financial institutions, which are the major sources of funds in a nation's domestic currency. In Japan, domestic financial institutions must participate in a yen Eurobond syndicate for the issue to succeed because they are the largest yen investors. The situation is similar elsewhere. If the government forbids the banks to participate, the issue must fail.

European currency unit The European currency unit (ECU) has recently become an important currency of denomination. The ECU is a composite currency comprised of a weighted basket of European currencies. The ECU exchange rate is an average exchange rate of all currencies in the basket. The ECU has attracted many borrowers from weak-currency countries (e.g., Italy, Belgium,

EXHIBIT 6.3
International Issues of Bonds
Breakdown by currency of issue (billions of U.S. dollars)

Issue	1982	1983	1984	1985	1986	1987	1988
Eurobond Issues by Currency							
U.S. Dollar	42.23	39.21	65.33	96.48	117.22	58.07	75.36
Deutsche Mark	3.25	4.04	4.32	9.49	16.87	15.02	23.67
European Currency Unit	0.82	2.19	2.94	7.04	6.96	7.40	11.33
Yen	0.50	0.23	1.19	6.54	18.67	22.56	15.84
Sterling	0.84	2.15	3.96	5.77	10.51	15.05	21.65
Australian Dollar	—	0.21	0.31	2.97	3.18	8.82	8.14
Canadian Dollar	1.20	1.07	2.20	2.82	5.36	6.00	12.86
French Franc	—	—	—	1.06	3.40	1.81	2.40
New Zealand Dollar	0.02	0.03	0.04	1.02	0.44	1.50	0.78
Other	1.47	0.97	1.43	2.24	4.34	4.28	5.13
Total	50.33	50.10	81.72	135.43	186.95	140.51	177.16
Foreign Issues by Market							
Switzerland	11.32	13.50	13.12	14.95	23.40	24.3	26.6
Japan	3.32	3.85	4.87	6.38	4.75	4.07	6.36
United States	6.02	4.73	4.29	4.65	6.06	7.41	9.74
West Germany	2.11	2.62	2.42	1.74	—	—	—
Netherlands	0.85	0.93	0.86	0.99	1.82	1.00	0.96
United Kingdom	1.13	0.86	1.65	0.96	0.32	—	0.16
Other	0.45	0.56	0.59	1.35	2.09	3.46	3.85
Total	25.20	27.05	27.80	31.02	38.44	40.25	47.67

Source: Financial Market Trends, Organization for Economic Coordination and Development, various issues.

and France), which cannot issue international bonds in their home currencies. For these borrowers the ECU reduces exchange risk relative to their home currency. At the same time, investors wanting to invest in nondollar bonds may directly diversify their portfolios of European currencies by investing in ECU-denominated bonds.

Types of instruments Most issues on the international bond market are fixed interest bonds. However, floating rate notes (FRNs) have become a sizable segment of the market, especially when interest rates are volatile. FRNs are usually issued in U.S. dollars. Japanese corporations rely heavily on convertible bonds, as do other borrowers. The many other types of instruments that have been issued on the international bond market are described in more detail below and in Chapter 7.

EXHIBIT 6.4
International Bond Issues
Breakdown by country of borrower (billions of U.S. dollars)

	1981	1982	1983	1984	1985	1986	1987	1988
Industrial Countries	40.9	63.1	60.3	91.9	141.1	200.3	156.5	199.0
United States	6.8	14.5	7.3	23.9	40.5	43.6	21.5	17.3
Japan	6.9	8.4	14.0	17.0	21.1	34.4	44.4	51.2
Developing Areas	4.9	5.0	2.5	3.6	7.9	4.2	3.1	4.2
Latin America	3.7	2.5	0.0	0.2	0.2	0.4	0.0	0.8
Asia	1.1	2.1	2.2	3.0	6.9	3.7	3.1	2.9
Middle East	0.2	0.4	0.2	0.4	0.4	0.1	0.0	0.5
Centrally Planned Countries	0.0	0.0	0.1	0.2	2.0	0.3	0.5	1.3
International Organizations	7.2	9.9	13.4	11.7	17.7	19.5	20.4	21.7
Total	53.0	78.0	76.3	107.4	167.7	224.3	180.8	224.8

Source: Data adapted from *World Financial Markets*, Morgan Guaranty, various issues, and *Financial Statistics*, OECD, various issues.

Borrowers The major borrowers on the international bond markets are industrial countries and supranational organizations (see Exhibit 6.4). U.S. and Japanese corporations are by far the heaviest borrowers. The governments of Canada and Scandinavia, and Scandinavian corporations are also heavy borrowers. High-risk borrowers have no access to this market, so that Latin American countries virtually dropped out after 1982. But note that supranationals such as the World Bank, European Investment Bank, Asian and African Development Banks, International Development Bank, and the European Economic Community are heavy borrowers in the international bond market, and part of their funds are, in turn, loaned to higher-risk countries. Starting in 1990, the deterioration of the economic and political situation in Eastern Europe has lead to drastic political changes in most countries of the region. The move to more liberal economic policies is accompanied by large financing needs. An international bank has been set up in 1990 by developed countries to assist the financing needs of Eastern European economies. This international organization, known as the BERD, is based in London and gives preferential treatment to private projects over public ones. It is likely to become a significant borrower on the international bond market.

Summary The world bond market is becoming more integrated across currencies. The Eurobond market in particular is opening up to a variety of currencies, including the French franc, Hong Kong dollar, and Australian dollar. Many governments are encouraging foreign borrowers to tap their national markets. For example, some governments have removed withholding taxes on domestic issues for foreign investors. Large market-makers perform an essential function in the world bond market because they deal simultaneously in both the European and national bond markets. Therefore, an investor wanting to buy domestic bonds, foreign bonds, or Eurobonds can do so through one financial institution and thereby receive equal tax treatment. In the future, current differences in costs and trading procedures and other impediments are bound to disappear as the internationalization of the world bond market continues.

MAJOR DIFFERENCES AMONG BOND MARKETS

A thorough technical knowledge of the various bond markets reduces an investor's trading costs and enhances his or her returns; it also helps one to understand better the risks involved. Because bond markets are still rapidly developing, new types of instruments and issuing techniques appear over the world all the time. For this reason, the following description of these markets is bound to become partially outdated over time; it is meant to serve chiefly as a broad guideline.

Types of Instruments

The variety of bonds offered to the international or even the domestic investor is amazing, due to the recent development of bonds with variable interest rates and complex optional clauses. This diversity is illustrated in the French bond market, where state or government agencies have issued the following types of bonds:

- Index-linked bonds, whose coupons or principal is indexed onto the price of gold, energy costs, the stock market index, or another index.
- Straight bonds with simultaneous call and put options. These bonds can be redeemed early at a set price by either the bondholder or the issuer.
- Straight bonds renewable at maturity into new straight bonds with the same coupon and terms.
- Straight bonds exchangeable for FRNs at the option of the bondholder or the issuer.
- FRNs exchangeable for straight bonds at the option of the bondholder or the issuer.
- Zero-coupon bonds.
- FRNs with a coupon linked to the average market long-term interest rate.
- FRNs with a coupon indexed to a variety of short-term interest rates. The coupon may be either post- or predetermined. If it is postdetermined, the investor knows the value of the coupon only on the payment date (in reference to the average interest rate over the coupon period). If it is

predetermined, the investor knows the value of the coupon for the coming coupon period (in reference to the interest rate during the previous coupon period). This reference interest rate may be an average over a period or a spot rate measured at a particular point in time.

□ Straight bonds with warrants to purchase similar bonds.

□ Straight bonds with warrants to purchase common stock or other types of assets.

□ Convertible bonds.

Whereas the U.S. and French bond markets are among the more innovative markets, the Eurobond market is surely the most creative of all. Investment bankers from many countries bring their expertise to this unregulated market. Each month new instruments appear or disappear regularly. Some of the more complex bonds are analyzed in Chapter 7.

The Eurobond market's major difference from domestic markets lies in its multi-currency nature. Japanese firms, for example, have frequently issued Swiss franc–denominated bonds convertible into common shares of a Japanese company. A foreign investor can benefit from purchasing this bond in any one of three situations:

□ a drop in the market interest rate on Swiss franc bonds (as on any straight Swiss franc bond);

□ a rise in the price of the company's stock (because the bonds are convertible into stocks), or

□ a rise in the yen relative to the franc (because the bond is convertible into a Japanese yen asset).

An example of such a Eurobond issue is presented in Exhibit 6.5. The tombstone in Exhibit 6.5 advertises a bond issued in 1986 by NKK, a Japanese company. Several points are worth noting: First, the underwriting syndicate is made up of banks from numerous countries (Japan, France, the United States, West Germany, the Netherlands, and Switzerland). The list of banks and countries is often much longer; it is not uncommon to see fifty or a hundred banks from all over the world participating in a large issue. Also note that U.S. commercial banks (Morgan Guaranty) participate, as well as U.S. investment banks (Morgan Stanley, Prudential-Bache). Note, however, that the British subsidiaries of the U.S. banks are involved and not U.S. head companies. This is easily recognized by the word *limited* at the end of the banks' names. Similarly, the Japanese and Swiss underwriters used a British-based company, with the exception of Yamaichi, which used a Benelux base. Another interesting feature of this bond is that it is a dual-currency bond: It is issued in yen (20 billion) with interest coupons fixed in yen (8%), but its principal repayment is fixed in U.S. dollars ($110,480,000). When this bond was issued numerous other borrowers issued yen/dollar dual-currency bonds, including the Federal National Mortgage Association (Fannie Mae).

EXHIBIT 6.5
Eurobond Tombstone

These securities have been sold outside the United States of America and Japan. This announcement
appears as a matter of record only.

<u>NEW ISSUE</u>   22nd January, 1986

Nippon Kokan Kabushiki Kaisha

8 per cent. Dual Currency
Yen/U.S. Dollar Bonds Due 1996

Issue Price: 101 per cent. of the Issue Amount

Issue Amount:	¥ 20,000,000,000
Redemption Amount at Maturity:	U.S. $110,480,000

Nomura International Limited	**Mitsubishi Trust & Banking Corporation** (Europe) S.A.
Prudential-Bache Securities International	**Yamaichi International (Europe) Limited**
Bankers Trust International Limited	**Crédit Lyonnais**
Credit Suisse First Boston Limited	**Dresdner Bank Aktiengesellschaft**
EBC Amro Bank Limited	**Fuji International Finance Limited**
Generale Bank	**Kleinwort, Benson Limited**
Lloyds Merchant Bank Limited	**Morgan Guaranty Ltd**
Morgan Stanley International	**Orion Royal Bank Limited**
Swiss Bank Corporation International Limited	**Union Bank of Switzerland (Securities)** Limited

S. G. Warburg & Co. Ltd.

Source: Euromoney, Euromoney Publications, July 1986. Reprinted with permission.

Issuing Techniques

Domestic bonds are usually underwritten by a syndicate of national banks. However, Dutch, British, Canadian, and Swiss government bonds are sold under a tender system, where banks place bids. In Great Britain, once an issue has been listed, the Bank of England often sells part of a gilts issue directly on the market through its broker. It also issues new branches of an old gilt with identical characteristics and sells those on the market. This technique, known as tapping the market, avoids a proliferation of different bonds.

Eurobonds are issued through an international syndicate of financial institutions. However, institutional investors may buy new bonds directly a few days before they are officially issued. This is the so-called gray market, which is described later in this chapter.

Dealing and Quotations

On European bond markets, orders are generally sent to the exchange floors through brokers. In the United States, trading usually takes place over the counter, although some bonds, especially foreign dollar bonds, are listed on the New York Stock Exchange. Trading of American bonds is transacted between *market-makers*, which are specialized financial institutions. Over-the-counter trading also takes place in some European markets (Switzerland, United Kingdom, West Germany, the Netherlands) for nongovernment issues. In Japan, bonds are both traded over the counter and on the securities exchanges.

In brokers' markets, bond buyers and sellers pay the same price, but must pay a commission to the broker. In the American system prices are net of commissions, but there is a bid-ask spread on all quotations.

Although the Eurobond market has no physical location, most of the bonds are listed on the Luxembourg stock exchange to satisfy the requirement of obtaining a public quotation at least once a year or quarter. However, very few transactions go through the exchange. Instead, Eurobond dealers created an around the clock market among financial institutions across the world that formed the Association of International Bond Dealers (AIBD). The geographical composition of the AIBD is shown in Exhibit 6.6. The prominent role of London in the AIBD is unmistakable. Swiss banks are the largest investors in the market, but because of a local stamp tax on all Swiss transactions, they often consummate their deals offshore. Settlement procedures vary from one country to the next.

Bonds are usually quoted on a price-plus-accrued-interest basis. This means the price is quoted separately (as a percentage of the bond's nominal value) from the percentage coupon accrued from the last coupon date to the trade date. The buyer pays (or the seller receives) both the market price of the bond and accrued interest. This means that the market price quoted is clean of coupon effect and allows meaningful comparisons between various bonds. Unfor-

EXHIBIT 6.6
Geographical Breakdown of AIBD Members

Locality	Number of members
United States	48
Belgium	33
Far East	33
France/Spain	52
West Germany/Austria	57
Italy	26
Luxembourg	63
Middle East	33
Netherlands	47
Scandinavia	55
Switzerland	141
United Kingdom	219

Source: Association of International Bond Dealers, 1988.

tunately, this method of quotation is not universal. Convertible bonds, index-linked bonds, or FRNs where the coupon is determined expost (at the end of the coupon period) are quoted with coupons attached. Even some straight bonds follow this convention, as in the UK gilt market, the market for UK government bonds.[2] There, bonds with more than five years to maturity are traded without any separate allowance for accrued interest (i.e., with the coupon attached). This means that the price quoted falls on the *ex-dividend* date, or *ex date*, the date when the bond trades without the next coupon payment. To make matters worse, the ex date is normally thirty-seven calendar days before each coupon date, plus or minus a couple of days to allow for weekends and vacations. An investor who buys the bond during this thirty-seven-day period does not receive the coupon. Instead, it goes to the previous bondholder. Furthermore, investors are allowed to trade *cum*, or ex-dividend, for a period of twenty-one days preceding the ex date. This is known as *special ex-dividend*. Exhibit 6.7 reproduces the unusual hypothetical market price behavior over time for a long-term UK gilt, assuming that the market interest rate stays constant. Tax effects should also be taken into account. Note also that when a UK gilt maturity is less than five years it is quoted on a price-plus-accrued-interest basis.

Bonds also differ in the way accrued interest is calculated. In the United States, straight bonds usually pay a semiannual coupon. The day-count method used in accrued-interest calculations is based on 30-day months in a 360-day year. In other words, the basic unit of time measurement is a month; it does not matter if the month is actually 28 or 31 days long. An investor holding a bond for one month receives $30/360$ or $\frac{1}{12}$ of the annual coupons ($\frac{1}{6}$ of the semiannual coupon). The same method is used in West Germany, Switzerland, and the

EXHIBIT 6.7
Market Price Behavior of a UK Gilt

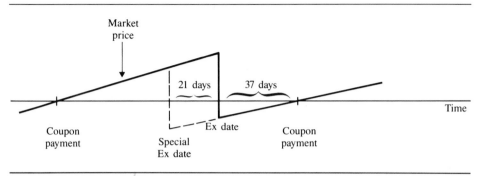

Netherlands. By contrast, the United Kingdom, Canada, and Japan use a day-count based on the actual number of days in a 365-day year, so that an investor receives accrued interest proportional to the number of days the bond has been held. Straight Eurobonds use the American convention regardless of their currency of denomination, so that a yen or sterling Eurobond uses a 30-day month in a 360-day year. On the other hand, Euro-FRNs use actual days in a 360-day year, which is also the convention used for short-term deposits. This follows naturally from the fact that FRN coupons are indexed to short-term interest rates. Straight Eurobonds pay annual coupons, while FRNs pay quarterly or semiannual coupons. The coupon characteristics of the major bond markets are summarized in Exhibit 6.8.

The issue of yields also needs to be addressed. Most financial institutions around the world calculate and publish yields-to-maturity on bonds (see definition in Chapter 7). Unfortunately the methods used for this calculation vary among countries, so that yields are not directly comparable. Most Europeans, for instance, calculate an annual, and accurate, actuarial yield-to-maturity using the AIBD-recommended formula. American (and often British) institutions publish a semiannual actuarial yield. For example, a U.S. bond issued at par with 12% coupons will pay $6 semiannually per $100 of face value, and is reported as having a semiannual yield-to-maturity of 12%.

Europeans would quote this bond as having a 12.36% (annual) yield-to-maturity because of the compounding of the two semester coupons. Common sense dictates that yields for all maturities and currencies be compared in an identical fashion. The tradition of using semiannual yields is understandably confusing for international investors.[3] The situation is even worse in Japan, where financial institutions tend to report yield-to-maturity based on simple-interest calculation. The sample formula given below shows how this is done.

$$\text{Yield} = \left(\text{Coupon rate} + \frac{100 - \text{Current price}}{\text{Years to maturity}}\right)\frac{100}{\text{Current price}}$$

EXHIBIT 6.8
Coupon Characteristics of Major Bond Markets (straight bonds)

Characteristic	United States	Canada	Japan
Usual Frequency of Coupon	semiannual	semiannual	semiannual
Day Count (month/year)	30/360	actual/365	actual/365

Characteristic	Australia	United Kingdom	Switzerland
Usual Frequency of Coupon	semiannual	semiannual	semiannual
Day Count (month/year)	actual/365	actual/365	30/360

Characteristic	West Germany	Netherlands	France
Usual Frequency of Coupon	annual	annual	annual
Day Count (month/year)	30/360	30/360	actual/365

Characteristic	Eurobonds	FRNs
Usual Frequency of Coupon	annual	quarter or semiannual
Day Count (month/year)	30/360	actual/360

This simple yield understates the true yield-to-maturity for bonds priced over par and overstates the yield for bonds priced below par. Again, the historical rationale for this incorrect formula is the ease of calculation.

Legal Aspects

Bonds are issued in either *bearer* or *registered* forms. On the Eurobond market, as well as in many European countries, the bearer of a bond is assumed to be its legal owner. In the United States and many other countries, owners must be registered in the books of the issuer. Share registration allows for easier transfer of interest payments and amortization. Coupons are usually paid annually on markets where bonds are issued in bearer form. This reduces the cost associated with coupon payments. Eurobond coupons in all currencies are paid this way.

Bearer bonds provide confidentiality of ownership, which is very important to some investors.

In many countries, investor purchase of foreign bonds is restricted. The motivation for these restrictions stems from exchange controls or attempts by governments to ensure domestic investor protection. In 1981 France imposed a special exchange rate (*devise titre*) for security transactions. This forced French investors to pay a currency premium to purchase and sell bonds, while their coupons could be cashed in at the normal exchange rate. This regulation was promulgated to curb capital outflows and defend the French franc. Similar exchange control measures have been imposed at times in other developed countries as well, including the United Kingdom (*dollar premium*), Belgium (*franc financier*), and the United States (Interest Equalization Tax).

The U.S. securities act is typical of government regulations designed to ensure that its domestic investors are protected. The act requires that all public issues of securities be registered with the Securities and Exchange Commission (SEC). Any bond not registered with the SEC cannot be sold to U.S. citizens at the time of issue. SEC registration is imposed to ensure that accurate information on bond issues is publicly available. Bonds issued in foreign markets and Eurobonds do not meet this requirement, but Yankee bonds do, because they undergo a simplified SEC registration. All other bonds cannot be purchased by U.S. citizens at the time of issue; they may only be purchased after they are seasoned (i.e., come to rest). Sometimes it is difficult to know when an issue is seasoned; usually three months, but sometimes a longer period such as nine months, is necessary. U.S. banks can participate in Eurobond issuing syndicates only if they institute a procedure guaranteeing that U.S. investors cannot purchase the bonds. This can be difficult because Eurobonds are issued in bearer form.

Fiscal Considerations

Fiscal considerations are important in international investment. Many countries impose withholding taxes on interest paid by their national borrowers. This means that a foreign investor is often taxed twice: once in the borrowing country (withholding tax) and again in the investor's home country through the usual income tax. Tax treaties help by allowing one to reclaim all or part of a withholding tax, but this is a lengthy and costly process. Avoiding double taxation, in fact, was a major impetus behind the development of the Eurobond market. And that is why today the official borrower on the Eurobond market is usually a subsidiary incorporated in a country with no withholding tax (e.g., the Netherlands Antilles). Of course, the parent must fully guarantee the interest and principal payments on the bond. Nevertheless, the trend seems to be toward the elimination of withholding taxes for foreign investors. In 1984 the United States and West Germany eliminated withholding taxes on foreign investment in their domestic markets. France also eliminated these taxes, but only on bonds

EXHIBIT 6.9
Summary of Withholding Tax Rates on Interest Payments in Selected Countries, 1988

Country	Minimum tax rate (percent)	Tax rate under U.S.–country tax treaty (percent)	Maximum tax rate (percent)
Australia	0	10	10
Canada	0	15	25
France	0	0–10	0–45
West Germany	0	0	0–25
Japan	10	10	20
Netherlands	0	0	0
Sweden	0	0	0
Switzerland	5	5	35
United Kingdom	0	0	0–30

issued after 1984. The United States allowed domestic corporations to borrow directly from foreigners on international markets without paying a 30% withholding tax. This removed the need to borrow through a subsidiary incorporate in the Netherlands Antilles or another tax free base. Similar regulations already existed in other countries. For example, France grants an exemption from French withholding tax to French companies borrowing abroad (provided the bonds are not offered to French residents).

Exhibit 6.9 displays national withholding taxes as of 1988. Depending on the nationality of the investor, part or all of this tax may be reclaimed. The exhibit is arranged from the point of view of a taxable U.S. investor, but similar rates apply to residents of other countries. Again, there is no withholding tax on Eurobonds. International tax treaties allow for the reduction of the withholding tax rate or a total or partial tax refund. Note that tax liability is sometimes more complex than is reflected in the exhibit. For example, all of the UK gilts except one (the war loan, which is taxed at 3.5%) are subject to a withholding tax that is frequently revised (the tax rate was in the 30 to 35% range in the mid-1980s). Foreign investors can claim a full refund for any of the taxes paid under most double taxation treaties. But more advantageous is the fact that foreigners can claim exemption on about half of the outstanding issues known as the FOT, or free-of-tax stocks. This exemption is obtained by applying to the UK government at least six weeks before the coupon payment.

International tax treaties allow foreign tax withheld to be credited against domestic income tax payment. The same treaties apply to stock dividend withholding tax, as was discussed in Chapter 4. Tax-exempt investors face the risk of loosing the tax withheld because they have no domestic tax to pay and therefore the foreign tax credit is lost. In many countries, tax-exempt investors such as pension funds can obtain a total exemption from withholding taxes or a direct tax refund in the foreign country; the final minimum tax rate is given in the first column of Exhibit 6.9. A notable exception is Japan where a minimum tax of 10% applies to all foreign investors. Foreign investors in Japan often resort to coupon hopping: They sell the Japanese bond just before the payment date and buy it back immediately thereafter. They incur no tax liability because the tax is only levied on the person receiving the coupon payment. Furthermore, there is a strong demand for coupons by Japanese institutions, so that a counterparty can easily be found and transaction costs are minimal.

The repeal of withholding taxes promotes a greater integration of Euro-pean and domestic markets, but not at the expense of the Euromarket. In 1984 and 1985 the Euromarket continued to grow despite the removal of these taxes on major national markets.

Bonds Indexes

Bonds indexes are less commonly available than stock indexes. This is probably because of the close correlation between all bond price movements when the interest rate fluctuates on a single currency market. However, total-return bond indexes serve many purposes and are increasingly used. A total-return index cumulates the price movement with accrued interest; it is a cumulative index of the total return on a bond portfolio.

These indexes are put to different uses: A bond index calculated daily for each bond market allows the quick assessment of the direction and magnitude of movements in the market. The assessment is much easier and more precise using an index than looking at the price quotations of a list of bonds when many of the bonds are not even traded on that day. An index allows for quick comparisons between various markets in different segments or currencies. Total-return bond indexes also are required to measure the performance of a bond portfolio in a domestic or multi-currency setting. This is usually done monthly or quarterly.

There are two approaches to the calculation of bond indexes. The first is to use a small but representative sample of actively traded bonds. Such an index provides good indications of short-term movements in the interest rate. The second is to build an exhaustive index covering all bonds in the market. Since many issues are not liquid and their prices may be old or out of line with the market, exhaustive market indexes tend to lag the interest rate movements, but they reflect the current valuation of a market portfolio. The first approach tends to be used to calculate daily indexes, and the latter, monthly indexes. Given the high correlation between all bond prices on a given market bond indexes tend be highly correlated, which is not the case for equity indexes. This is illustrated in Exhibit 6.10, which compares the monthly total return (income plus price appreciation) on a deutsche mark Eurobond index: The first index is calculated monthly by Salomon Brothers in New York, and the second one is calculated

EXHIBIT 6.10
Total Return Bond Indexes Variation, January 1984 to June 1986
Deutsche mark Eurobond index

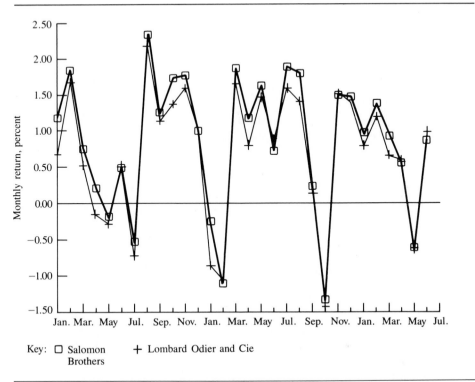

Key: □ Salomon   + Lombard Odier and Cie
         Brothers

Source: Lombard Odier and Cie, July 1986. Reprinted with permission.

daily by Lombard Odier and Cie in Geneva. Despite marked differences in index composition, the performance of the indexes is very close. This is not the case for equity indexes, as illustrated in Exhibit 4.7.

As for equity indexes, there are two major sources of bond indexes: domestic and international. In many countries, domestic institutions calculate local bond indexes weekly, monthly, and sometimes daily. Examples of such institutions are the following:

United States	Shearson/Lehman, Salomon Brothers, Merril Lynch
United Kingdom	Financial Times
France	Crédit Lyonnais, CDC-FININFO
Switzerland	Pictet, Vontobel, Lombard Odier

International investors find the indexes calculated by these institutions difficult to use because they must be obtained from numerous sources that are often difficult to access. Also, their construction and frequency of calculation make it difficult to compare them.

Several institutions have developed consistent bond indexes for the major domestic and Eurobond markets:

- Salomon Brothers has published monthly indexes for a long time on all major bond markets. They are now calculated daily. Their indexes are extensively used for performance measurement. Total return indexes take into account both the price movement and the income earned. They are published monthly in *Euromoney*.

- Lombard Odier and Cie has published daily total-return as well as price-only indexes since 1982. They are published daily in the *Wall Street Journal* (*Europe*).

- *The Financial Times* publishes daily quotes on "benchmark" bonds representative of each market.

- Several banks have developed international bond indexes reported in their monthly publications (Merrill Lynch, First Boston Credit Suisse, Chase, etc.).

- Intersec, an American international investment consulting firm, publishes monthly indexes in *Institutional Investor*.

- The AIBD publishes total-return and price-only indexes for the Eurobond market.

- Other institutions are publishing weekly indexes (price-only) on various segments of the Eurobond market (Kredietlux in Luxembourg, Vontobel in Zürich). Other institutions are likely to produce international bond indexes in the future, given the size of the world bond market and the lack of a single established standard.

All these institutions and many others report average yields for various market segments.

THE EUROBOND MARKET

Of all the bond markets in the world, the Eurobond market is certainly the most attractive to the international investor. It avoids most national regulations and constraints. Because of its important role in international investment, we will examine in some detail how Eurobonds are issued and traded.

The Issuing Syndicate

Eurobonds are sold in a multi-stage process. The issue is organized by an international bank called the *lead manager*. This bank invites several *co-managers* to form the *management group* (from five to thirty banks usually). For large issues there may be several lead managers. The managers prepare the issue, set the final conditions of the bond, and select the *underwriters* and *selling group*. One of the managers is appointed as the principal paying agent and fiscal agent. A large portion of the issue is directly subscribed by the management group.

The underwriters are invited to participate in the issue on the basis of their regional placement power. Their number varies from 30 to 300 and comprises international banks from all regions of the world. Together with the management group, they guarantee final placement of the bonds at a set price to the borrower.

The selling group is responsible for selling the bonds to the public. It consists of managers, underwriters, and additional banks with a good selling base. Note that a participant may be, at the same time, manager, underwriter, and seller. Separate fees are paid to compensate for the various services. The total fee ranges from 1.25 to 2.5%. Unlike their U.S. counterparts, Eurobond underwriters are not obligated to maintain the bond's market price at or above the issue price until the syndicate is disbanded. This means that bonds are often placed at a price below the issue price. There is considerable price discrimination among clients, and selling members may pass along part of their fee to the final buyer of the bond.

The Timetable of a New Issue

Unlike national markets, the Eurobond market has neither registration formalities nor *waiting queues*. A new issue may be placed within three weeks. A typical timetable is depicted in Exhibit 6.11.

First the lead manager gets together with the borrower to discuss the terms of the bond (amount, maturity, fixed or floating rate, and coupon). The terms generally remain provisional until the official offering date. During this period the lead manager arranges the management syndicate and prepares various documents, one of which is a preliminary prospectus called, at this stage, a *red herring*. On the *announcement day* the managers send telexes describing the proposed bond issue and inviting banks to join the underwriting and selling groups. Potential underwriters are sent the preliminary prospectus. A week or two later the final terms of the bond are set, and the syndicate commits itself to the borrower. A final prospectus is printed, and the bonds are publicly offered on the *offering day*. At the end of a public placement period of about two weeks, the subscription is closed on the *closing day*, and the bonds are delivered in exchange for cash paid to the borrower. A *tombstone* is later published in international newspapers to advertise the successful issue and list the participating banks.

After the closing day, the bonds can be publicly traded. However, bond trading actually takes place well before the closing day. A gray market for the bonds starts before the final terms have been set on the offering day; trading is contingent on the final issue price. That is, bonds are traded in the gray market at a premium or discount relative to the future price. For example, a quote of

EXHIBIT 6.11
Timetable of a New Issue

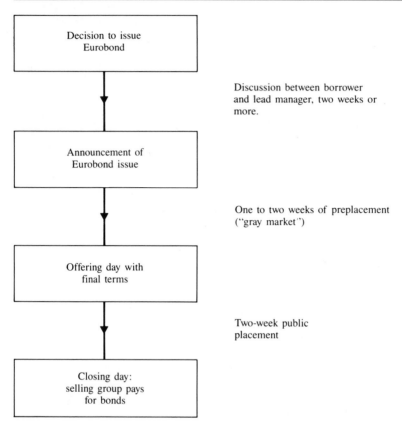

Total elapsed time; five to six weeks

less $\frac{1}{4}$ means that the bonds are exchanged at a price of $99\frac{1}{4}\%$ if the future issue price is set at $99\frac{1}{2}\%$. This is a form of forward market for bonds that are not yet in existence. The gray market is often used by members of the selling group to resell part of their bond allocation at a discount below the issue price but possibly at a net profit if their fee is large enough.

Dealing in Eurobonds

The Eurobond secondary market is truly international and comprises an informal network of market-makers and dealers. A market-maker quotes a net price to a financial institution in the form of a bid and ask price. No commissions are charged.

All market-makers and dealers in Eurobonds are part of the AIBD based in Zurich. The AIBD bears some similarities to the U.S. National Association of Securities Dealers (NASD). But whereas NASD is under the supervision of the Securities and Exchange Commission, the AIBD is purely self-regulated and enjoys no government intervention.

Eurobond Clearing System

Let's assume that a Scottish investment manager wants to buy $100,000 worth of a specific Eurobond. The investment manager calls several market-makers to get their best quotations and concludes the deal at the lowest price quoted. The trade is settled in seven calendar days, and the transaction is cleared through one of the two major clearing systems, Euroclear or Cedel.

Both systems are owned by a group of financial institutions. Euroclear, which handles about two-thirds of the total volume, was founded and is operated by Morgan Guaranty from Brussels. Cedel is based in Luxembourg and was created by a group of Eurobond traders to compete with Morgan Guaranty's Euroclear. Both systems operate in a similar fashion. Each member has both bond accounts and cash accounts in each of the currencies used to denominate Eurobonds. All transactions are entered in the books without any physical movement of the securities. Both systems cover more than 7000 different securities. German banks prefer to deposit their deutsche mark Eurobonds in a domestic group of depositary banks, the Kassenvereine, which have direct links with Euroclear and Cedel. Similarly, most Swiss franc bonds are deposited in Switzerland, usually with the local clearing system SIGA. The whole clearing system is highly efficient because there are electronic bridges between Euroclear and Cedel as well as between the various domestic clearing systems (SICOVAM in France, NECIGEF in the Netherlands, CIK in Belgium, and others).

All transactions are performed on a net basis. In other words, the market-maker quotes a bid-ask spread and charges no commission. The typical spread for a straight dollar bond is 50 basis points or 0.5% (a basis point is one-hundredth of a percentage point) for a normal ticket of 100 to 500 securities (a $100,000 to $500,000 transaction). This spread increases for deutsche mark straight bonds (between 0.5 and 0.75%) and reaches 1% for Swiss franc bonds and bonds denominated in other currencies. The spread for floating rate notes is generally on the order of 0.25% and is larger than 1% for convertible bonds.

The above spread figures are averages. The spread is larger for small transactions and may vary for each bond, depending on market conditions. The private investor is charged a commission by his or her bank on top of this spread.

Clearing and custody charges must also be paid. Euroclear and Cedel collect a transaction fee for each book entry; a schedule of these fees is shown in Exhibit 6.12. They also charge a custody fee for holding the securities. The custody fees are a function of a client's transaction volume: If the member bank maintains a large bond turnover, the custodial fee is nil.

EXHIBIT 6.12
Schedule of Transaction Costs in Euroclear and Cedel Systems, 1987

Transaction	Euroclear (dollars)	Cedel (dollars)
Transfer of Securities between Members of the System	1.00	1.00
Transfer of Securities against Payments between Members of the System	1.50	1.50
Transfer of Securities against Payments between the Two Systems (Bridge Euroclear–Cedel)	4.00	4.00
Deposit of Security	free	free
Removal of Security from the System	12.50	12.50

SWAPS

A *swap* is an exchange of periodic cash flows between two parties. The origin of swaps may be traced back to the *parallel* or *back-to-back* loans, which were popular in the 1970s. In a back-to-back loan two companies exchange loans in two different currencies. For example, a French company lends French francs for five years to a U.S. company at a rate of 10%. In turn the U.S. company lends an equivalent amount of U.S. dollars to the French company at a rate of 8%, with the same schedule. The two companies have thereby exchanged both the principal and the interest payments. The French company has exchanged a stream of cash flows in French francs for a stream of cash flows in U.S. dollars at a fixed exchange rate. This is, in a sense, a long-term forward currency contract.

Two problems arise with back-to-back loans: (1) They appear on the balance sheet for accounting and regulatory purposes, although they effectively offset each other. (2) Default by one party does not release the other party from its obligation to make its contractual payments. In 1981 the currency swap was designed[4] taking into account these two problems. Soon, interest rate swaps and mixed currency–interest rate swaps developed.

Description

Currency swaps A *currency swap* resembles a back-to-back loan. It is an exchange of liabilities in two different currencies, but it is packaged into a single transaction, as opposed to two separate loans. A typical currency swap could be organized as follows:

A French company would like to borrow U.S. dollars to finance a foreign investment but is little known outside of France. Similarly, a U.S. company

EXHIBIT 6.13
Currency Swap

Principal exchange (in millions)

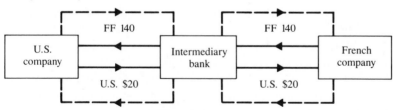

Key: Cash flow year 0 ——————
     Cash flow year 5 — — — — —

Yearly interest exchange (in millions)

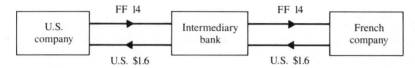

needs French francs for its local subsidiary, but has much easier access to the
U.S. bond market. An intermediary bank specialized in swaps may assist in
getting the two parties together and arranging a U.S. dollar/French franc
currency swap. Under the swap agreement the French company contracts to pay
the U.S. company principal and interest on its U.S. debt, while the U.S. company
contracts to pay the French company principal and interest on its French debt.
The two contracts are conditional, so that if one party defaults the other party is
released from further obligation. In this exchange the swap exchange rate is
FF/$ = 7.00, and the interest rate is 10% in French francs and 8% in U.S.
dollars with a maturity of five years. Each year the U.S. company pays to the
French company an annual interest of FF 14 million (10% of the French franc
principal), while the French company pays an annual interest of $1.6 million (8%
of the U.S. dollar principal). After five years the principals of $20 million and FF
140 million will be swapped back.[5] This swap is diagrammed in Exhibit 6.13.

A currency swap can be seen as a package of forward currency contracts.
(The pricing of swaps is discussed in Chapter 7.) For example, the above swap
with annual interest payments is a package of five forward currency contracts.
The year-one forward commitment is for $1.6 million; the implicit forward
exchange rate is equal to the ratio of the sums exchanged, or FF/$ = 8.75
(FF 14/$1.6). The year-five forward commitment is for $21.6 million (principal
plus last interest payment); the implicit forward exchange rate is equal to the

ratio of the sums exchanged or FF/$ = 7.13 (FF 154/$21.6). Currency swaps are used to manage the long-term currency exposure of companies and financial institutions. A company with a current long-term debt in currency A can engage in a currency swap to swap it into a debt in currency B if the company is afraid of an appreciation of currency A. In some swaps only interest coupons are exchanged, not the principal payments.

Interest rate swaps An *interest rate swap* is the exchange of liabilities in the same currency but based on two different interest rates. The most common interest rate swaps are U.S. dollar swaps involving a fixed interest rate and a floating rate. The floating rate index used is generally the six-month London interbank offered rate (LIBOR); the treasury bill rate is also used. Other swaps involve two floating rates; these are often referred to as *basis-rate swaps*. A typical example is the exchange of a LIBOR-indexed liability for a treasury bill rate–indexed liability. Another example is the exchange of liabilities indexed on the one-month and the six-month LIBOR.

Interest rate swaps do not involve exchange of the principal, since the same amount and currency is involved on both sides of the swap. These interest rate swaps sometimes have an optionlike payoff. For example, there could be a ceiling on the floating rate, allowing for a maximum level of the floating interest rate. These options are described in Chapter 9.

Currency–interest rate swaps A *currency–interest rate swap* is the exchange of liabilities in two different currencies, one with a fixed interest rate, the other with a floating interest rate. For example, a company could decide to swap a five-year French franc liability with a fixed interest rate of 10% with a five-year dollar liability at the six-month LIBOR plus 0.25%. Exhibit 6.14 describes such a currency–interest rate swap for 20 million U.S. dollars (FF 140 million). The floating rate (LIBOR plus 0.25%) is applied to a principal of $20 million U.S. dollars.

Such a swap can be seen as a combination of a French franc/U.S. dollar currency swap as presented above and a U.S. dollar–interest rate swap, exchanging a $20 million fixed interest rate liability for a floating rate (LIBOR plus 0.25%) liability.

The Market

The dollar–interest rate swap started after the currency swaps but it represents the largest share of the swap market. Interest rate swaps in French francs, Swedish kronor, British sterling, deutsche marks, and Dutch guilders have also been arranged. It is estimated that a sizable portion of Eurobond issues are swapped. Swaps cut across borders: Interest rate swaps often involve a U.S. domestic bond issue and a Eurobond issue.

EXHIBIT 6.14
Currency–Interest Rate Swap

Principal exchange (in millions)

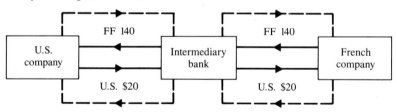

Key: Cash flow year 0 ——————
     Cash flow year 5 — — — — —

Yearly interest exchange (in millions)

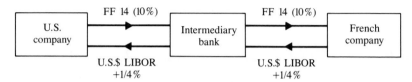

The motivation for a swap Companies use swaps[6] to manage their long-term exposure to currency and interest rate risks, especially when they are faced with risks to existing liabilities. For example, if a corporation borrowed in Swiss francs two years ago and is concerned about anticipated strong appreciation of the Swiss franc, a U.S. dollar/Swiss franc swap can be used to transform the Swiss franc liability into a U.S. dollar liability.

Interest rate swaps can be used to alter the exposure of a portfolio of assets or liabilities to interest rate movements. They are typically used when assets or liabilities cannot be traded, as is the case for bank loans.

Take the example of a French company that borrowed 100 million U.S. dollars a year ago at 9.5%. The long-term U.S. dollar interest rate has started to drop and the French company believes that it will continue to fall. To take advantage of this drop in interest rates the company decides to enter an interest rate swap in U.S. dollars. It swaps 100 million U.S. dollars at a fixed interest rate of 9% for a floating rate equal to the six-month LIBOR. In effect the French company is now protected against a down movement in interest rates. Conversely, a reverse swap is arranged if one believes a rise in interest rates is due.[7] Futures contracts on bonds can also be used to hedge interest rate exposure, but they need to be rolled over frequently and require administrative attention because of the marking-to-market procedure described in Chapter 8.

The usual argument for the use of swaps in new borrowing is cost saving. The main motivation in the early stage of the market was to take advantage of borrowing cost differentials to raise funds cheaply. A classic currency swap operates as follows: A supranational[8] borrower can tap the U.S. dollar market on favorable terms but would prefer to borrow Swiss francs because of the low interest rate in that market. Alternatively, a U.S. corporation can borrow on attractive terms in the foreign Swiss franc market but needs dollars. The two parties engage in a swap agreement whereby the supranational borrower taps the U.S. dollar market and swaps the proceeds for the low–interest rate Swiss francs borrowed by the U.S. corporation. Each party is bound to benefit from this swap by obtaining funds more cheaply than if they had directly accessed their desired-currency market.

It was not uncommon to achieve a seventy-five basis-point reduction in interest rate thanks to a combined swap-borrowing arrangement. However, these cost savings based on the comparative advantage of some companies in some market segments are a form of market inefficiency. Financial arbitrage, such as a swap, exploits these market inefficiencies. However, as the volume of swaps increases, these inefficiencies are bound to disappear; they are arbitraged away. As a swap trader observed:

> "...at the outset of the market, a 'AAA' issuer could reasonably expect to achieve 75–100 basis points below LIBOR on a bond/swap; under current conditions, this same issuer might expect only 25–30 basis points below.... Many issuers now find it more cost-effective to approach the floating rate note market than the bond/swap market."

> *Source:* Bankers Trust Company, "The International Swap Market," Supplement to *Euromoney*, September 1985.

Many swap dealers believe that the growth of the market depends on the ability to identify new arbitrage opportunities as they develop in world markets and exploit them. Some of these temporary or persistent arbitrage opportunities are caused by the regulatory and fiscal environment. An example can be found in the yen market, where the Japanese regulatory pressure is strongly felt.

Until recently, three Japanese regulatory and fiscal situations could have lead to an interesting packaging of securities. These three situations were:

1. The Ministry of Finance limited the amount of nonyen bonds held by Japanese institutions such as pension funds.

2. Zero-coupon bonds were taxed as nonincome-generating assets. At maturity the difference between the face value and purchase price of the bond was taxed as a capital gain.

3. A dual currency bond issued in yen, with interest payments in yen but principal repayment in a foreign currency, qualified as a yen bond for purpose of the yen limit imposed by the Ministry of Finance. This was attractive to Japanese institutions as a legal way to invest in foreign currency assets.

In response to this regulatory and fiscal environment a corporation wanting to borrow U.S. dollars could instead have engaged in the following operations:

☐ Issue a five-year dual-currency bond with an 8% interest coupon in yen and principal repayment in dollars. The face value would be 50 million U.S. dollars and the issue amount would be 10 billion yen.

☐ Issue a zero-coupon yen bond with the same maturity as the dual-currency bond and a face value of 10 billion yen. There would be no interest payment; simply a principal repayment of 10 billion yen.

☐ Enter into an agreement to swap a five-year yen fixed-rate loan of 10 billion yen for a U.S. dollar liability (yen/dollar currency swap).[9]

Let's look at the economic position taken. The combination of the zero-coupon and dual-currency loan is equivalent to a straight yen bond plus a U.S. dollar zero-coupon bond with a face value of $50 million. The reasoning is simple if one looks at the cash flows by currency:

	Yen	*Dollars*
Yearly interest	8% of 10 billion yen	0%
Principal repayment	10 billion yen	$50 million

To get back to purely dollar borrowing, the corporation would have had to swap the yen obligation of 10 billion yen into a U.S. dollar obligation (as indicated in the third operation above). The issue of the two bonds would have capitalized on a regulatory and fiscal attraction to Japanese investors, but the final product for the corporation would have been a U.S. dollar loan, preferably at a cheaper cost than a straight U.S. dollar loan.

Swaps also contribute to the integration of financial markets by creating contracts that do not currently exist in the marketplace. They make the market more complete. Currency swaps are a typical example of long-term forward contracts that did not exist previously.

In summary, the market for swaps developed both to exploit international financial arbitrage opportunities and to offer unique tools for currency and interest rate management.

Evolution of the market Swaps are an attractive source of off–balance-sheet earnings for commercial banks and investment banks alike. They also facilitate other types of businesses, such as Eurobond underwriting. Commercial banks tend to consider swaps an extension of their traditional credit activities as an intermediary. They stress their expertise in assessing credit risk and their ability to carry long-term market and credit risks. They also rely on their large customer base to find swap counterparts. In contrast, investment banks consider swaps negotiable securities. They attempt to remove all default risk from a swap and standardize the contract as much as possible. They stress their trading and hedging expertise.

It should be stressed that the credit risk of a swap is rather small.[10] It does not apply to the principal, but only to the differential in interest payments and, in the case of currency swaps, to the differential of principal repayments due to currency movements. Clearly the risk of a currency swap is higher than that of an interest rate swap. Because of their large capital base commercial banks are more willing to assume long-term credit risk than investment banks, who frequently request collaterals.

The secondary market for swaps has evolved unevenly because many swap contracts are highly customized. Furthermore, the other party must agree to the sale of the swap, and often objects because of the change in credit risk. Three other possibilities are open to a party wanting to get out of a swap contract:

1. Agree on a voluntary termination with the original counterparty. This popular agreement is simple and only implies a lump-sum payment to reflect the changes in market conditions. Once this cash payment is settled the counterparty can always look for another swap at current market conditions if it wants to maintain the same economic position. This cash termination is negotiated between the two parties.

2. Write a *mirror swap* with the original counterparty. A swap is reversed by writing an opposite swap contract with the same maturity and amount but at current market conditions. For example, company *A* enters into a seven-year swap agreement with bank *B*. *A* receives LIBOR and pays 10.5% fixed. A year later the two parties could write a six-year mirror swap whereby *A* receives 9.5% and pays LIBOR to *B* (the current swap conditions). The difference from a termination is that the settlement is paid over the remaining six years (1% per year) and some credit risk remains on the differential interest rate payment.

3. Write a *reverse swap* in the market with another counterparty. This is the easiest deal to arrange but has two drawbacks: First, it is unlikely and expensive to find a swap that exactly offsets the previous one in terms of payment frequencies, price reset, and floating rate base. Second, engaging in another swap doubles the credit risk.

Investment banks encourage the development of the secondary market by standardizing swaps and eliminating credit risk. After all, swaps are long-term futures contracts and they could be traded as futures on an organized exchange. Credit risk would be eliminated by a margin system with a marking-to-market procedure, as described in Chapter 8. Investment banks also attempt to eliminate credit risk by collateralization. They incorporate collateral provisions in the swap contract, giving the intermediary the right to call for an amount of collateral equal to the credit exposure on the contract.

At present, swaps are used by corporations and banks primarily to manage the currency and interest rate exposure of their assets and liabilities. The minimum size of the contracts (a few million dollars), as well as the lack of a developed secondary market, does not make them attractive to the average investor. The standardization of swap contracts could change that situation.

SUMMARY

1. The international bond market is divided into three broad market groups: domestic bonds, foreign bonds, and Eurobonds. While domestic and foreign bonds are issued and traded on a single national market, Eurobonds belong to an unregulated international market where banks from all over the world participate.

2. The total world bond market capitalization has passed the $6000 billion mark. U.S. dollar–denominated bonds account for about half of the world market, and Japanese yen bonds for about 20%. Bonds denominated in European currencies account for more than one-fourth of the world market.

3. The market for international bonds has been growing very rapidly. The U.S. dollar dominates as a denomination currency, but several other currencies are also used. The ECU, a composite basket of the European currencies, has been extensively used in the recent past. The Eurobond market is a free and innovative market. All types of instruments can be found with imaginative interest rates and multi-currency clauses.

4. Issuing and dealing practices differ among bond markets across the world. Yield calculation varies greatly between countries and markets. International investors must be aware of these practical differences.

5. Foreign withholding taxes on interest income are being progressively removed throughout the world. Where such taxes exist, international tax treaties allow them to be claimed as a tax credit against domestic income tax, or to be used to get a tax refund from the withholding country. Eurobonds are exempt from any withholding tax.

6. The Eurobond market is an informal network of investment and commercial banks of all nationalities. New issues are made rapidly, since, in the absence of supervising authorities, no special documents need to be prepared by the borrowing firm or underwriting syndicate. An international clearing system ensures efficient settling of all transactions.

7. Swaps have rapidly developed in the 1980s. Currency swaps involve the exchange of liabilities in two different currencies. Interest rate swaps involve the exchange of two liabilities in the same currency, one with a fixed interest rate, the other with a floating rate. Currency–interest rate swaps involve the exchange of a fixed interest rate in one currency for a floating interest rate in another currency. A sizable percentage of Eurobond issues is driven by swap agreements.

Swaps are used to manage the long-term exposure of a company to currency and interest rate risk.

QUESTIONS AND PROBLEMS

1. What is the difference between a foreign bond and a Eurobond?

2. What is the attraction of an ECU bond?

3. Let's consider the NKK dual-currency bond shown in Exhibit 6.5. It is a bond quoted in yen at 101%. What would happen to the market price of the bond if the following scenarios took place?

☐ The market interest rate on (newly issued) yen bonds drops significantly.

☐ The dollar drops in value relative to the yen.

4. What are the potential biases of the simple interest calculation used in Japan? Take the example of two straight yen Eurobonds with the same maturity of five years. Bond *A* has a coupon of 12% and bond *B*, a coupon of 8%. The current market interest rate on yen bonds is 10%. These two bonds have the same yield-to-maturity of 10% and are correctly priced at $107.58 for bond *A* and $92.42 for bond *B*. What would be the yield-to-maturity indicated by the simple interest calculation?

5. Two bond indexes of the same market tend to give similar total return indications even if their composition is quite different. Why?

6. A German bank has the following portfolio of loans in U.S. dollars:

Assets	*Liabilities*
$50 million of a five-year loan at LIBOR plus 0.5%	$10 million of a five-year loan at a fixed rate of 9%

The German bank fears a long-term depreciation of the U.S. dollar relative to the deutsche mark and a rise in U.S. interest rates. What type of swap arrangement should it contract? Would you suggest another strategy if the bank expects that the drop in the dollar value will come in the near future but does not expect a long-term weakening trend?

NOTES

1. The Interest Equalization Tax was imposed on interest paid to U.S. bondholders by foreign borrowers. The supposed purpose was to equalize the after-tax interest rate paid by U.S. and foreign borrowers. This tax did not apply to some borrowers such as those in Canada, less developed countries, and supranationals such as the World Bank.

2. British traders use the world *stock* where Americans use the word *bond*. This original trading practice was partly eliminated in 1986, which was welcome news for international investors, but sad for traditionalists and finance historians.

3. The rationale for this method is that it is easy to calculate the yield for a bond issued at par with semiannual coupons. However, the use of an annual actuarial yield makes much more sense and enables direct comparison between instruments and markets. The actuarial (or discounting) method of calculating a yield-to-maturity is described in Chapter 7.

4. The World Bank initiated the first currency swap. The literature on swaps include T. S. Arnold, "How to Do Interest Rate Swaps," *Harvard Business Review*, September/October 1984; J. Bicksler and A. Chen, "An Economic Analysis of Interest Rate Swaps," *Journal of Finance*, July 1986; and various publications prepared by *Euromoney*.

5. In practice only the cash flow difference is exchanged. Suppose the French franc has dropped to FF/$ = 7.50 in year one. Then the French franc value of the interest payment of the French company to the U.S. counterparty is equal to $1.6 million × 7.50, or FF 12 million when valued at the current spot exchange rate. This FF 12 million is to be compared with the FF 14 million interest payment owed by the U.S. company. The U.S. company simply remits to the French company the FF 2 million difference in cash flow.

6. A good description of the market for swaps can be found in a detailed study by the Bank for International Settlements, *Recent Innovations in International Banking*, April 1986.

7. As mentioned in Chapter 7, a drop in interest rates increases the present value of a fixed-rate debt obligation, whereas a rise in interest rates reduces the present value.

8. Supranational borrowers such as the World Bank, the EEC, or the European Investment Bank are not favorites of Swiss bankers. A typical interest rate swap is a highly rated European bank raising fixed interest rate debt in the Eurobond market and swapping this debt to a lower rated U.S. corporation that raised floating rate funds from the international banking market.

9. Such an example has also been presented by C. Smith, C. W. Smithson, and L. M. Wakeman, "The Evolving Market for Swaps," *Midland Corporate Finance Journal*, Spring 1986.

10. A good analysis of swap credit risk and how banks manage their exposure is provided in Bank for International Settlements, *Recent Innovations in International Banking*, April 1986, pp. 52–55.

BIBLIOGRAPHY

Arnold, T. S., "How to Do Interest Rate Swaps," *Harvard Business Review*, September/October 1984.

Bank for International Settlements, *Recent Innovations in International Banking*, April 1986.

Bruslerie, H. de la, *Euro-Obligations*, Paris: C.L.E.T., 1984.

————. *Gestion Obligataire Internationale*, Economica, Paris, 1990.

Dufey, G. and I. Giddy, *The International Money Market*, Englewood Cliffs, NJ: Prentice Hall, 1978.

Eiteman, D. K., "International Capital Market," in N. Roussakis (ed), *International Banking: Principles and Practices*, Westport, CT: Praeger, 1983.

Euromoney, various publications on international bond markets, swaps, etc., London: Euromoney Publications.

George, I. and I. Giddy, *International Finance Handbook*, New York: Wiley, 1983.

Grabbe, J. O., *International Financial Markets*, New York: Elsevier, 1986.

Kemp, L. J., *A Guide to World Money and Capital Markets*, New York: McGraw Hill, 1982.

Kerr, I., *A History of the Eurobond Market: The First 21 Years*, Euromoney Publications, 1984.

Mitello, F. C., "Swap Financing, A New Approach to International Transactions," *Financial Executive*, October 1984.

Park, Y. S. and J. Zwick, *International Banking in Theory and Practice*, Reading, MA: Addison-Wesley, 1985.

Reed, H. C., *The Preeminence of International Financial Centers*, Westport, CT: Praeger, 1981.

Smith, C. N., C. W. Smithson, and L. M. Wakeman, "The Evolving Market for Swaps," *Midland Corporate Finance Journal*, Spring 1986.

7

Bonds: Concepts and Techniques

In Chapter 2 we established the case for diversification in international bond markets. We found that foreign bonds reduce the risk of a global portfolio. Furthermore, we found that active international fixed-income management can achieve superior performance, if a manager is skilled at forecasting interest rates and currency movements.

International fixed-income investment requires both a familiarity with the markets described in Chapter 6 and a thorough knowledge of the techniques required to manage bond portfolios. We begin this chapter by reviewing the main concepts and actuarial techniques used in fixed-income portfolio management. We also consider the dimension of multi-currency analysis. The rest of this chapter presents some of the more complex bonds issued worldwide and ideas about how they should be analyzed.

STRAIGHT BOND PRICES AND YIELDS

Bond portfolio management requires the use of mathematical techniques. International bond management adds a new dimension to these techniques, namely, a multi-currency strategy. It also implies the analysis of a large variety of unusual bonds, floating rate notes, currency option bonds, and other instruments.

The following section could appear in any textbook that deals with domestic investment. As such, it is only briefly presented here. It is followed by a more detailed analysis of the techniques used in international portfolio management, especially the comparison of international yield curves, and an analysis of special bonds.

Bond Valuation Techniques: A Review

Yield-to-maturity The theoretical value of a bond is determined by computing the present value of all future cash flows generated by the bond discounted at an appropriate interest rate. Conversely, one may calculate the internal rate of return, or *yield-to-maturity* (YTM), of a bond on the basis of its current market price and its promised payments.

For example, a bond that promises a payment of $F_1 = \$110$ one year from now with a current market value of $P = \$100$ has a yield-to-maturity r given by

$$P = \frac{F_1}{1+r} \tag{7.1}$$

$$100 = \frac{110}{1+r}.$$

Hence

$$r = 0.10 = 10\%.$$

Similarly, one may compute the yield-to-maturity of zero-coupon bonds maturing in t years using the formula

$$P = \frac{F_t}{(1+r)^t} \tag{7.2}$$

where r is expressed as a yearly interest rate. The term $1/(1+r)^t$ is the discount factor for year t. The yield-to-maturity is defined as the interest rate at which P dollars should be invested today in order to realize F_t dollars t years from now.

$$P(1+r)^t = F_t$$

For example, a two-year zero-coupon bond paying $F_2 = \$100$ two years from now and currently selling at a price $P = \$81.16$, has a yield-to-maturity r given by

$$81.16 = \frac{100}{(1+r)^2}.$$

Hence

$$r = 0.11 = 11\%.$$

Yield curves The yields-to-maturity of two zero-coupon bonds in the same currency but with different maturities are usually different. However, bonds with similar characteristics (risks, coupons, and maturities) should provide the same return. Graphing the yields-to-maturity on bonds with different maturities allows us to draw a *yield curve*. The yield curve shows the yields-to-maturity

EXHIBIT 7.1
Yield Curve for Zero-Coupon Bonds

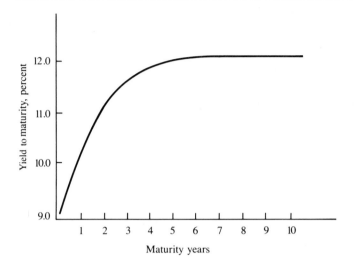

Maturity years

computed on a given date as a function of the maturity of the bonds. It provides an estimate of the current *term structure* of interest rates. To be meaningful a yield curve must be drawn from bonds with identical characteristics, except for their maturity.

A good example of a yield curve can be drawn for zero-coupon bonds with government guarantees and no call or *sinking fund* clauses. This is a default-free yield curve. Two zero-coupon bonds are represented as two points on the hypothetical yield curve in Exhibit 7.1. Other yield curves can be drawn for risky bonds, e.g., those with an AA quality rating or denominated in foreign currencies.

Forward interest rates Yield-to-maturity is a sort of average rate of interest on a bond held to maturity. YTM assumes a constant rate of interest over the life of a bond, but as we have already seen, interest rates are contingent on the maturity of a bond. For example, the yields-to-maturity on one-year and two-year zero-coupon bonds, r_1 and r_2, are generally different.

Now we can introduce the notion of forward interest rates: Forward interest rates are future one-year interest rates implied by long-term interest rates.

The yield-to-maturity on a t-year bond, r_t, may be thought of as the rollover of one-year investments until the bond expires. Let's use R_1 to represent the interest rate on a one-year bond maturing in a year, and R_2 to represent the forward interest rate on a one-year bond maturing in two years (i.e., issued one year from now). Similarly, R_3, R_4, etc. represent the forward interest rates on one-year bonds maturing three, four, or however many years from now. The values of the forward rates are determined by the following set of equations:

$$(1 + R_1)(1 + R_2) \cdots (1 + R_t) = (1 + r_t)^t. \tag{7.3}$$

Note that R_1 must equal r_1. The next forward interest rate, R_2, is easily derived from the yield curve knowing the yields-to-maturity on a one-year and a two-year bond.

$$(1 + r_1)(1 + R_2) = (1 + r_2)^2.$$

Hence

$$1 + R_2 = \frac{(1 + r_2)^2}{(1 + r_1)}$$

and so on for $R_3, R_4, \ldots, R_t$.

Going back to our original example, the forward interest rate one year from now is given by

$$1 + R_2 = \frac{(1.11)^2}{1.10} = 1.12009.$$

Hence

$$R_2 \approx 12\%$$

when

$$r_1 = 10\% \text{ and}$$
$$r_2 = 11\%.$$

In order to borrow at this forward rate one can simply combine two transactions. At time zero, borrow for two years at $r_2 = 11\%$, and simultaneously lend for one year at $r_1 = 10\%$. Nothing happens during the first year, since the borrowing and lending are mutually offsetting. After one year we are left in a borrowing position at a rate R_2 such that

$$1 + R_2 = \frac{(1 + r_2)^2}{1 + r_1}.$$

In other words, the one-year interest rate must move to 12% in the year 2001 for an investor to be indifferent to buying a two-year bond in 2000 or buying a one-year bond and rolling it over in 2001. Many investors believe that the implied forward rate reflects expectations about changes in the short-term interest rate.[1] The forward interest rate structure implied by the yield curve depicted in Exhibit 7.1 may be easily computed and is shown in Exhibit 7.2.

EXHIBIT 7.2
Implied Forward Interest Rates

N maturity (years)	1	2	3	4	5
N-years interest rate (percent)	10	11	11.5	11.75	11.9
Implied one-year forward interest rate (percent)	10	12	12.52	12.50	12.50

Valuing a bond with coupons The theoretical value of a coupon-paying bond is more difficult to assess. It may be considered the present value of a stream of cash flows consisting of each coupon payment and the principal reimbursement. Since the cash flows occur at different times, they should be discounted at the interest rate corresponding to their date of disbursement. Accordingly, the coupon to be paid in one year should be discounted at the one-year interest rate on the yield curve, $\left(\dfrac{1}{1 + r_1}\right)$; the coupon to be paid in two years should be discounted at the two-year rate, $\left(\dfrac{1}{1 + r_2}\right)$, and so forth. In essence then, a coupon-paying bond is a combination of bonds with different maturities. For example, a ten-year $100 bond with an annual coupon of ten dollars is a combination of ten bonds, each with a nominal value of $10 and a maturity of one to ten years, and a bond with a nominal value of $100 and a ten-year maturity. As we will later see, the *duration* of this coupon-bond is less than the maturity of the final payment because it is a weighted average of the maturities of this combination of bonds.

One may still define the yield-to-maturity of a coupon bond as the internal rate of return, r, which equates the discounted stream of cash flows to the current bond market price. For an annual coupon bond, the equation is as follows:

$$P = \frac{C_1}{1 + r} + \frac{C_2}{(1 + r)^2} + \cdots + \frac{C_n}{(1 + r)^n} \tag{7.4}$$

where $C_1, C_2, \ldots, C_n$ are the coupons $1, 2, \ldots, n$ years from now, including the final reimbursement. In practice, coupons may be paid semestrally or quarterly, and a valuation may be made at any time during the coupon period. This calls for the more general valuation formula to determine yield-to-maturity, which is shown below:

$$P = \frac{Ct_1}{(1 + p)^{t_1}} + \frac{Ct_2}{(1 + p)^{t_2}} + \cdots + \frac{Ct_n}{(1 + p)^{t_n}} \tag{7.5}$$

where p is the daily yield,[2] i.e., $(1 + p)^{365} = 1 + r$, and $t_1, t_2, \ldots, t_n$ are the dates on which the cash flows occur, expressed in number of days from the

EXHIBIT 7.3
Yield Differentials Between High- and Low-Coupon Government Bonds
Weekly data, June 1982 to June 1983

		Yield Differentials (basis points)		
Country	Representative bonds	Average	Maximum	Minimum
Japan	8 '86 vs. 6.6 '87	−50	−23	−95
Switzerland	$5\frac{3}{4}$ '93 vs. $3\frac{3}{4}$ '92	53	68	30
United Kingdom	$15\frac{1}{4}$ '96 vs. 12 '98	34	92	23
United States	$16\frac{1}{8}$ '86 vs. $12\frac{3}{4}$ '87	12	54	−10
Canada	$11\frac{1}{4}$ '89 vs. 10 '89	12	33	−29
West Germany	$10\frac{3}{4}$ '91 vs. $8\frac{1}{2}$ '92	6	16	−1

Source: J. Hanna and T. Q. Hung, "Coupon Based Trading Strategies," *Bond Market Research*, Salomon Brothers Inc., August 1983. Reprinted with permission.

current date. Cash flows include all payments, including coupons and reimbursement.

The maturity of a bond is generally defined as the date on which the final payment is made on the bond, although its duration is less. This implies that the yield-to-maturity on a coupon bond can differ from that on a zero-coupon bond with the same maturity. In an upward sloping yield curve, the YTM on a correctly priced coupon bond should be less than that of a zero-coupon bond because it has a shorter duration.[3] In a downward sloping yield curve, the reverse is true.

But two other factors affecting yield-to-maturity should be taken into account. The first stems from the fact that coupons and capital gains usually have a different tax status. That is, investors must generally pay more taxes on income than on capital gains; therefore, they prefer low-coupon bonds. Conversely, investors require a higher YTM from high-coupon bonds to compensate for this tax effect. It should be remembered, however, that this tax effect is not present to the same degree in all countries. Exhibit 7.3 shows the average yield differential for high- and low-coupon government bonds with comparable maturity in six different domestic markets. What we find is that YTM is an increasing function of the coupon rate in all countries except Japan.[4]

A second factor, particularly important in the Eurobond market, is the use of *call* provisions (see below). Low-coupon bonds offer greater call protection than high-coupon bonds. This is because low-coupon bonds must sell at a higher market price than high-coupon bonds with a similar maturity in order to provide a comparable yield-to-maturity. Conversely, high-coupon bonds are more likely to be called (repaid at a set price) by the issuer, a risk that must be offset by a higher YTM for the investor.

Duration The cash flows on a coupon bond are periodically paid over the life of the bond in the form of coupons and, ultimately, a principal reimbursement. The duration of a bond is defined as its average maturity. It is a time-weighted average where each date is weighted by the present value of the cash flow paid by the bond on that date. On the coupon date duration, D, is computed as follows:

$$D = \frac{1}{P}\left(1\frac{C_1}{1+r} + 2\frac{C_2}{(1+r)^2} + \cdots + t\frac{C_t}{(1+r)^t} + \cdots + n\frac{C_n}{(1+r)^n}\right)$$

(7.6)

or

$$D = \frac{\displaystyle\sum_{t=1}^{n} t\frac{C_t}{(1+r)^t}}{\displaystyle\sum_{t=1}^{n} \frac{C_t}{(1+r)^t}}$$

(7.7)

where the final cash flow, C_n includes the coupon and the principal repayment. Duration is easily computed on dates other than coupon dates using a daily compounding formula like Eq. (7.5).

Duration is a more precise definition of the average maturity of a coupon bond. It gained wide use when it was recognized that it also measures bond-price sensitivity to interest rate movements. The percentage change in price induced by a small change, dr, in interest rate (for example, a ten-basis-point increase where $dr = 0.10\%$) is given by

$$\left(\frac{1}{P}\right)\left(\frac{dP}{dr}\right) = -\frac{1}{P}\sum_{t=1}^{n} t\frac{C_t}{(1+r)^{t+1}} = -D\frac{1}{1+r} = -D^*.$$

(7.8)

$D^* = \dfrac{D}{1+r}$ is often called *interest rate sensitivity* or *modified duration*. The only difference between this and the former measure is the multiplicative constant $\dfrac{1}{1+r}$. For the remainder of the chapter, the latter definition of duration will be used:[5] the measure of the sensitivity of the price of a bond to interest rate movements.

A bond with a duration of 7.2 rises in price on the order of 0.72% when the interest rate drops by ten basis points (0.10%):

Percent change in $P = -D^* \times$ Change in interest rate.

Let's consider two bonds, one with a duration of 7.2, and the other with a duration of 10. The second bond is more sensitive to interest rate movements, up and down, than the first one. Their relative sensitivity is the ratio of their duration, $\dfrac{10}{7.2}$.

Note that mathematically, a coupon-bearing bond with duration of N years has the same sensitivity to changes in interest rates as an N-year zero-coupon bond. That is, a coupon bond with ten-year final maturity and a duration of 7.2 would react to changes in interest rates as a zero-coupon bond with 7.2 years remaining.

Two words of caution are in order here. First, the sensitivity of the bond as measured by its duration is an exact actuarial measure. Yet, the price sensitivity of a bond price varies with the level of interest rates themselves. This means that for large changes in the market interest rate, $D^*(r)$ does not stay constant. Nonetheless, exact calculations of $D^*(r)$ can be performed. Second, the underlying assumption of Eq. (7.8) is that the whole term structure of interest rates moves by the same amount, dr. More complex multi-factor duration models have been developed that assume different shifts for short- and long-term interest rates. But empirical evidence indicates that Eq. (7.8) performs just as well as the more complex models.[6]

The interest rate sensitivity or risk of a portfolio is the weighted average of the durations of individual bonds.

Sinking fund Many bonds are not repaid *in fine*, that is, in a lump at maturity. Instead, they are progressively amortized over their maturity through a sinking fund provision. Three methods are used by issuers for early bond redemption:

Lot drawing at par. Following a grace period part of the bond issue is repaid according to a fixed schedule. The bonds to be repaid are drawn at random and reimbursed at par value.

Market repurchase. Part of the bond issue is repaid according to a fixed schedule by which it is purchased in the market at market prices.

Issuing of serial bonds. Serial bonds each have a serial number, and each series has a different maturity and yield. Investors know at issue which bond will be reimbursed and when. This method is seldom used because each series represents a different bond, which reduces the liquidity of the issue.

Sometimes a combination of methods is used. For example, the issuer may have the option to meet the redemption schedule by either drawing bonds at par or repurchasing them in the market. This flexibility greatly benefits the issuer because it allows him or her to choose the cheapest redemption method possible at any given time. Conversely, it is a disadvantage to the investor.

For each bond purchased, an investor can compute the expected cash flows, taking into account the probability each year of being reimbursed. From these cash flows he or she can compute an internal rate of return. This is the yield obtained by an investor who, holding a large number of shares of a bond issue, knows exactly how many bonds will be drawn each year.

A bond with a mandatory redemption schedule has a smaller duration than a *bullet bond* with a similar maturity. The *average life* (AL) of a bond is usually defined as the average maturity of the whole issue. Average life takes into account the fact that some bonds are reimbursed early, others late, which makes it a weighted average of the maturities on each bond. Unlike duration, the calculation of the average life takes into account only the principal repayments, not the coupon. Also, it is only a linear average without discounting.

Worldwide, there is some confusion over the correct definition of yield-to-maturity for a bond with contractual amortization. Some institutions compute the YTM on Eurobonds as if there were no sinking fund. In actuality, this is a *yield-to-final-maturity* (YFM) and it is equal to YTM only for those bonds that are reimbursed on the final date. It does not measure the expected yield on either a typical bond or portfolios containing the bond. These same institutions often call *yield-to-average-life* (YTAL) what we would call YTM, i.e., the actuarial yield that takes the mandatory sinking fund into account. This computation is clearly a more exact measure of the expected rate of return on the bond. The YTM computed without reference to the mandatory redemption schedule is misleading. The difference between the two measures YFM and YTAL can be large for bonds selling at a price either far above or far below par value. Early redemption at par improves the true yield-to-maturity if a bond is selling under par in the market, but reduces it if the bond is selling over par in the market. This feature does not apply if the bond is repurchased within the market (though there may be temporary upward pressure on its market price). An option to repurchase a bond in the market or drawing a bond at par always reduces the true yield-to-maturity.

To illustrate this, we reproduce in Exhibit 7.4 the average life, duration, and yield-to-maturity for three hypothetical bonds *with a similar final maturity of ten years*. The three bonds are

1. A zero-coupon bond trading at 32.2.

2. A 10% coupon (annual) bond, repaid in full in ten years. This bullet bond currently trades at 88.7.

3. A 10% coupon (annual) bond with sinking fund determined by lot drawing at par. The bond is redeemed in equals tranche amounting to one-tenth of all bonds each year. This sinking fund bond currently trades at 92.7.

Note that all three bonds have the same final maturity. They were issued five years ago, and early redemption only applies to the third bond. The three bonds have the same yield-to-maturity of 12%, once the coupons and redemption schedule are taken into account. The zero-coupon bond A has a (modified) duration equal to 8.93 (10 years divided by $1 + r = 1.12$), which greatly exceeds that of the 10% coupon-bond B with a maturity of 10 years and a duration of 5.85 years. Bond C has an average life of 5.5 years because of the sinking fund and a duration of only 3.67 years. This last bond is much less sensitive to changes in interest rates than the zero-coupon bond A with identical final maturity.

EXHIBIT 7.4
Characteristics of Three Bonds with Similar Final Maturity

Bond	Market price (percent of par)	Final maturity (years)	Average life (years)	Yield-to-final maturity (percent)	Yield-to-maturity (percent)	Interest-Rate sensitivity (duration)
A. Zero-Coupon	32.2	10	10	12	12	8.93
B. Coupon Bond	88.7	10	10	12	12	5.85
C. Coupon Bond with Sinking Fund	92.7	10	5.5	11.25	12	3.67

The true yield-to-maturity on each of these bonds is 12% when the sinking fund schedule is taken into account. An institution calculating only the yield-to-final-maturity would find a yield of 11.25% for bond *C*, while its true YTM is 12%, if one takes into account the fact that the bond is redeemed progressively.

Of course, there is no reason for these three bonds to have the same YTM, since they are so different in duration. The zero-coupon bond carries much more interest risk than the sinking fund bond and should have a higher YTM in an upward-sloping yield curve.

Call options Bonds are sometimes issued with a call or other options. This is very common in the Eurobond markets, but less so in certain domestic markets, such as the British gilt market.

The most common call option is the right given to the issuer to call back the bond at a given date at a price set in the bond contract. This is profitable to the issuer if the market interest rate falls because he or she can redeem high-coupon bonds and issue new bonds with a lower coupon.

Many other options are also found in the international market. For example, currency-option bonds give the investor an opportunity to benefit from currency movements. Bond options such as these are analyzed below.

Quality spreads The interest rate required by a bondholder is a function of the default risk assumed: the greater the risk, the higher the yield that the borrower must pay. This implies that yields reflect a quality spread over the default-free rate.

In some countries, credit-rating agencies assess the creditworthiness of borrowers with respect to specific obligations. The rating is based on both the likelihood of default and the nature, provisions, and protection afforded by specific obligations. Although such credit ratings are routinely provided on the U.S. bond market, they are rare on other national markets (with the exception of the United Kingdom and Japan). Standard and Poor's and Moody's now provide credit ratings on most international bonds (foreign bonds and Eurobonds). Exhibits 7.5A and B give the ratings scales used by these two agencies and Exhibit 7.6 shows some sample documents these agencies prepare for international bonds.

Governments are much heavier borrowers than corporations in the international market. To assess the creditworthiness of corporate borrowers, traditional analysis can be used, but for governments, the task is trickier. That is why commercial banks and supranational lenders such as the World Bank have developed special techniques for forecasting sovereign default and assessing country risk. These techniques often rely on statistical methods. Two publications, *Euromoney* and *Institutional Investor*, regularly provide investors with country-risk rankings. *Euromoney* ranks countries according to the average spreads they pay on their Euromarket borrowing. *Institutional Investor* surveys the lending officers of the largest banks in order to establish their country ranking. To be sure, no method is perfect. The spread over the London interbank offered rate (LIBOR) depends partly on market conditions at the time of borrowing. When markets are liquid, the spread is reduced for every borrower. Moreover, front-end and management fees should, to some extent, be taken into consideration. Also, the popularity-poll approach of the *Institutional Investor* survey introduces some bias into its ranking. As shown in Exhibit 7.7, country-risk rankings sometimes differ according to the analysis techniques used. For example, the French government is considered more risky than the Singaporean government according to the *Euromoney* ranking but not according to the *Institutional Investor* ranking.

It should be clear that the currency borrowed can affect default risk. For example, there is little risk of the French government defaulting on French franc bonds because it has the power to print its own money.

There is no consensus on the credit ratings of corporations and governments. The Swiss market, which is the second-largest international bond market, seems to favor private corporations over supranational entities and governments. Swiss, British, and American assessments of creditworthiness for certain European borrowers can differ quite markedly at times. Several money-management institutions, in fact, have developed their own credit-rating methods. This implies that the link between a quality spread on a bond yield and its credit rating by an agency is not as close as it is in the United States.

Specific International Techniques

International bond investment demands special analysis techniques. Several of the more commonly used techniques are described below.

Bond issues in a specific currency are sometimes found in several markets. For example, U.S. dollar bonds are issued on both the domestic U.S. market and the Eurobond markets. There are several reasons for this. One is that foreign firms often prefer to raise money on the Eurobond market rather than the Yankee bond market, the U.S. market for foreign borrowers, simply to avoid

EXHIBIT 7.5A
Moody's Long-Term Debt Ratings

Many of the entities described in this publication may have more than one issue of long-term debt. The long-term debt rating shown is the highest long-term rating assigned to that entity's debt by Moody's.

Aaa

Bonds that are rated **Aaa** are judged to be of the best quality. They carry the smallest degree of investment risk and are generally referred to as *gilt edged*. Interest payments are protected by a large or by an exceptionally stable margin and principal is secure. While the various protective elements are likely to change, such changes as can be visualized are most unlikely to impair the fundamentally strong position of such issues.

Aa

Bonds that are rated **Aa** are judged to be of high quality by all standards. Together with the **Aaa** group they comprise what are generally known as high-grade bonds. They are rated lower than the best bonds because margins of protection may not be as large as in **Aaa** securities, fluctuation of protective elements may be of greater amplitude, or there may be other elements present that make the long-term risks appear somewhat larger than the **Aaa** securities.

A

Bonds that are rated **A** possess many favorable investment attributes and are to be considered upper-medium-grade obligations. Factors giving security to principal and interest are considered adequate, but elements may be present that suggest a susceptibility to impairment some time in the future.

Baa

Bonds that are rated **Baa** are considered as medium-grade obligations (i.e., they are neither highly protected nor poorly secured). Interest payments and principal security appear adequate for the present, but certain protective elements may be lacking or may be characteristically unreliable over any great length of time. Such bonds lack outstanding investment characteristics and in fact have speculative characteristics as well.

Ba

Bonds that are rated **Ba** are judged to have speculative elements; their future cannot be considered as well assured. Often the protection of interest and principal payments may be very moderate, and thereby not well safeguarded during both good and bad times over the future. Uncertainty of position characterizes bonds in this class.

B

Bonds that are rated **B** generally lack characteristics of the desirable investment. Assurance of interest and principal payments or of maintenance of other terms of the contract over any long period of time may be small.

Caa

Bonds that are rated **Caa** are of poor standing. Such issues may be in default or there may be present elements of danger with respect to principal or interest.

Ca

Bonds that are rated **Ca** represent obligations that are speculative to a high degree. Such issues are often in default or have other marked shortcomings.

C

Bonds that are rated **C** are the lowest-rated class of bonds, and issues so rated can be regarded as having extremely poor prospects of ever attaining any real investment standing.

Source: Moody's International Bond Review, July 1986. Reprinted with permission.

Moody's applies numerical modifiers, **1**, **2**, and **3** in each generic rating classification from **Aa** through **B** in its corporate bond rating system. The modifier **1** indicates that the security ranks in the higher end of its generic rating category; the modifier **2** indicates a mid-range ranking; and the modifier **3** indicates that the issue ranks in the lower end of its generic rating category.

EXHIBIT 7.5B
Standard and Poor's Guide to International Ratings

Standard and Poor's debt rating is a current assessment of the creditworthiness of an obligor with respect to a specific obligation. This assessment may take into consideration obligors such as guarantors, insurers, or lessees.

The debt rating is not a recommendation to purchase, sell, or hold a security, inasmuch as it does not comment on market price or suitability for a particular investor.

The ratings are based on current information furnished by the issuer or obtained by S + P from other sources it considers reliable. S + P does not perform an audit in connection with any rating and may, on occasion, rely on unaudited financial information. The ratings may be changed, suspended, or withdrawn as a result of changes in, or unavailability of, such information, or for other circumstances.

The ratings are based, in varying degrees, on the following considerations:

1. Likelihood of default. Capacity and willingness of the obligor as to the timely payment of interest and repayment of principal in accordance with the terms of the obligation.

2. Nature and provisions of the obligation.

3. Protection afforded by, and relative position of, the obligation in the event of bankruptcy, reorganization, or other arrangement under the laws of bankruptcy and other laws affecting creditors' rights.

AAA

Debt rated **AAA** has the highest rating assigned by Standard & Poor's. Capacity to pay interest and repay principal is extremely strong.

AA

Debt rated **AA** has a very strong capacity to pay interest and repay principal and differs from the highest-rated issues only to a small degree.

A

Debt rated **A** has a strong capacity to pay interest and repay principal, although it is somewhat more susceptible to the adverse effects of changes in circumstances and economic conditions than debt in higher rated categories.

BBB

Debt rated **BBB** is regarded as having an adequate capacity to pay interest and repay principal. While it normally exhibits adequate protection parameters, adverse economic conditions or changing circumstances are more likely to lead to a weakened capacity to pay interest and repay principal for debt in this category than in higher rated categories.

BB, B, CCC, CC

Debt rated **BB**, **B**, **CCC**, or **CC** is regarded, on balance, as predominantly speculative with respect to capacity to pay interest and repay principal in accordance with the terms of the obligation. **BB** indicates the lowest degree of speculation and **CC** the highest degree of speculation. While such debt will likely have some quality and protective characteristics, these are outweighed by large uncertainties or major risk exposures to adverse conditions.

C

This rating is reserved for income bonds on which no interest is being paid.

D

Debt rated **D** is in default, and payment of interest and/or repayment of principal is in arrears.

Plus(+) or minus(−)

The ratings from **AA** to **B** may be modified by the addition of a plus or minus sign to show relative standing within the major rating categories.

N.R.

Indicates no rating has been requested, that there is insufficient information on which to base a rating, or that S + P does not rate a particular type of obligation as a matter of policy.

Debt obligations of issuers outside the United States and its territories are rated on the same basis as domestic corporate and municipal issues. The ratings measure the creditworthiness of the obligor to repay in the currency of denomination of the issue. However, S + P does not assess the foreign exchange risk that the investor may bear.

Source: Standard and Poor's International Credit Week, October 1985. Reprinted with permission.

EXHIBIT 7.6
Bond Review Published

International Bond Issues – Continued

Type of Debt	Coupon	Maturity	Moody's Rating	Amount Issued	Currency	Date Issued
Credit National						
Yen Gtd Bonds	8	1995	Aaa	20000.0	Yen	8/5/85
Euronts	9⅛	1993	Aaa	150.0	USD	1/20/86
Flt Rt Euronotes		1993	Aaa	175.0	ECU	9/17/85
Credit Suisse (Bahamas) Limited						
Gtd Eurobonds	10½	1990	Aaa	150.0	USD	3/10/83
Crocker National Bank						
Euronts	10½	1988	A1	75.0	USD	3/15/83
Zero Cpn Euronotes	0	1992	A1	225.0	USD	2/15/82
Cummins International Finance						
Gtd Euro C S D	6¼	1986	Baa3	15.0	USD	9/15/71
Gtd Euro C S D	5	1988	Baa3	20.0	USD	7/15/68
Cummins Overseas Finance						
Gtd Sub Euronotes	15½	1991	Baa2	50.0	USD	12/15/81
Cutler-Hammer World Trade Inc						
Gtd Eurobonds	8	1987	A2	15.0	USD	6/15/72
Dai-Ichi Kangyo Fin (Hong Kong)						
Gtd Flt Rt Nts		1996	Aaa	150.0	USD	4/17/84
Daiwa Securities Co Ltd						
Eurobonds	2¾	1991	Aa2	120.0	USD	
Dana International						
Gtd S F Eurodeb	8	1987	A2	20.0	USD	3/15/72
Dart & Kraft Finance N.V.						
Gtd Eurobonds	11¾	1989	Aa1	7.0	K.Dol.	2/26/82
Gtd Eurobonds	15¼	1988	Aa1	10.0	N.Z.Dol.	8/'8/83
Gtd Sub Euronotes	7¾	1998	Aa2	85.0	USD	11/7/83
Dart & Kraft Financial Corp.						
Eurobonds	10¼	1996	Aa1	100.0	USD	12/5/85
Eurobonds	16¼	1988	Aa1	60.0	N.Z.Dol.	8/7/85

Source: Moody's International, July 1985. Reprinted with permission.

Rating	Issuer / Euroissue	Amount Million	Year Issued	Support	Interest Dates	First Call	Lead Mgr.	Listing
	Credit Nationale *(Gtd:Republic of France)*							
AAA	floating rate bonds due 1988	US$75	1978	Gtd	Jan. 11, Jul. 11	1984	BNP	Lux
AAA	11.375% notes due 1991	ECU50	1984	Gtd	Feb. 24	None	CLYN	Lux
AAA	12.25% notes due 1993	ECU50	1983	Gtd	Apr. 22	None	CLYN	Lux
AAA	floating rate notes due 1994	US$200	1982	Gtd	Mar. 9, Sep. 9	1985	BPPB	Lux
AAA	10.375% notes due 1994	ECU50	1984	Gtd	Dec. 28	None	CLYN	Lux
AAA	floating rate notes due 1995	£100	1983	Gtd	Dec.	1991	HAMB	Lon
AAA	8% dual currency Yen/$ bonds due 1995	¥20,000	1985	Gtd	Sep. 4	None	NOMI	Lux
AAA	8.875% notes due 1995	ECU50	1985	Gtd	Jun. 28	None	CLYN	Lux
AAA	floating rate notes due 2000	US$500	1985	Gtd	Feb. 20, Aug. 20	None	CSFB	Lux
	Credit Suisse (Bahamas) Ltd. *(Gtd: Credit Suisse)*							
AAA	10.5% debentures due 1990	US$150	1983	Gtd	Mar. 15	None	CSFB	Lux
	CSX Corporation							
A	11.5% notes due 1992	US$100	1985	—	Jun. 12	1990	CSFB	Lux
	Cummins Int'l. Fin. Corp. *(Gtd: Cummins Engine Co. Inc.)*							
BBB	5% conv. sub. debs. due 1988	US$20	1968	Gtd-sub	Feb. 1, Aug. 1	Conv	FBC	Lux
	Cummins Int'l. Fin. N.V. *(Gtd: Cummins Engine Co. Inc.)*							
BBB	6.25% conv. sub. debs. due 1986	US$15	1971	Gtd-sub	Apr. 1, Oct. 1	Conv	FBC	Lux
	Cummins Overseas Fin. N.V. *(Gtd: Cummins Engine Co. Inc.)*							
BBB +	15.5% notes due 1991	US$50	1981	Gtd	Dec. 15	1987	CSFB	Lon
	Cutler-Hammer Int'l. Fin. Inc. *(Gtd: Cutler-Hammer Inc.)*							
A −	8% debs. due 1987	US$15	1972	Gtd	Jun. 15	1980	MCI	Lux
	Dana International Fin. Co. *(Gtd: Dana Corp.)*							
A	8% debs. due 1987	US$20	1972	Gtd	Mar. 1	1979	MLPF	Lux
	Dart & Kraft Fin. N.V. *(Gtd: Dart & Kraft Inc.)*							
AA	11.75% bonds due 1989	KD7	1982	Gtd	Mar. 1	1984	KIIC	Lux
AA −	7.75% sub. debs. due 1998	US$85	1983	Gtd-sub	Nov. 30	None	MGTY	Lux

Source: Standard & Poor's International Credit Week, October 1985. Reprinted with permission.

EXHIBIT 7.7
Risk Ranking for a Selected List of Localities as of April 1984

Locality	Institutional Investor ranking	Euromoney ranking
United States	1	1
Switzerland	2	1
Japan	3	1
West Germany	4	1
United Kingdom	5	1
Canada	6	6
Australia	9	8
France	11	18
Singapore	12	15
Hong Kong	22	29

U.S. regulations. Differential tax treatment also encourages the development of parallel bond markets (see Chapter 6). By purchasing Eurobonds, foreign investors can avoid the withholding tax that is sometimes imposed on them in national markets. Confidentiality is another consideration, at least for those private investors who prefer to remain anonymous. This is possible on the Eurobond market, but not on some domestic markets. These factors, in turn, influence the yield differential between various market segments in the same currency.

Another important aspect of the international bond market is its large number of nonstandard issues. A sizable portion of the U.S. dollar Eurobond market is made up of floating rate notes commonly referred to as floaters or FRNs. Technical analysis of FRNs is quite different from that of fixed interest bonds. International bankers are extremely inventive in this area, and as a result there is a large number of bonds in all currencies with unusual clauses and options, including renewable bonds, currency options, and dual-currency bonds. New instruments appear almost daily; therefore, investors must develop the ability to analyze innovative bonds quickly. The analysis of FRNs and *fancy* bonds is discussed later in this chapter.

The multi-currency dimension is the major complication of international bond investment. A strategic approach implies decisions about currencies and maturities and requires the use of analytical tools to merge interest and exchange rate analysis.

International yield curve comparisons A term structure of interest rates exists for each currency. Investors focus on the yield curve for government bonds. However, other yield curves may be drawn beside the default-free term structure, depending on the quality of the bond and the market sectors. Yields-to-

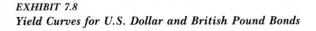

EXHIBIT 7.8
Yield Curves for U.S. Dollar and British Pound Bonds

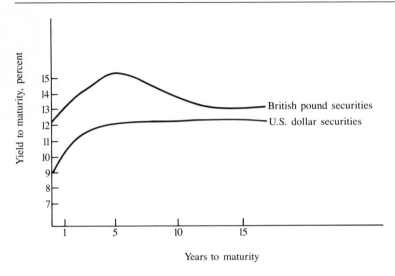

Years to maturity

maturity generally differ across currencies. As we discussed in Chapter 1, international interest rate differences are caused by a variety of factors, including differences in national monetary–fiscal policies and inflationary expectations. Furthermore, the interest rate differential for two currencies is not constant over the maturity spectrum.

Term structures for U.S. dollar and British pound bonds are given in Exhibit 7.8. These are hypothetical yield curves for government securities, which are meant to serve as an illustration. We see from the exhibit that the U.S. short-term interest rate is much lower than the British rate. The British yield curve peaks at around five years, and thereafter the difference in yield between the two curves goes from 300 basis points down to approximately 80 basis points for very long-term bonds. These two yield curves are not atypical: For some dates the yield curve may be upward sloping in one currency and downward sloping in others. Yield curves for various currencies are shown in Exhibit 7.9.

Clearly, the difference in yield curves between two currencies is caused by foreign exchange expectations. Otherwise arbitrage would occur between bonds denominated in different currencies. This key relation between interest rate differences and exchange rate expectations for a given maturity is the subject of our next discussion.

Implied forward exchange rates The purpose of this section is to introduce the analytical tools that can help a manager to choose an optimal investment strategy given a particular exchange rate–interest rate scenario. Our main

EXHIBIT 7.9
Yield Curves for Various Currencies Based on Eurobond Yields

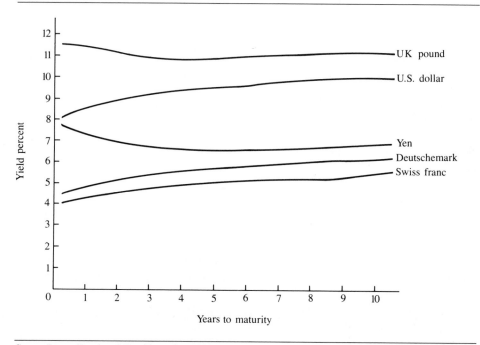

Source: James Capel and Co., November 1985.

objective is to determine the implication for exchange rates of yield differentials on bonds denominated in different currencies but with similar maturities. In other words: How do we compare exchange rate movements and yield-to-maturity differentials?

A higher yield in one currency is often compensated, expost, by a depreciation in this currency, and in turn, an offsetting currency loss on the bond. It is important to know how much currency movement will exactly compensate the yield differential. This subject was already discussed for short-term instruments in Chapters 1 and 3.

Let's consider a one-year treasury bill with an interest rate r_1 in domestic currency, and r_1^* in foreign currency. The current exchange rate is S, expressed as the domestic currency value of one unit of a foreign currency. One year from now the exchange rate must move to a level F_1 in order to make the two investments identical, i.e., have the same total return. In Chapter 1 we called the forward exchange rate F_1. It is expressed as follows:

$$1 + r_1 = (1 + r_1^*)\frac{F_1}{S}.$$

(7.9)

The implied offsetting currency depreciation is given by

$$\Delta S_1 = \frac{F_1 - S}{S} = \frac{(r_1 - r_1^*)}{1 + r_1^*}.$$

As an illustration, assume that the dollar one-year interest rate is $r_1 = 10\%$, the pound one-year interest rate is $r_1^* = 13\%$, and the current exchange rate is $S = 2.00$ dollars per pound.

From Eq. (7.9) we see that the forward exchange rate equals

$$F_1 = S\frac{1 + r_1}{1 + r_1^*} = 2.0\frac{1.10}{1.13} = 1.947.$$

The implied offsetting currency movement is therefore equal to:

$$\Delta S_1 = \frac{(1.947 - 2.0)}{2.0} = -2.65\%.$$

Thus, a 2.65% depreciation of the pound will exactly offset the yield advantage on the British investment.

Similarly, we can calculate implied forward exchange rates on two-year zero-coupon bonds as well as on bonds of longer maturity. By comparing the yield curves in two currencies, we can derive the term structure of implied forward exchange rates, and therefore of implied appreciation or depreciation. The implied forward exchange rate for a t-year bond is given by Eq. (7.10):

$$\frac{F_t}{S} = \left(\frac{1 + r_t}{1 + r_t^*}\right)^t. \tag{7.10}$$

The implied currency appreciation or depreciation over the t-year period is equal to

$$\Delta S_t = \left(\frac{1 + r_t}{1 + r_t^*}\right)^t - 1.$$

The calculations for the term structures shown in Exhibit 7.8 are given in Exhibit 7.10 and Exhibit 7.11. We find that the implied pound/dollar exchange

EXHIBIT 7.10
Implied Forward Exchange Rates and Offsetting Currency Depreciation (U.S. dollar per British sterling)

Maturity (years)	1	2	3	4	5	6	7
Sterling Yield (percent)	13.00	13.75	14.25	14.75	15.00	14.80	14.20
Dollar Yield (percent)	10.00	11.00	11.50	11.75	11.90	11.95	12.00
Forward Exchange Rate (dollar/pound)	1.947	1.904	1.859	1.799	1.745	1.720	1.754
Currency Depreciation (percent)	2.65	4.78	7.05	10.06	12.75	14.00	12.73

rate initially declines with time (pound depreciation). On a five-year investment, the break-even exchange rate is £1 = $1.745, a 12.75% depreciation of the pound. In other words, an investor would get a similar five-year return on the British and U.S. bond investments if the pound were to depreciate 12.75% by the end of the period. Note that this result holds only for investments having this five-year maturity.

These simple calculations assume that we use yield curves for zero-coupon bonds. The formulas are slightly more complicated if we use the yield curves for coupon bonds, because we must assume that the coupons are reinvested each year or semester until final maturity. Computations for coupon bonds are given in the appendix at the end of the chapter.

Currency swaps can be considered a package of forward currency contracts corresponding to each exchange of cash flows. The implied forward rates can be calculated in this fashion.

Applications The implied forward exchange rate is not a forecast, but rather a break-even point. It provides investors with a yardstick against which to measure their own foreign-exchange forecasts. In our hypothetical example, U.S. dollar bond investments are clearly not attractive if we expect a depreciation of the U.S. dollar relative to the British pound. By the same token, a 20% depreciation of the pound makes British bonds unattractive whatever their maturity.

In order to pick bond maturities we examine the term structure of implied forward exchange rates shown in Exhibit 7.11. If exchange rate trends are our major concern, a long-term investment (over seven years) in British pounds bonds is unattractive because the maximum implied depreciation obtains for less than seven years. It should be remembered, however, that this result is atypical. Most implied exchange rate curves are not bumped like that for British pound; usually they just slope upward or downward.

Another illustration of the use of this concept is found in comparing the U.S. dollar and Swiss franc bond market in 1984. In August 1984 ten-year bond yields for U.S. dollar and Swiss franc bonds of comparable quality were 12.25% and 5%, respectively. This disparity in yields suggests that the U.S. dollar would have to depreciate by 50% in order to make the Swiss investment attractive. In other words, the Swiss franc would have to move from roughly $0.4 to $0.8. Although this is not impossible, few investors at the time would have taken the risk of betting on so weak a dollar.

A more precise scenario analysis can be performed for individual bonds. Consider an investor from the United Kingdom who wants to buy bonds

8	9	10	11	12	13	14	15
13.80	13.50	13.20	13.10	13.00	13.00	12.95	12.90
12.00	12.05	12.10	12.10	12.10	12.10	12.10	12.10
1.760	1.781	1.814	1.814	1.798	1.802	1.799	1.798
11.97	10.93	9.30	9.31	10.11	9.87	10.05	10.12

EXHIBIT 7.11
Implied Forward Exchange Rates and Offsetting Currency Depreciation

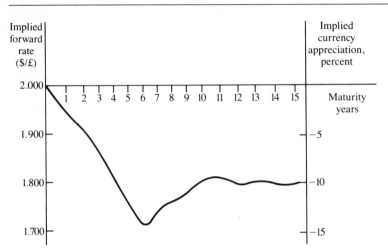

denominated in a foreign currency, say Euro-deutsche marks. Bonds are available on the market, with a variety of coupons and sinking fund provisions. In order to evaluate them, our investor should posit several scenarios for the British pound/deutsche mark exchange rate over time. Actuaries can compute the expected pound return for each bond, given these scenarios; by translating each bond payment at the expected exchange rate on the payment date. For example, a rapid deutsche mark appreciation over the next two years followed by a period of stable exchange rate would make high-coupon short-term Euro-deutsche mark bonds very attractive.

Banks are interested in bonds for both lending and borrowing, and several banks in Europe prepare tables simulating a variety of currency scenarios (i.e., one-time depreciation, trends, and combinations) and their influence on bond returns. A final step is to engage in active currency hedging on bonds, as explained in Chapter 10.

FLOATING RATE NOTES

Investment bankers on the international bond market are notoriously inventive when it comes to escaping domestic regulations. U.S. commercial bankers, on the other hand, are very active in floating new issues abroad. Investment bankers bring domestic expertise from around the world to bear on the international market, and that is why it boasts so many sophisticated techniques. This sophistication is evident in the incredible diversity of bonds issued, which in turn, makes the analysis all the more difficult and technical.

Apart from the straight bonds discussed earlier, there are two other major categories of bonds: index-linked bonds and bonds with options.

Indexation

Several types of index-linked bonds are found on both domestic markets and international markets. In countries with high and volatile inflation, bonds indexed either to inflation or to the price of a specific commodity are common. In 1981, for instance, the UK government started issuing index-linked gilts. Both the coupon payments and the final payment at maturity of these bonds are adjusted in line with changes in the UK retail price index. The French and Danish governments have issued bonds indexed to the price of gold (*gold bonds*), while Mexican firms have issued bonds indexed to the price of oil (*petro bonds*). Other countries have issued inflation-indexed bonds, but these issues mainly attract local investors.

In the Eurobond market private corporations have occasionally indexed coupons to some quantity or price index. For example, Club Meditérranée issued a U.S. dollar bond with a coupon indexed to both the average price of a vacation in their American-zone villages and their occupancy rate. An analysis of index-linked bonds is performed for a French gold bond in Chapter 11.

The most common index-linked bonds are floating rate notes. The coupon paid on these bonds is indexed to some variable interest rate. Floating rate notes do not exist on all national bond markets, but this is rapidly changing. France, where a large variety of FRNs have recently been issued, is a notable example. The clauses used in interest rate indexation are also very diverse, as we see from the examples that follow:

□ The coupon may be indexed to a short- or a long-term interest rate.

□ The reference interest rate may be a recent value or a yearly or quarterly average.

□ The coupon may be pre- or postdetermined, i.e., either the coupon is known for the coupon period in reference to the interest rate valid at the start of the period, or the coupon is set on the payment date in reference to the current interest rate.

□ The spread over the reference interest rate may be multiplicative or additive.

□ Minimum and/or maximum values for the reference rate may be specified.

These diverse clauses make accurate valuation of an FRN a difficult but valuable exercise.

Floating rate notes were first issued on the U.S. domestic market with a coupon set at a spread over the treasury bill rate. Dollar-denominated FRNs are usually in great demand by U.S. thrift institutions because of the development of money-market deposit accounts and the rapid growth of the U.S. FRN market.

The largest FRN market is the U.S. dollar international market. Euro-dollar FRNs represented 40% of all new U.S. dollar issues in the international bond

EXHIBIT 7.12
Cumulative Total Return Indexes
December 30, 1977 = 100

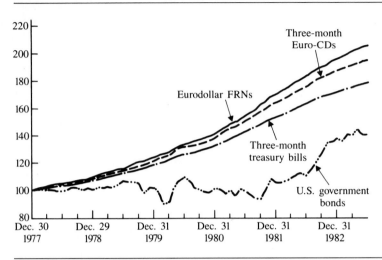

Source: J. Hanna and G. Pariente, *International Bond Market Analysis*, Salomon Brothers, July 1983. Reprinted with permission.

market in 1985. There is also a significant market for floating rate notes in Euro-sterling (British pound) and Swiss francs. Eurobond FRNs are generally indexed to the London interbank offered rate,[7] which is the short-term deposit rate on Euro-currencies. The coupon on Eurobond FRNs is usually reset every semester.

FRN prices behave quite differently from straight bond prices, which adjust to fluctuations in the market interest rate. The price of a straight bond must go down if the market interest rate goes up in order to maintain a competitive yield-to-maturity. By contrast, floaters have coupons that adjust to interest rates, so the coupons react to interest rate movements rather than the bond price. This means that FRNs exhibit great price stability when compared to straight bonds. The difference in volatility is illustrated in Exhibit 7.12, which shows the comparative performance (from December 1977 to mid-1983) of FRNs, U.S. government bonds, Euro-CDs, and three-month treasury bills. All indexes assume that the income is reinvested. We see from the exhibit that the annualized standard deviation of returns on Euro-FRNs (1.5% per year) is historically much less than that on either U.S. government bonds (12.1% per year) or Euro-dollar straight bonds (8.9% per year), though it is comparable to that of domestic- or Euro-CDs (1.5% per year).

From a theoretical point of view, we may ask why there is any price variability at all on floating rate bonds. It turns out that there are several major reasons for this variability, which we will illustrate by taking examples from the Euro-dollar market.

Spread over Index

Borrowers must offer a spread, or margin, over the reference interest rate. This spread is determined by the credit quality of the borrower: The more risky the borrower, the higher the spread that must be paid. As with any other debt instrument, the price performance of FRNs depends on the market perception of the borrower's credit standing. Changes over time in a borrower's credit standing affect the price of outstanding bonds.

For top-quality issuers the spread is very small ($\frac{1}{8}$% or $\frac{1}{16}$%). This is because some of them, like banks, can easily borrow in the Euro-dollar short-term deposit market at LIBOR.[8] The minimum spread paid by these top-quality issuers changes only slightly over time in response to market conditions. This, in turn, affects the bond price of all outstanding FRNs. From 1981 to 1982, for example, institutional investors such as pension funds, savings institutions, and insurance companies entered the Euro-FRN market and accepted a lower minimum spread because the yield was still more attractive than that on money-market investment alternatives such as CDs and commercial paper. All outstanding FRN prices benefited from this narrowed market spread.

On the U.S. domestic market, no corporation can borrow as cheaply as the U.S. Treasury, so that even top-quality borrowers must pay a sizable spread over the treasury bill rate, which is lower than LIBOR. In recent years the yield differential between LIBOR and treasury bills has fluctuated between one and five percentage points. The differential widens when there is a risk of disruption in the banking system. Not surprisingly, the yield on U.S. treasury bills is very low (relative to LIBOR) when the U.S. government is the only safe borrower in U.S. dollars: The government can always print money to pay its debts. Unfortunately, FRN issuers lack that privilege, so that their credit quality is lower. That is why domestic FRNs indexed to treasury bill rates are not an attractive investment during panicky periods. They are as risky as Euro-FRNs, but provide a much lower yield, with the result that their prices drop. This happened in 1982 during the so-called flight to quality, when investors feared Less Developed Countries (LDC) bankruptcies and a collapse of the international banking system. For a time, the treasury bill-versus-LIBOR yield differential reached 400 basis points, and the price of U.S. domestic FRNs dropped by 5%, yet Euro-FRNs remained stable. In fact, U.S. domestic FRNs indexed to treasury bills always exhibit more price volatility than Euro-FRNs indexed to LIBOR, although domestic issues limit price variability by employing more frequent coupon

EXHIBIT 7.13
Price Volatility: Eurodollar Versus Domestic FRNs
Semiannual, long maturity

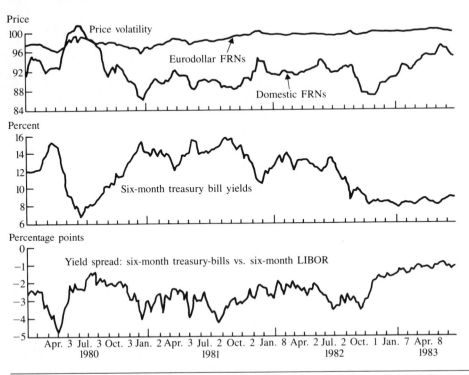

Source: J. Hanna and G. Pariente, *International Bond Market Analysis*, Salomon Brothers, July 1983. Reprinted with permission.

revisions that have adjustable spreads and put clauses. This is shown in Exhibit 7.13.

It pays to be careful in selecting the reference interest rate for an issue. In order to limit price variability, an index should behave like the short-term interest rate available on a typical top-quality borrower in the FRN market.

Maturity

Research shows that long-term floaters are usually more volatile than short-term floaters. FRNs with long maturities also tend to sell at a discount relative to those with short maturities. Several phenomena help to explain this observation.

The first one is technical. FRNs are protected against movements in market interest rates, though they are sensitive to variations in required spread, as we discussed above. Without going into actuarial formulas, it should be clear that the longer the maturity, the more sensitive a bond is to changes in the required spread. The FRN coupon is not fully indexed to the market-required yield, because the interest rate component is indexed but the spread is fixed over the life of the bond. Note that bonds have been issued with spreads that vary over time but are fixed and known at issue. Other bonds have a spread that can be revised according to market conditions on new issues. If the market-required spread changes over time, the FRN behaves partly like a fixed-coupon bond precisely because of this feature. And we know that technically, long-term bonds are more sensitive than short-term bonds to changes in market yield. By contrast, short-term bonds are repaid sooner, and this drives their prices close to par.

A second explanation has to do with credit risk. Market perceptions of credit risk are more likely to change over longer periods of time. If the credit risk premium is an increasing function of time to maturity, the FRN price should increase with time. This stems from the fact that the coupon spread over the index rate is constant, while the market-required spread, which is influenced by the credit risk premium, falls as the bond nears maturity.

Reset Date

FRN coupons are periodically reset. The rollover may be annual (as in France), semiannual, or quarterly. The semester is the most common revision period. This means that the coupon is fixed at the reset, or rollover, date for the coming six months. Therefore, the bond tends to behave like a short-term fixed-coupon bond until the next reset date. FRN prices are more volatile just after the reset date because that is when they have the longest fixed-coupon maturity. FRNs with a semiannual reset date tend to be more volatile than FRNs with quarterly reset dates, while FRN prices tend to be most stable on the reset dates.

This is illustrated in Exhibit 7.14 for the price of a Midland Bank FRN with a semiannual reset. Note that in December 1980 the six-month Euro-dollar rate climbed over 20% just after the coupon on the bond had been reset. This induced a 2% drop in the bond price. By contrast, the rollover prices are stable but increasing over time. This pattern may be explained by both the time-to-maturity effect discussed above and a general decreasing trend in the minimum spread over LIBOR from 1979 to 1983.

Other factors such as minimum coupons, sinking fund, and call provisions may also affect FRN prices.

BONDS WITH OPTIONS

A variety of option clauses may now be found on all domestic bond markets, but with varying frequency. A *call option* permits an issuer to redeem a bond early at a set price. It is the most common option clause in many markets, but is still unusual in the French bond market and in many government bond markets,

EXHIBIT 7.14
Eurodollar FRNs: The Stability of Rollover Date Prices
(Midland Bank, May 1987)

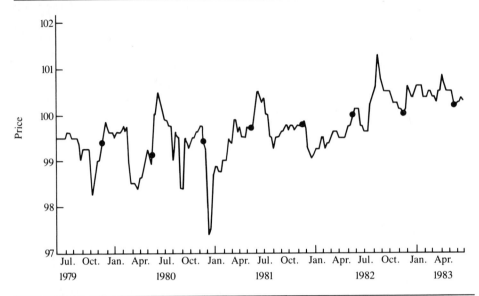

Source: J. Hanna and G. Pariente, *International Bond Market Analysis*, Salomon Brothers, July 1983. Reprinted with permission.

including those in Europe and Japan. A call option works to the advantage of the bond issuer whenever the market interest rate drops because the issuer can call back the bond at a preset price and issue a new bond at a lower market rate. Conversely, this feature works to the disadvantage of the bondholder. In the absence of a call, the market price of a bond goes up when the market interest rate goes down. This is not so when a bond has a call because of the risk that the issuer will call the bond back. As such, the presence of a call deprives the investor of an opportunity for capital gain.

Some bonds are issued with a *put option*, which entitles the bondholder to redeem the bond at a preset price. It is to the bondholder's advantage to do so whenever interest rates go up and the bond price concomitantly drops. Some bonds, such as French and Belgian bonds, have both call and put options with different exercise prices.

The international bond market has seen a large number of innovative option clauses introduced in recent years. Other common options are

- bonds convertible into the common stock of the issuer;
- bonds exchangeable for bonds with longer maturity;
- bonds issued with warrants, i.e., with the option to buy more bonds with the same characteristics at a preset price;

□ bonds with warrants for common stock; and

□ floating rate bonds convertible into fixed interest rate bonds and vice versa.

The advantage of an option clause is that the investor has the right to exercise it when it can yield the most benefit. It protects against risk without affecting the return on investment if the risk does not materialize. When an option has value to the holder, as with a put option, it can be issued at an interest rate lower than the market yield for straight bonds of comparable quality. The investor loses in terms of yield what is gained in terms of risk protection. A major challenge for the investor is determining the value of each option clause. Pricing of the bonds requires knowing how much interest rate reduction the market will accept as compensation for the option.

When an option is controlled by the bond issuer, e.g., a call provision, it is exercised only in the issuer's best interest, which means to the disadvantage of the bondholder. That is why a bond with a call option must offer a higher interest rate than a comparable straight bond.

Option Clause Valuation

A call provision is the easiest to value. Let's consider a perpetuity issued at par in the year 2000 with a coupon of 12%. The bond is callable in 2005 at a price of $100. Let's now assume that in 2004 interest rates have dropped. The very-long-term market rate is 10% and the one-year interest rate is 9%. The term structure of interest rates is therefore upward sloping. Recalling Eq. 7.4, the market price of a perpetuity without a call option is easily computed[9] as follows:

$$P = \frac{C}{r}$$

where C is the coupon and r is the interest rate.
Here

$$P = \frac{12}{0.10} = 120.$$

There is a high probability that this bond will be called the following year at a price of $100. If the bond is certain to be called, it should be valued in 2004 as a one-year bond yielding a one-year return of 9%. Its market price should be $102.75 so that it provides a yield-to-next-call of 9%:

$$P = \frac{100 + 12}{1.09} = 102.75.$$

In practice, we would expect the bond to be called while the market long-term interest rate stays below 12%. Given the 10% rate for the year ahead, it seems likely, but not certain, that the call will be exercised. The market price of this bond should be close to $102.75.

Determining a precise theoretical market value requires an option valuation model similar to the Black-Scholes[10] model presented in Chapter 9. Conceptually, the call option price we derive from the option model should be subtracted from the straight bond price ($120, in this example). Once the volatility of the bond's price has been estimated, the theoretical value of an option to repurchase the bond at a price P_E while it currently quotes P can be calculated. Let's call this value $P_0(P)$. Then, the theoretical value of the bond is equal to the value of the bond without the option clause (*naked bond*) minus the value of the option. The value of the naked bond is simply the present value of all coupon and principal payments discounted at the current market interest rate. In the example, the value of the naked bond is $P_N = \$120$. In this simple approach, the theoretical value of the callable bond is given by the following equation:

$$P = P_N - P_0(P_N). \tag{7.11}$$

As shown in Chapter 9, the option value can be broken down into two parts: (1) the intrinsic value, which is the value of the option if it were exercised immediately, and (2) the time value of the option. The intrinsic value is equal to 0 if the naked bond is worth less than the callable price P_E; it is equal to the difference between the bond price and the callable price (otherwise, $P_N - P_E$). Of course, the coupon should also be taken into account.

The formula becomes more complicated if the call option can be exercised at various dates in the future. Brennan and Schwartz[11] have provided general valuation formulas for bonds with put and call options.

It should be stressed that the concept of a single yield-to-maturity on a callable bond becomes very fuzzy because of the uncertainty as to what the maturity will actually be. Practitioners often choose the minimum of the yield-to-next-call and the yield-to-maturity without the call. In other words, they assume that the most pessimistic scenario will take place. This convention tends to systematically underestimate the true expected YTM because interest rates can move widely before the call is exercisable. A year before the call date, exercise of the call may seem unlikely (high yield-to-next-call relative to YTM), but a year later interest rates could drop, so that it would be to the issuer's advantage to exercise the call. If that happened, the expost yield for the investor would turn out to be the higher, and not the lower, of the two alternatives.

Currency Option Bonds

Because international investors invest in several currencies, some bond option clauses address currency risks. Bonds with these clauses are said to have a *currency option*. During the early 1970s certain bonds were issued with a deutsche mark/sterling currency option. This particular option gives the bondholder the right to receive principal, premium (if any), and interest payments in either sterling or deutsche marks, whichever is more advantageous to the investor. Both the coupon rate and the sterling/deutsche mark exchange rate are fixed during the life of the bond. In June 1972 Rothmans International issued a twenty-year sterling/deutsche mark bond of this type with a coupon rate of 6.25% and a fixed exchange rate of 7.80 deutsche marks per sterling. The bond was issued in sterling so that each £1000 bond paid an annual coupon of either £62.50 or DM 487.5, whichever the bondholder preferred. The exchange rate of 7.80 deutsche marks for a British pound was roughly the market exchange rate at the time of issue. Ten years later in 1982 the sterling/deutsche mark exchange rate had dropped by 50% down to roughly 3.90 deutsche marks per sterling. Naturally, investors preferred their interest payments in deutsche marks at that time, since a coupon of DM 487.5 represented £125, or twice the amount the coupon paid in sterling. For all practical purposes, the Rothmans International bond had become a deutsche mark bond with a coupon of 6.25%, because it is very unlikely that sterling will return to its 1972 exchange rate of 7.80 deutsche marks. Moreover, as of 1982 the sterling coupon rate of this bond was a full 12.50%, since the bondholder could convert the coupon of DM 487.5 at the market exchange rate of 3.90 deutsche marks per sterling and thereby receive 125 sterling for an initial investment of £1000.

A currency option bond benefits the investor, since he or she can always select the stronger currency. On the other hand, the interest rate at issue is always lower than the interest rate paid on single-currency straight bonds denominated in either currency. A call redemption clause usually protects the issuer against a large movement in one of the currencies. Only a few currency option bonds have been issued lately, since they are considered too risky by issuers.

In 1972 Rothmans should have paid approximately 10% on a straight sterling bond and 8.75% on a straight deutsche mark bond. It should be obvious that the currency option bond must be issued at a coupon below the lowest of the two interest rates if the option clause is to be of any value. In our case, a Rothmans bond investor ended up with a deutsche mark bond with a coupon of 6.25%, while he or she could have obtained 8.75% on a straight deutsche mark bond. On the other hand, the investor is better off than if he or she had bought a 10% straight sterling bond.

The value of such a currency option bond can be broken down into two elements: the value of a straight 6.25% deutsche mark bond; and the value of an option to swap a 6.25% deutsche mark bond for a 6.25% sterling bond at a fixed exchange rate of 7.8 DM/£. So, the value of this bond is the sum of the value of a straight bond plus the value of an option on a currency swap contract. Basically, the issuer is writing the currency swap option. Of course, the bond value could also be seen as the sum of a straight 6.25% sterling bond plus an option for a 6.25% £/DM currency swap. The major difficulty in valuing such a bond is the theoretical valuation of the currency swap option.

Feiger and Jacquillat[12] studied the application of option theory to currency option bonds. As with any option model, they found that the value of a currency option bond depends mainly on two factors: (1) the parameters set in the option clauses, such as the conversion rate and exercise data, and (2) the volatility of the exchange rate.

Dual-Currency Convertible Bonds

A more common currency option clause is found in bonds issued in one currency and convertible into common stocks (or bonds) quoted in another currency. Japanese issuers have frequently issued bonds in U.S. dollars (or sterling, deutsche marks, Swiss francs, etc.) convertible into shares of the Japanese company. For example, Toshiba, a Japanese electronics firm, issued bonds denominated in Swiss francs and convertible into shares of Toshiba quoted in yen with a fixed rate of currency conversion. The bond issue is described in Exhibit 7.15. The currency conversion rate is fixed at ¥ 103.44 = SF 1, and the stock conversion price determines exactly how many common stocks can be acquired if the SF 5000 bond is converted. At conversion, one common share of Toshiba is exchanged for 4.3407 Swiss francs–worth of bonds (449/103.44). So, for one bond of denomination SF 5000, the bondholder can get 5000/4.3407 = 1152 shares of Toshiba. Note that the U.S. dollar–based investor has three profit potentials:

1. The investor benefits if the Swiss interest rate drops and the Swiss franc rises relative to the investor's home currency (i.e., the dollar); this is true of any Swiss franc bond.

2. The investor benefits if Toshiba stock prices go up significantly. He or she will convert the bond and benefit from the difference between the conversion price and the share market price.

3. The investor benefits if the yen goes up significantly relative to the Swiss franc because he or she can exchange the Swiss franc asset (the bond) for a yen asset (common stock).

These convertible bond issues also include a call provision, which makes the fair valuation of these bonds difficult.

SPECIAL ISSUING TECHNIQUES

New issuing techniques continue to appear (and disappear) on the international bond market as issuers adjust to changing markets. The most interesting are motivated by currency selection and speculation. These bonds focus on the currency element, but they have no optional clauses as those described above.

EXHIBIT 7.15
Bond Description

INTERNATIONAL BONDS SERVICE

PART 2   **TOSHIBA**

| ADDED TO SERVICE | UP-DATED TO 26 APR.1984 | **2% CONV. 1984-92** |

TOSHIBA CORPN. (JAPAN)
2% CONVERTIBLE BONDS 1984-92.
Sw.Fr.100m. issued at 100% in April 1984 for redemption 30 September 1992.

CONVERTIBLE INTO COMMON STOCK OF TOSHIBA CORPN.

BUSINESS
The Group is engaged primarily in the development, manufacture and sale of a wide variety of consumer electronic and electrical products, heavy apparatus and industrial electronic products ond systems.

PRINCIPALS
Swiss Credit Bank; Swiss Bank Corpn.; Union Bank of Switzerland; Swiss Volksbank; Banque Leu S.A.; Groupement des Banquiers Privés Genevois; A. Sarasin & Cie.; Société Privée de Banque et de Gérance; Groupement de Banquiers Privés Zurichois; Union des Banques Cantonales Suisses; Nomura (Switzerland) Ltd.; Daiwa (Switzerland) S.A.; Mitsui Finanz (Schweiz) AG; Bank of Tokyo (Schweiz) AG; Deutsche Bank (Suisse) S.A.

CONVERSION & PAYING AGENTS
Swiss Credit Bank; Swiss Bank Corpn.; Union Bank of Switzerland; Swiss Volksbank; Banque Leu S.A.; Groupement des Banquiers Privés Genevois; A. Sarasin & Cie.; Société Privée de Banque et de Gérance; Groupement de Banquiers Privés Zurichois; Union des Banques Cantonales Suisses; Bank of Tokyo (Schweiz) AG; Deutsche Bank (Suisse) S.A.

INTEREST
Payable semi-annually on 31 March and 30 September without deduction of tax. The first interest payment will be made on 30 September 1984 in respect of the period from 8 May 1984 to 30 September 1984.

REDEMPTION
a)Mandatory.
Redeemable at par on 30 September 1992; no sinking fund.

b)Optional.
Upon 90 days' notice, as a whole only, on 30 September 1989 or any subsequent coupon date at the following redemption prices:

Coupon Date	%
30 Sept.1989	102
31 Mar. 1990	101-1/2
30 Sept.1990	101
31 Mar. 1991	100-1/2

and thereafter at par.
Co. may redeem all outstanding Bonds on or after 30 September 1988, if for at least 30 consecutive trading days, ending 15 days prior to redemption, the closing price of shares of Co.'s Common stock was at least 150% of effective Conversion Price. Such repayment will be made at the following redemption prices:

6-month Period Commencing	%	6-month Period Commencing	%
30 Sept.1988	103	31 Mar. 1990	101-1/2
31 Mar. 1989	102-1/2	30 Sept.1990	101
30 Sept.1989	102	31 Mar. 1991	100-1/2

and thereafter at par.

CONVERSION
Convertible from 8 June 1984 to 21 September 1992 into shares of Common stock of Toshiba Corpn. at an initial price of Y.449 per share (Y.103.44 = Sw.Fr.1). Fractions arising upon conversions will not be issued nor any cash adjustment be made.

DENOMINATIONS
Sw.Fr.5,000: Sw.Fr.100,000.

QUOTED
Zurich, Basle, Geneva, Lausanne and Berne.

DELIVERY
Europe.

BONDSPEC CODE
TSHE.

Source: Extel Statistical Service, April 1984. Reprinted with permission.

Dual-Currency Bonds

In 1983 and 1984, dual-currency bonds were popular. These bonds were mainly issued on the Swiss foreign bond market. A typical dual-currency bond is a straight foreign Swiss franc issue with interest paid in Swiss francs and principal repaid in U.S. dollars. The amount of dollars repaid is determined at issue with reference to the current Swiss franc/U.S. dollar exchange rate. U.S. and Canadian corporations used this technique to tap the Swiss market, which was the second-largest bond market in the world after the U.S. dollar market. The issuer of a dual-currency bond can convert his or her Swiss francs into U.S. dollars on the spot foreign-exchange market, hedge the stream of Swiss francs coupon payments on the forward exchange market (or through a bank), and thereby borrow U.S. dollars at a cheaper rate than is directly possible in the U.S. dollar market. Swiss-based investors were attracted to the issues by the opportunity for limited currency speculation (on only the principal) that they provided. Those who invested were betting on an appreciation of the dollar. Note that there is no option involved in dual-currency bonds because all of their terms are fixed at issue.

Recently, a large number of Japanese yen/U.S. dollar bonds have been issued. These bonds are issued and pay interest in yen, but are reimbursed for a fixed dollar amount. Borrowers are Japanese corporations, but also non-Japanese entities such as the U.S. Federal National Mortgage Association (Fannie Mae). These bonds are attractive to Japanese investors because they are considered as yen bonds for regulatory purposes. The Ministry of Finance imposes limits on the amount of foreign currency bonds held by Japanese institutions. Dual-currency bonds allow investors to hold a dollar-linked asset, although it qualifies as a yen bond for regulatory purposes.

The value of a dual-currency bond can be broken down into two parts:

1. A stream of year coupon payments. The current value of this stream of cash flow is obtained by discounting at the yen interest rate.

2. A dollar zero-coupon bond for the final dollar principal repayment. The current value of this single cash flow is obtained by discounting at the dollar interest rate.

Partly Paid Bonds

Partly paid bonds are issued in several currencies to attract foreign investors with expectations of downward currency and interest rate movements. This type of bond is only partly paid by the investor at the time of issue and fully paid after a delay of a several months. Of course, the terms of the issue are fixed on the issuing date.

Let's consider the example of a British investor who would like to lock in the high U.S. interest rate on currently issued bonds, but fears a short-term drop in the value of the dollar. This investor may find a partly paid U.S. dollar bond issue attractive; she locks in the high interest rate but fully subscribes the bond only in a few months, with the intention of using fewer sterlings to invest the same amount of U.S. dollars.

Partly paid bulldog sterling as well as foreign Swiss franc issues have also been offered.

The value of a partly paid bond can be broken down into two parts:

1. The value of a straight bond for the part that is paid up immediately.

2. A forward contract on a long-term bond for the part that is subscribed later. The maturity of the forward bond contract is the date of final liberation.

Because a forward contract requires no capital investment, it is not exposed to a down movement in the currency of denomination.

European Currency Unit and Special Drawing Right Bonds

European currency unit (ECU) and special drawing right (SDR) bonds are securities issued in a basket of currencies. The ECU is, by far, the most successful composite currency. In recent years, in fact, the ECU has surpassed the Dutch guilder and the Canadian dollar as a currency of denomination for new issues in the Eurobond market.

The ECU is the weighted average of the currencies of the European Monetary System (EMS). Its value relative to the U.S. dollar is computed daily. ECU bonds pay an interest that is related to the weighted average of the interest rates of EMS members. A composite currency allows investors, especially European investors and borrowers, to limit currency risk. For a French investor, for example, the ECU is less volatile than any one of its currency components, such as the deutsche mark or Dutch guilder. Moreover, whenever the French franc devalues with respect to other European currencies, the French franc value of the ECU correspondingly rises (even though this effect is dampened by the fact that the French franc is part of the basket). In short, the ECU is an attractive investment alternative to single foreign currencies because it is less sensitive to the volatility of a single currency and it is revalued in the event of a depreciation of the investor's home currency. The ECU market is also quite attractive, from a risk viewpoint, for European borrowers. Of course, an ECU bond should be valued as a portfolio of bonds in proportion to the ECU weights.

Swaps

Swaps were described in Chapter 6. A currency swap is the exchange of a liability in one currency (say, U.S. dollars) for a liability in another currency (say, French francs). The stream of coupons and principal payments are swapped at

EXHIBIT 7.16
Currency Swap as a Package of Forward Currency Contracts (in millions)

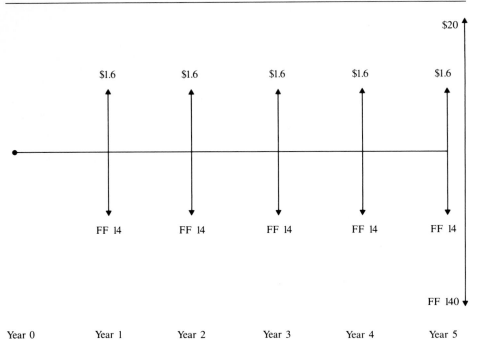

the spot exchange rate at the time of payment, and only the cash flow differential, if any, is transferred.

A currency swap can be broken down into a series of forward currency contracts for each cash flow. For example, let's consider the swap introduced in Chapter 6. Twenty million U.S. dollars are swapped against 140 million French francs. The spot exchange rate is FF/$ = 7.00, the interest rate on dollars and francs are 8% and 10%, respectively. The maturity of the contract is five years and interest coupons are swapped once a year. This swap can be treated as a package of five forward contracts with maturity from one to five years as depicted in Exhibit 7.16.

At the time of issue interest rates in the two currencies are set, so that there is no actual exchange of money. In our example, $20 million is worth FF 140 million at the current exchange rate, and no money need be exchanged to enter into this swap agreement. In a sense, the market value of this currency swap is zero on the contracting day. However, the market value of this swap will change because of movements in interest rates and the spot exchange rate. The question is: How should we value a swap in the secondary market? For example, assume that a corporation bought this swap contract to pay dollars and receive French francs and wants to sell it a year later: How should we price this swap?

Two approaches can be used:

1. We can price the swap as a sum of forward currency prices.[13] In other words, we can unbundle the package of forward currency contracts. There are two problems with this approach. First, it is not obvious that a fixed bundle of contracts would be exactly priced as the sum of its components, because markets are incomplete and the unbundling of packages of contracts is difficult. Second, forward contracts are not frequently traded for long-term maturities, so that forward currency rates have to be inferred from interest rate yield curves as discussed previously. As a matter of fact, it is more common to derive forward currency prices from swap prices rather than the reverse.

2. Swaps can be treated as a portfolio of two bonds, short in one currency and long in the other. Basically, the swap is treated as a back-to-back loan. The value of this hedged portfolio changes if interest rates in either of the two currencies move or if the spot exchange rate moves. Let's denote $P_1(r_\$)$ and $P_2(r_{FF})$ the respective values of the dollar and French franc bonds, given the current market interest rates, $r_\$$ and r_{FF}, on bonds in the two currencies. Then, the franc value of the swap, given the spot exchange rate, S, expressed as French francs per dollar is

$$\text{Swap value} = P_2(r_{FF}) - SP_1(r_\$).$$

This is the value of a swap to pay dollars and receive French francs. The dollar value is deducted from the franc value by dividing by the spot exchange rate, S.

An application of the previous example will illustrate this formula. At the time of issue the two interest rates were equal to the market yield-to-maturity on five-year government bonds in dollars (8%) and francs (10%). Assume that a year later long-term rates have dropped to 7% on U.S. dollar default-free bonds and 8% on French franc default-free bonds; these are yields-to-maturity on four-year maturity bonds. The spot exchange rate has dropped to FF/$ = 6.8.

We now value separately the two bonds implied in the swap. In other words, we treat the swap as a back-to-back loan. The dollar bond was worth $20 million (its par value) when the swap was contracted with a dollar interest rate of 8% $[P_1(8\%) = 20$ million]. A year later the bond is worth $20.677 million at the current market yield of 7%. This is the present value of a stream of yearly coupons of $1.6 million and a principal of $20 million repaid in four years, discounted at 7%. Similarly, the French franc bond was worth FF 140 million (its par value) when the swap was contracted with a franc interest rate of 10% $[P_2(10\%) = 140$ million]. A year later the bond is worth FF 149.274 million at the current market yield of 8%. This is the present value of yearly coupons of FF 14 million and a principal of FF 140 million repaid in four years, discounted at 8%. The value of the swap (to pay dollars and receive francs) is equal to

$$\text{Swap value (in francs)} = 149.274 \text{ million} - (6.8 \times 20.677 \text{ million})$$
$$= 8.670 \text{ million}.$$

In dollars, the swap is worth $1.275 million.

The only practical problem in this approach is determining the relevant market interest rates used on both sides of the swap. For example, the French yield could be equal to the government bond yield plus twenty basis points.

Interest rate swaps can be valued likewise using a hedge portfolio of a fixed rate bond and a floating rate bond. The same applies to a mixed currency–interest rate swap.

PORTFOLIO STRATEGIES

The diversification benefits brought by an international bond portfolio are stressed in Chapter 2. The approach to international bond diversification, present here, may be passive or active.

Passive Management

Index funds In a passive approach the manager builds a world index fund. The ideal world bond index would consist of all securities contained in the markets, with each issue weighted by its market capitalization. An example of such an index for the U.S. domestic market is the Shearson Lehman Corporate/Government Bond Index which indicates the performance of the U.S. investment grade institutional bond market. The task of constructing a portfolio tracking such a world bond index is formidable, since the index would contain more than 100,000 securities quoted over the world. It is not possible to hold a portfolio including all securities in their market value proportions. A practical alternative is to group bonds in homogeneous groups. A homogeneous group is defined as bonds with similar characteristics and holding period returns. These portfolios can be formed by picking one or more liquid issues from each group. The weighting of the securities would be proportional to the weights of the groups they represent. For example, the Swiss franc market could be divided in five groups by category of issuers and then by maturity (short, medium, and long-term). The five categories of borrowers might be:

- foreign states and supranationals (EEC, world, bank, etc.);
- foreign corporations;
- the Swiss Confederation and cantons;
- Swiss banks and finance companies; and
- Swiss industrial and services.

Note that the portfolio sampling concentrates on liquid issues, since some rebalancing is required to reflect changes in the market composition. Most of the issues are not actively traded so that rebalancing is limited as much as possible. Because interest rate movements are the major cause of all bond price variation (in any currency), the index is not too difficult to track. Furthermore, the stratified sampling accounts for changes in quality spread. Two major problems in the bond index fund approach are the large number of fancy bonds with callable clauses and the poor liquidity of the market for most issues. The technical aspects of bond indexation are discussed in Seix and Akhoury (1986).[14]

A third problem with this approach is the selection of bond indexes recognized worldwide. Some domestic bond markets publish daily, weekly, or monthly bond indexes, but they are not internationally comparable. As mentioned in Chapter 6, a few institutions now publish consistent bond indexes for domestic and international markets. Institutional investors tend to limit their international investments to top-quality risks such as the best sovereign borrowers.

Despite all the technical problems, the great advantage of passive bond management is retaining the benefits of international diversification while reducing transaction costs.

Immunization Immunization strategies are passive in the sense that they are a straightforward, disciplined application of simple and technical rules. Immunization is a strategy designed by pension funds or life insurance companies to construct and manage bond portfolios such that bond values are always in line with the value of their liabilities.

In cash-flow matching, the most direct method a manager selects a portfolio of bonds such that the cash inflow (coupons plus repayments) exactly matches the expected cash outflow of the liabilities (pension plan or life insurance). Matching cash inflow and outflow precisely is difficult and often infeasible. The exact replication of cash flow is often impossible to find in the bond market; it might also lead to a dangerous concentration in a few bonds with little risk diversification.

A practical alternative to cash flow matching is building a portfolio such that its value exactly matches that of the liabilities for any change in the interest rate. The institution could simply achieve this objective by selecting a portfolio of bonds with a duration and initial present value equal to the duration and present value of the schedule liability cash flows. Note that a change in interest rate, as well as the investment time, will change the duration of both assets and liabilities, so that the portfolio of bonds must be continuously adjusted to maintain immunization.

As mentioned above, the single duration measure is strictly valid only if there are parallel shifts in the term structure (i.e., if the yield-to-maturity on all bonds changes by the same amount when interest rates change). If these yields change by different amounts, the relative changes in bond values will not be exactly proportional to the duration and the fund will not be perfectly immu-nized. Some equilibrium models[15] of the bond market have been developed assuming that interest rates follow a "multi-factor" model allowing for twists in the term structure of interest rates. These models lead to multi-factor measures of duration. However, all empirical tests indicate that the simple measure of interest rate sensitivity appears to be very effective in immunizing portfolios and performs as well as the more sophisticated alternatives of the multi-factor models.[16]

The theory of immunization assumes that the only source of risk is interest rate risk. In practice, however, many managers attempt to improve their performance by investing in bonds with default risk (i.e., corporate bonds or municipals). The process for default risk does not lend itself to the application of duration analysis. The application of immunization techniques to non-default-free bonds is expected to lead to imperfect results and should be used with caution. Similarly the calculation of the duration for a bond with option clauses (e.g., early call option) is not simple; such calculations require an option valuation model for each optional clause. Again the duration estimates for a bond with optional clauses should be used with caution, and it might be preferable to limit immunization strategies to straight, default-free bonds.

Financial futures are used to adjust the duration of a bond portfolio. The calculation of the duration of a financial futures contracts such as a Treasury Bill or Treasury Bond is straightforward. Banks are extensive users of future contracts to immunize the interest risks caused by a mismatch of duration between their assets and liabilities.

A pure immunization strategy is passive in the sense that it is purely technical and does not involve any forecast about interest rates. Some active strategies might be designed to attempt to improve the performance of the fund. These strategies imply that the managers choose a portfolio duration different from the riskless duration and according to their forecasts about interest rates. For example, they will choose a lower duration if they expect a rise in interest rates compared to the market consensus implied in the term structure of interest rates. *Contingent immunization* strategies are designed to guarantee a predesignated minimum return and foster the likelihood of slightly higher returns.[17] Of course, the minimum return is less than that promised by a pure immunization strategy.

Immunization strategies are developed for a single currency. Multicurrency liabilities exist for pension plans of multinational firms or for life insurance companies operating in several countries; in this situation, immunization strate-gies should be applied for each currency separately.

Active Management

An active management of international bond portfolios, requires both a good technical knowledge of the various domestic and Eurobond markets and some ability to forecast interest rates and currencies. The neutral position, assuming no forecasting ability, should be market capitalization weights in the major currencies; deviations from these weights are induced by specific forecasts.

As for common stocks, the observation that all bonds issued in a given currency behave very similarly, tends to justify a top-down currency approach. For an international investor, the major differences in performance are caused by the selection of currency markets. All fixed-interest bond prices are influenced by changes in interest rates in the respective currencies as well as the translation in the domestic currency. For example, the dollar performance of all British pound bonds is primarily influenced by two factors: movements in British interest rates and movements in the pound/dollar exchange rate. In comparison, the difference in performance within a market segment is relatively small.

Typically an active management of multi-currency bond portfolios is broken into three stages:

1. portfolio analysis,

2. strategic analysis, and

3. bond selection and arbitrage techniques.

Portfolio analysis The portfolio analysis stage provides the manager or trustee with a good synthesis of the current composition of the portfolio and its exposure (sensitivity) to the various risks involved. It is important to get the breakdown of the portfolio by currency, type of borrower, maturity, etc . . . . The information typically printed for each holding is:

- □ issuer name;
- □ coupon (annual or semester);
- □ maturity date;
- □ call or sinking fund provision (yes or no);
- □ credit rating;
- □ market price;
- □ yield-to-maturity;
- □ yield-to-next-call;
- □ duration;
- □ average life;
- □ capital invested (in local currency);
- □ accrued interest;
- □ total value in base currency (capital plus accrued interest); and
- □ percentage of portfolio value.

Some summary information should be provided by currency. The duration measures the rough estimate of the portfolio's sensitivity to interest rate movements.

This portfolio analysis might be linked to a valuation system designed to compute the fair market value of bonds. Usually the valuation system works by isolating the important characteristics of bonds and then estimating market values for them using sophisticated techniques involving option models. The analysis starts from an estimation of the term structure of default-free bonds and then takes into account:

- □ call or other interest rate related options;
- □ quality spreads;
- □ default risks;
- □ liquidity; and
- □ tax effects.

Strategic analysis The investment strategy is based on forecasted scenarios for interest rates and currencies. Note that exchange rate movements are correlated, to some extent, with interest rate changes so that the two forecasts are not independent. Given the current portfolio, one can simulate the effect of a scenario on the value of the portfolio. This simulation also suggests which securities to sell and buy given the forecasted scenario. The three basic inputs are:

- □ changes in the term structure for each currency;
- □ changes in quality or sector yield spreads (i.e., changes in the spread between the domestic and Euromarket segments); and
- □ changes in exchange rates.

This analysis suggests a revision in the multicurrency bond asset allocation. A comparison between the forward interest rates implied in the market yield curves and the manager forecasts of future interest rates indicates the preferred duration of the portfolio in each currency. This simulation model also allows for a sensitivity or risk analysis.

Bond selection and arbitrage techniques Numerous techniques are proposed to add value to the performance of the basic strategy. Some specialized trading techniques are used to provide incremental returns with very little risk (e.g., securities lending). These techniques evolved over time and are too specialized to be described here.

Valuation techniques are used to detect the cheapest bonds to buy (undervalued) when the portfolio has to be rebalanced. Spread analysis is often used to assess the relative value of two securities with fairly similar characteristics. This spread analysis can even lead to an arbitrage between two bonds. The idea is very simple. Two bonds with close characteristics trade at very similar prices and yield-to-maturity. Each day a manager computes the spread between the two bond prices and plots them. Because of market inefficiencies the spread is likely to be high above (or below) its average (normal) value at some point in time. This is the time to arbitrage one bond against the other. This spread analysis is conducted in terms of yield-to-maturity rather than in terms of prices.

Other bond portfolio management techniques are more complex and involve instruments such as futures or option contracts. For example, one might wish to invest in foreign bonds hedged against currency risks. All these hedging techniques involving other types of instruments allow for monitoring and adjusting the exposure of a bond portfolio to various sources of risk; they are presented in Chapter 8.

SUMMARY

1. We started with a review of the concepts and techniques used in analyzing straight bonds. Yield curves and duration are important concepts in bond management. A comparison of yield curves in different currencies allows one to assess the exchange rate movement implicit in bond yield differentials in two currencies. An investor should compare this implicit exchange rate with a personal forecast of the exchange rate fluctuations over the maturity of the bond.

2. Credit ratings of borrowers are available on the Eurobond market and on a few national markets. Governments, who are the largest borrowers, are rated by the research departments of banks, as well as by various agencies and publications. The assessment of sovereign risk often differs among the various rating organizations.

3. Floating rate notes (FRNs) are bonds with a coupon indexed to some interest rate. Their price is much less volatile than that of a straight bond, but still exhibits some volatility because of the indexation technique.

4. Many bonds are issued with various option clauses. The valuation of these option clauses is important, especially on the international market, where numerous currency option clauses can be found. In a currency option bond, the bondholder can choose to receive coupon and principal payments in either of two currencies at a predetermined exchange rate. Two-currency convertible bonds are very common in the international market. These bonds are issued in one currency, but convertible into common stocks of a company from a country with a different currency. These bonds can be valued as the sum of a straight bond plus an option.

5. Special types of bonds and issuing techniques designed for the multi-currency investor are found in the Eurobond market. The major ones are dual-currency bonds, partly paid bonds, ECU and SDR bonds, and currency swaps. A currency swap is the exchange of liabilities in two different currencies. These swaps can be valued as a package of forward currency contracts. More practically, they can be valued as a hedged portfolio of two bonds, long in bonds of one currency and short in bonds of the other currency. Interest swaps and currency–interest rate swaps can be valued likewise.

6. International bond investment strategies are complex because of the large variety of available instruments. Active strategies start from forecasts on exchange rate movements and changes in the term structure of interest rates in each currency. Bond selection techniques are then applied to each market segment.

QUESTIONS AND PROBLEMS

1. What are the yield-to-maturity and duration for the following bonds:

  □ a zero-coupon bond reimbursed at $100 in 10 years and currently selling at $38; and

  □ a straight bond reimbursed at $100 in 10 years with an annual coupon of 10% selling at $110.

2. Calculate the implied forward rates as was done in Exhibit 7.10, but assume that the yield curves are par yield curves, i.e., yield curves derived from coupon bonds selling at par rather than from zero-coupon bonds.

3. Some of the yields given in Exhibit 7.9 are as follows:

Maturity	U.S. dollar	Deutsche mark	Japanese yen	Swiss franc	British pound
1 Month	7.94	4.44	7.81	4.06	11.50
6 Months	8.00	4.69	7.50	4.25	11.50
12 Months	8.31	4.81	7.19	4.31	11.31
5 Years	9.78	6.40	6.82	5.40	10.90
7 Years	10.16	6.75	7.00	5.45	11.00
10 Years	10.33	6.80	7.33	5.70	11.14
Spot Exchange Rate (per U.S. Dollar)	—	2.50	200.00	2.10	0.70

Calculate the implied dollar forward exchange rates assuming that the interest rates apply to zero-coupon bonds.

4. A young investment banker considers issuing a DM/$ currency option bond for a AAA client and wonders about its pricing. Our banker knows that currency swap options are available on the market and that they could help set the conditions on the bond issue. As a first step, he decides to study a simple case: a one-year bond. The current market conditions are as follows:

  □ one-year dollar interest rate: 10%;

  □ one-year deutsche mark interest rate: 7%;

  □ spot DM/$ exchange rate: $1 = DM 2.

Our banker could issue a bond in dollars at 10%, in deutsche marks at 7%, or a currency option bond at an interest rate to be determined. One-year currency options are negotiated on the over-the-counter market. A one-year currency option to exchange one dollar for two deutsche marks is quoted at 4%, i.e., four cents per dollar. This is a European option (see Chapter 9), which can only be exercised at maturity. The one-year forward exchange rate is

$$F = 2\left(\frac{1 + 7\%}{1 + 10\%}\right)$$

As mentioned in Chapter 2, the forward discount is approximately equal to the interest rate differential. Given these data, what should the interest rate be on a one-year DM/$ bond? How would you determine how to set the interest rate on an n-year currency bond?

5. A five-year currency swap involves two AAA borrowers and has been set at current market interest rates. The swap is for $100 million against DM 200 million at the current spot exchange rate of DM/$ = 2.00. The interest rates are 10% in dollars and 7% in deutsche marks, or annual swaps of $10 million for DM 14 million. A year later the interest rates have dropped to 8% in U.S. dollars and 6% in deutsche marks and the exchange rate is now DM/$ = 1.9. What should the market value of the swap be in the secondary market? Assume now that this was instead a currency–interest rate swap where the dollar interest is set at LIBOR plus $\frac{1}{8}$. What would the market value of the currency–interest rate swap be if the above market conditions prevailed a year later?

NOTES

1. For a description of the various theories on forward interest rates, expectations, and risk premia, see W. Sharpe, *Investments*, Englewood Cliffs, NJ: Prentice Hall, 4th ed, 1987.

2. As mentioned in Chapter 6, different countries have different traditions in adjusting for annual yields. The British (and sterling Eurobonds) use a 365-day year, whereas Americans (and U.S.-dollar Eurobonds) use a 360-day convention.

3. The yield-to-maturity should be equal on similar bonds with the same duration rather than same final maturity. For a more detailed explanation of this well-known result, see Sharpe, *op. cit.*

4. One explanation for this phenomenon is that insurance companies, which are large investors in Japan, prefer coupon income to capital gains for accounting and regulatory reasons.

5. For a detailed discussion of duration, see G. Bierwag, G. Kaufmann, and A. L. Toevs, "Duration: Its Development and Use in Bond Portfolio Management," *Financial Analysts Journal*, July/August 1983; H. G. Fong and K. J. Fabozzi, *Fixed Income Portfolio Management*, Homewood, IL: Dow Jones-Irwin, 1985; and G. Bierwag,

G. Kaufmann, and A. L. Toevs (eds), *Innovations in Bond Portfolio Management: Duration Analysis and Immunization*, JAI Press, 1983.

6. See J. Nelson and S. Schaefer, "The Dynamics of the Term Structure and Alternative Portfolio Immunization Strategies," in G. Bierwag, G. Kaufmann, and A. L. Toevs (eds), *op. cit.*

7. The London interbank offered rate is the rate at which banks offer to lend on Euro-deposits. Some FRNs are indexed to the London interbank bid rate (LIBID), the rate that a bank is willing to pay on Euro-deposits. Others are indexed to the LIMEAN, which is the mean of LIBID and LIBOR. (The spread between LIBID and LIBOR is generally approximately $\frac{1}{8}$%.)

8. Banks often issue FRNs for regulatory reasons. For example, FRNs are classified as capital in France and the United Kingdom and help banks meet their reserve and ratio requirements. Japanese banks are required to cover part of their short-term international lending with long-term financing.

9. Remember that the value of a perpetual bond with coupon C and market interest rate r is given by the formula:

$$P = \frac{C}{1 + r} + \frac{C}{\left(1 + r\right)^2} + \cdots = \frac{C}{r}$$

10. See F. Black and M. Scholes, "The Pricing of Options and Corporate Liabilities," *Journal of Political Economy*, June 1973. Option pricing is discussed in Chapter 9.

11. See M. Brennan and E. Schwartz, "Savings Bonds, Retractable Bonds and Callable Bonds," *Journal of Financial Economics*, January 1977. A put option could be valued likewise.

12. See G. Feiger and B. Jacquillat, "Currency Option Bonds Puts and Calls on Spot Exchange and the Hedging of Contingent Claims," *Journal of Finance*, December 1979. An analysis of currency option bonds on three currencies or with default risk is provided by R. Stulz, "Options on the Minimum or the Maximum of Two Risky Assets: Analysis and Applications," *Journal of Financial Economics*, July 1982.

13. See C. Smith, C. Smithson, and L. Wakeman, "The Evolving Market for Swaps," *Midland Corporate Finance Journal*, May 1986.

14. See C. Seix and R. Akhoury, "Bond Indexation: The Optimal Quantitative Approach," *Journal of Portfolio Management*, Spring 1986.

15. See J. Cox, J. Ingersoll and S. Ross, "Duration and Measurement of Basis Risk," *Journal of Business*, January 1979; M. Brennan and E. Schwartz, "Duration, Bond Pricing and Portfolio Management," in G. O. Bierwag, G. Kaufman and A. Toevs, (eds), *Innovation in Bond Portfolio Management: Duration Analysis and Immunization*, Greenwich, CT: J.A.I. Press, 1983; S. Schaeffer and J. Nelson, "Dynamics of the Term Structure and Alternative Portfolio Immunization Strategies," in Bierwag, Kaufman and Toevs, *op. cit.*

16. Many empirical studies are presented in G. O. Bierwag, G. Kaufman and A. Toevs, (eds), *Innovation in Bond Portfolio Management: Duration Analysis and Immunization*, Greenwich, CT: JAI Press, 1983.

17. See M. Leibowitz and A. Weinberger, "Continent Immunization," *Financial Analysts Journal*, November/December 1982 and January/February 1983.

BIBLIOGRAPHY

G. Bierwag, G. Kaufmann, and A. L. Toevs, "Duration: Its Development and Use in Bond Portfolio Management," *Financial Analysts Journal*, July/August 1983.

G. Bierwag, G. Kaufmann, and A. L. Toevs (eds), *Innovations in Bond Portfolio Management: Duration Analysis and Immunization*, Greenwich, CT: JAI Press, 1983.

F. Black and M. Scholes, "The Pricing of Options and Corporate Liabilities," *Journal of Political Economy*, June 1973.

M. Brennan and E. Schwartz, "Savings Bonds, Retractable Bonds and Callable Bonds," *Journal of Financial Economics*, January 1977.

G. Feiger and B. Jacquillat, "Currency Option Bonds Puts and Calls on Spot Exchange and the Hedging of Contingent Claims," *Journal of Finance*, December 1979.

H. G. Fong and F. J. Fabozzi, *Fixed Income Portfolio Management*, Homewood, IL: Dow Jones-Irwin, 1985.

J. Nelson and S. Schaefer, "The Dynamics of the Term Structure and Alternative Portfolio Immunization Strategies," in G. Bierwag, G. Kaufmann, and A. L. Toevs (eds), *Innovations in Bond Portfolio Management: Duration Analysis and Immunization*, JAI Press, 1983.

W. Sharpe, *Investments*, Englewood Cliffs, NJ: Prentice Hall, 4th ed, 1987.

C. Smith, C. Smithson, and L. Wakeman, "The Evolving Market for Swaps," *Midland Corporate Finance Journal*, May 1986.

R. Stulz, "Options on the Minimum or the Maximum of Two Risky Assets: Analysis and Applications," *Journal of Financial Economics*, July 1982.

Chapter 7: Appendix
Advanced Section on Implied
Forward Rates

Implied Forward Exchange Rate on a Par-Yield Curve

Let's consider the yield curve for coupon bonds selling at their par value. Our aim is to calculate the terminal value of a bond investment, assuming that all coupons are reinvested in the same currency until maturity. Let's call V_t this final value for a domestic t year bond and V_t^* for a foreign t year bond. The implied forward exchange rate F_t for maturity t is given by

$$\frac{F_t}{S} = \frac{V_t}{V_t^*} \tag{7.A1}$$

Let's compute the value of V_t in one currency assuming we know the par yield curve r_t. V_t is equal to the sum of the final repayment (and coupon) plus all reinvested coupons, so V_t can be decomposed into its components v_1 to v_t. For a unit investment (say, \$1) the final payment is equal to

$$v_t = 1 + r_t$$

The annual coupon, which equals r_t, is paid every year. Now, we must determine the interest rate at which this coupon is reinvested. We know that a coupon paid in year $t - 1$ is reinvested for one year, but we do not know at what rate it will be reinvested. The most natural assumption is that it will be reinvested at the forward interest rate derived from the term structure. As we saw above, the one-year forward interest rate from the period $t - 1$ to t is R_t. It is calculated using Eq. (7.A2):

$$(1 + R_t) = \frac{(1 + r_t)^t}{(1 + r_{t-1})^{t-1}} \tag{7.A2}$$

where we should recall that

$$1 + r_1 = 1 + R_1 \text{ and}$$

$$(1 + r_t)^t = (1 + R_1)(1 + R_2)\ldots(1 + R_t).$$

Therefore, the final value, in local currency, of the reinvested coupon from year $t - 1$ is equal to

$$v_{t-1} = r_t(1 + R_t) = r_t \frac{(1 + r_t)^t}{(1 + r_{t-1})^{t-1}}.$$

Similarly, the final value, in local currency, of the reinvested coupon from year $t - 2$ is equal to

$$v_{t-2} = r_t(1 + R_t)(1 + R_{t-1}) = r_t \frac{(1 + r_t)^t}{(1 + r_{t-2})^{t-2}}$$

and so on. For the first coupon paid at the end of the first year, we have

$$v_1 = r_t \frac{(1 + r_t)^t}{1 + r_1}.$$

This gives us the final value, in local currency, of our bond investment, V_t:

$$V_t = v_t + v_{t-1} + \cdots + v_1.$$

A similar computation can be performed for V_t^*, and Eq. (7.A1) gives the value of the implied exchange rate F_t.

8

Futures

Speculative investments offer financial leverage. The capital invested is less than the price of the underlying asset, allowing one to multiply the rate of return on the underlying asset. Because of this leverage, speculative investments may be used either to take better advantage of a specific profit opportunity or to hedge a portfolio against a specific risk.

Investments used in these ways are usually traded on futures and options markets, which allow an investor to speculate, or hedge risk, without much capital investment. Other types of leveraged investments exist in the form of private contracts between two parties. Once signed, these contracts are not easily traded. The scope of this book is limited to financial markets; therefore we only consider publicly available investments such as option and futures contracts.

This chapter describes futures, and options are covered in the next chapter. Strategies using futures and options to cash in on specific forecasts or to hedge specific risks are studied in Chapters 10 and 11.

MARKETS AND INSTRUMENTS

The Principle of a Futures Contract

In a *futures* or *forward contract*, all terms of a goods exchange are arranged on one day but the actual physical delivery takes place at a later date. More precisely, a futures or forward contract is a commitment to purchase or deliver a specified quantity of goods on a designated date in the future for a price determined competitively when the contract is transacted.

Let's consider the gold futures traded on the commodity exchange in New York. Contracts on the exchange specify delivery of 100 troy ounces; all futures prices are quoted per unit, here, per ounce of gold. On December 1, 1983, one could have bought a futures contract for delivery in April 1984 at a price of $420 per ounce. This means that the buyer of the futures contract was obliged to buy 100 ounces of gold in April from the seller of the contract, who likewise was obliged to sell to the buyer. The seller may pick the actual date of delivery during the month of April. The amount of money transacted was $42,000. Exchanges offer contracts with different delivery months: On the commodity exchange in New York (COMEX) gold futures are traded with delivery months in February, April, June, August, October, and December over a two-year period.

A futures contract is simply a commitment to buy or sell. There is no money exchanged when the contract is signed. Therefore, in order to ensure that each party fulfills its commitment, some form of deposit is required. This is called the *margin*. The exchanges set a minimum margin for each contract, but brokers often require larger margins from clients. In fact, two types of margins are required: When the client first enters a contract an *initial margin* must be posted. The amount depends on the volatility of the contract price and hence on the risk being taken. It typically varies from 1 to 10%, depending on the commodity. The initial margin on our gold contract was $1500 for a 100-ounce contract. The *maintenance margin* is the minimum level below which the margin is not allowed to fall once losses on the contract value have been taken into account. The maintenance margin is usually 70 to 80% of the initial margin, but is often equal to the initial margin on non-American futures exchanges. Margins are usually deposited in the form of cash, and the broker pays no interest. But brokers often allow large customers to use interest-bearing securities such as treasury bills as deposits. In that case, there is no opportunity cost associated with a futures contract investment, since the margin position continues earning interest.

Futures prices fluctuate every day, and even every instant. For this reason, all contract positions are *marked to market* at the end of every day. If net price movements induce a gain on the position, the customer immediately receives cash in the amount of this gain. Conversely, if there is a loss, the customer must cover the loss. As soon as a customer's account falls below the maintenance margin, the customer receives a *margin call* to reconstitute the margin. If this is not done immediately, the broker will close the position on the market. The following example illustrates how this works.

Assume that a customer buys an April contract in gold at $420 per ounce on December 1 and puts up an initial cash margin of $1500. The maintenance margin is $1200. The next day the futures price moves down to $415, and the position is marked to market. The customer loses $5 per ounce, or $500 per contract. This amount is debited from his cash position, which is reduced to $1000. The customer receives a margin call for $500 to reconstitute the initial margin to $1500. The next day the futures price moves up to $425 per ounce, and the customer's cash account is credited $1000 [(425 − 415)100 ounces]. The cash account now has a balance of $2200 and the customer may draw up to $700 from the account.

The procedure of marking to market implies that all potential profits and losses are immediately realized. This is a major difference between futures and forward contracts. Practically every day futures contracts are cancelled and replaced by new contracts with a delivery price equal to the new futures price, that is, the settlement price at the end of the day. In our gold example, the contract was replaced at the end of the second day by a new April contract with a delivery price of $415 instead of $420.

The internationalization of futures markets started in 1984. Some exchanges have linked their operations on identical contracts. For example, the Chicago Mercantile Exchange (CME) and the Singapore International Monetary Exchange (SIMEX) created a mutual offset system for their currency and Euro-dollar contracts in September 1984. This interexchange trading system allows a market participant to open a position on one exchange and liquidate that position on another exchange during two different trading sessions. These links provide additional trading hours for investors around the globe. In 1989, the CME announced its intention to develop GLOBEX, a computerized trading system that would allow international, round-the-clock trading. MATIF, the largest futures exchange in Europe, has decided to join GLOBEX. The CBT is studying the development of a competing global computerized trading system called AURORA.

Futures Versus Forward Contracts

Like futures contracts, forward contracts are made in advance of delivery. But a forward contract is a private agreement between two parties. It is not possible to resell a forward contract, since there is no secondary market for it. For the same reason, forward contracts cannot be marked to market, and the customer has to wait for the delivery date to realize the profit or loss on the position. The margin is set initially and never revised. This leads to fairly large initial margins, in order to cover the risk over the life of the contract.

Futures contracts have succeeded because they are standardized. A clearing house handles the two sides of a transaction. For any transaction two contracts are written: one between the buyer and the clearing house, and one between the clearing house and the seller. Through this procedure all contracts are standardized in terms of name of the other party, as well as size and delivery date. To cancel a position the customer simply has to reverse the trades by selling contracts previously bought or buy back contracts previously sold. This creates a highly liquid market in standardized contracts. Forward contracts do not offer the same liquidity because all contracts are different in terms of size, delivery date, and name of the other contracting party. Even if a reverse trade was possible in the forward market (and it would require an identical amount and delivery date), the customer has to carry both contracts until the delivery date,

EXHIBIT 8.1
Major Differences Between Forward and Futures Contracts

Forward contracts	Futures contracts
1. Customized contracts in terms of size and delivery dates.	1. Standardized contracts in terms of size and delivery dates.
2. Private contract between two parties.	2. Standardized contract between a customer and a clearing house.
3. Impossible to reverse a contract.	3. Contract may be freely traded on the market.
4. Profit or loss on a position is realized only on the delivery date.	4. All contracts are marked to market; profits and losses are immediately realized.
5. Margins are set once, on the day of the initial transaction.	5. Margins must be maintained to reflect price movements.

since both are private commitments with two different parties. The reverse trade locks in the profit (or loss) on the initial contract, but this profit (or loss) will only be realized on the delivery date. Exhibit 8.1 summarizes the major differences between the two types of markets.

It should be stressed that futures contracts are seldom used for physical delivery. These contracts are used to hedge, or take advantage of, price movements rather than to delay the sale or the purchase of goods. Most customers reverse their position in the futures market before expiration of the contract.

Commodities

There has always been a need for future markets in commodities with volatile spot prices. Farmers and harvest buyers have long used futures markets to hedge price risks arising from climatic conditions. A large variety of commodities are now traded on futures markets throughout the world, including perishable goods such as soybeans or live cattle, metals such as copper or silver, energy sources such as oil, and a variety of financial contracts, which are described below. For each commodity the quality and quantity of the product traded are precisely specified; similarly, the location and conditions of delivery are clearly defined.

The same commodity is often traded on several futures markets, although the quality of the commodity may vary slightly from one market to the next. Take gold, for instance. Gold bullion is traded on several futures and forward markets throughout the world. Futures contracts in gold bullion of 100 troy ounces are traded on the following major markets:

- New York Commodity Exchange (COMEX),
- International Monetary Market of the Chicago Mercantile Exchange (IMM),
- Chicago Board of Trade (CBT),
- Midamerica Commodity Exchange,
- London International Financial Futures Exchange (LIFFE),
- Hong Kong, and
- Singapore International Monetary Exchange (SIMEX).

Forward transactions can also be arranged on the major spot gold markets, i.e., London and Zurich.

Currencies

The *interbank foreign exchange market* is usually considered the largest market for forward or futures transactions in currencies, although there are no statistics available on its trading volume. As seen in Chapter 3, this forward market is closely linked to that of Euro-currency deposits because of the technical relationship between forward exchange rates and interest rate differentials between two currencies. It is also very large and efficient and boasts minimal transaction costs for normal transactions ($1 million or more). Moreover, the market is open around the clock with participants throughout the world.

As mentioned above, forward contracts are not standardized, and there is no organized secondary market. Currently, forward contracts are usually negotiated with maturities of one month, two months, three months, six months, or twelve months, but contracts with other maturities can also be arranged. Because the length of the contracts rather than the delivery date is fixed, each day a new contract is traded on the market. For example, someone buying a one-month contract on June 2 with maturity July 1 cannot resell it on June 6, since one-month contracts traded on this day expire on July 5.

Furthermore, these contracts involve two private parties, and a reverse transaction to cover the position is not possible, so that the contract has to be held until delivery. Of course it is possible to cover economic positions by making an offsetting transaction on a contract with the same delivery date, but as we just mentioned, these contracts are usually not traded on the interbank market. To assist a customer, a bank may propose a forward contract tailored to the customer's needs, and charge a large commission for this service. In the foregoing example a bank would propose a forward contract with a maturity of twenty-five days expiring on July 5. The Eurobond currency swaps described in Chapters 6 and 7 are a form of forward exchange rate contract. They involve swapping at a fixed exchange rate a series of cash flows denominated in one

EXHIBIT 8.2
Quotations for Currency Futures

```
Currency Futures
                                        Lifetime      Open
          Open  High  Low Settle Change High  Low  Interest
   BRITISH POUND (IMM)—25,000 pounds; $ per pound
Sept 1.4735 1.4820 1.4675 1.4765 − .0125 1.5435 1.3240 28,123
Dec  1.4630 1.4695 1.4560 1.4650 − .0125 1.5360 1.3250    881
   Est vol 8,877; vol Fri 16,430; open int 29,024, +329.
   CANADIAN DOLLAR (IMM)—100,000 dlrs.; $ per Can $
Sept  .7244 .7247 .7239 .7246 +.0011  .7305  .6809  8,529
Dec   .7210 .7215 .7205 .7212 +.0011  .7285  .6790  1,675
Mar87 .7175 .7182 .7175 .7178 +.0011  .7256  .6770    393
   Est vol 763; vol Fri 1,004; open int 10,670, −41.
   JAPANESE YEN (IMM) 12.5 million yen; $ per yen (.00)
Sept  .6238 .6288 .6230 .6282 +.0072  .6317  .4690 44,512
Dec   .6270 .6321 .6264 .6314 +.0072  .6348  .4720  1,511
Mar87  ....  .... .6350 +.0072  .6354  .5850    295
   Est vol 16,968; vol Fri 21,955; open int 46,318, −2,247.
   SWISS FRANC (IMM)—125,000 francs-$ per franc
Sept  .5601 .5663 .5593 .5657 +.0084  .5717  .4790 29,502
Dec   .5631 .5688 .5612 .5680 +.0083  .5743  .4878  2,124
   Est vol 18,735; vol Fri 26,630; open int 31,660, −1,690.
   W. GERMAN MARK (IMM)—125,000 marks; $ per mark
Sept  .4587 .4632 .4577 .4631 +.0063  .4675  .3762 42,469
Dec   .4610 .4652 .4601 .4654 +.0063  .4703  .4090  1,107
   Est vol 19,655; vol Fri 29,266; open int 43,670, −835.
```

Source: Wall Street Journal (Europe), July 16, 1986, © copyright 1986, Dow Jones & Co., Inc. All rights
reserved worldwide. Reprinted with permission.

currency for a series of cash flows denominated in another currency. This swap
may be regarded as a package, or strip, of forward currency contracts on each of
the coupon and principal payment dates. This currency swap market allows for
long-term currency hedging. The forward and futures markets cover contracts
ranging from one month to two years in length, whereas swaps extend this
range to ten years.

Futures markets in currencies follow the same rules as commodity futures.
The International Monetary Market of the Chicago Mercantile Exchange trades
in futures contracts[1] for French francs, Canadian dollars, Dutch guilders,
Mexican pesos, British pounds, Japanese yen, deutsche marks, and Swiss francs.
Active trading takes place in the last four currencies. As shown in Exhibit 8.2, all
prices are expressed in U.S. dollars per unit of foreign currency. One could have
bought one deutsche mark contract with a December delivery wherein one
would have agreed to buy 125,000 deutsche marks in December for a price of
0.4654 dollars per deutsche mark. If the deutsche mark appreciated and went
above 0.4654 dollars by December, the buyer would have made a profit; if not,
the buyer would have taken a loss.

The currency futures quotations[2] shown in Exhibit 8.2 illustrate the type of
information available in the international financial press. For example, the
bottom of the table gives futures prices for the deutsche mark contracts. All
contract prices are given per unit of goods traded, i.e., one deutsche mark. The
December contract opened at 0.4610 dollars per deutsche mark and closed, or
settled, at 0.4654. The high and low price of the day were 0.4652 and 0.4601

dollars. The *change* gives the price change from the settlement price on the previous day. The settlement price is also the price used for the marking-to-market procedure. The buyer of one December deutsche mark contract would have gained $787.50 from the previous day of quotation (DM 125,000 × 0.0063$/DM). The *open interest* is the amount of contracts outstanding.

The advantage of currency futures is that the investor may transact in small amounts for reasonable transaction costs. Moreover, the market is very liquid. An investor may engage in active currency exposure management, since clearing procedures allow him or her to cover positions at any time by reverse transactions in the futures contracts. In addition, the margins are less than on the interbank market, and the procedure of marking to market allows an investor to realize a profit or a loss immediately rather than having to wait until delivery. As with commodity futures, few contracts result in actual delivery because reverse trades are usually made to cancel the position before the delivery date.

Some currency and gold futures contracts are traded in several markets throughout the world (e.g., London, Singapore, Chicago Mercantile Exchange). Trading links between the markets allow positions that are opened in one market to be liquidated in another. This permits around-the-world around-the-clock trading.

Futures contracts usually express the exchange rate of the U.S. dollar relative to another currency. A Swiss investor wanting to hedge the currency risk of British assets has to take two positions: one in British pounds (relative to U.S. dollars) and the other in Swiss francs (relative to U.S. dollars). For example, to hedge British assets against the risk of a pound depreciation relative to the Swiss franc, an investor would sell British pound futures and buy Swiss franc futures.

In general, forward and futures currency contracts are used by investors to manage their exposure to currency risk. Their purposes range from hedging exchange risk on the foreign part of their portfolio to pure speculation on currencies.

Interest Rate Futures

The most actively traded futures contracts in the world are interest rate futures such as Euro-dollar contracts or U.S. treasury bonds. These futures are used by commercial banks and money managers to hedge their interest rate exposure, i.e., to protect their portfolios of loans, investments, or borrowing against adverse movements in interest rates. They are also used by speculators as leveraged investments based on their forecasts of movements in interest rates.

Organized markets for interest rate futures exist for instruments in several currencies. Following the United States and the United Kingdom, most countries with a major bond market have either already developed, or are in the

EXHIBIT 8.3

Quotations for Interest Rate Futures

EURODOLLAR (IMM)—$1 million; pts of 100%								
						Yield		Open
	Open	High	Low	Settle	Chg	Settle	Chg	Interest
Sept	93.56	93.63	93.54	93.61 + .04		6.39 −	.04	76,011
Dec	93.46	93.55	93.43	93.53 + .06		6.47 −	.06	38,366
Mr87	93.26	93.35	93.25	93.34 + .07		6.66 −	.07	19,393
June	93.00	93.08	92.98	93.08 + .07		6.92 −	.07	10,705
Sept	92.71	92.80	92.70	92.79 + .07		7.21 −	.07	6,757
Dec	92.42	92.51	92.42	92.51 + .07		7.49 −	.07	5,110
Mr88	92.15	92.23	92.14	92.24 + .08		7.76 −	.08	4,970
June	91.89	91.96	91.88	91.98 + .08		8.02 −	.08	1,632
Est vol 31,938; vol Fri 40,189; open int 16 2,944, +422.								

TREASURY BONDS (CBT)—$100,000; pts. 32nds of 100%								
Sept	99-16	100-17	98-31	100-14 + 34		7.956 −	.107	164,959
Dec	98-23	99-23	98-05	99-20 + 34		8.038 −	.109	23,623
Mr87	97-28	98-28	97-14	98-26 + 34		8.121 −	.110	5,197
June	97-15	98-02	97-15	98-01 + 34		8.202 −	.111	3,372
Sept	96-14	97-11	96-14	97-09 + 34		8.280 −	.113	2,517
Dec	96-13	96-23	96-08	96-20 + 34		8.350 −	.114	1,288
Mr88	95-28	96-03	95-21	96-01 + 34		8.413 −	.116	1,266
June	....	....	....	95-16 + 34		8.471 −	.116	759
Sept	94-24	95-03	94-24	95-01 + 34		8.522 −	.117	304
Dec	....	....	....	94-19 + 33		8.570 −	.114	112
Est vol 200,000; vol Fri 222,906; open int 203,397, +6,152.								

process of developing, a futures market for long-term bonds, and sometimes short-term paper.

Active U.S. dollar markets currently exist in three-month U.S. treasury bills and Euro-dollar deposits for short-term interest rates, and in twenty-year 8% treasury bonds for long-term rates. Other futures contracts have been introduced for certificates of deposit (CDs), commercial paper, five- and ten-year treasury bonds, and the mortgage bonds known as Ginnie Maes, or GNMA. Similarly, the London International Financial Futures Exchange offers a three-month sterling deposit contract, a three- to four-and-a-half-year 12% UK gilt contract, and a twenty-year 12% UK gilt contract. The Paris Bourse (MATIF) proposes a fifteen-year 10% government bond contract and a three-month treasury bill contract. The Tokyo Stock Exchange offers contracts on ten-year bonds with a 6% yield. The Sydney Futures Exchange proposes contracts for three-month Australian bills and ten-year Australian bonds. Euro-dollar contracts are traded on several exchanges in the United States, Canada, London, and Singapore. These interest rate futures markets are growing rapidly throughout the world, and new contracts are continually created to fit the needs of banks and investors.

The quotation method used for these contracts is difficult to understand, but tends to be similar among countries. Quotations for U.S. interest rate futures are given in Exhibit 8.3. Contracts on short-term instruments are quoted at a discount from 100. At delivery, the contract price equals 100 minus the interest rate of the underlying instrument. For example, three-month Euro-dollar contracts are denominated in units of $1 million; the price is quoted in points of 100%. For this reason the September contract in Exhibit 8.3 is quoted at 93.61% on the IMM. The price of 93.61% is linked to an interest rate on three-month Euro-dollar deposits of 6.39% (100 minus 93.61). If the three-month interest rate at delivery is less than 6.39%, the buyer of the contract at 93.61% will make a profit.

This quotation method is drawn from the treasury bill market. However, further calculations are required to derive the profit or loss on such a futures position, since the interest rates for three-month instruments are quoted on an annual basis. The true interest paid on a three-month instrument is equal to the annual yield divided by four. Therefore, the profit or loss on one unit of a Euro-dollar contract (or any other three-month financial contract) equals the futures price variation divided by four. The total gain or loss on one contract is therefore equal to

$$\text{Gain (loss)} = \left(\frac{\text{Futures price variation}}{4} \right) \text{Size of contract}.$$

Assume that in September the Euro-dollar interest rate drops to 6% on the delivery date. The futures price will be 94% on that date. The profit to the buyer of one contract is

$$\text{Gain} = \left(\frac{94\% - 93.61\%}{4} \right) \$1 \text{ million} = \$975.$$

The same quotation technique is used for treasury bills and other short-term interest rate contracts.

The quotation method for contracts on long-term instruments is quite different. The contract is usually defined in reference to a theoretical bond of well-defined characteristics, usually called a *notional bond*. For example, the U.S. treasury bond contracts traded on the Chicago Board of Trade as well as on the LIFFE are defined in reference to a notional treasury bond with an 8% yield and a twenty-year maturity. The contract is to buy or deliver 100,000 U.S. dollars of par value of any U.S. treasury bond that has a minimum life of fifteen years and is noncallable over that period. However, the futures price quoted applies strictly to the notional twenty-year 8% coupon bond. If the seller of a contract wants to physically deliver a bond, the seller can do so with any U.S. treasury bond that has a maturity of more than fifteen years and is noncallable for fifteen years. The price received for a specific bond is equal to the settlement price of the notional bond adjusted by a conversion factor that takes into account the different characteristics in terms of coupon and maturity of the bond delivered.

For example, a high-coupon security is worth more than a comparable low-coupon bond. Basically the conversion factor[3] equals the present value of the bond discounted at 8%. Thus, bonds with coupons in excess of 8% have conversion factors greater than one. Bonds with coupons below 8% have conversion factors less than one. The invoice price of a delivery is therefore equal to the futures settlement price times the contract size times the conversion factor:

$$\begin{array}{ccccc} \text{Principal} = & \text{Futures} & \times \text{Contract} & \times & \text{Conversion} \\ \text{invoice} & \text{settlement} & \text{size} & & \text{factor.} \end{array}$$

The delivery invoice is adjusted for accrued interest on the delivered bond. At each point in time some bonds will be cheaper to deliver than others: their invoice cost will be less than that for other securities. Futures prices tend to correlate most closely with the price of the cheapest-to-deliver security.

As shown in Exhibit 8.3 the quotations are expressed in points and thirty-seconds of 100%. The quotation is in percentage of the par value of the bond. For example, the December 1986 contract of treasury bonds settled at $99\frac{20}{32}$ on July 14. The change from the previous day's settlement price was $\frac{34}{32}$, or more than one percentage point (100 basis points). This exhibit also gives the calculated yield-to-maturity and its change from the previous day. With a price of $99\frac{20}{32}$, the notional bond has a yield-to-maturity of 8.038%. Because of the inverse relationship between the long-term interest rate and the market price of a bond (see Chapter 7) the buyer of a bond contract gains if the interest rate drops (the bond price rises) and loses if the interest rate rises. The gain or loss is simply equal to the futures price variation, in percent, times the size of the contract. In our illustration, the gain made on one U.S. treasury-bond contract from the previous trading day is equal to

$$\text{Gain} = \frac{34}{32}\% \times \$100,000 = \$1062.50.$$

The degree of international interest in financial futures is illustrated by the fact that the most active futures contract in terms of dollar value of the underlying security is the Euro-dollar contract. As shown in Exhibit 8.3, the total dollar value of Euro-dollars exchanged in July 1986 was $31,938 \times \$1$ million = $31.9 billion, as opposed to $20 billion for U.S. treasury bonds. In 1987, Euro-dollar contracts dominated any other futures contract, financial or nonfinancial, throughout the world in terms of amount of the underlying asset. Futures contracts in the Japanese government bond are also very active; in 1987 the par value of bonds traded daily was comparable to that of U.S. treasury-bond contracts.

Some interest rate contracts are negotiated outside organized exchanges. Future rate agreements (FRA) are private contracts usually written by banks, which guarantee a client the borrowing or lending interest rate at a future time. On the expiration date of the FRA, the bank pays the interest rate difference between the agreed rate and the interest rate prevailing in the marketplace at the time. It should be stressed that the FRA is disconnected from the actual lending or borrowing. The bank simply pays, or receives, the interest rate difference at maturity, but does not lend to, or borrow from, the client. The FRAs allow a client to lock in a future interest rate, so that they can be used in the same way as interest rate futures. However, FRAs are customized contracts that cannot be traded until maturity. Their advantage is that they can be tailored to the client's needs both in terms of exact expiration date and type of interest rate desired (e.g., six-month Euro-dollar or twelve-month CD). In turn, the bank attempts to hedge its position using other FRAs or interest rate futures.

Interest rate swaps described in Chapters 6 and 7 are also akin to forward contracts. As mentioned above, they may be considered long-term packages of forward contracts.

Stock Index Futures

Stock index contracts are linked to a published stock index. The contract size is a multiple of the index. For example, the dollar size of the Standard and Poor's 500 contracts traded on the Chicago Mercantile Exchange is 500 times the S + P 500 index. As with all futures contracts, the futures price depends on the expected final settlement price, since the futures price converges at expiration toward the spot price of a good or financial instrument. The unique characteristic of stock index futures is that the underlying good, the stock index, does not exist physically as a financial asset. As a result all final settlements take place in cash rather than by delivery of a good or security. On the delivery date, the buyer of a stock index contract receives the difference between the value of the index and the previous futures price. The procedure works as if the contract was marked to market on the last day, with the final futures price replaced by the stock index value. The cash delivery procedure avoids most of the transaction costs involved in buying and selling a large number of stocks. That is why cash settlement is sometimes used for other financial futures contracts. Euro-dollar futures contracts have a cash settlement, and many new contracts are being created with cash settlement rather than physical delivery.

Numerous stock index contracts are available in both the United States and other countries, including the United Kingdom, Brazil, Australia, Hong Kong, and Singapore. Futures or forward markets for individual stocks also exist in some stock markets such as Rio de Janeiro and Paris. The most active contracts are described in Exhibit 8.4. These indexes are usually broadly based to allow for broad participation in the market. One exception is the Chicago Maxi Market index, which consists of only twenty stocks. It is favored because it closely tracks the Dow Jones index and it is easier to arbitrage, given the small number of stocks involved.

All stock index futures prices are expressed as the value of the underlying index. As an illustration, let's assume that the December contract of the Sydney All Ordinary index contract is 1150. The next day this contract quotes at 1170.

EXHIBIT 8.4
Major Stock Index Contracts Worldwide, 1989

Contract	Index specifications	Futures value multiplier
CME, S + P 500	weighted index of top 500 industrial stocks on NYSE	$500 × index
CBOT, Maxi Market	weighted index of top 20 stocks on NYSE	$250 × index
TFE, TSE 300	weighted index of top 300 Canadian stocks on TSE	Canadian $10 × index
LIFFE, FTSE 100	weighted index of top 100 British stocks on LSE[a]	£25 × index
SFE, All Ordinary	weighted index of top 250 Australian stocks	Australian $100 × index
HKFE, Hang Seng	weighted index of top 33 shares on Hong Kong Stock Exchange	Hong Kong $50 × index
Nikkei–Dow Jones Osaka and SIMEX,	unweighted index of top 225 shares on Tokyo Stock Exchange	¥1000 × index
Tokyo, TOPIX	weighted index of Japanese Stocks on TSE.	¥10,000 × index
MATIF CAC40	weighted index of top 40 French stocks	FF200 × index

[a]The futures price quotation is the index divided by ten.

The gain in Australian dollars for the holder of one contract is equal to

$$\text{Gain} = (1170 - 1150)\,A\,\$100 = A\,\$2000.$$

In general

$$\text{Gain (loss)} = \frac{\text{Futures price}}{\text{variation}} \times \frac{\text{Contract value}}{\text{multiplier}}.$$

One may wonder why stock index futures have become so popular. The reason is that, like any other futures contracts, stock index futures offer an investor leverage. One can speculate on or hedge stocks with only a small cash investment equal to the margin. The specific advantage of a stock index contract is that an investor can directly invest in the stock market in a broad sense, without having to bear the specific risk of individual securities. Let's consider an investor who is bullish on an economy but has no knowledge or expectations about individual firms in that economy. What the investor wants is a diversified portfolio that will appreciate with the market rather than a few individual issues, which are vulnerable to specific factors. He has two alternatives: He may either buy an index fund with the associated costs or he may buy stock index futures. Stock index futures are a convenient, highly liquid, and relatively inexpensive way to get a position similar to that of a well-diversified portfolio. They can even be used to *short the market*.

There are numerous situations in which stock index futures are useful:

☐ Because of their leverage and liquidity, they allow for active up-and-down speculation.

☐ Large institutional investors may hedge their portfolios by selling stock index contracts when they anticipate a decline in the market. Hedging avoids the large transaction costs involved in rapidly liquidating a large portfolio. Moreover, the hedge can be undone instantly should expectations be revised.

☐ An investor may be very bullish on specific companies and expect their stock price performance to outperform the market. However, the market as a whole may decline, pushing all stock prices down. The investor can hedge the associated market risk of the selected securities by taking a short position in stock index futures contracts.

☐ Institutions that move large sums of money in the stock market use these contracts to immediately take a position in the market, while slowly lining up sellers of shares at the best price. Even if the stock market goes up before the purchase program is completed the institution benefits from the rise thanks to its *long position* in stock index futures. An alternative strategy is to ask brokers and dealers for a firm price immediately; because brokers require a certain amount of time to line up buyers, they charge a marked-up asking price. This compensates them for the risk of the market going up while they are lining up buyers. With stock index futures the need for this procedure, and the risk premium required, is eliminated. The same applies to institutions wanting to sell large portfolios.

☐ Foreign investors are interested in stock index futures to reduce cash movements between countries and manage their currency risk exposure better. This is illustrated in Chapter 10.

FUTURES VALUATION

Payoff Structure

A whole term structure of futures prices is quoted for every asset. For example, the term structure of gold futures prices for December 1, 1983, is given in Exhibit 8.5. In the spot (cash) market an ounce of gold traded for $400. The futures price quoted on the COMEX for delivery April 1984 was $420, with a

EXHIBIT 8.5
Gold Contract of 100 Troy Ounces on the COMEX; Futures Price per Ounce on
December 1, 1983

Delivery date	Futures price (dollars)
December 1983	403
February 1984	413
April 1984	420
June 1984	428
August 1984	435
October 1984	444
December 1984	452
February 1985	457
April 1985	467
June 1985	475
August 1985	485
October 1985	493

margin of $15 per ounce. Since gold is traded in contracts of 100 ounces, the total margin for one contract was $1500. It is clear that the financial leverage is on the order of 28, i.e., 420 over the margin deposit of 15. In other words, a 10% gold price appreciation would have been transformed into a 280% profit on the capital invested (less commissions and taxes). In a sense, the gold beta of this speculative position (i.e., the rate of return sensitivity to a gold price movement) is equal to 28, the financial leverage:

$$\frac{\mathrm{d}M}{M} = \beta \frac{\mathrm{d}G}{G}$$

where

β is equal to G/M, or the financial leverage
M is the amount of margin, and
G is the price of gold.

Potential gains or losses on the position may be represented either in dollars per ounce or in rate of return as a function of the price of gold at maturity (see Exhibit 8.6). It is clear that the loss may exceed 100% (the original margin).

The Basis

A futures price approaches the spot price at delivery, though not during the life of the contract. The difference between the two prices is called the *basis*:

Basis = Futures price − Spot price.

Futures valuation models determine a theoretical value for the basis. The basis for perishable goods depends on complex factors that are often difficult to

EXHIBIT 8.6
Potential Gain–Loss Structure as a Function of Gold Price

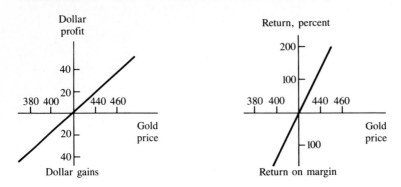

forecast, including harvesting cycles and expected crop sizes. But the bases for financial contracts such as currencies, interest rates, stock indexes, or gold depend on much simpler factors.[4]

The theoretical value of the basis is constrained by the existence of profitable riskless arbitrage between the futures and the spot markets for the good. This arbitrage is often referred to as a *cash and carry* and is illustrated below for several types of futures. Taxes and transaction costs can make futures prices deviate from their arbitrage values.

Gold futures If the futures price gets to be too high relative to the price of gold in the spot market, operators start an arbitrage involving spot and futures positions. They buy cash gold and sell gold futures contracts. As an illustration, assume that the February futures 1984 price given in Exhibit 8.5 was $430 instead of $413. Furthermore, assume that the annual interest rate on three-month borrowing was 12% (or 3% for three months) and that gold storage costs were equal to forty cents per ounce, per month. An arbitrager could have bought spot gold at $400 per ounce, financed the purchase at a 12% interest rate, and stored gold until the end of February. A February futures contract would have been sold at the same time the spot was purchased, for a futures price of $430. At the end of February the spot gold would have been used for delivery of the futures contract. The final result would have looked as follows:

Spot purchase	
Cash	$400.00
Financing cost (3%)	12.00
Storage cost (0.40 × 3 months)	1.20
	$413.20
Futures sale	$430.00
Net profit	$16.80

Arbitrage takes place to eliminate this profit opportunity. Prices adjust until the futures price is such that the basis is inferior or equal to the *carrying costs*, which are the costs of storage, insurance, and financing the spot purchase. Financing and storage costs are, in turn, linked to the quantity of goods and the length of time they are stored. Storage costs may be either fixed or a function of the value insured (the spot price). As a matter of fact, the basis generally approximates carrying costs. If it were significantly less, sophisticated investors would sell gold from their hoardings and replace it with gold futures contracts. Therefore, arbitrage implies that the basis should be close to carrying costs. We assume that the margin is interest bearing, so that there is no financing opportunity cost associated with depositing it.

If we denote F the futures price for delivery at time t, and S the current spot price, a simple theoretical value of the basis is given by

$$\text{Future price} = F = S(1 + r) + k(t, S), \text{ or}$$

$$\text{Basis} = F - S = Sr + k(t, S) \tag{8.1}$$

where

r is interest rate over the period t, and

k is the cost of storage, which is a function of t and S.

As an illustration, assume as above that the three-month interest rate is 3% (12% annual) and the cost of storage is \$0.40 per ounce per month. Then the basis should be equal to \$13.2:

$$F - S = (400 \times 3\%) + (0.40 \times 3) = 13.2.$$

To simplify the mathematical formula, we refer in this chapter to interest rates over the time period considered. If annual rates are used instead, they have to be adjusted by multiplying by the number of days in the period and dividing by 360. For example, the 12% annual rate translates into

$$r = 12\% \frac{90}{360} = 3\%.$$

Commissions should not be neglected in this arbitrage. They are often quite large and affect the theoretical valuation model given above. Moreover, contract prices for different delivery dates may be negotiated at different times of the day, which means that they may be based on different spot prices. Combined with the cost of arbitrage, this introduces apparent discrepancies into the term structure of the futures prices we see published in newspapers. This problem arises more frequently in markets that either are illiquid or have little trading activity on certain delivery dates.

Note that the basis increases with the maturity of the contract, as illustrated in Exhibit 8.5. Similar arbitrage valuation models hold for other financial futures.

Currency futures A futures pricing argument was already developed in Chapter 3. It has been shown that the currency futures exchange rate cannot differ from the spot exchange rate adjusted by the interest rate differential in the two currencies.

Let's take an example where the spot exchange rate S is FF/\$ = 8.00, the U.S. dollar one-year interest rate is $r_\$ = 10\%$, and the French franc one-year interest rate is $r_{FF} = 14\%$. Then the one-year futures rate, F, has to be equal to 8.2909. To illustrate again how the arbitrage works, let's suppose for a moment that the futures rate is only FF/\$ = 8.10. Then the following (riskless) arbitrage would be profitable for a French investor:

Borrow \$1 and transfer it into
French francs on the spot market: FF 8.00

Invest the francs for a year
at 14% with an income of   <u>1.12</u>

                                   FF 9.12

Sell a futures contract to repatriate
enough of these francs to cover the
dollars borrowed plus the financing
cost, i.e., \$1.10. At delivery, \$1.10
will be obtained for FF 8.10 × 1.10   FF 8.91

The FF net profit is   FF 0.21

Arbitrage will take place until the futures rate is such that

$$F = S\frac{1 + r_{FF}}{1 + r_\$}, \text{ or}$$

$$\text{Basis} = F - S = S\frac{r_{FF} - r_\$}{1 + r_\$}.$$

(8.2)

In the example, the futures rate must be equal to FF/\$ = 8.2909.

Interest rate futures

Bonds
A similar arbitrage reasoning holds for bond futures. Let's consider the example in which a British investor has the choice to buy a bond future with delivery in three months or a long-term bond selling at 100% in the cash market with a coupon equal to the current long-term yield, r_L, of 12%. The three-month short-term interest rate, r_S, is equal to 8%. If the futures price is too high, say a

future price of 99.8, the investor should work the following arbitrage:

Buy the bond in the cash market	-100
Incur three months financing costs (at 8%)	-2
Receive three months of bond accrued interest (at 12%)	$+3$
	-99
Sell bond futures (at 99.8) and take delivery in three months	99.8
Net profit	0.8

Clearly the basis has to be equal to the difference between the short- and long-term interest rates (-1% in this example) to rule out any obvious arbitrage opportunities. The bond futures price will be below spot prices if the yield curve is upward sloping (long-term interest rates above short-term rates).

The previous example is, however, somewhat misleading. First, there are several bonds that can be used for delivery, so that the basis must be calculated for each of these bonds; these bases are usually referred to as the *cost of carry*. In each cost-of-carry calculation, the futures price should be adjusted by the conversion factor. Second, whereas the seller of a futures contract may deliver any of the acceptable bonds, the buyer of a futures contract must accept the bonds chosen by the contract's seller. The seller will generally choose the bond cheapest to deliver, which means that the futures prices are generally influenced by the cost of carry of the bond cheapest to deliver. The option to choose the cheapest bond to deliver is a definite advantage to the contract's seller (or short). The relative value of deliverable bonds changes when the interest rate changes. The option to choose the bond to be delivered is impounded in futures prices bidding them down.[5] This may make the futures look inexpensive compared to the cash value of bonds. Conversely, the futures yield may appear high compared to the average bond yield as found on the cash market.

Short term deposit

Short-term interest rate futures create a deposit commencing several months hence. Their valuation is somewhat difficult because the futures are written on a security that has not been issued and therefore has no spot price. For example, the September Euro-dollar indicated in the July 14 quotations in Exhibit 8.3 relates to a three-month deposit that will start in September. Even if three-month bills are traded in July, these are not the bills that will be issued in September. This is a marked difference from other financial contracts, where the underlying security is simultaneously traded in the cash market. (Stock index futures have no underlying securities, but the spot value of the index can easily be calculated at any moment in time.) The short-term interest rate futures are often referred to as *forward/forward rates*; the valuation of such a contract is usually obtained by observing two interest rates currently quoted in the market.

Assume that we want to determine the futures interest rate on the above September Euro-dollar contract. As of July 14 the contract is deliverable in about two months; since the contract is written on a three-month deposit, the final maturity takes place in five months (two plus three). Buying the futures contract in July is equivalent to a contract to lend Euro-dollars for three months in September (two months from now) at the futures interest rate. This is similar to lending in July for five months and simultaneously borrowing for two months. Therefore, the futures interest rate, r_F, is given by the formula

$$1 + r_F = \frac{1 + r_m}{1 + r_d}. \tag{8.3}$$

where

r_F is the futures interest rate,

r_m is the current interest rate to maturity (five months, in the example), and

r_d is the current interest rate to delivery (two months, in the example).

As mentioned above, since interest rates are usually quoted on an annual basis, they should be multiplied by the time to maturity: r is equal to the annual interest rate multiplied by (period = days/360). Annual interest rates are calculated over 365 days, rather than 360, in a few countries such as the United Kingdom, France, and Japan. It might be useful to work this formula through an example.

Let's assume that the five-month annual interest rate is equal to 6.3% and the two-month annual interest rate is equal to 6.068%. The interest rate over the periods are

$$r_m = 6.3\% \frac{5}{12} = 2.6250\% \text{ and}$$

$$r_d = 6.068\% \frac{2}{12} = 1.0113\%.$$

So, by Eq. (8.3) we find that

$$1 + r_F = \frac{1.026250}{1.010113} = 1.015975.$$

Hence, $r_F = 1.5975\%$ and the annual interest rate is

$$1.5975 \frac{12}{3} = 6.39\%.$$

Therefore the futures price should be equal to 100% minus the interest rate of 6.39%, which is 93.61.

Stock index futures Again, the basis for stock index futures is determined by an arbitrage argument. The basis should be equal to the opportunity cost of directly buying the stocks in the cash market; the cost of financing the stocks is linked to the short-term interest rate, while the arbitrager receives the dividend yield, which is not paid on the futures contract. The theoretical value is given by

$$F = S(1 + r_{\mathrm{S}} - r_{\mathrm{D}}) \tag{8.4}$$

where

r_{D} is the dividend yield,
r_{S} is the financing cost (short-term interest),
S is the spot value of the stock index, and
F is the futures value of the stock index.

If the futures price was much larger than this theoretical value (the futures quotes at a large premium), an arbitrager could buy the index and sell the futures. At expiration, he or she would receive the value of the futures, F, plus the dividend yield on the index, Sr_{D}, while he or she would have spent the value of the spot index plus the financing of the spot position ($S + Sr_{\mathrm{S}}$). Arbitrage takes place until the receipt and expenses are equal, as in Eq. (8.4).

Transaction costs to build the arbitrage make all these valuation models somewhat approximate. This is more vividly the case for stock index futures where a large number of different securities have to be transacted to build an arbitrage. Buying and selling programs take place anyway and may affect the stock prices on the delivery date.[6]

Futures and Forward

The pricing relations described above ought to be better verified for forward than for futures contracts. This is because forward contracts have a fixed margin that is not revised over the life of the contract. So far, we have assumed that the initial margin was deposited in the form of interest-bearing securities, so that there was no financing cost for this margin. However, futures contracts are marked to market, so that any loss on the futures position must be paid for and financed. This financing cost is uncertain because it depends on the future price variation. Also, the interest rate used to finance this margin may vary over time.[7] It has been shown that futures and forward prices should be equal if the interest rates are constant over the life of the contract. If interest rates are uncertain, the correlation of interest rate and asset price movements has been shown to be an important variable in the relationship between forward and futures prices.[8]

Other futures contract quirks affect futures pricing. For example, many contracts traded in the United States can be delivered at any time during the delivery month, so that the exact maturity of the contract is uncertain.

Bond contracts traded on the Chicago Board of Trade have an *implied put option* or *wild card play*. The seller may choose to deliver securities on any day during the delivery month. The invoice price is based on the futures settlement price at the close of trading (2:00 P.M. in 1986). But the seller has until 8:00 P.M. the same day to decide whether or not to deliver, during which time the bonds continue to be traded in the cash market. If bond prices drop sharply between 2 and 8 P.M., the seller may buy cheap bonds in the cash market that can be used to deliver at the settlement price fixed at 2:00 P.M. Of course, this option affects future pricing[9] and lowers the value of the futures contract.

HEDGING WITH FUTURES

Leveraged securities allow hedging of specific risks with minimal capital investment. Hedging the risk of an individual asset is easy if futures contracts on that specific asset exist. A U.S. investor holding 1000 ounces of gold bullion may sell ten 100-ounce gold futures contracts when the outlook for gold becomes poor. This action will basically remove the uncertainty linked to gold price fluctuations. However, futures contracts do not exist for every asset, so that somewhat imperfect hedging strategies have to be designed. The major question is: Which futures contracts should be used and in what amount? This problem is all the more important in portfolios with an international asset allocation and numerous sources of risk.

As an illustration, let's consider a Swiss manager worried about the British bond part of his portfolio. The manager might fear an increase in British interest rates, while forecasting a strong British pound relative to the Swiss franc. This would lead the manager to selectively hedge against the British interest rate risk, while retaining the British pound currency exposure. Similarly, the manager might be bullish on a few U.S. companies, while fearing an adverse movement in both the general level of U.S. stock prices and the value of the U.S. dollar. Multi-currency risk management is addressed in Chapter 10; whereas we focus here on the hedging approach to a single national market (commodity, equity, or fixed income).

A hedge can generally be classified as a *cash hedge* or an *anticipatory hedge*. A cash hedge is the hedging of an existing position in the spot (cash) market. An anticipatory hedge involves hedging a cash position that has not yet been taken but is expected to be taken in the near future. A cash hedge generally involves selling futures contracts to cover a cash position and is usually referred to as a *short hedge*. In contrast, an anticipatory hedge generally involves buying futures contracts in anticipation of a cash purchase. This is usually referred to as a *long hedge*, since the investor is long in futures contracts.

Examples in fixed-income management may illustrate these two types of hedges. Financial futures are often used by bond portfolio managers following an active strategy when they fear a sudden, adverse move in interest rates. Futures contracts allow them to adjust a position quickly, without incurring the high transaction costs involved in rapidly rebalancing a portfolio. Two examples illustrate how this works:

Short hedge. An investor has a portfolio of treasury bonds with a face value of $1 million worth $769,000 in the market. She is worried that the weekly money supply figure, announced on Thursday, will push long-term interest rates up. Rather than sell the bond portfolio, the investor can temporarily hedge the portfolio against interest rate movements by selling ten treasury bond contracts on the CBT (one contract for each $100,000 in face value). The futures price for a December contract is $76\frac{16}{32}\%$, which is the price of a theoretical 8%-coupon treasury bond. The investor's portfolio of treasury bonds may be used as collateral. If long-term interest rates go up, the futures price will drop, and the investor will show a profit because her contracts will be marked to market.

One week later the futures price drops to 76 and the market value of the treasury bond portfolio falls to $764,000. The profit on the ten futures contracts is

$$\left(76\frac{16}{32}\% - 76\%\right) \times \$100,000 \times 10 = \$5000.$$

This realized profit offsets the loss of value on the bond portfolio, as illustrated in Exhibit 8.7.

Long hedge. A Swiss portfolio manager has just learned that a client will add $1 million to his account in a week. This cash flow will be invested in short-term Euro-dollar deposits. The current short-term interest rates on the Euro-dollar market are at 10%, but the manager is afraid that interest rates will drop before the cash flow is received and invested. In order to lock in the 10% interest rate the manager buys one Euro-dollar futures contract on the London International Financial Futures Exchange (LIFFE). Recall that short-term futures contracts are quoted as 100 minus the annual interest rate, even for three-month deposits. The futures price on the LIFFE is 90.

EXHIBIT 8.7
Short Hedge

Cash market		*Futures market*
September 1	holds $1 million of a bond at 76.9% ($769,000)	sells $1 million of treasury bond futures at 76.5% ($765,000)
September 8	holds $1 million of a bond at 76.4% ($764,000)	buys $1 million of treasury bond futures at 76% ($760,000)
	Gain − $5000	+ $5000

One week later the three-month interest rate drops to 9% and the Euro-dollar futures price is 91. The cash flow has arrived and is invested at the current 9% interest rate. The futures contract may then be resold at a profit. The profit per unit is equal to the futures price variation $(91 - 90)$ divided by four, because the annual yield must be converted to a quarterly rate for a three-month instrument. The total realized profit on one contract is therefore

$$\tfrac{1}{4}(91\% - 90\%)\$1,000,000 = \$2500.$$

Meanwhile, the cash flow is invested at 9% with a return after three months of

$$\$1,000,000 \times 9\% \times \tfrac{1}{4} = \$22,500.$$

Compared to the 10% interest rate initially contemplated (an interest income of $25,000), there is an opportunity loss of $2500, but the realized profit on the futures contract exactly offsets this opportunity cost. In other words, the manager has locked in the initial high interest rate of 10%. This strategy works perfectly only if the maturity of the deposit or loan is three months and if the starting date corresponds exactly to the delivery date. Unfortunately, this is seldom the case for real transactions. Short-term interest rate futures can sell after a good hedge despite the mismatched dates and maturities. However, cross-hedge risk is introduced, as discussed below.

It should be stressed that hedging with futures allows the reduction, or even the elimination, of the price uncertainty. However, it works both ways: It also reduces the chance of a gain in case of a favorable move in the price of the cash position. In the short-hedge example, the manager will not benefit from a drop in interest rates because a loss on the futures position will offset a gain on the cash position.

Unfortunately, perfect hedges as shown in these two examples are usually difficult to build. In a hedge, risk is eliminated to the extent that the gain (loss) on the futures position exactly offsets the loss (gain) on the cash position. A perfect hedge is generally impossible to construct because futures prices are not perfectly correlated to their spot prices and futures contracts do not exist for all assets to be hedged.

Problems

Basis risks In a few cases one can find futures contracts written on the asset that needs to be hedged, as is the case for gold bullion. Even then, a perfect hedge will only work if the futures and spot prices of the asset vary exactly in parallel. Unfortunately, the basis, i.e., the difference between the futures and the spot prices, tends to vary in an unpredictable manner. The basis is linked to the cost of carrying a futures versus a spot arbitrage position and can be positive or negative. As shown above, the basis should, in theory, be equal to the difference between the income from the deliverable asset and the cost of borrowing this asset (short-term interest rate plus storage costs, for commodities).

Fluctuations in interest rates lead to variations in the basis. In the case of gold futures, the basis increases if short-term interest rates rise. The basis for most financial instruments involves a spread between two rates. For example, the basis for stock index futures is linked to the spread between the short-term interest rate and the dividend yield on the stock index. The basis for bond futures is linked to the spread between the short-term and long-term interest rates. Fluctuations in the spread induce variations in the basis. Therefore, a futures price will not exactly track the spot price of the underlying asset. Also, the basis, as calculated in the valuation formulas above, is only an arbitrage condition that holds within transaction costs. Even if interest rates do not move the basis can fluctuate within the transaction cost band before arbitrage occurs. For example, buy (or sell) stock market arbitrage programs are automatically triggered if the basis (premium or discount) in stock index futures reaches the transaction cost band. The uncertainty about the variation in the basis creates basic risk, which precludes the possibility of establishing a perfect hedge. Strictly speaking, only unexpected variations in the basis create a risk; the basis is expected to converge to zero at delivery. The basis risk is a function of the time to expiration of the futures contract: the longer the maturity of the contract the larger the basis. This is a major reason why investors tend to hedge with near-term contracts despite the commissions involved in rolling over the hedge, if desired, at the expiration of the futures contract.

The perception of basis risk depends on the investment horizon set by the investor. One usually attempts to preserve capital on a daily basis and reduce the daily volatility of a portfolio. In a few cases, investors care only about the value of the portfolio at specific dates, say, end of quarter. One would then try to hedge with futures contracts expiring on the date nearest to the investment horizon in order to minimize basis risk. Note that basis risk disappears totally if one shorts futures contracts whose delivery dates coincide exactly with the investment horizon. This happens because, on that delivery date, the futures price is equal to the spot price and all uncertainty in the basis is resolved.

The existence of basis risk is illustrated in Exhibit 8.8. A gold bullion position is hedged by selling futures contracts of equal amounts of ounces. The spot gold price is $400 per ounce, while the futures price is $413. Many things can happen in a week, and gold prices may go up or down. Gold price risk will be fully hedged because the futures contract is precisely written on gold bullion, the asset being hedged. However, the basis may fluctuate. Several scenarios are presented in Exhibit 8.8, which indicates the net gain or losses per ounce on the fully hedged position. We use the February futures given in Exhibit 8.5.

EXHIBIT 8.8
Hedge and Basis Risk
Profit and loss per ounce under various scenarios of a short hedge

Scenario		Cash (spot) market		Futures market		Basis
Drop in Gold Price						
December 1	buy	400	sell	413		13
December 8	sell	380	buy	393		13
		− 20		+ 20		change = 0
		Net = 0				No change in basis
December 1	buy	400	sell	413		13
December 8	sell	380	buy	396		16
		− 20		+ 17		change = + 3
		Net = − 3				Basis increases
December 1	buy	400	sell	413		13
December 8	sell	380	buy	391		11
		− 20		+ 22		change = − 2
		Net = + 2				Basis decreases
Increase in Gold Price						
December 1	buy	400	sell	413		13
December 8	sell	420	buy	433		13
		+ 20		− 20		change = 0
		Net = 0				No change in basis
December 1	buy	400	sell	413		13
December 8	sell	420	buy	436		16
		+ 20		− 23		change = + 3
		Net = − 3				Basis increases
December 1	buy	400	sell	413		13
December 8	sell	420	buy	431		11
		+ 20		− 18		change = − 2
		Net = + 2				Basis decreases

If the basis remains unchanged, the return on the position is always zero[10] and all gold price risk is eliminated. The only uncertainty borne is that of a change in the basis. As shown in Exhibit 8.8, the net gain is equal to the change in basis whatever the movement in the price of gold. The asset price risk is fully eliminated because the futures contract is precisely written in the asset to be hedged and the only risk borne on this position is basis risk. A short hedger will gain if the basis decreases (a negative basis gets smaller in absolute value, or even becomes positive) and will lose if the basis increases. The reverse holds true for a long hedger.

Cross hedging Unfortunately, futures contracts exist for only a few assets; the chance of matching a futures contract to a specific portfolio of bonds or stocks is slim. A *cross hedge* has to be constructed in order to hedge the volatility of a specific security in a portfolio. A cross hedge means that the futures contract used is different from the initial asset to be hedged. For example, a UK Gilt (long-term government bond) contract can be used to hedge a specific British corporate bond. Clearly the cross hedge will be established so that the price of the selected futures contract most closely correlates with the price of the initial asset. A few examples of cross hedges on individual assets are the following:

- □ Use Euro-dollar contracts to hedge Euro-CDs.
- □ Use gold bullion contracts to hedge gold price uncertainty in a Canadian gold mining stock.
- □ Use deutsche mark futures contracts to hedge Dutch guilders.
- □ Use UK stock index contracts to hedge a specific British stock portfolio.

The prices of the two instruments involved in the cross hedge do not correlate perfectly, so that cross-hedge risk is introduced. For example, the spread between Euro-CDs and Euro-dollar rates may increase, or the specific UK stock portfolio may have a worse performance than the general market index.

Cross-hedge risk can seldom be avoided on portfolios of securities. The only exceptions are portfolios that are specifically designed to track a given market index (e.g., the Standard and Poor's 500) for which futures contracts are available. Hedging each individual security in the portfolio would be a costly and unfeasible task, since few futures contracts exist for individual assets. Instead, the strategy is to hedge homogeneous groups of securities (e.g., UK stocks or U.S. bonds) with global futures contracts such as stock index contracts or government bond contracts.

The combination of basis and cross-hedge risk means that a perfect hedge can seldom be established, which means that an optimal hedging strategy has to be designed to get the best possible hedge.

Hedge Ratio

The result of a hedging strategy depends on finding the proper *hedge ratio*, because price movements of the asset and of the futures are often of different magnitudes. The hedge ratio is usually defined as the ratio of the principal (face value) of the futures contracts used to hedge relative to the principal (face value) of the cash asset position.

The multiplicity of asset types and contracts makes it difficult to give an encompassing definition of the hedge ratio; the one used here fits interest rate futures. In the two examples illustrating short and long hedges, the investors had to hedge a position with a face value of $1 million. In both cases they hedged using futures with a $1 million face value, so that the hedge ratio was equal to one. The application of this definition to other types of assets is somewhat difficult, especially when cross hedges are involved.

A practical and general extension of the hedge ratio definition is as follows:

$$\text{Hedge ratio} = \frac{\text{Number of contracts} \times \text{Size of contract} \times \text{Spot price}}{\text{Market value of asset position}}$$

$$= \frac{N \times \text{Size} \times S}{V} \tag{8.5}$$

where

N is the number of futures contracts used to hedge;

Size of contract is the quantity of assets (e.g., 100 ounces of gold or 125,000 deutsche marks), or the face value of securities (e.g., $100,000 worth of treasury bonds or $1,000,000 worth of Euro-dollars), or the stock

index multiplier (e.g., $500 times the S + P 500);
S is the spot price of the asset; and
V is the market value of the cash asset position.

It is easy to check that this definition of a hedge ratio is consistent with the previous one for fixed-income securities where $\frac{V}{S}$ is the face value of the cash assets, and $N \times \textit{Size}$ is the face value of the futures contracts. This definition equally applies to gold and other commodities. If an investor holds 1000 ounces of gold (spot price, $400 per ounce) and decides to short ten contracts of 100 ounces (futures price $413 per ounce), the hedge ratio is equal to one, since

$$\text{Hedge ratio} = h = \frac{N \times \text{Size} \times S}{V} = \frac{10 \times 100 \times 400}{400,000} = 1.$$

The hedge ratio for a stock portfolio can be calculated in a similar fashion. Note, however, that for stock portfolios the notion of physical quantities (as with a single commodity) or face value (as with bond portfolios) becomes very fuzzy. In this definition, S represents the spot price of the index. Let's consider a portfolio of U.S. stocks with a market value of $1.5 million, hedged with twenty Standard and Poor's 500 futures contracts. The spot value of the S + P 500 is $150, while the futures price is $155. The hedge ratio is then equal to one:

$$\text{Hedge ratio} = h = \frac{N \times \text{Size} \times S}{V} = \frac{20 \times 500 \times 150}{1,500,000} = 1.$$

The determination of an optimal hedge ratio is a controversial issue.[11] The method used depends on what the investor wants to optimize as well as on the stochastic behavior of asset prices. The methods currently used are listed below. The appendix at the end of this Chapter focuses on determining the optimal hedge ratio for a bond portfolio, which is somewhat more technical than determining one for commodities and stocks. Examples of hedging a gold and a stock investment will be used below.

The naive approach: equal position In the naive approach, the principal value of futures contract is chosen to be equal to the principal value of the asset position. The hedge ratio is therefore one. This is the traditional approach in commodities in which hedging is based on the exact quantity of goods held. Brochures prepared by futures exchanges often suggest this hedging strategy. It makes sense for commodities in which futures are traded on an identical commodity. However, if the quality of the commodity differs among the cash futures or if cross hedges are required, this hedging strategy may not be optimal. For example, we may be hedging a small-company stock portfolio with S + P 500 futures. A higher hedge ratio would be required because small-company stocks are more volatile than the S + P 500 index.

The naive approach: dollar matching A variant of the naive approach is to build a futures position so that its dollar market value will be equal to that of the asset position. Instead of matching quantities in position, we match dollar market values. The two hedge ratios differ because the futures price is different from the spot price.

Using gold as an example, our investor would sell $400,000 worth of gold futures, or approximately 9.69 contracts (for the purpose of this illustration, we assume that futures contracts can be fractionated), since each futures contract has a market value of $413 × 100 ounces = $41,300. Therefore, 9.69 contracts will match the cash position of 1000 ounces at $400. The resulting hedge ratio is

$$\text{Hedge ratio} = \frac{9.69 \times 100 \times 400}{400,000} = 0.969.$$

Similarly, the small-companies' investor would sell $1.5 million worth of S + P futures contracts. At market value this would amount to 19.355 contracts, since each contract has a market value of 500 × 155 = $77,500. The resulting hedge ratio is

$$\text{Hedge ratio} = \frac{19.355 \times 500 \times 150}{1,500,000} = 0.968.$$

This dollar-matching strategy assumes that the percentage price movements of spot and futures prices are identical. The equal-position and dollar-matching strategies differ because of the difference between futures and spot prices. The equal-position approach makes more sense. We know that a futures price may be broken down into two parts: the spot price and the basis. The basis is moved by factors that may be quite independent from movements in the spot price, so that the basis component does not provide a hedge against uncertainty in the spot price. Hedges should be constructed to have equal spot value, as in the equal-position approach.

This naive approach may be acceptable for direct hedges when futures exist for the asset to be hedged. However, better strategies have to be used for cross hedges or even when basis risk is significant.

Minimum variance approach Because of cross-hedge and basis risks, it is usually impossible to build a perfect hedge. One objective is to search for minimum variability in the value of the hedged portfolio.[12] Investors usually care about the rate of return on their investment and the variance thereof. So, if they decide to hedge, investors would like to minimize the variance of the return on the hedged portfolio. It is shown in the appendix that the optimal hedge ratio is equal to the covariance of the asset, or portfolio, return to be hedged with the return on the futures, divided by the variance of the return on the futures:

$$\text{Hedge ratio} = h = \frac{\sigma_{PF}}{\sigma_F^2}. \tag{8.6}$$

This optimal hedge ratio can be estimated as the slope coefficient of the regression of the asset, or portfolio, return on the futures return:

$$R_p = a + hR_F \tag{8.7}$$

where R_p is the return on the asset or portfolio, R_F is the return on the futures and a is a constant term. The futures return is defined as the futures price change divided by the spot price. (See a discussion in the appendix.)

The minimum-variance hedge ratio for gold is likely to be close to one: gold spot and futures prices are strongly correlated, with a regression slope of one. This is not the case for many cross hedges. Take the example of our small-companies portfolio. The optimal hedge is derived by regressing the portfolio return on the stock index return. This hedge ratio is the traditional beta used in modern portfolio theory. A slight difference is that we use the index futures return instead of the index return. This introduces a very small difference.

Let's consider a portfolio of small stocks that is more volatile than the market. It tends to amplify the movement in the market index by 50%. In other words, its β relative to the market is equal to 1.5, the slope of the regression of the portfolio return on the market index return. The minimum-variance optimal hedge ratio is equal to 1.5. Whenever the market drops by X% the portfolio tends to drop by 1.5X%.

Utility-based approach The objective set thus far has been to minimize the volatility of the hedge position. But this may be achieved at the expense of sacrificing expected return. More general theories of hedging[13] attempt to maximize expected utility rather than simply minimize risk. The optimal hedging strategy depends on the investor's utility function, so that no general practical results can be found. In the traditional mean-variance approach, an investor would attempt to minimize risk and maximize expected return simultaneously.

Hedging market risk Financial futures are often used to hedge against market risk. The hedge allows the elimination of market risk while retaining specific risk. This is a typical portfolio approach with stocks and bonds. A few examples may illustrate this point.

1. An investor thinks that a couple of companies are undervalued. She will then buy the stocks of these companies and simultaneously sell stock index futures to avoid the risk of a slide in the stock market. When the mispricing of these companies is corrected, our investor will profit regardless of the movement in the market level. If she invests $1 million in these stocks, she should follow these two steps:

□ Calculate the regression slope, β, of her portfolio return with the stock index return. Since the β of a portfolio is the weighted average of the βs of the individual companies, the portfolio β can easily be calculated from the company β values published by many brokers and research services. Assume that the β of the portfolio is equal to 1.5 in this case.

□ Sell Standard and Poor's 500 futures. The hedge ratio should be 1.5. Each contract has a multiplier of $500, and the spot value of the index is 150. The number of contracts required is given by Eq. (8.5) assuming that the hedge ratio is 1.5.

$$1.5 = \frac{N \times 500 \times 150}{1,000,000}$$

where N is the number of contracts. Hence, our investor should sell twenty contracts.

If the coefficient β stays constant over time, the portfolio will be well hedged against stock market risk.

To illustrate the working of such a hedge, let's consider an American who wants to purchase shares of Australian natural resources companies (mines, etc.). He believes that this portfolio of stocks will strongly outperform the Australian stock market. The beta of this portfolio is estimated at 1.15. He wants to acquire protection against adverse movements in the Australian stock market, and sells futures contracts on the All Ordinary Stock Index. The current level of the stock index is 1140, and the December futures are quoted at 1150. He decides to buy a natural resources stock portfolio of A$1 million and to sell ten contracts. The number of contracts is again derived from Eq. (8.5). Since All Ordinary Stock Index contracts have a multiplier of A$100 and the beta is equal to

1.15, the number of hedging contracts is given by

$$1.15 = \frac{N \times 100 \times 1140}{1,000,000}.$$

Hence, $N = 10.09$, or approximately 10 contracts.

The portfolio is now protected against a down movement in the market. A month later the market drops by 10%, while the portfolio only loses 6.9%. A market drop of 6% is implicit in the loss of 6.9% incurred on a portfolio with a beta of 1.15, since 6.9% = 1.15 × 6%. The outcome of the operation is given below:

	Futures market	*Stock market*
September 1	sell 10 December All Ordinary Futures at 1150	buy natural resource stock ($\beta = 1.15$), cost = A $1,000,000
October 1	market declines 10%, but natural resources decline 6.9%	
	buy 10 December All Ordinary Futures at 1036	sell natural resource stocks, proceeds = A $931,000
	profit on futures = A $114,000	loss on stocks = A $69,000
	Net profit on trade = A $45,000	

Despite the fact that the value of the stocks fell, because the market as a whole fell further, the short futures created a greater profit than the loss incurred on the stocks. A profit would also show if the stock market rose (instead of falling) and the natural resource stocks appreciated more than the market, adjusted for beta. For example, assume that the market rose 10% but natural resource stocks rose by 16.1%. A market rise of 14% is implicit in the gain of 16.1% incurred on a portfolio with a beta of 1.15, since 16.1% = 1.15 × 14%.

	Futures market	*Stock market*
October 1	buy 10 December All Ordinary Futures at 1264	sell natural resource stocks, proceeds = A $1,161,000
	loss on futures = A $114,000	profit on stocks = A $161,000
	Net profit on trade = A $47,000	

Note that the hedge allows the investor to benefit not from the market appreciation, but from the differential performance of the natural resource stocks. Because of the basis, the percentage movement in futures prices is somewhat different from that of the spot stock index.

2. An investor expects the spread between Eurobond yields and U.S. treasury bond yields to narrow, i.e., she expects the price of Eurobonds to rise

relative to that of treasury bonds. However, she is uncertain about the prospects of
general interest rate levels. She should therefore buy Eurobonds and sell treasury bond futures. The hedge ratio can be determined as shown in the appendix.

3. A gold bug believes that some Canadian gold mines and French gold-linked bonds are undervalued. He should buy a portfolio of these assets, calculate their β relative to gold price movements, and use this β as the hedge ratio. The sale of gold futures will protect the portfolio against adverse movements in the gold price, while allowing the investor to cash in on the correction of the securities mispricing.

SUMMARY

1. Futures and forward contracts offer high financial leverage and liquidity.

2. Futures contracts are standardized in terms of size and delivery dates. They may be freely traded on the market. They are marked to market every day so that profits and losses are immediately realized.

3. Forward contracts are private contracts between two parties. They are customized in terms of size and delivery date and have to be held until delivery. The margin is set once and never revised.

4. There is a very large interbank forward exchange market as well as a significant currency futures market for the major currencies. All other commodities and financial instruments tend to be traded in futures rather than forward contracts.

5. Futures and forward contracts have a symmetrical payoff structure.

6. Futures and forward prices are usually broken down into the spot, or cash, price of the asset plus a basis. The basis is referred to as a discount, or premium, for currency or stock index contracts.

7. The major question in futures valuation is how to determine the theoretical value of the basis. This is usually done using an arbitrage argument taking offsetting positions in the spot and futures or forward markets. The cost of carrying this arbitrage puts limits on the basis. In all cases, the basis tends to reflect the financing cost of holding a cash position minus the income lost, if any, in holding a futures position. Various technical aspects render the valuation of bond futures more difficult.

8. Futures and forward contracts are used to hedge assets or portfolios of assets against price risk. Several types of hedges can be designed. Two major decisions are the contracts to be used and the amount of hedging. Since few futures contracts exist, investors must often engage in cross hedging by using contracts that are close, but not identical, to the assets to be hedged. The aim is

to use contracts whose futures price most closely correlates with that of the assets to be hedged.

9. Perfect hedges can seldom be created because of basis risk (unexpected fluctuations in the basis) and cross-hedge risk (imperfect correlation between the asset and the contract). Various strategies for optimal hedging in a single-currency context have been proposed. These strategies range from a naive approach to a minimum-variance optimization approach.

QUESTIONS AND PROBLEMS

1. Derive a theoretical price for each futures contract below and indicate why and how the market price should deviate from this theoretical value. In each case, consider one unit of underlying asset. The contract expires in exactly three months and the annual interest rate on 3-month bills is 12%. All rates quoted are annualized.

Gold futures	spot gold price = $400 per ounce; cost of storage = $0.50 per ounce per month
Currency futures	$/DM spot exchange rate = 50 cents per deutsche mark; 3-month deutsche mark interest rate = 4%
Bond futures (8% notional)	current long-term yield = 10%
Euro-dollar futures	6-month Euro-dollar interest rate = 10%
Stock index futures	current value of stock index = 240; dividend yield = 4%

2. A money manager holds $50 million worth of top-quality Eurobonds denominated in dollars. Their face value is $40 million, and most issues are highly illiquid. She fears a rise in U.S. interest rates and decides to hedge using U.S. treasury bond futures. Why would it be difficult to achieve a perfect hedge? (List the various reasons.)

3. In the above example, the average modified duration of the Eurobond portfolio is four years. The manager shares the market view that Eurobond yields for top-quality issues will closely track the yield on U.S. treasury bonds. The current futures price is 80 and the modified duration of the notional bond is nine years. What hedge ratio would you recommend? What about using a combination of different futures contracts?

4. An investor wants to invest in a diversified portfolio of Japanese stocks but can only invest a rather small sum. Our investor also worries about fiscal and transaction-cost considerations. Why would futures contracts on the Nikkei/Dow Jones index be an attractive alternative?

5. A manager holds a diversified portfolio of British stocks worth £5 million. He has short-term fears about the market, but feels that it is a sound long-term investment. He is a firm believer in betas, and his portfolio's beta is equal to 0.8. What are the alternatives open to temporarily reduce the risk on his British portfolio?

NOTES

1. The contract sizes on the International Monetary Market are 250,000 French francs; 100,000 Canadian dollars; 125,000 Dutch guilders; 1 million Mexican pesos; 25,000 British pounds; 12.5 million Japanese yen; 125,000 deutsche marks; and 125,000 Swiss francs. The trading volume has been rapidly growing and is catching up with the volume on the forward market. Over a billion-dollars worth of each of the major currencies is typically traded every day. For example, 16,968 contracts of 12.5 million yen were traded on July 14, 1986, which amounts to roughly $3 billion.

2. Exhibit 3.3 gave similar quotations for forward exchange rates.

3. A detailed description of the delivery mechanisms may be found in Chicago Board of Trade, *Interest Rate Futures for Institutional Investors*, October 1985, and various pamphlets by the futures exchanges. See also D. Fitzgerald, *Financial Futures*, Euromoney Publications, 1983; and R. W. Kolb, *Interest Rate Futures*, Richmond: Dame Inc., 1982.

4. A more detailed analysis of financial futures may be found in S. J. Khoury, *Speculative Markets*, Woodbridge, IL: McMillan Pubns., 1984; N. Rothstein (ed), *The Handbook of Financial Futures*, New York: McGraw Hill, 1984; R. W. Kolb, *Interest Rate Futures*, Richmond: Dame Inc., 1982; R. W. Kolb and G. Gay (eds), *Interest Rate and Stock Index Futures and Options*, Financial Analysts Research Foundation, 1985; D. Fitzgerald, *Understanding Interest Rate Futures*, Euromoney Publications, 1983, and P. Laufman, *Handbook of Futures Market: Commodity, Financial Stock Indices and Options*, New York: Wiley, 1986.

5. See K. Garbade and W. L. Silber, "Futures Contracts in Commodities with Multiple Varieties: An Analysis of Premiums and Discounts," *Journal of Business*, July 1983; G. D. Day and S. Manaster, "The Quality Option Implicit in Futures Contracts," *Journal of Financial Economics*, September 1984; and S. Benninga and M. Smirlock, "An Empirical Analysis of the Delivery Option, Marking to Market and the Pricing of Treasury Bond Futures," *Journal of Futures Markets* 5(3), Fall 1985.

6. A more detailed analysis of stock index futures may be found in N. Weiner, *Stock Index Futures*, New York: Wiley, 1984; W. Nix and S. Nix, *The D. J. Irwin Guide to Stock Index Futures*, Homewood, IL: Irwin, 1984; R. W. Kolb and G. Gay (eds), *Interest Rate and Stock Index Futures and Options*, Financial Analysts Research Foundation, 1985; B. Cornell and K. French, "Taxes and the Pricing of Stock Index Futures," *Journal of Finance*, June 1985; F. Fabozzi and G. Kipnis (eds), *Stock Index Futures*, Homewood, IL: Dow Jones-Irwin, 1984; D. Modest and M. Sundaresan, "The Relationship Between Spot and Futures Prices in Stock Index Markets," *Journal of Futures Market*, 3(1), Spring 1983; B. Cornell and K. French, "The Pricing of Stock Index Futures," *Journal of Futures Market*, Spring 3(1), 1983.

7. For literature on futures and forward pricing, see F. Black, "The Pricing of Commodity Contracts," *Journal of Financial Economics*, March 1976; R. A. Jarrow and G. S. Oldfield, "Forward Contracts and Futures Contracts," *Journal of Financial Economics*, December 1981; J. Cox, J. Ingersoll, and S. Ross, "The Relation Between Forward and Futures Prices," *Journal of Financial Economics*, December 1981; and S. Richard and M. Sundaresan,

"A Continuous Time Equilibrium Model of Forward Prices and Futures Prices in a Multigood Economy," *Journal of Financial Economics*, 9, December 1981.

8. B. Cornell and M. Reiganum, in "Forward and Futures Prices: Evidence from the Foreign Exchange Market," *Journal of Finance*, December 1981, studied the relationship between futures and forward exchange rates; they found no significant discrepancies. Using simulations, most authors conclude that stocks and interest rates and marking to market should have minimal effects on equilibrium prices: futures and forward prices should be very close. See, for example, D. Modest, "On the Pricing of Stock Index Futures," *Journal of Portfolio Management*, Summer 1984.

9. See A. Kane and A. J. Marcus, "Valuation and Optimal Exercise of the Wild Card Option in the Treasury Bill Futures Market," *Journal of Finance*, March 1986.

10. The expected return on the position is really the risk-free interest rate. The basis should progressively converge toward zero on the delivery date. If interest rates do not move, it can be shown that the expected daily change on this fully hedged position is the daily interest rate. This can be easily deducted by looking at the pricing equation, (Eq. 8.1).

   The daily posting of marked-to-market margins renders the theoretical analysis more complicated for futures than for forward contracts.

11. A review of the various hedging strategies may be found in R. W. Kolb and G. Gay, *Interest Rate and Stock Index Futures and Options*: *Characteristics, Valuation and Portfolio Strategies*, Financial Analysts Research Foundation, Monograph 18, 1985; E. Schwarz, J. Hill, and T. Schneeweis, *Financial Futures*: *Fundamentals, Strategies and Applications*, Homewood, IL: Irwin, 1986. See also R. W. Anderson and J. P. Danthine, "Cross-Hedging," *Journal of Political Economy*, December 1981. G. Gay, R. Kolb, and R. Chiang, "Interest Rate Hedging: An Empirical Test of Alternative Strategies," The *Journal of Financial Research*, March 1983.

12. This approach was originally introduced for commodities by L. Johnson, in "The Theory of Hedging and Speculation in Commodity Futures," *Review of Economic Studies*, 27, October 1960 and J. L. Stein, in "The Simultaneous Determination of Spot and Futures Prices," *American Economic Review*, 51, December 1961. It was formalized by L. Ederington, in "The Hedging Performance of the New Futures Markets," *Journal of Finance*, 34, March 1979. It is discussed in all futures textbooks and in numerous articles such as S. Figlewski, "Hedging with Stock Index Futures: Theory and Application in a New Market," *Journal of Futures Market*, 5, Summer 1985; R. Nelson and R. Collins, "Hedging's Performance," *Journal of Futures Market*, 5, Spring 1985; R. W. Gray and D. Rutledge; "The Economics of Commodity Futures Markets: A Survey," *Review of Marketing and Agricultural Economics*, 39(4), 1971; and B. Wardrep and J. F. Buck, "The Efficacy of Hedging with Financial Futures: A Historical Perspective," *Journal of Futures Market*, 2(3), Summer 1982.

13. R. W. Anderson and J. P. Danthine, in "Cross-Hedging," *Journal of Political Economy*, December 1981; S. Benninga, R. Eldor, and I. Zilcha in "The Optimal Hedge Ratio in Unbiased Futures Markets," *Journal of Futures Market*, 4(2), Spring 1984, show that the minimum-variance hedge is also an optimal hedge ratio if the futures prices are unbiased predictors of spot prices.

14. See J. Hill and T. Schneeweis, "A Note on Hedging Effectiveness of Foreign Currency Futures," *Journal of Futures Markets*, 1, 1981; S. Benninga, R. Eldor, and I. Zilcha, "The Optimal Hedge Ratio in Unbiased Futures Markets," *Journal of Futures Market*, 4(2), Spring 1984.

15. Running a regression on price levels results in significant autocorrelation of residuals. Running a regression on price changes results in heteroscedasticity.

16. The advantages of this approach are discussed in A. L. Toevs and D. Jacob, *Interest Rate Futures: A Comparison of Alternative Hedge Ratio Methodology*, Morgan Stanley, 1984; and "Futures and Alternative Hedge Ratio Methodologies," *Journal of Portfolio Management*, Spring 1986. Also, see G. Gay and R. W. Kolb, "The Management of Interest Rate Risk," *Journal of Portfolio Management*, Winter 1983.

17. For details on the application and refinement of this approach, see A. L. Toevs and D. Jacob, *op. cit.* They also discuss the relative advantages of the various methods. The duration of the cheapest-to-deliver bond is often used instead of that of the notional bond.

BIBLIOGRAPHY

Anderson, R. W., and J. P. Danthine. "Cross-Hedging," *Journal of Political Economy*, December 1981.

Benninga, S., and M. Smirlock. "An Empirical Analysis of the Delivery Option, Marking to Market and the Pricing of Treasury Bond Futures," *Journal of Futures Markets*, 5(3) Fall 1985.

Black, F. "The Pricing of Commodity Contracts," *Journal of Financial Economics*, March 1976.

Chicago Board of Trade. *Interest Rate Futures for Institutional Investors*, October 1985.

Cornell, B., and K. French. "The Pricing of Stock Index Futures," *Journal of Futures Market*, 3(1) Spring 1983.

Cornell, B., and K. French. "Taxes and the Pricing of Stock Index Futures," *Journal of Finance*, June 1985.

Cornell, B., and M. Reiganum. "Forward and Futures Prices: Evidence from the Foreign Exchange Market," *Journal of Finance*, December 1981.

Cox, J., J. Ingersoll, and S. Ross. "The Relation Between Forward and Futures Prices," *Journal of Financial Economics*, December 1981.

Day, G. D., and S. Manaster. "The Quality Option Implicit in Futures Contracts," *Journal of Financial Economics*, September 1984.

Ederington, L. "The Hedging Performance of the New Futures Markets," *Journal of Finance*, 34, March 1979.

Fabozzi, F., and G. Kipnis (eds). *Stock Index Futures*, Homewood, IL: Dow Jones-Irwin, 1984.

Figlewski, S. "Hedging with Stock Index Futures: Theory and Application in a New Market," *Journal of Futures Market*, 5, Summer 1985.

Fitzgerald, D. *Financial Futures.* Euromoney Publications, 1983.

Garbade, K., and W. L. Silber. "Futures Contracts in Commodities with Multiple Varieties: An Analysis of Premiums and Discounts," *Journal of Business*, July 1983.

Gay, G., R. Kolb, and R. Chiang. "Interest Rate Hedging: An Empirical Test of Alternative Strategies," *The Journal of Financial Research*, March 1983.

Gray, R. W., and D. Rutledge. "The Economics of Commodity Futures Markets: A Survey," *Review of Marketing and Agricultural Economics*, 39(4) 1971.

Jarrow, R. A., and G. S. Oldfield. "Forward Contracts and Futures Contracts," *Journal of Financial Economics*, December 1981.

Johnson, L. "The Theory of Hedging and Speculation in Commodity Futures," *Review of Economic Studies*, 27, October 1960.

Kane, A., and A. J. Marcus. "Valuation and Optimal Exercise of the Wild Card Option in the Treasury Bill Futures Market," *Journal of Finance*, March 1986.

Khoury, S. J. *Speculative Markets*, Woodbridge, IL: McMillan Pubns., 1984.

Kolb, R. W. *Interest Rate Futures*, Richmond: Dame Inc., 1982.

Kolb, R. W. *Understanding Financial Futures*, Glenview, IL: Scott Foresman, 1985.

Kolb, R. W., and G. Gay (eds). *Interest Rate and Stock Index Futures and Options*, Financial Analysts Research Foundation, 1985.

Kolb, R. W., and G. Gay. *Interest Rate and Stock Index Futures and Options: Characteristics, Valuation and Portfolio Strategies*, Financial Analysts Research Foundation, Monograph 18, 1985.

Laufman, P. *Handbook of Futures Market: Commodity, Financial Stock Indices and Options*, New York: Wiley, 1986.

Modest, D., and M. Sundaresan, "The Relationship Between Spot and Futures Prices in Stock Index Markets," *Journal of Futures Market*, 3(1) Spring 1983.

Nelson, R., and R. Collins. "Hedging's Performance," *Journal of Futures Market*, 5, Spring 1985.

Nix, W., and S. Nix. *The D. J. Irwin Guide to Stock Index Futures*, Homewood, IL: Irwin, 1984.

Richard, S., and M. Sundaresan. "A Continuous Time Equilibrium Model of Forward Prices and Futures Prices in a Multigood Economy," *Journal of Financial Economics*, 9, December 1981.

Rothstein, N. (ed). *The Handbook of Financial Futures*, New York: McGraw Hill, 1984.

Schwarz, E., J. Hill, and T. Schneeweis. *Financial Futures: Fundamentals, Strategies and Applications*, Homewood, IL: Irwin, 1986.

Stein, J. L. "The Simultaneous Determination of Spot and Futures Prices," *American Economic Review*, 51, December 1961.

Toevs, A. L. and D. Jacob. "Futures and Alternative Hedge Ratio Methodologies," *Journal of Portfolio Management*, Spring 1986.

Wardrep, B. and J. F. Buck. "The Efficacy of Hedging with Financial Futures: A Historical Perspective," *Journal of Futures Market*, 2(3) Summer 1982.

Weiner, N. *Stock Index Futures*, New York: Wiley, 1984.

Chapter 8: Appendix
Advanced Section

DERIVATION OF THE MINIMUM-VARIANCE HEDGE RATIO

Let's consider a portfolio of assets with market value V. This portfolio is hedged selling N futures contracts of a specific size. The spot and futures prices are S and F.

From period 0 to period t, the profit (or loss) on the hedged position is given by

$$\text{Profit} = (V_t - V_0) - [N \times \text{Size} \times (F_t - F_0)] \tag{8.A1}$$

Introducing the hedge ratio h

$$h = \frac{N \times \text{Size} \times S_0}{V_0},$$

we have

$$\text{Profit} = (V_t - V_0) - \left[\frac{N \times \text{Size} \times S_0}{V_0} \left(V_0 \frac{F_t - F_0}{S_0} \right) \right]. \tag{8.A2}$$

The rate of return on the hedged position, R_H, is equal to

$$\text{Rate of return hedged} = R_H = \frac{V_t - V_0}{V_0} - \left[\left(\frac{N \times \text{Size} \times S_0}{V_0} \right) \left(\frac{F_t - F_0}{S_0} \right) \right] \tag{8.A3}$$

where

R_H is the rate of return on hedged portfolio,
R_P is the rate of return on asset portfolio,
R_F is the rate of return on futures $\dfrac{F_t - F_0}{S_0}$, and
h is the hedge ratio.

Eq. (8.A3) is equivalent to

$$R_H = R_P - h R_F.$$

The variance of return is equal to

$$\sigma_H^2 = \sigma_P^2 + h^2 \sigma_F^2 - 2h \sigma_{PF} \tag{8.A4}$$

where σ_H^2, σ_P^2, and σ_F^2 are the variances of R_H, R_P and R_F, respectively; and σ_{PF} is the covariance of R_P and R_F. Setting the derivative of σ_H^2 to zero, one can see that the variance of the hedged position is minimized for a hedge ratio given by

$$2h\sigma_F^2 = 2\sigma_{PF}, \text{ so}$$

$$h = \frac{\sigma_{PF}}{\sigma_F^2}. \tag{8.A5}$$

Note that this optimal hedge ratio is also the slope of the regression:

$$R_P = a + hR_F \tag{8.A6}$$

The minimum-variance strategy is sometimes applied to price changes or price levels rather than rates of return, depending on the investor's risk-minimization objective. Rates of return are generally used in portfolio theory, since one generally cares about returns per dollar (or other unit of currency) invested. Even if some investors cared about only absolute dollar losses, they would still be better off estimating the optimal hedge ratio by running a regression such as in Eq. (8.A6). As pointed out by Hill and Schneeweis (1981) and Benninga, Eldor, and Zilcha (1984),[14] the econometric properties of price levels or price changes requires the estimation of h using a regression on percentage price changes, i.e., rates of returns.[15]

Estimation Problems

The optimal hedge ratio is usually estimated on past data. Besides the econometric problems mentioned above, the procedure is only helpful to the extent that the past provides useful information on the future. A few months of daily or weekly data are required to estimate the regression slope. If the composition of the asset portfolio is frequently rebalanced, a past estimation of the optimal hedge ratio may be useless for the current portfolio. Therefore, the method used to estimate h should be forward looking rather than backward looking. Even if the composition of the asset portfolio stays constant the regression slope can be unstable with a low R^2. This is typically the case for the βs of stocks. This means that the hedge will be imperfect expost and that great care should be devoted to estimating the optimal hedge ratio. This topic is detailed below for bond portfolios.

Multi-Contract Hedging

Investors may want to hedge simultaneously several types of risk. For example, the value of a gold-linked bond is influenced both by movements in long-term yields and gold prices (see Chapter 11). The holder of such a bond might sell treasury bond futures and gold futures. The minimum-variance hedge ratios are obtained by running a multiple regression:

$$R_P = a + h_1 R_{F1} + h_2 R_{F2} \tag{8.A7}$$

where h_1 and h_2 are the hedge ratios on each of the two futures contracts and a is a constant term. A joint estimation of the two hedge ratios is required, since the two futures prices tend to be correlated. In our example, gold prices are negatively correlated with movements in interest rates.

HEDGING STRATEGIES WITH BONDS

There exist a large variety of bonds, but only a few bond futures contracts. Therefore, hedging a bond portfolio is a difficult task. In this section we recall the various methods used to determine optimal hedge ratios, while focusing on those methods that are specific to bond management.

The Naive Approach

The simplest approach to hedging bond portfolios is to sell futures contracts with a face value equal to that of the bond portfolio, thereby attaining a hedge ratio of one. A simple example based on a single bond can illustrate the differences in hedging strategies according to the approach followed. In practice, managers care about diversified portfolios of bonds rather than single issues. Let's consider a Treasury bond with a 12% coupon maturing in 2010, on June 1. This bond is priced at 90 percent of par value. The September treasury bond futures trade at 70 percent of par value. Assume that the investor holds $1 million of face value of the bond. By definition of the hedge ratio, the equal-position hedge requires the investor to sell a number of contracts, N, such that the hedge ratio is equal to one in Eq. (8.5):

$$\frac{N \times 100,000 \times 90\%}{900,000} = 1.$$

Hence, $N = 10$ contracts. This hedge would work well if the cash and futures positions experience the same price change.

Another alternative would be to match the dollar values of the cash and futures positions. This hedge would work well if the two positions experienced the same percentage return (rather than the same price change). Here the hedge ratio is equal to

$$h = \frac{90}{70} = 1.286.$$

The hedger should sell 12.86 contracts for each $1 million of bond face value.

Since the 12% treasury bond maturing in 2010 is deliverable for the futures contract, a minor variation in the dollar-matching approach is to use the conversion factor. This bond has a conversion factor of 1.30, which means that it will be worth 1.3 times the futures price at delivery. This method is only applicable if the bond is deliverable. Furthermore, the hedge works well only if this bond is the cheapest to deliver, since futures prices tend to track more closely the price of the cheapest-to-deliver security. The conversion factor method cannot be applied to general bond portfolios.

Although the above methods are very convenient, they seldom provide efficient hedging.

Minimum-Variance Approach

To apply the minimum-variance approach to hedging a bond portfolio one would collect a few months of daily data on the portfolio values and futures prices. A regression of the portfolio's return, R_P, on the futures return, R_F, is run over the data set

$$R_P = a + hR_F$$

For example, the slope of the regression in our illustration is equal to 1.15. Note that this hedge ratio is quite different from the dollar-matching value of 1.286. The number of contracts to be sold is equal to N such that

$$\frac{N \times 100,000 \times 90\%}{900,000} = 1.15.$$

Hence, $N = 11.5$ contracts.

However, this method suffers from several problems: First, the slope estimate is likely to be unstable and reflect past relations. A change in the bond portfolio composition would affect the future slope coefficient. Second, the relationship between the two regression variables R_P and R_F is not expected to be linear. Remember that a bond price is a complex function of the interest rate. Interest rate changes will affect R_P and R_F differently. Indeed the coefficient h is likely to be a complex function of the interest rate and move over time.

This regression method is theoretically questionable and impractical, since it necessitates the collection of a large number of daily observations on each portfolio. A specific method has been developed to assess the optimal hedge ratio for bond portfolios. It is usually referred to as the instantaneous price sensitivity approach or duration approach.[16]

Instantaneous Price Sensitivity

The objective of a good minimum-variance hedge strategy is to offset any unexpected price change in the bond portfolio with price changes in the futures position. Actuarially, we know how a bond price reacts to a change in interest rates. The instantaneous price sensitivity, D^*, has been described in Chapter 7. The absolute value, D^*, is equal to the standard duration divided by one plus the yield-to-maturity on the bond. The sensitivity D^* is often referred to as modified duration:

$$\frac{dV}{V} = -D^*dr$$

where dr is the instantaneous change in interest rate, and dV the change in value of a bond or portfolio of bonds. Since a similar duration, D_F^*, exists for the notional bond futures, an optimal hedge can be constructed as the ratio of the price sensitivity of the bond portfolio to the price sensitivity of the futures contract. Then the optimal hedge ratio is equal to

$$h = \frac{SD_P^*}{FD_F^*} \qquad\qquad (8.A8)$$

where D_P^* and D_F^* are the modified durations for the portfolio and futures, and S is the average price of the bond portfolio.

In the example, the modified duration of the 12% treasury bond maturing in 2010 is equal to 6.5 years, while the notional bond in the futures contract has a modified duration of 7.1 years. Hence, the optimal hedge ratio is equal to

$$h = \frac{90 \times 6.5}{70 \times 7.1} = 1.177.$$

Note that this instantaneous price sensitivity approach gives results equal to those of the dollar-matching approach when the duration of the portfolio is equal to that of the notional bond.

The advantage of this approach is that it is forward looking.[17] It can easily be applied to a portfolio by calculating the weighted average duration of the portfolio. This is easy, since duration figures are routinely available from commercial services and brokers; no historical data is required. On the other hand, the hedge is supposed to work only instantaneously for small movements in interest rates. As the durations vary, the hedge ratio should be readjusted periodically.

Note that the instantaneous price sensitivity approach assumes that the interest rate is the only source of uncertainty and that there are parallel shifts in the term structure of interest rates. Indeed, the concept of duration relies on the assumption of parallel shifts in the term structure. An example of a situation where this method is not expected to provide a perfect hedge is the hedging of a corporate bond portfolio of three-years' duration using twenty-year treasury bond futures; changes in the corporate-government interest rate spread, plus twists in the term structure, would lead to unexpected returns on the hedged position.

9

Options

Option contracts,[1] like futures contracts, are leveraged investments. They offer an attractive risk structure and are used for hedging and speculation. But their main advantage is that, because of their risk-return characteristics, they can be used to insure an existing portfolio.

Bonds and many other financial contracts include one or several optional clauses, so that the valuation of options is a very important task in finance. In this chapter we first describe the options market and its instruments. We then discuss the risk-return characteristics of options and their valuation. Finally, we briefly touch on the technique of insuring with options.

THE MARKETS AND INSTRUMENTS

The Principle of an Option

In general, an option gives to the buyer the right, but not the obligation, to buy or sell a good, whereas the option seller must respond accordingly. Many different types of option contracts exist in the financial world. The two major types of contracts traded on organized options exchanges are *calls* and *puts*.

A call gives to the buyer of the option contract the right to buy a specified number of units of an underlying asset, at a specified price called the *exercise* or *strike price*, on or before a specified date called the *expiration date* or *strike date*. A put gives to its buyer the right to sell a specified number of units of an underlying asset at a specified price on or before a specified date. In all cases the seller of the option contract, the *writer*, is subordinate to the decision of the buyer, and the buyer exercises the option only if it is profitable to him or her. The buyer of a call benefits if the price of the asset is above the exercise price at expiration. The buyer of a put benefits if the asset price is below the exercise price at expiration.

The complete definition of an option must clearly specify how the option can be exercised. A European-type option can only be exercised on a specified date, usually the expiration date. An American-type option can be exercised by the buyer at any time until the expiration date. American options are used on most of the organized options exchanges in the world. Both types of options can be freely traded at any time until expiration.

Organization of the market Before 1973 and the creation of the Chicago Board of Options Exchange (CBOE), options contracts were private contracts between two parties. The contracts were generally not standardized, and there was little or no secondary market activity. It was simply too difficult or costly to find someone to take over the obligation of a specific option contract. The procedure introduced by the CBOE revolutionized options trading and stimulated tremendous development of the market worldwide. The organization of the market for listed, or traded, options is somewhat similar to that of the futures market. An *options clearing corporation* plays a central role. All option contracts are represented by bookkeeping entries on the computers of clearing corporations. As soon as a buyer and a seller of a particular contract decide to trade, a clearing corporation steps in and breaks down the deal into two option contracts: one between the buyer and the clearing corporation acting as seller, and the other between the seller and the clearing corporation acting as buyer. This procedure completely standardizes the contracts. It allows one to close a position by simply *selling out* the options held, while a seller may *buy into* a previous position. If a buyer decides to exercise an option, the clearing corporation randomly selects a seller of the option and issues an exercise notice. Specific selection rules are set by each exchange.

In most cases, investors offset their position by making a reverse trade before the expiration date. Option buyers usually find it more profitable to resell an option on the market than to exercise it. But there are times when exercising an option is more profitable, such as when a large dividend is about to be paid on the underlying stock.

Some of the old options markets still offer only private nontraded options, but these markets are steadily disappearing. For example, dealers in the American over-the-counter market received authorization from the Securities and Exchange Commission to organize a Chicago-type options market for over-the-counter stocks. The Paris Bourse has also transformed its traditional options market into a Chicago-type market. Notable exceptions to this trend are the markets for currency options. Banks have begun writing European-type currency options tailored to the specific needs of commercial customers. This interbank market has successfully developed despite competition from the listed currency options market, which got its start on the Philadelphia Stock Exchange, and is now found on markets in London, Chicago, Amsterdam, Singapore, Sydney, Montreal, and other places.

Listed options markets can be found all over the world and are growing quickly. International links between options exchanges have also developed. For example, the European Options Exchange (EOE) in Amsterdam is linked to exchanges in Montreal, Vancouver, and Sydney, allowing around-the-clock trading in gold, silver, and currency options.

Trading in listed options The option to buy an asset has a price that must be paid at the time of contracting. The price of an option, usually called the *premium*, fluctuates over time depending on the value of the underlying asset and other parameters (discussed below). Option quotations are given in the press as illustrated in Exhibits 9.1, 9.2, and 9.3. An option is usually defined by the underlying asset, the exercise price, and the expiration month. Several options are usually traded on the same asset. Looking at London-traded options on BP in Exhibit 9.1, one finds that on July 14, 1986, nine calls and nine puts were traded for three exercise prices (500, 550, and 600 pence) and three expiration months (July, October, and January). The premium for the January 550 call option was 55, while that for the October 600 put was 50. At the time of the transaction buyers of the January call paid 55 pence per share. The standard size of an option contract is usually 100 shares, so that buyers of one January 550 BP call contract paid $100 \times 55 = 5500$ pence, or 55 pounds. At expiration, the buyer would have exercised the call option only if the BP share price had been higher than the exercise price of 550. In Exhibit 9.1 the closing price of a BP share is given in the first column below the name of the underlying asset. The option buyer would have profited if the difference between the share price and the exercise price had been larger than the initial investment, namely, the premium of 55 pence. The investor could also have resold the option at any time after the initial purchase. Whether this investment resulted in a profit or a loss depended on the evolution of the option premium.

One must be careful when directly comparing published option prices, since they may be based on transactions taking place at different times of the day. The underlying asset price can change over the course of a day, thereby changing the option price.

The various quotations from Chicago, London, and Amsterdam are published in slightly different formats, as shown in Exhibits 9.1 to 9.3, but they all include the same information. In the United States and the United Kingdom the first three option prices listed are for calls, and the latter three, for puts. On the European Options Exchanges in Amsterdam (Exhibit 9.2) the three prices in each row apply either to a call, if the underlying asset name is followed by a *C*, or to a put, if it is followed by a *P*. The current price of the underlying asset is given in all tables. It appears under the asset name in U.S. and British quotations and in the last column on the EOE. The information on the EOE is slightly more complete: The publication indicates the number of contracts traded each day. Note that some options were not traded on July 14. A nontraded option is indicated by a dash (—) on European exchanges. In the United States, however, a nontraded option is often indicated by the letter *r*, if the option was not traded during the day, or an *s*, if the option does not exist, but is included to complete the matrix format of the publication. Each exchange

EXHIBIT 9.1
Options Quotation in London

LONDON TRADED OPTIONS

Option		CALLS			PUTS		
		July	Oct.	Jan.	July	Oct.	Jan.
Allied Lyons	300	32	45	55	1	7	8
(*333)	330	8	25	38	8	18	25
	360	2	12	20	33	38	40
B.P.	500	65	75	90	1	6	10
(*563)	550	20	40	55	4	19	27
	600	1½	17	30	40	50	57
Cons. Gold	420	24	47	57	3	22	30
(*434)	460	3	28	38	34	47	55
	500	1	11	23	70	77	84
Courtaulds	260	26	36	45	1	5	9
(*286)	280	8	25	31	4	10	15
	300	2	14	22	18	22	27
	330	1	6	14	48	49	50
Com. Union	280	33	38	—	1	3	—
(*312)	300	13	27	37	4	12	14
	330	2	14	24	20	26	28
Cable & Wire	600	90	120	140	1	10	13
(*685)	650	40	77	900	3	22	32
	700	10	35	60	20	45	55
	750	1	20	38	65	70	80
Distillers	600	145	160	—	1	4	—
(*740)	650	95	115	—	2	10	—
	700	45	70	—	4	25	—
G.E.C.	180	14	28	36	1	5	8
(*192)	200	3	16	22	10	15	18
	220	1	8	13	30	32	34
Grand Met.	360	—	—	55	—	—	13
(*383)	382	9	27	—	9	23	—
	390	—	—	38	—	—	30
	420	1	12	25	43	48	50
I.C.I.	850	147	160	182	2	4	7
(*994)	900	97	112	140	2	9	15
	950	47	78	105	4	24	30
	1000	13	50	72	17	42	52
Land Sec.	300	39	52	60	1	3	5
(*339)	330	10	30	39	3	10	15
	360	1½	13	21	24	26	29
Marks & Spen.	180	19	28	35	1	4	7
(*197)	200	3	16	23	5	12	16
	220	0½	7	14	24	26	27
Shell Trans.	700	78	100	117	1½	7	14
(*778)	750	30	60	82	5	18	27
	800	7	30	52	27	47	52
Trafalgar House	280	8	22	30	7	16	19
(*281)	300	2	10	18	22	28	30
	330	1	4	10	52	52	53

Option		July	Aug.	Sept.	Oct.	July	Aug.	Sept.	Oct.
FT-SE	1550	58	75	—	—	5	11	—	—
Index	1575	38	55	73	—	8	22	27	—
(*1599)	1600	20	38	53	82	17	33	38	52
	1625	90	27	42	65	33	45	55	70
	1650	3	20	35	52	57	62	70	84
	1675	2	15	23	38	80	83	87	100
	1700	1	—	—	—	105	—	—	—
	1750	1	—	—	—	155	—	—	—

Source: Financial Times, July 15, 1986. Reprinted with permission.

---

has a fixed cycle of expiration months. Because active trading takes place in the last month of an option, some exchanges have introduced options expiring at the end of the current month.

Option combinations Investors can assemble various types of options into combinations that have such colorful names as *straddles*, *strips*, *straps*, and *butterfly*

EXHIBIT 9.2
Options Quotations on European Options Exchange

EUROPEAN OPTIONS EXCHANGE

Series		Aug. Vol.	Aug. Last	Nov. Vol.	Nov. Last	Feb. Vol.	Feb. Last	Stock
GOLD C	$370	15	1	21	4.80	—	—	$346
GOLD P	$320	4	0.50	—	—	20	4.50	"
GOLD P	$330	—	—	20	3.50	—	—	"

Series		Sept. Vol.	Sept. Last	Dec. Vol.	Dec. Last	March Vol.	March Last	Stock
SILV C	$550	8	19	5	19A	—	—	$505
SILV P	$550	—	—	20	35	—	—	"
£/FL C	Fl.355	25	10.50	—	—	—	—	FL.366.25
£/FL C	Fl.365	1	5.50	5	7.50	—	—	"
£/FL C	Fl.385	—	—	10	2	—	—	"
£/FL P	Fl.350	8	1.30	—	—	—	—	"
£/FL P	Fl.355	25	2.50	—	—	—	—	"
£/FL P	Fl.360	13	4.30	—	—	—	—	"
£/FL P	Fl.370	15	10.50	—	—	—	—	"
£/FL P	Fl.380	8	18	—	—	—	—	"
$/FL C	Fl.240	150	10	—	—	—	—	FL.246.55
$/FL C	Fl.245	12	6.50	—	—	—	—	"
$/FL C	Fl.250	111	4.200	1	7.20	—	—	"
$/FL C	Fl.255	5	2.90	—	—	—	—	"
$/FL C	Fl.260	44	1.70	1	3.80	—	—	"
$/FL C	Fl.265	—	—	7	2.50	—	—	"
$/FL C	Fl.270	8	0.50	—	—	—	—	"
$/FL P	Fl.235	4	1.70	—	—	—	—	"
$/FL P	Fl.240	11	3.40	5	6.80A	—	—	"
$/FL P	Fl.245	44	5.30	—	—	—	—	"
$/FL P	Fl.250	2	7.50	—	—	—	—	"
$/DM C	Dm.225	20	3	—	—	—	—	DM.218.75

Series		July Vol.	July Last	Oct. Vol.	Oct. Last	Jan. Vol.	Jan. Last	Stock
ABN C	Fl.600	278	8	136	27	41	41A	Fl.606
ABN P	Fl.600	25	1.80	108	17	44	20	"
AEGN C	Fl.110	207	0.20	21	4.50	20	7.50A	Fl.106.20
AEGN P	£1.115	208	8.50	10	9.50	—	—	"

TOTAL VOLUME IN CONTRACTS: 31,767

A=Ask   B=Bid   C=Call   P=Put

Source: Financial Times, July 15, 1986. Reprinted with permission.

spreads. A straddle is the combination of one put and one call on the same asset with the same exercise price and the same expiration date. A strip is the combination of one call and two puts with similar exercise prices and expiration dates. A strap is the combination of two calls and one put with similar characteristics. More complex combinations involve calls and puts with different exercise prices or expiration dates.

Options on futures versus options on spot So far we have discussed only options that require the physical delivery of an asset when they are exercised. Recently, options on futures contracts have been introduced. The buyer of a futures option has the right to buy (call) or sell (put) a specified futures contract. When the option is exercised, the writer, or seller, of the option pays the buyer the difference between the current price of the futures contract and the exercise price of the option. This cash settlement must be paid because futures contracts are marked to market every day.

EXHIBIT 9.3
Currency Options Quotations

Currency Options
Philadelphia Exchange

Option & Underlying	Strike Price	Calls—Last			Puts—Last		
		Jul	Aug	Sep	Jul	Aug	Sep
12,500 British Pounds-cents per unit.							
BPound	135	r	s	r	r	s	0.30
148.57	.140	r	s	8.70	r	s	0.90
148.57	.145	r	r	5.35	r	1.30	2.70
148.57	.150	r	1.75	2.60	r	3.80	5.20
148.57	.155	r	0.50	1.05	r	r	r
148.57	.160	r	0.15	r	r	r	r
50,000 Canadian Dollars-cents per unit.							
CDollr	...74	r	r	0.19	r	r	r
62,500 West German Marks-cents per unit.							
DMark	.. 43	r	r	2.95	r	r	0.21
46.06	...44	r	2.25	r	r	r	0.26
46.06	...45	r	1.42	1.78	r	0.30	0.61
46.06	...46	r	0.86	1.23	r	0.78	r
46.06	...47	r	0.41	0.77	r	r	r
46.06	...48	r	0.19	0.42	r	r	r
46.06	...49	r	s	0.26	r	s	r
6,250,000 Japanese Yen-100ths of a cent per unit.							
JYen	...54	r	s	r	r	s	0.04
62.57	...56	r	r	6.50	r	r	r
62.57	...57	r	r	r	r	r	0.16
62.57	...58	r	r	4.68	r	r	0.19
62.57	...59	r	r	r	r	0.14	r
62.57	...60	r	r	3.16	r	0.21	r
62.57	...61	r	r	2.46	r	0.43	0.74
62.57	...62	r	1.15	1.77	r	0.70	1.21
62.57	...63	r	0.87	1.32	r	1.16	r
62.57	...64	r	r	0.90	r	r	r
62.57	...65	r	0.35	r	r	r	r
62,500 Swiss Francs-cents per unit.							
SFranc	...53	r	r	r	r	r	0.32
56.39	...54	r	r	r	r	0.22	r
56.39	...55	r	r	r	r	0.42	0.88
56.39	...56	r	r	r	r	1.00	r
56.39	...57	r	0.74	1.10	r	r	r
56.39	...58	r	0.41	0.65	r	r	r
56.39	...60	r	0.14	0.38	r	r	r

Total call vol. 9,885 Call open int. 325,104
Total put vol. 9,966 Put open int. 282,224
r—Not traded. s—No option offered.
Last is premium (purchase price).

Chicago Board Options Exchange

Option & Underlying	Strike Price	Calls—Last			Puts—Last		
		Jul	Aug	Sep	Jul	Aug	Sep
25,000 British Pounds-cents per unit.							
BPound	140	r	r	r	r	r	0.95
148.63	.145	r	r	r	r	1.55	2.35
148.63	.150	r	1.60	2.35	r	r	r
125,000 West German Marks-cents per unit.							
DMark	.. 45	r	1.16	1.73	r	r	r
46.07	...47	r	r	0.59	r	r	r
12,500,000 Japanese Yen-100ths of a cent per unit.							
JYen	... 60	r	r	3.17	r	0.32	r
62.58	...62	r	1.37	1.82	r	r	r
62.58	...63	r	0.88	1.26	r	r	r
62.58	...64	r	r	r	r	2.13	r
62.58	...65	r	0.28	r	r	r	r
125,000 Swiss Francs-cents per unit.							
SFranc	...54	r	r	r	r	0.18	r
56.38	...55	r	r	r	r	0.37	0.68
56.38	...56	r	1.10	r	r	0.80	r
56.38	...58	r	0.38	r	r	r	r

Total call volume 2,279 Total call open int. 17,250
Total put volume 804 Total put open int. 12,837
r—Not traded. s—No option offered.
Last is premium (purchase price).

Currency Futures Options

EURODOLLAR (CME) $ million; pts. of 100%

Strike Price	Calls—Settle			Puts—Settle		
	Sep-c	Dec-c	Mar-c	Sep-p	Dec-p	Mar-p
9300	0.63	0.64	0.64	0.03	0.13	0.32
9325	0.41	0.48	0.50	0.06	0.22	0.42
9350	0.23	0.33	0.37	0.12	0.30	....
9375	0.12	0.22	0.27	0.26	0.42	....
9400	0.06	0.13	0.19	0.44	....	0.82
9425	0.02	0.08	0.13	0.65	....	....

Est. vol. 3,327, Fri.; vol. 3,913 calls, 10,563 puts
Open interest Fri.; 53,723 calls, 41,282 puts

BRITISH POUND (CME) 25,000 pounds; cents per pound

Strike Price	Calls—Settle			Puts—Settle		
	Sep-c	Dec-c	Mar-c	Sep-p	Dec-p	Mar-p
1425	6.40	7.35	....	1.30	3.50	5.20
1450	4.75	6.00	....	2.10	4.60	6.40
1475	3.35	4.80	5.50	3.20	5.80	7.70
1500	2.25	3.80	4.55	4.60	7.25	9.10
1525	1.50	2.95	....	6.30	8.80	10.70
1550	0.95	2.25	3.05	8.20	10.55	....

Est. vol. 2,078, Fri.; vol. 1,073 calls, 338 puts
Open interest Fri.; 23,645 calls, 11,949 puts

W. GERMAN MARK (CME) 125,000 marks, cents per mark

Strike Price	Calls—Settle			Puts—Settle		
	Sep-c	Dec-c	Mar-c	Sep-p	Dec-p	Mar-p
44	2.54	3.14	....	0.25	0.67	0.94
45	1.79	2.48	2.96	0.49	0.98	1.26
46	1.16	1.91	2.39	0.85	1.37	1.66
47	0.71	1.44	1.95	1.40	1.88	2.16
48	0.41	1.06	1.55	2.09	2.48	....
49	0.25	0.81	....	2.91	....	....

Est. vol. 4,329, Fri.; vol. 4,152 calls, 2,193 puts
Open interest Fri.; 49,122 calls, 38,721 puts

SWISS FRANC (CME) 125,000 francs; cents per franc

Strike Price	Calls—Settle			Puts—Settle		
	Sep-c	Dec-c	Mar-c	Sep-p	Dec-p	Mar-p
55	2.18	3.02	....	0.61	1.26	....
56	1.55	2.46	3.06	0.98	1.66	....
57	1.06	1.95	2.57	1.47	2.13	2.49
58	0.70	1.54	2.14	2.13	2.70	....
59	0.45	1.21	....	2.86	3.28	....
60	....	....	....	....	....	....

Est. vol. 2,419, Fri.; vol. 1,087 calls, 886 puts
Open interest Fri.; 17,936 calls, 17,574 puts

JAPANESE YEN (CME) 12,500,000 yen; cents per 100 yen

Strike Price	Calls—Settle			Puts—Settle		
	Sep-c	Dec-c	Mar-c	Sep-p	Dec-p	Mar-p
61	2.45	3.36	....	0.65	1.26	1.68
62	1.82	2.76	....	1.01	1.65	....
63	1.29	2.24	2.99	1.47	2.10	....
64	0.90	1.80	2.54	2.06	....	....
65	0.61	1.43	....	2.76	....	....
66	....	....	....	....	....	....

Est. vol. 3,797, Fri.; vol. 2,614 calls, 1,221 puts
Open interest Fri.; 25,142 calls, 16,569 puts

STERLING (LIFFE)—b-£25,000; cents per pound

Strike Price	Calls—Settle			Puts—Settle		
	Sep-c	Dec-c	Mar-c	Sep-p	Dec-p	Mar-p
140	8.38	9.06	9.67	0.93	2.81	4.47
145	4.87	6.11	6.98	2.42	4.86	6.78
150	2.43	3.88	4.85	4.98	7.63	9.65
155	1.03	2.32	3.26	8.58	11.07	13.06
160	0.37	1.30	2.11	12.92	15.05	16.91
165	0.11	0.69	....	17.66	19.44	....

Actual Vol. Monday, 798 Calls, 238 Puts.
Open Interest Friday; 3,147, Calls, 4,389 Puts.
b-Option on physical sterling.

For some financial instruments one can find both options on an asset and options on futures contracts in that asset at the same time, as is the case for interest rate, currency, and stock index options. Futures options are usually listed on futures exchanges.

The Different Instruments

Stock options Trading in listed options started with options on common stocks. Markets have developed throughout the world to the point where options on most active stocks are now traded. Options have also been introduced for stocks of smaller companies that have attractive characteristics such as high growth or membership in a specialized industry. In the United States the volume of shares traded through options is often larger than the volume of the actual stocks traded on the New York Stock Exchange.

Stock options are usually protected against capital adjustments such as splits, but not against dividend payments, which is why it can be more profitable to exercise a stock option just before a dividend is paid than to keep it and loose the dividend.

Commodity options Options are also traded on certain commodities; the most active trading takes place in gold and silver options, which many money managers use for their gold-linked assets. In the past, private commodity options have been successfully offered, especially by Credit Suisse First Boston. But they have been steadily replaced by listed options traded on many exchanges, including the European Options Exchange, the New York Commodity Exchanges, Amex Commodity Corporation, Chicago Board of Trade, and the exchanges in London, Montreal, Vancouver, and Hong Kong.

It should be stressed that some of the exchanges trade in bullion options, which require physical delivery of the metal, while others trade in gold futures contracts.

Interest rate options Options are traded on U.S. debt instruments such as treasury bonds, treasury bills, and certificates of deposit (CDs). Similar options exist in a few other countries with developed bond markets, including the Netherlands and the United Kingdom. Options on treasury bills require the delivery of a current bill issued during the week of settlement, whereas options on treasury bonds require delivery of a specific bond on the Chicago Board of Options Exchange. But a more active market has developed for options on futures contracts in treasury bonds. Futures contracts allow for a more-liquid and less-costly exercise procedure.

Besides these exchange-traded options, some interest rate options are negotiated over the counter. These tend to be longer-term options on short-term interest rates. They often take the form of *caps* and *floors*. The basic contract in an interest rate cap option is an agreement between the buyer and the seller of the option stating that if a chosen index such as the three-month London interbank offered rate (LIBOR) is above the agreed exercise price at prespecified dates in the future, then the seller will reimburse the buyer for the additional interest cost until the next specified date. (LIBOR is the short-term Euro-dollar interest rate most commonly used in floating rate notes and loans.) A floor option has the reverse characteristics. A five-year cap on the three-month LIBOR can be broken down into a series of nineteen European options with quarterly strike dates. The option premium may be paid in the form of a single front-end price (e.g., 2% of the amount specified in the option) or a yearly cost paid up regularly (e.g., 0.5% per year).

As an illustration, consider a five-year 10% cap on the three-month LIBOR for $1 million. The current LIBOR is 8%, and the yearly cap premium is 0.5%. If the LIBOR stays below 10% over the next five years, the cap option will be useless. Conversely, if the LIBOR rises above 10% by some of the specified exercise dates, the seller will pay the difference in interest costs. Let's assume that the LIBOR rises to 12%. The cap buyer then receives a payment in the amount of the difference between the market LIBOR (12%) and the exercise price (10%). In this case the quarterly payment is

$$\$1,000,000\left(\frac{12\% - 10\%}{4}\right) = \$5000.$$

The motivation for engaging in these caps and floors contracts is financial costs insurance. The contracts are most often used by companies as an insurance against a rise in interest costs on existing floating rate borrowings. The options are usually written by banks with extensive international underwriting activities. These banks often hedge their option writing by borrowing funds at a variable rate with an interest cap. For example, a bank may engage in the following operations:

- Lend money to company A at the LIBOR + $\frac{7}{8}$%.
- Borrow money from investors at the LIBOR + $\frac{3}{8}$% with a cap at 10%.
- Sell a cap option at 10% to company B for $\frac{1}{2}$% per year.

As seen in Exhibit 9.4, a bank has hedged its cap writing and ends up with a margin of 1%. An alternative for the bank might simply have been to lend to company A at the LIBOR plus $\frac{7}{8}$% and borrow from investors at the LIBOR plus $\frac{1}{8}$% without any cap. In effect the margin would have been equal to $\frac{3}{4}$% ($\frac{7}{8}$% − $\frac{1}{8}$%). The cap packaging allows the bank to increase its profit margin without taking additional risks.

Collars, which offer both a floor and a ceiling on interest rates, have also been introduced on the international market. They are another attractive instrument for management of long-term interest rate risk.

As seen with swaps, these complex packagings are quite common in international finance. Their use requires expertise on the part of bankers and a good understanding of the pricing of these multiple options.

EXHIBIT 9.4
Hedging the Sale of a Cap

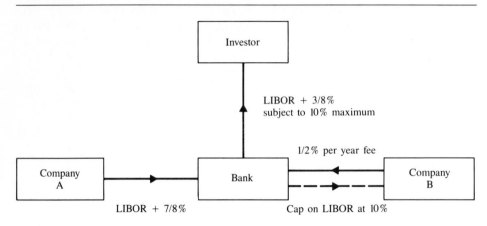

Over-the-counter dollar options are available against most bases such as the Euro-dollar LIBOR, CDs, treasury bills, commercial paper, and prime rates. However, the most active contracts are those for the three- and six-month LIBOR. Dealers writing options on bases other than the LIBOR tend to hedge their position using the three-month LIBOR. They tend to charge fairly high costs to buyers because they assume the mismatch risk. Nondollar caps and floors are also available in deutsche marks and sterling.

The great advantage of these nontraded options is their maturity, which extends from a year to ten years or more. However, they tend to involve large sums of money and are designed for corporations, rather than small private investors.

Stock index options Options on stock indexes have developed in several countries in the Americas, Europe, and the Far East. Exhibit 9.1 shows quotations for the UK *Financial Times* index. Stock index options are options on the level of the index. The contract size is equal to the index times a *multiplier* set by the exchange. For example, the Standard and Poor's 500 options traded on the Chicago Mercantile Exchange have a contract multiplier of 500. In other words, the investment required to purchase one contract is equal to the premium multiplied by $500. All settlement procedures require cash, rather than physical delivery of an index.

Some options (e.g., options traded on the CBOE, the American Exchange, and the New York Stock Exchange) are directly linked to an index value, while others are options on futures contracts of stock indexes (e.g., options on the New York Futures Exchange and the Chicago Mercantile Exchange). Options listed on futures exchanges are usually futures options, while options listed on stock exchanges are usually spot options.

Currency options Markets in currency options have become essential for coping with the volatility of the U.S. dollar. As shown in Exhibit 9.3, currency options are now traded on markets throughout the world, including markets in the United States, London, Amsterdam, Hong Kong, Singapore, Sydney, Vancouver, and Montreal. In all of these markets three types of contracts are negotiated:

1. Over-the-counter currency options are not tradeable and can only be exercised at maturity, that is, they are European-type options. Commercial customers often turn to a bank when they need a large number of options of this type for a specific date. For example, a German car exporter may expect a payment of $10 million three months from now on September 7. Listed options do not offer this specific expiration date, and the amount involved (500 contracts) may be too large for the volume of transactions on the exchange. Moreover, a commercial exporter would not be interested in the possibility of early exercise or sale of the options, anyway. Once the bank has written the option, it uses forward contracts or listed currency options to hedge actively the position it has created. Options are also written for longer terms (over two years) than the maturity available on the exchange-listed options.

2. In the early 1980s the Philadelphia Stock Exchange introduced option contracts on currencies. When a currency option is exercised, foreign currency must be delivered to a bank account, usually in the country whose currency the delivery is made in.

3. Other listed currency options are options on currency futures contracts. For example, the Chicago Mercantile Exchange trades options on its own currency futures.

As shown below, the price of an option on spot and futures exchange rates may differ slightly. Technical differences are also important. For example, spot currency options on the Philadelphia Stock Exchange expire on the Saturday before the third Wednesday of the month (i.e., around the middle of the month). But futures currency options on the Chicago Mercantile Exchange stop trading two Fridays before the third Wednesday of the month (i.e., at the start of the month).

Currency options are quoted in several ways. In the United States, options are quoted in terms of U.S. dollars per unit of foreign currency. For example, in Exhibit 9.3 the call deutsche mark August 45 quoted in Philadelphia is an option contract giving to the investor the right to buy 62,500 deutsche marks at an exercise price of 45 cents per deutsche mark on or before mid-August. At the time, the spot exchange rate was 46.06 cents per deutsche mark and the premium was 1.42 cents per deutsche mark. If the deutsche mark had gone up, the price of the option would have increased, and the holder of the call would have profited. One could also have bought a deutsche mark put, which would have given to the investor the right to sell 62,500 deutsche marks at a fixed exercise price. For example, the put deutsche mark August 45 was worth 0.30 cent per deutsche mark. If the deutsche mark had depreciated (i.e., if its value had gone down in terms of U.S. dollars), the holder of the put would have profited. Remember that currency options traded in the United States are options written on a foreign currency, so that the prices of the currency and of the option are expressed in U.S. dollars and cents just like a U.S. stock option. There are different conventions in different countries.

Other instruments with options Many securities have option features. Among the most common securities with options are the following:

- *Warrants* are like long-term call options. They are traded securities issued by a firm whose stock serves as the underlying asset of the option. While *stock warrants* are more common, *bond warrants* are also found, especially on the Eurobond market and in France. A bond warrant is a security giving to the holder the right to buy a given bond at a specified exercise price over the life of the warrant. The terms stipulated in the warrant are sometimes complex. For example, the exercise price can vary over time.

- *Convertible bonds* are bonds convertible into another security at the option of the bondholder. The most common convertibles are bonds that are convertible into common stock of the firm that issued them. These securities trade on most national capital markets and on the Eurobond market.

- *Bonds with optional clauses* are very common on all markets. As discussed in Chapter 6, many bonds are issued with a call provision, which gives the issuer the right to call back, or reimburse, the bondholder at a specified price. Bonds with put options give to the bondholder the right to force the issuer to reimburse the bondholder at a specified price.

OPTION VALUATION

Profit and Loss at Expiration

The profit and loss structure of an option that is held until expiration is shown in Exhibit 9.5. The exercise price is assumed to equal the current spot price of gold, which is $400. The premium is $10, and commissions are ignored. All profits and losses are expressed in dollars per ounce of gold.

Exhibits 9.5A and B show the profit structures for long and short positions on an underlying asset. We see from the diagram that the profit structures on these two positions exactly mirror each other. This stems from the fact that for any dollar gain in the price of gold the buyer of gold earns a dollar profit, while the seller loses a dollar.

The profit structures for options must take premiums into account. The buyer and the writer of a call option have opposite profit opportunities at expiration. The maximum loss for an option buyer is limited to the premium,

EXHIBIT 9.5
Profits and Losses from Various Positions

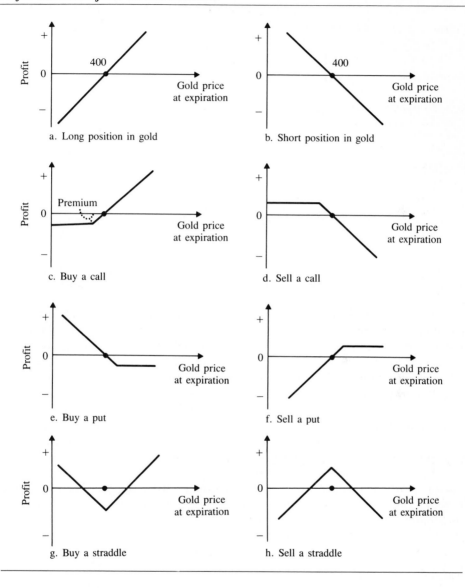

a. Long position in gold

b. Short position in gold

c. Buy a call

d. Sell a call

e. Buy a put

f. Sell a put

g. Buy a straddle

h. Sell a straddle

EXHIBIT 9.6
Potential Return on a Call Option

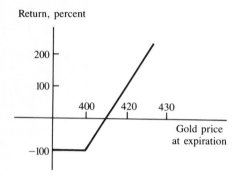

while the profit may be quite large. The reverse holds true for the option writer, which is why Exhibits 9.5C and D also are mirror images of each other.

Another way of saying this is that the risk structure of options is asymmetric when compared to a direct investment in the spot or futures market. That is, though the option buyer risks losing the premium, the seller of that same option bears the risk of an almost unlimited loss.

The six basic positions of buying or selling an asset, a call, or a put may be combined in complex investment strategies. For example, buying a call and a put with the same exercise price is called a straddle. Its profit structure is shown in Exhibit 9.5G. The attraction of this strategy is that a substantial gold price movement in either direction will generate a profit. Another strategy for achieving the same thing is to buy two calls and sell short the underlying asset (in this case, gold). This does not mean that all securities or combinations of securities with similar profit structures have exactly the same price. They may differ in exercise price and amount of capital invested, but their risk-return structures are similar and their market values are linked.

To be sure, Exhibit 9.5 depicts only examples of securities that are held until expiration. However, option buyers usually resell contracts before maturity, and sellers, likewise, repurchase them. The rate of return on a call option is depicted in Exhibit 9.6.

Valuation Models

Option premiums fluctuate so rapidly as a function of price movements in underlying assets that computerized models are necessary to properly value them. These models are so extensively used by traders and money managers that simple versions of them can be found even on programmable hand-held calculators.

EXHIBIT 9.7
Option Intrinsic Value

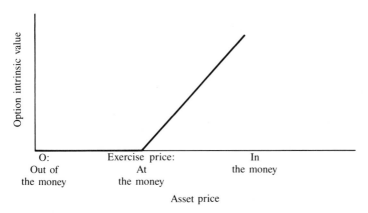

Asset price

In order to understand how options are valued, recall both the parameters that determine option premiums and the famous valuation formula proposed by Black and Scholes.[2]

Most options traded in the world are American options in the sense that they can be exercised any time before expiration, which means premiums must at least equal the profit one could obtain by immediately exercising the option. *Intrinsic value* is the value of an option that is immediately exercised. A rational option buyer would never exercise an option when the underlying asset price is below the exercise price because he or she would lose money. An option exercised under such circumstances is said to be *out of the money*, and the intrinsic value of the option is zero. When an asset price is above the exercise price, the option is said to be *in the money*, and its intrinsic value is the difference between the asset price and the exercise price. The intrinsic value of an option as a function of asset price is shown in Exhibit 9.7.

An option will generally sell above its intrinsic value. For example, a gold option with a strike, or exercise, price of $400 is worth $10 when the spot price of gold, the underlying asset, is $402. The difference between the option premium and its intrinsic value is usually referred to as the *time value* of the option. Here, the intrinsic value is $2 ($402 − $400) and the time value is $8 ($10 − $2). The major valuation problem is to determine the time value of an option.

On all markets option premiums vary with the underlying asset prices along a curve similar to that shown in Exhibit 9.8. For very low values of the asset price relative to the exercise price, the intrinsic value is zero and the time value of the option is close to zero, since the probability that the option will ever be exercised is almost zero. For very high asset prices relative to the exercise price, the option premium is almost equal to the option's intrinsic value. The option is almost sure to be exercised at expiration, since it is unlikely that the asset price

EXHIBIT 9.8
Option Value as a Function of Asset Price

will ever drop below the exercise price; therefore, the time value of the option is close to zero and the premium approaches the intrinsic value. When the asset price is in the neighborhood of the exercise price, the time value of the option may be large and the premium is well above its intrinsic value. In the example above, the time value is $8. If the gold price goes up, say, to $450, the option holder will benefit from the price appreciation; on the other hand, the investor will be protected from a fall in gold prices because his or her maximum loss is limited to the option premium: if gold drops to $300, the investor will lose only $10. This attractive asymmetric risk structure calls for a positive time value.

Note that the slope of a tangent to the curve shown in Exhibit 9.8 gives the instantaneous reaction of the option premium to a change in the asset price. This slope is usually called delta (δ).

On all markets, option premiums vary with asset prices along a curve similar to that shown in Exhibit 9.8. Investigators have found that option values depend on just four variables. The influence of each of these variables on a call option is explained below.

Exercise price. We have seen that the value of an option depends critically on its exercise price, E, relative to its current asset (e.g., gold) price, $G(G/E)$. The higher the exercise price, the lower the premium for options on the same asset that have an identical expiration date.

Interest rate. The value of a call option is an increasing function of the interest rate. Buying a call enables an investor to lay claim to an asset, while making a much smaller capital investment. Options reduce the opportunity of financing cost for claiming an asset. Naturally, as interest rates rise, this characteristic of options becomes more valuable, thereby raising the price of the option; in a sense, the present value of the asset to be purchased at expiration is reduced.

Volatility. The value of an option increases with the volatility of the underlying asset because options are perfectly protected against downside risk. The buyer can never lose more than the premium paid. Yet simultaneously, the buyer may potentially realize big gains on the upside. The more volatile the asset, the larger the expected gain on the option and, hence, the larger its premium.

Time to expiration. The value of an option is an increasing function of the time to expiration. There are two reasons for this. First, the leveraging advantage mentioned above increases with time. Second, the opportunity for the underlying asset price to far exceed the exercise price increases over time. Of course there is also an increased opportunity for the asset price to drop by more, but once again, the call holder's loss is always limited to the premium paid. Time, therefore, compounds both the interest rate and volatility effects described above.

All the determinants of option premiums, except underlying asset volatility, can be measured precisely. Underlying asset volatility is represented by the standard deviation of returns (or its squared value, the variance) and must be estimated.

From these four parameters, a simple valuation model for call options can be constructed. The most famous valuation model was developed by Black and Scholes and is currently used on option markets worldwide. It is available on a variety of computer time–sharing systems, financial packages, and even hand-held calculators. The reason valuation models are so necessary is that a small change in the underlying asset price can cause an immediate, large percentage change in the option premium. The Black–Scholes formula is based on an arbitrage model for a European-type call option. It assumes that no commissions, taxes, or dividends are paid, the interest rate is constant and risk-free, and the return on the asset follows a normal distribution with a constant variance, σ^2. Under these assumptions, a call premium may be valued by the following, relatively simple, formula:

$$P_0 = GN(d) - Ee^{-rt}N(d - \sigma\sqrt{t}) \qquad (9.1)$$

where

$$d = \frac{\ln(G/E) + (r + 0.5\sigma^2)t}{\sigma\sqrt{t}}$$

and where

> G is the price of the asset (e.g., gold),
>
> E is the exercise price,
>
> r is the risk-free interest rate expressed on a continuous compounding basis,
>
> σ is the standard deviation of the asset's annual rate of return,
>
> t is the time to expiration (in years),
>
> e is 2.71828,
>
> ln   is the natural logarithm, and
>
> $N(d)$ is the probability that a deviation less than d will occur in a normal distribution with a mean of zero and a standard deviation of one.

A polynomial approximation of $N(d)$ is often used on computers in the following form:

$$N(d) = 1 - \left[0.5(1 + 0.04986734d + 0.0211410061d^2 + 0.0032776263d^3\right.$$
$$\left. + 0.000380036d^4 + 0.0000488906d^5 + 0.0000005383d^6)^{-16}\right].$$

The derivation[3] of this formula is generally based on an arbitrage construction using options and their underlying asset. The hedge is constructed by looking at the derivative of the option premium with respect to the underlying asset's price. In Exhibit 9.8, this derivative would be δ, the slope of the tangent to the option value at any given point. The inverse of this slope is usually called the *hedge ratio*, h. A good hedge can be formed by buying one unit of the underlying asset and selling h units of the option. Alternatively, one could buy one unit of the option and sell δ units of the underlying asset. By construction, this hedge portfolio should not be sensitive to small changes in the asset's price. The hedge ratio continually changes with the asset's price, so that the composition of the hedge portfolio should be continually rebalanced. The expected return on this riskless portfolio should be equal to the risk-free interest rate. This reasoning leads to a differential equation whose solution has been given above. Other authors[4] have derived the theoretical value of an option using a binomial process.

Applying the Black–Scholes formula is straightforward once the variance of the asset over the life of the option, σ^2, has been estimated. It can be estimated either from past data or through other prospective methods. Though it is the only estimated variable in the formula, it is an important one.

In some cases, particular characteristics of the underlying asset require revision of the formula. Buying options on bonds, for example, does not allow one to claim the accrued interest, whereas buying a bond does. Some options are not written on assets, but on indexes or prices such as futures prices or exchange rates. To accommodate these differences, slight changes are required in the arbitrage model used to derive the valuation formula. The changes made in the model to accommodate currency options are discussed in the appendix.

These valuation formulas provide useful approximations. With the help of computers, they can be used to continually adjust premium estimates, thereby reflecting changes in underlying asset prices and allowing for rapid management of a position. Unfortunately, several of the assumptions required by the Black–Scholes model are not actually valid in the real world: interest rates and variances are not constant and stocks pay dividends that are not precisely known ahead of time. It is therefore sometimes profitable to exercise an option before its expiration date. For example, it is occasionally profitable to exercise a stock option before a dividend payment or a currency option that is deep in the money.

Since the Black–Scholes formula assumes no early exercise, its theoretical value is clearly incorrect. The problem is even more pronounced for put options.[5] Transaction costs and taxes also undermine the Black–Scholes model. Some of these imperfections are taken into account in more sophisticated formulas, but an exact analytical model for option premiums will never exist. However, it appears that Black–Scholes–type formulas provide a good practical approximation of option pricing.[6] Computer valuation programs can simulate various scenarios for the underlying asset's price and thereby indicate the best investment alternative given the manager's expectations. Such models assist in the day-to-day management of a complex position, so that a manager can understand how sensitive his or her total position is to changes in key parameters over time.

INSURING WITH OPTIONS

Options provide a unique tool with which to insure portfolios. Insurance means that a portfolio is protected against a negative performance while it retains its positive performance potential. By contrast, hedging removes both negative and positive performance potentials. An example will illustrate this concept.

An investor holds 1000 ounces of gold. On December 1, the spot price is equal to $400 per ounce and the premiums of put gold options are as reproduced in Exhibit 9.9. Our investor decides to buy ten put options February 400. The premium is equal to $8 per ounce, so that the total cost is equal to

10 options × 100 ounces × $8 = $8000.

If the price of gold goes up by the end of February, the options will be worthless. It is useless to have the right to sell at $400 gold that is worth more on the spot market. However, if the price of gold drops, the investor will use the option to sell her gold holdings at $400 per ounce. The net value of the insured portfolio as a function of the future price of gold is given in Exhibit 9.10. The value of the portfolio is always greater than $400,000 minus the premium cost of $8000. This premium is the insurance cost.

Several different options could be chosen. An out-of-the-money option such as the put February 390, is less costly, but only protects the portfolio for gold prices below $390 per ounce. In-the-money options provide better protection at a higher cost, as seen in Exhibit 9.11. An insurance could be sought for a longer time horizon, but naturally the premium is higher given the larger time value of the option.

Selling a call would not provide a good protection, since the option to exercise lies with the buyer of the call. However, dynamic strategies for changing the options position when the spot price of gold moves may be implemented. Also investors may replicate a put position even if such a contract is not traded. These synthetic securities may be created by combining several other securities or adopting dynamic buy and sell strategies.[7]

The above example assumes that the option is held until expiration. In many cases the option will be sold in the market before expiration; the total insurance cost is simply the difference in the time values of the option. In some cases, options, instead of futures, are used to hedge portfolios. Hedging is

EXHIBIT 9.9
Premiums of Put Options on Gold
Contracts of 100 ounces, premium per ounce

Strike price	Expiration Month		
	February	May	August
390	2.00	5.00	7.00
400	8.00	10.00	12.00
410	13.00	14.00	15.00

EXHIBIT 9.10
Value of the Insured Portfolio for Various Scenarios of the Price of Gold

Price of gold (dollars per ounce)	Value of the portfolio (dollars)
380	392,000
390	392,000
400	392,000
410	402,000
420	412,000
450	442,000

EXHIBIT 9.11
Value of Insured Portfolios with Different Options

Price of gold	Value of the Portfolio (dollars insured with)		
(dollars per ounce)	Feb. 390	Feb. 400	Feb. 410
380	388,000	392,000	397,000
390	388,000	392,000	397,000
400	398,000	392,000	397,000
410	408,000	402,000	397,000
420	418,000	412,000	407,000
450	448,000	442,000	437,000

designed to eliminate the uncertainty of a future outcome, whereas insurance is designed to eliminate only the negative outcomes. Of course, there is a cost to the attractive risk-return characteristic of insurance. The use of options for hedging and insurance is further discussed in the next chapter.

SUMMARY

1. Options, like futures, are leveraged investments, but they have an attractive asymmetric risk-return characteristic. Calls and puts are the major types of options traded on organized exchanges. Combinations of options and other securities allow the creation of numerous positions designed to capitalize on specific expectations about return and risk. Customized options can be arranged, especially for currencies and interest rates, with long-term horizons extending up to ten or fifteen years. These customized options are only written by banks for large amounts.

2. Exchange-traded options are written on all types of financial instruments including commodities, currencies, individual stocks, stock indexes, and fixed-income securities. Options on spot assets as weil as on futures contracts also exist.

3. The valuation of options is somewhat complex and depends on the underlying asset. Analytic valuation models have been derived for European-type options, which cannot be exercised until expiration. They offer an operational approximation for American-type options, which can be exercised any time, as is the case for most options traded in the world.

4. Options can be used to invest in a specific security or market, while limiting the downside risk potential. They are also used to insure an existing portfolio. For example, buying a put on an asset (or portfolio) allows the reduction, or elimination, of loss in case of a drop in value of an asset. In-the-money options offer better protection than out-of-the-money options, but at a higher cost.

QUESTIONS AND PROBLEMS

1. An American investor believes in the depreciation of the dollar and buys one call option in deutsche marks at an exercise price of 45 cents per deutsche mark. The option premium is 1 cent per deutsche mark or $625 per contract of 62,500 deutsche marks (Philadelphia):

- For what range of exchange rates should the investor exercise the call option on the last day of the call life?

- For what range of exchange rates will the investor realize a net profit, taking the original cost into account?

- If the investor had purchased a put with the same exercise price and premium, instead of a call, how would you answer the previous two questions?

2. The average premium on currency calls has decreased, while the premium on currency puts has increased. Why?

3. If the average premium on gold call options declines, does it mean that they are becoming undervalued and therefore should be bought? Using valuation models, give at least two possible causes for this decline in an efficient market.

4. You would like to protect your portfolio of British equity against a down movement of the British stock market. What are the relative advantages of stock index futures and options? Should you prefer in-the-money or out-of-the-money options?

5. Titi, a Japanese company, issued a six-year Eurobond in dollars convertible to shares of the Japanese company. At time of issue, the long-term bond yield on straight dollar bonds was 10% for such an issuer. Instead, Titi issued bonds at 8%. Each $1000 par bond is convertible into 100 shares of Titi. At time of issue, the stock price of Titi is 1600 yen and the exchange rate is 100 yen = 0.5 dollar ($/¥ = 0.005).

- Why can the bond be issued with a yield of only 8%?
- What would happen if
    the stock price of Titi increases;
    the yen appreciates; or
    the market interest rate of dollar bonds drops?
- A year later the new market conditions are as follows:
    The yield on straight dollar bonds of similar quality has risen from 10% to
    11%.
    Titi stock price has moved up to ¥ 2000.
    The exchange rate is $/¥ = 0.006.
    What would be a minimum price for the Titi convertible bond?

□ Could you try to assess the theoretical value of this convertible bond as a package of other securities such as a straight bond issued by Titi, options or warrants on the yen value of Titi stock, and futures and options on the dollar/yen exchange rate?

NOTES

1. A good analysis of options may be found in J. Cox and M. Rubinstein, *Options Markets*, Englewood Cliffs, NJ: Prentice Hall, 1985; D. Galai, R. Geske, and S. Givots, *Option Markets: Theory and Evidence*, Reading, MA: Addison-Wesley, 1988; and R. A. Jarrow and A. Budd, *Option Pricing*, Englewood Cliffs, NJ: Prentice Hall, 1983.

2. See F. Black and M. Scholes, "The Pricing of Options and Corporate Liabilities," *Journal of Political Economy*, 81(3) May/June 1973, pp. 637–654.

3. See F. Black and M. Scholes, "The Pricing of Options and Corporate Liabilities," *Journal of Political Economy*, 81(3) May/June 1973. See also R. Merton, "A Rational Theory of Option Pricing," *Bell Journal of Economics and Management Science*, Spring 1973; R. A. Jarrow and A. Budd, *Option Pricing*, Englewood Cliffs, NJ: Prentice Hall, 1983; and D. Galai, R. Geske, and S. Givots, *Option Markets: Theory and Evidence*, Reading, MA: Addison-Wesley, 1987.

4. See J. Cox and M. Rubinstein, *Option Markets*, Englewood Cliffs, NJ: Prentice Hall, 1985; or W. Sharpe, *Investments*, Englewood Cliffs, NJ: Prentice Hall, 1987.

5. A review of some of the problems can be found in J. Cox and M. Rubinstein, *op. cit.*, and in C. Smith, "Option Pricing: A Review," *Journal of Financial Economics*, January/March, 1976.

6. This is shown in the foreign-currency options market by K. Shastri and K. Tandon in "On the Use of European Models to Price an Option on Foreign Currencies," *Journal of Futures Markets*, Spring 1986; and by J. Bodhurta and G. R. Courtadon in "Efficiency Tests of the Foreign Currency Options Market," *Journal of Finance*, March 1986. Tests for other markets are presented in D. Galai, R. Geske, and S. Givots, *op. cit.*

More complex models have been proposed. Numerical analysis must be used to derive solutions. This is a costly and computer time–consuming approach. See M. Brennan and E. Schwartz, "The Valuation of American Put Options," *Journal of Finance*, May 1977; and J. Cox, S. Ross, and M. Rubinstein, "Option Pricing: A Simplified Approach," *Journal of Financial Economics*, September 1979. Some analytical formulas have been derived by R. Roll, "An Analytical Formula for Unprotected American Call Options with Known Dividends," *Journal of Financial Economics*, November 1977; and R. Geske and H. Johnson, "The American Put Valued Analytically," *Journal of Finance*, December 1984.

7. See J. Cox and M. Rubinstein (1985) *op. cit.* and M. Rubinstein and H. Leland, "Replicating Options with Positions in Stock and Cash," *Financial Analysts Journal*, July/August 1981.

8. For a straightforward derivation of the Black–Scholes valuation formula for currency options, see M. Garman and S. Kohlagen, "Foreign Currency Option Values," *Journal International Money and Finance*, December 1983; and J. O. Grabbe "The Pricing of Call and Put Options on Foreign Exchange," *Journal of International Money and Finance*, December 1983.

9. The formula for European-type options on futures contracts has been derived by F. Black in "The Pricing of Commodity Contracts," *Journal of Financial Economics*, March 1976.

10. Tests of the Black–Scholes and other models can be found in J. Bodhurta and G. R. Courtadon, "Efficiency Tests of the Foreign Currency Options Market," *Journal of Finance*, March 1986; and K. Shastri and K. Tandon, "On the Use of European Models to Price an Option on Foreign Currencies," *Journal of Futures Markets*, Spring 1986.

BIBLIOGRAPHY

F. Black, "The Pricing of Commodity Contracts," *Journal of Financial Economics*, March 1976.

F. Black and M. Scholes, "The Pricing of Options and Corporate Liabilities," *Journal of Political Economy*, 81(3) May/June 1973, pp. 637–654.

J. Bodhurta and G. R. Courtadon, "Efficiency Tests of the Foreign Currency Options Market," *Journal of Finance*, March 1986.

M. Brennan and E. Schwartz, "The Valuation of American Put Options," *Journal of Finance*, May 1977.

J. Cox, S. Ross, and M. Rubinstein, "Option Pricing: A Simplified Approach," *Journal of Financial Economics*, September 1979.

J. Cox and M. Rubinstein, *Options Markets*, Englewood Cliffs, NJ: Prentice Hall, 1985.

D. Galai, R. Geske, and S. Givots, *Option Markets: Theory and Evidence*, Reading, MA: Addison-Wesley, 1988.

M. Garman and S. Kohlagen, "Foreign Currency Option Values," *Journal of International Money and Finance*, December 1983.

R. Geske and H. Johnson, "The American Put Valued Analytically," *Journal of Finance*, December 1984.

J. O. Grabbe, "The Pricing of Call and Put Options on Foreign Exchange," *Journal of International Money and Finance*, December 1983.

R. A. Jarrow and A. Budd, *Option Pricing*, Englewood Cliffs, NJ: Prentice Hall, 1983.

R. Merton, "A Rational Theory of Option Pricing," *Bell Journal of Economics and Management Science*, Spring 1973.

R. Roll, "An Analytical Formula for Unprotected American Call Options with Known Dividends," *Journal of Financial Economics*, November 1977.

M. Rubinstein and H. Leland, "Replicating Options with Positions in Stock and Cash," *Financial Analysts Journal*, July/August 1981.

W. Sharpe, *Investments*, Englewood Cliffs, NJ: Prentice Hall, 1987.

K. Shastri and K. Tandon, "On the Use of European Models to Price an Option on Foreign Currencies," *Journal of Futures Markets*, Spring 1986.

C. Smith, "Option Pricing: A Review," *Journal of Financial Economics*, January/March, 1976.

Chapter 9: Appendix:
Valuing Currency Options

Traditional option valuation models can be readily adapted to currency options.[8] The main revision stems from the fact that the opportunity cost to invest in a foreign currency is not the domestic risk-free rate, as for an ordinary asset, but rather the interest rate differential (domestic minus foreign). The intuitive explanation for this is that the direct investment in a foreign currency costs the domestic interest rate (to finance the purchase of currency) but earns the foreign interest rate. This leads to a simple revision of the Black–Scholes formula, Eq. (9.1). For a European-type call option the revised formula is

$$P_0 = e^{-r^*t}\left[SN(d) - e^{-rt}EN(d - \sigma\sqrt{t}\,) \right] \qquad (9.A1)$$

where

S	is the exchange rate (the domestic currency price of one unit of foreign currency),
E	is the exercise price,
r and r^*	are the domestic and foreign interest rates expressed on a continuous compounding basis,
$N(X)$	is the probability that a deviation of less than X will occur in a unit normal distribution,
d is	$\dfrac{\ln(S/E) + (r - r^* + 0.5\sigma^2)t}{\sigma\sqrt{t}}$,
t	is the time to expiration, and
σ	is the standard deviation of percentage exchange rate changes.

This formula can also be written as a function of the forward, or futures, exchange rate, rather than the spot exchange rate. With continuous compounding, the interest rate parity relation between the forward rate, the spot rate, and the interest rate differential is written as

$$F = Se^{(r - r^*)t}. \qquad (9.A2)$$

This implies that the valuation of the option premium may be written as

$$P_0 = e^{-rt}\left[FN(d) - EN(d - \sigma\sqrt{t}\,) \right] \qquad (9.A3)$$

where

$$d = \frac{\ln\,(F/E) + 0.5\sigma^2 t}{\sigma\sqrt{t}}.$$

Note that this formula equals the Black–Scholes formula for options on currency futures.[9] Therefore, a European-type option on spot exchange rate or on futures exchange rate should have the same value. This is not the case for an American-type option, which can be exercised any time before expiration. Although the spot and futures exchange rates converge at expiration, they are not equal during the life of the option. Depending on the value of the basis (futures discount or premium), an American-type option on spot exchange rates (as traded in Philadelphia) may be worth more or less than an American-type option on futures exchange rates (as traded in Chicago).

In the valuation formula for European-type currency options, the coefficient δ is equal to

$$\delta = e^{-rt}N(d).$$

Valuing a currency put is identical to valuing a currency call because of the inverse relationship between exchange rates. A put on the pound/dollar rate is identical to a call on a dollar/pound rate.

The above formula was derived by Black and Scholes for European-type options, which cannot be exercised before expiration. In reality, however, listed currency options can usually be exercised at any time before expiration. And unlike many other call options, it is sometimes more profitable to do so. This is true, for example, for deep-in-the-money calls or put options, when the foreign interest rate is much higher (or lower) than the domestic interest rate. In general, in fact, the probability of early exercise increases with the interest rate differential, especially for in-the-money options. The intuitive explanation for this is that it is better to exercise a call immediately and invest at a high foreign interest rate than wait until expiration and, in the meantime, earn a low domestic interest rate on the cash to be converted. When the probability of early exercise increases, the premium becomes driven by the conversion value of the option, so that the Black–Scholes formula systematically underestimates it. Under those circumstances, we must use more complicated models involving numerical estimation techniques.[10]

Other things being equal, the value of an option decreases over time. Intuitively, this relationship between time and the value of an option makes sense for two reasons. First, the cash investment in the option is less than the amount required to buy the security, which means that money is left over to invest elsewhere. The longer the time to expiration, the more valuable this financing advantage is. Second, the longer the time to expiration, the more likely it is that there will be a large positive move in the price of the underlying security. Of course, large adverse moves are just as likely to occur, but this does

EXHIBIT 9.12
Volatility Profile of Spot Currencies

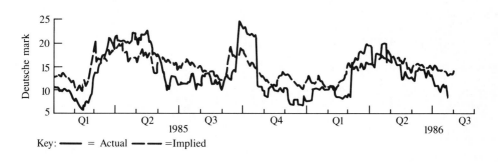

Key: ——— = Actual — — — =Implied

Source: Monthly Review of Futures and Options, July 1986, Salomon Brothers Inc. Reprinted with permission.

not affect the option buyer because his or her loss is limited to the premium. For currency options, the time premium component is usually less than it is for stock options because the financing opportunity cost for currency options is only the interest rate differential, not the domestic risk-free rate. But the second component, i.e., security price volatility of the time premium, is still present, and that is why the premium tends to decline over time.

The premium of a currency option is affected by the interest rate differential and, more importantly, by the estimated volatility of the exchange rate. Exchange rate markets go through periods of calm and periods of turbulence, depending on the international environment. Options can be considered as undervalued by an investor if his or her volatility assessment is more than that of the market. Option valuation models can be used to estimate the market assessment of the exchange rate volatility implied in current option premiums. Basically, one would use models such as Eq. (9.A1) and solve for σ given the premium P_0. This is routinely done by most option dealers. Exhibit 9.12 shows the evolution of the volatility of the \$/DM exchange rate changes as calculated by Salomon Brothers. The solid line is the actual volatility based on the standard deviation of percentage exchange rate movements in the past 20 days. The dashed line is the estimated annualized volatility implied in the nearby option premium traded in Philadelphia. The expost volatility measure moved between 5 and 25% per year. Clearly the market assessment implied in option premiums is influenced by the recent behavior of the spot market but, being forward looking, the implied volatility tends to smooth the past volatility. The implied volatility fluctuated in a narrower range of 10 to 20% per year. Some investors use these charts to determine periods when options look under- or overvalued.

10

Currency Risk Management

The traditional and most consistent international investment strategy is first to decide on an international asset allocation. An allocation breaks down a portfolio by both asset class (short-term deposit, bond, equity, commodity) and country or currency of investment (U.S. dollar, British pound, French franc). The resulting allocation can be used to form a matrix of currencies and asset classes. Ten percent of a typical portfolio's value may be allocated to Japanese stocks, 5% to deutsche mark bonds, and so forth. Specific bonds and stocks are selected using the various techniques discussed in previous chapters. Once a portfolio is structured it must be managed according to changes in expectations. For example, periodical revisions of the forecasted earnings of specific companies can lead to equity arbitrage within a portfolio. More common revisions in expectations, however, are the result of macroeconomic variables. News of economic growth or changes in money supply may cause a manager to alter his or her asset allocation, at least temporarily. But frequent reallocation can lead to heavy transaction costs, especially on bonds and some illiquid foreign stocks.

Leveraged instruments such as options and futures are used domestically to hedge risks that arise suddenly. They protect a manager from being forced to arbitrage or liquidate a large part of his or her portfolio. For example, interest rate futures or options may be used to hedge a long-term bond portfolio if fears about a rise in interest rates materialize. Similarly, a domestic manager who is heavily invested in bonds but suddenly becomes bullish on the stock market can immediately act on his or her expectation by buying stock index futures or options and thereafter slowly switching his or her portfolio from bonds to stocks. This technique reduces transactions costs, gives to the manager time to select the best stocks, and locks in potential profits on the anticipated rise in the stock market. Moreover, if after a few days the manager changes his or her mind about how well the stock market will perform all the manager needs do is close his or her futures and options position and stick with the initial portfolio allocation. These and other short-term risk management techniques are extensively used in both the United States and other countries where speculative instruments on stocks and bonds exist (see Chapter 8). The use of financial futures and options in controlling portfolio risk is described in textbooks that deal with domestic investment. <u>The most important area of risk management in international investment is *currency risk*.</u>

<u>This chapter</u> is devoted to the art of fine-tuning an international portfolio, so that it will benefit from both sudden changes in expectations and market uncertainties. <u>Its focus is currency risk management.</u>

Most portfolio managers are often confronted with practical problems such as the following:

- An investor holds a portfolio of French stocks on which he is bullish, but he is concerned that the franc may drop sharply in the wake of local elections. On the other hand, the franc may also appreciate strongly if the election goes the other way.
- An investor holds British gilts. She expects the long-term UK interest rate to drop, which in turn, would cause a depreciation of the pound.
- An investor would like to buy KLM stock because he is very bullish about the Dutch airline, but he is concerned that the Dutch guilder may depreciate.
- A British investor specializes in forecasting monetary variables such as interest and exchange rates. Which strategies should she choose to capitalize on her forecasts?

This chapter is intended to assist the reader in better handling these kinds of situations.

HEDGING WITH FUTURES OR FORWARD CURRENCY CONTRACTS

Either futures or forward currency contracts may be used to hedge a portfolio. They differ in several ways, which are outlined in Chapter 8, but more importantly, both types of contracts allow a manager to take the same economic position. Therefore, in this chapter *futures* will denote both futures and forward contracts.

The Basic Approach: Hedging the Principal

<u>Hedging with futures or forward contracts</u> is very simple. <u>One takes a position with a foreign exchange contract that is the reverse of the principal being hedged.</u> In other words, a citizen of country A who wants to hedge a portfolio of

assets denominated in currency B would sell a futures contract to exchange currency B for currency A. The size of the contract would equal the market value of the assets hedged. For example, a U.S. investor with £1 million invested in British gilts (Treasury bonds) would sell futures for £1 million worth of dollars. The direction of a foreign exchange rate contract is often confusing because it involves the exchange rates of two currencies.

On the International Monetary Market at the Chicago Board of Trade one can buy and sell contracts of £25,000 where the futures price is expressed in dollars per pound. The same-size contract is also found on the London International Financial Futures Exchange (LIFFE). Let us assume that on September 12 our U.S. investor buys futures with delivery in December for 1.95 dollars per pound; the spot exchange rate is 2.00 dollars per pound. In order to hedge his £1 million principal the investor must sell a total of forty contracts. Now let us assume that a few weeks later the futures and spot exchange rates drop to $1.85 and $1.90, respectively, while the pound value of the British asset rises to 1,010,000. To help the U.S. investor assess the value of his portfolio we introduce the following notation:

V_t — value of the portfolio of *foreign assets to hedge* measured in foreign currency at time t (e.g., £1 million),

V_t^* — value of the *portfolio of foreign assets* measured in domestic currency (e.g., $2 million),

S_t — spot exchange rate: domestic currency value of one unit of foreign currency quoted at time t (e.g., 2.00 $/£), and

F_t — futures exchange rate: domestic currency value of one unit of foreign currency quoted at time t.

Exhibit 10.1 shows that as the pound value of the British assets appreciates by 1%, the sterling exchange rate drops by 5%, causing a loss in dollar value on the portfolio of 4.05%. In dollar terms, this loss in portfolio value is $81,000, as we see below

$$V_t^* - V_0^* = V_t S_t - V_0 S_0. \tag{10.1}$$

EXHIBIT 10.1
Relationships Between Portfolio Value and Rate of Return

	Period 0	Period t	Rates of return (percent)
Portfolio Value (in pounds), V	1,000,000	1,010,000	1
Portfolio Value (in dollars), V^*	2,000,000	1,919,000	−4.05
Exchange Rate ($/pounds), S	2.00	1.90	−5
Futures Rate ($/pounds), F	1.95	1.85	—

Hence

$$\$1,919,000 - \$2,000,000 = (\pounds1,010,000 \times \$/\pounds1.90)$$
$$- (\pounds1,000,000 \times \$/\pounds2.00)$$
$$= -\$81,000.$$

On the other hand, the realized gain on the futures contract sale is $100,000, as shown below

$$V_0^*(-F_t + F_0) = \text{Realized gain.} \tag{10.2}$$

Hence

$$\pounds1,000,000 \times \$/\pounds(1.95 - 1.85) = \$100,000.$$

Therefore, the net profit on the hedged position is $19,000, as we see below:

$$\text{Profit} = V_t^*S_t - V_0^*S_0 + V_0^*(F_0 - F_t). \tag{10.3}$$

Hence

$$\text{Profit} = \$100,000 - \$81,000 = \$19,000.$$

The rate of return in dollars on the hedged position is

$$\text{Return} = \frac{19,000}{2,000,000} = 0.95\%.$$

This position is almost perfectly hedged, since the 1% return on the British asset is transformed into a 0.95% return in U.S. dollars despite the drop in value of the British pound. The slight difference between the two numbers is explained by the fact that the investor hedged only the principal (£1 million), not the price appreciation or the return on the British investment (equal here to 1%). The 5% drop in sterling value applied to this 1% return exactly equals $1\% \times 5\% = 0.05\%$.

The efficiency of a hedge depends on the return on the hedged assets. The larger the return, the less efficient the hedge. This is seen by examining the rate of return on the hedged position. It is necessary to introduce some further notations to better understand the technical effects of exchange rate movements. Let us call R, R^*, and s the rates of return on V, V^*, and S, and let's call R_F the variation on the futures exchange rate as a proportion of the spot exchange rate, that is, $R_F = (F_t - F_0)/S_0$. The relationship between dollar and pound returns on the foreign portfolio is as follows:

$$R^* = R + s(1 + R). \tag{10.4}$$

Hence

$$-4.05\% = 1\% - 5(1.01)\%.$$

The cross-product term $sR = 0.05\%$ explains the difference between the return on the portfolio and the return on the futures position. The currency

R_F = the variation on the futures exchange rate as a proportion of the spot exch rate

R^* = Rate of return of portfolio value in domestic currency.

contribution, $R^* - R$, is equal to exchange rate variation plus the cross-product sR. When the value of the portfolio in local currency fluctuates widely, the difference is significant. So the question is what the exact amount hedged should be to reduce or fully eliminate the influence of the currency movement.

Optimal Hedge Ratio

The objective of a currency hedge (see the appendix) is to minimize the influence of an exchange rate depreciation. This is usually taken to mean the following: A currency hedge should achieve on a foreign asset the same rate of return in domestic currency as can be achieved on the local market in foreign currency terms. For example, a U.S. investor would try to achieve a dollar rate of return on a British gilts portfolio equal to what he or she could have achieved in terms of sterling. Creating a perfect currency hedge is equivalent to nullifying a currency movement and translating a foreign rate of return directly into a similar domestic rate of return.

As shown in Chapter 8, the rate of return on a hedged position is equal to

$$R_H = R^* - hR_F \tag{10.5}$$

where R_H is the rate of return on a portfolio hedged against currency risk and h is the hedge ratio as defined in Chapter 8.

The optimal amount to hedge is determined by finding the value of h such that the hedged return in domestic currency terms, R_H, equals the return in foreign currency terms, R. Substituting the value of R^* given in Eq. (10.4) into Eq. (10.5), we find

$$R_H = R + s(1 + R) - hR_F.$$

Therefore, the objective of a hedging policy is to minimize the variance of the return differential $R_H - R$, where

$$R_H - R = s(1 + R) - hR_F. \tag{10.6}$$

We will now study the operational implications of this currency hedging strategy starting with a simple case and moving on to a more general case.

No basis risk Let's first assume that the basis (see Chapter 8) remains constant. Then the rate of return on a futures contract, $R_F = (F_t - F_0)/S_0$, is equal to the spot exchange rate movement, $s = (S_t - S_0)/S_0$. Eq. (10.6) can now be written as

$$R_H - R = s(1 + R - h). \tag{10.7}$$

The optimal hedge ratio h is most easily determined for assets that have nonstochastic returns, such as interest-bearing securities with fixed prices (e.g., short-term deposits). To eliminate the influence of currency translation one must hedge both the principal and the expected return on the principal $(1 + R)$. In the previous example, the investor should ideally have hedged £1,010,000 had he been able to anticipate that the return would be 1% on his British gilts. When the return on foreign assets is uncertain, however, an investor should take into account the covariance between exchange rates and asset returns.

We saw in Chapter 1 that, in practice, stock prices have little correlation with exchange rates, so that the last covariance term may dropped. The optimal hedge for stocks, therefore, includes both the principal and any expected dividend payment or price appreciation. Where there are unexpected price movements an investor's holding of futures contracts should be adjusted to reflect the change in market value of the foreign stock portfolio.

Bond portfolios are generally more sensitive to exchange rate movements because of the link between exchange rates and interest rates. In the introduction, we described a U.S. investor who was expecting a decline in British interest rates (rise in bond prices) leading to a depreciation of the pound. This scenario implies that there is a negative covariance between R and s. The hedging implications of this covariance are studied in the appendix.

Basis risk   - Int rate diff between forward + Spot

The basis

Forward and futures exchange rates are directly determined by two factors: the spot exchange rate and the interest rate differential between two currencies. (This was discussed in Chapters 3 and 8.) The forward discount or premium, which is the percentage difference between the forward and the spot exchange rates, equals the interest rate differential for the same maturity as the forward contract. In futures jargon, we say the basis equals the interest rate differential. If we express the exchange rate in sterling as the dollar value of one pound (e.g., $/£ = 2.00$) and call $r_\$$ and $r_£$ the interest rates in dollars and pounds, respectively, with the same maturity as the futures contract, the relation known as interest rate parity is

$$\frac{F}{S} = \frac{1 + r_\$}{1 + r_£} \quad \text{and}$$

$$\frac{F - S}{S} = \frac{r_\$ - r_£}{1 + r_£}. \tag{10.8}$$

Because this relation is the result of arbitrage on very liquid markets, it technically holds at every instant. On the forward interbank of Euro-currency markets, banks only trade in short-term interest rates. There, forward prices are simply quoted to clients by applying the interest rate parity formula. When a forward contract is written for a client, the bank simply takes an offsetting position in the Euro-currency market. Arbitrage between futures and forward prices ensures that interest rate parity applies to futures contracts as well. Note that such an exact valuation of the basis does not work for futures or forward contracts on other commodities and instruments: Arbitrage transaction costs are much higher in other markets, and optional clauses exist in many other futures contracts. As discussed in Chapter 8, bond futures are an extreme case where basis valuation is a rather difficult exercise. Forward and futures currency contracts are an interesting exception, since the basis is precisely defined as the interest rate differential and changes in the interest rate differential have a strong influence on currency movements.

Minimum-variance hedge

The optimal hedge ratio is equal to the covariance of the currency contribution $(R^* - R)$ with the futures return R_F divided by the variance of the futures return (see Eq. 8.6 and the Chp. 10 appendix). A correlation between currency movements and changes in the interest rate differential will lead to an optimal hedge ratio different from one. This is because a component of the futures return is the change in interest rate differential or basis. Accordingly, the hedge ratio should compensate for this correlation.

The correlation between futures and spot exchange rates is a function of the futures contract term. Futures prices for contracts near maturity closely follow spot exchange rates because at this time the interest rate differential is a small component of the futures price. To illustrate, let us consider the futures price of British pound contracts with one, three, and twelve months left until delivery. The spot exchange rate is currently $2.00 per pound, and the interest rates and the calculated values for the futures are as given in Exhibit 10.2. The one-month futures price should equal $2.00 plus the one-month interest rate differential applied to the spot rate. The interest rate differential for *one month* equals the annualized rate differential of -4% divided by 12:

$$F = S + S\frac{r_\$ - r_£}{1 + r_£} = 2.00 - 2.00\frac{\frac{4}{12}\%}{1 + \frac{14}{12}\%}.$$

EXHIBIT 10.2
Importance of Interest Rate Differentials to Futures Prices

	Maturity one month	Three months	Twelve months
Pound Interest Rate (percent)	14	13.5	13
Dollar Interest Rate (percent)	10	10	10
Futures Price (dollars)	1.993	1.983	1.947
Interest Rate Component (dollars)	−0.007	−0.017	−0.053

Spot rate: £1 = $2.00.

Hence

$$F = 1.993 .$$

We see then that even though the interest rate differential is very large, its effect on the one-month futures price is minimal because the spot exchange rate is the driving force behind short-term forward exchange rate movements. This is less true for longer-term contracts. More specifically, a reduction of 1% (100 basis points) in the interest rate differential causes a futures price movement of approximately 0.25% ($\frac{3}{12}$) for the three-month contracts and 1% ($\frac{12}{12}$) for the one-year contract, as compared to 0.08% ($\frac{1}{12}$%) for the one-month contract.

Hedging Strategies

A major decision in selecting a futures or forward currency hedge is the choice of contract terms. Short-term contracts track the behavior of the spot exchange rates better, have greater trading volume, and offer more liquidity than long-term contracts. On the other hand, short-term contracts must be rolled over if a hedge is to be maintained for a period longer than the initial contract.

For longer-term hedges, a manager can choose from three basic contract terms:

1. short-term contracts, already mentioned above, which must be rolled over at maturity;
2. contracts with a matching maturity, that is, with a maturity matching the expected period for which the hedge is to maintained; and
3. longer-term contracts with a maturity extending beyond the hedging period.

Futures contracts for any of the three terms may be closed by taking an offsetting position on the delivery date. This avoids actual physical delivery of a currency. Exhibit 10.3 depicts three such hedging strategies for an expected hedge period of six months. The choice of strategy depends on the evolution of

EXHIBIT 10.3
Three Hedging Strategies for an Expected Hedge Period of Six Months

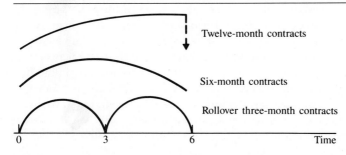

interest rates. Long-term contracts are more attractive if the interest rate differential (domestic minus foreign) falls in absolute value. *Ceteris paribus*, a drop in the interest rate differential means lower futures prices (relative to spot prices), which is beneficial to the seller of a futures contract.

Another consideration in picking a hedging strategy is transaction costs. Rolling over short-term contracts generates more commissions because of the larger number of transactions involved. Also, the number of futures contracts used in order to reflect changes in the market value of the hedge portfolio should be frequently adjusted to reflect changes in the asset value.

Longer hedges can be built using currency swaps, which can be arranged with horizons up to a dozen years long. However, currency swaps are primarily used by corporations in the currency management of their assets and liabilities. Portfolio managers usually take a shorter horizon.

Portfolio of Currencies

Cross hedges are sometimes used for closely linked currencies. For example, a U.S. investor could use deutsche mark futures to hedge a currency risk on Dutch stocks, since the Dutch guilder and the deutsche mark are strongly correlated. Futures and forward currency contracts are only actively traded for the major currencies. International portfolios are often invested in assets in Spain, Italy, Norway, Sweden, Singapore, and other countries where futures and forward contracts are not traded in the domestic currency. In these cases, one must try to find contracts on other currencies that are closely correlated with the investment currencies.

Investment managers sometimes fear the depreciation of only one or two currencies in their portfolio and, therefore, hedge currency risk selectively. Other managers fear that their domestic currency will appreciate relative to all foreign currencies. For example, the strong U.S. dollar appreciation from January 1983 to March 1985 was realized against all currencies. This domestic currency appreciation induced a negative currency contribution on all foreign portfolios. Foreign stock investments had outstanding performances, but an overall currency hedge on their foreign investments would have drastically improved their performance by nullifying the negative currency contribution to the total dollar performance of non-U.S. portfolios.

Systematic currency hedging also reduces the total volatility of the portfolio, as seen in Chapter 2.[1] A complete foreign currency hedge can be achieved by hedging the investments in each foreign currency. But this is unfeasible for many currencies and very cumbersome administratively. Also, it is not necessary to hedge all of each currency component in a multi-currency portfolio. In a portfolio with assets in many currencies, the residual risk of each currency gets partly diversified away. Optimization techniques can be used to construct a hedge with futures contracts in only a few currencies (e.g., the yen, deutsche mark, and sterling). Although the residual risk of individual currencies is not fully hedged, the portfolio is well protected against a general appreciation of the home currency.[2] Another alternative is to use futures on a basket of currencies such as the European currency unit.

The stability of the estimated hedge ratios is of crucial importance in establishing effective hedge strategies especially when cross-hedging is involved. Empirical studies indicate that hedges using futures contracts in the same currency as the asset to be hedged are very effective but that the optimal hedge ratios in cross-hedges that involve different currencies are quite unstable over time.[3]

INSURING AND HEDGING WITH OPTIONS

Two approaches are used for reducing currency risk exposure with options. The traditional method exploits the asymmetric risk-return characteristic of an option, so that it is used as an insurance vehicle. The second, and more dynamic, approach takes into account the relationship between the option premium and the underlying exchange rate. This second approach is closer to a hedging strategy.

Insuring with Options

Many investors continue to focus on the characteristics of options at expiration. Currency options are purchased in amounts equal to the principal to be hedged. As with currency futures, it is not easy to determine which options to use because they involve the rate of exchange between two currencies. Our previous example described a U.S. investor with £1 million of British assets. Let us assume that on the Philadelphia Stock Exchange he buys British pound puts for December at 200. A British pound put gives him the right, but not the obligation, to sell British pounds at a fixed exercise price with payment in dollars. Similarly, a British pound call gives him the right to buy British pounds with U.S. dollars. We should note that a call to buy British pounds with U.S. dollars is equivalent to a put to sell U.S. dollars for British pounds. Options markets in some countries sometimes offer reverse contracts, so that investors must be sure that they understand the position they are taking. In all cases, however, a good hedge implies buying options (puts or calls), not selling or writing them.

Returning to our example, the spot exchange rate is 2.00 U.S. dollars per pound. The exercise price for the December put is 200 cents per pound (or 2 dollars per pound), and the premium is 6 cents per pound. On the Philadelphia Stock Exchange, one contract covers £12,500, so that the investor must buy 80 contracts to hedge £1 million. In this traditional approach puts are treated as insurance devices. If the pound drops below $2.00 at expiration, a profit will be made on the put that exactly offsets the currency loss on the portfolio. If the pound drops to \$1.90, the gain on the put at expiration is

$$80 \times 12{,}500 \times (2.00 - 1.90) = \$100{,}000.$$

The advantage of buying options over buying futures is that options simply expire if the pound appreciates rather than depreciates. For example, if the British pound moves up to \$2.20, the futures contract will generate a loss of \$200,000, nullifying the currency gain on the portfolio of assets. This does not happen with options that simply expire. Of course, one must pay a price for this asymmetric risk structure, namely, the premium, which is the cost of having this hedging insurance.

Note that the premium keeps an investor from having a perfect hedge. In the previous example, the net profit on the put purchase equals the gain at expiration minus the premium. If we call P_0 the premium and E the exercise price, the net dollar profit on the put at the time of exercise t is

Net dollar profit $= V_0(E - S_t) - V_0 P_0$, that is,

Net dollar profit = Value option (Exercise price − Spot price)

− Value option (Premium).

Hence

$$\pounds 1{,}000{,}000 \times \$/\pounds(2.00 - 1.90) - \pounds 1{,}000{,}000 \times \$/\pounds 0.06 = \$40{,}000.$$

This profit does not cover the currency loss on the portfolio (equal to roughly \$100,000) because the option premium cost \$60,000. It would have been even less profitable if the pound had dropped to only \$1.95. An alternative solution is to buy out-of-the-money puts with a lower exercise price and a lower premium. But with those, exchange rates would have to move that much more before a profit could be made on the options. In short, what is gained in terms of a lower premium is lost in terms of a higher exercise price.

In fact, the traditional approach does not allow for a good currency hedge except when variations in the spot exchange rate swamp the cost of the premium. Instead, this approach uses options as insurance contracts, and the premium is regarded as a sunk cost. Note, however, that options are usually resold on the market rather than left to expire, and when the option is resold part of the initial insurance premium is recovered. On the other hand, the approach still exploits the greatest advantage of options, namely, that an option can be allowed to expire if the currency moves in a favorable direction. Options protect a portfolio in case of adverse currency movements, as do currency futures, and maintain its performance potential in case of favorable currency movements, while futures hedge in both directions. The price of this asymmetric advantage is the insurance cost implicit in the time value of option.

Dynamic Hedging with Options

Listed options are continually traded, and positions are usually closed by reselling the put in the market instead of exercising it. The profit on a position is the difference between the two market premiums and, therefore, completely dependent on market valuation. The modern approach to currency option hedging recognizes this fact, and is based on the relationship between changes in option premiums and changes in exchange rates.

The definition of a perfect currency option is simple and similar to the one given previously. A perfect hedge is a position where every dollar loss from currency movement on a portfolio of foreign assets is covered by a dollar gain in the value of the options position.

We know that an option premium is only indirectly related to the underlying exchange rate. Exhibit 10.4 shows the relationship we usually observe. Beginning with a specific exchange rate, say, $\$/£ = 2.00$, a put premium can go up or down in response to changes in the exchange rates. The slope of the curve at point A denotes the elasticity of the premium to any movements in the dollar exchange rate. In Exhibit 10.4 the premium is equal to 6 cents when the exchange rate is 200 U.S. cents per pound, and the tangent at point A equals -0.5. This slope is usually called delta, as described in Chapter 9.

In this example, a good hedge would be achieved by buying two sterling puts for every sterling of British assets. One sterling put is defined here as a put option on one unit of British currency. One contract includes several unit puts,

EXHIBIT 10.4
Value of a Pound Puts in Relation to the Exchange Rate

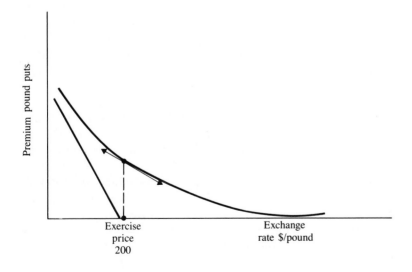

Premium pound puts

Exercise price 200

Exchange rate $/pound

depending on the contract size. If the pound depreciated by 1 U.S. cent, each put would go up by approximately 0.5 cent, offsetting the currency loss on the portfolio. In general, if n sterling options are purchased, the gain on the options position is

$$\text{Gain} = n(P_t - P_0)$$

where P_t is the put value at time t and P_0 is the put value at time zero. For small movements in the exchange rate,

$$P_t - P_0 = \delta(S_t - S_0).$$

Hence a good currency hedge is obtained by holding $n = -V_0/\delta$ options. The hedge ratio is equal to $-\frac{1}{\delta}$. The profit on the options position is then equal to $-V_0(S_t - S_0)$, which offsets the currency loss on the portfolio. In the first approximation, the pound value of the portfolio is assumed not to move.

We must emphasize that δ and the hedge ratio vary[4] with the exchange rate, so that the number of options held must be adjusted continually. This is both impractical and expensive because of transaction costs. In reality, a good hedge can be achieved only with periodical revisions in the options position, i.e., when there is a significant movement in the exchange rate. Between revisions, options offer their usual asymmetric insurance within the general hedging strategy. This strategy may be regarded as a mixed hedging-insurance strategy.

Implementing such a strategy requires a good understanding of option valuation and the precise estimation of the hedge ratio. As with futures, the strategy should take into account the expected return on the foreign portfolio as well as its correlation with exchange rate movements.

Hedging Strategies

Hedging strategies with options can be more sophisticated than those with futures for two reasons: The hedge ratio of options fluctuates, while it is constant for futures; and an investor can play with several maturities and exercise prices with options only.

The following example illustrates a dynamic strategy. At time zero, an investor buys n currency puts to hedge a portfolio of British assets. If the pound depreciates, options protect the portfolio but its δ changes. For example, the slope δ could move to -0.8 if the pound drops to 1.95. Then the hedge ratio should be equal to $\frac{1}{0.8} = 1.25$. To avoid over hedging, the investor must either sell some puts or switch to options with a lower exercise price (and lower delta); in both cases a profit will be realized. A typical strategy is to keep a fixed number of options, but replace in-the-money options with cheap out-of-the-money options to maintain the same hedge ratio. If the pound later reverses its down trend, the puts will become worthless; however, most of the profit will have been previously realized and saved.

A hedging strategy can combine futures and options.[5] Futures markets are very liquid and charge low transaction costs. Options offer the advantage of an asymmetric risk structure but have higher costs, in terms of both the fair price for this insurance risk structure and their transaction costs.

If a hedging decision is necessary because an investor faces an increasing volatility in exchange rates and doesn't have a clear view of the direction of change, currency options are a natural strategy. In the scenario described in the introduction, French elections created uncertainties about the future of the franc. In that case, options would have allowed the investor to hedge a drop in the franc while maintaining the opportunity to profit in case it rose.

Where the direction of a currency movement is clearly forecasted, currency futures provide a cheaper hedge. In setting the hedge, however, one should take into account the expected return on the portfolio and its correlation with currency movements.

OTHER METHODS FOR MANAGING CURRENCY EXPOSURE

Many methods are used to reduce currency exposure and to take positions in foreign markets without incurring excessive exchange risk. First, an investor can rearrange a portfolio so as to increase its risk level in a foreign market without increasing its currency exposure. For stocks, this means buying equities with higher betas (relative to the market index) and selling those with lower betas. This makes the portfolio more sensitive to local market movements without increasing its sensitivity to currency fluctuations. For bonds, this means adjusting the duration of the foreign portfolio to play on foreign interest rates without increasing its currency exposure.

An international portfolio manager who wants to invest in countries where the currency is expected to weaken has a couple of choices. He or she can buy common stock outright and hedge the exchange risk with currency futures or options, or the manager can take the less-costly alternative and buy options on the stock. For example, a U.S. investor may want to buy call options on the British firm ABC rather than ABC shares. The reason is simple: If ABC stock goes up by the same percentage as the British pound drops, the dollar value of a direct investment in ABC stock will remain unchanged. On the other hand, options on ABC will yield both a pound profit and a dollar profit. Currency fluctuations affect only the translation of the profit into dollars, not the principal. The price quotations given in Exhibit 10.5 illustrate how this strategy works.

The dollar profit of buying one share of ABC is zero because the currency loss on the principal offsets the capital gain in pounds. If the investor had instead purchased an option, the profit per share would have been $36 despite the currency loss. Also, note that the initial investment in options is only $16.50 compared to $300 for shares. The difference could have been invested in U.S. cash instruments. Since the initial foreign currency investment in an option is

EXHIBIT 10.5
Price Quotations on ABC shares

	Prices		Price
	December 1	January 15	variation (percent)
Dollars per pound	1.50	1.25	
Pounds per dollar	0.667	0.80	+20
ABC stock (in pounds)	200	240	+20
ABC stock (in dollars)	300	300	0
ABC February 200 Options (in pounds)	11	42	
ABC February 200 Options (in dollars)	16.5	52.5	

very small, the currency impact is always limited to the direct investment in the asset.

A similar approach can be used to invest in an entire foreign market rather than just specific securities. This is done by buying stock index futures or options. Like regular stock futures, stock index futures limit an investor's foreign currency exposure to the margin. Any realized profit can be immediately repatriated in the domestic currency. For example, a Swiss investor who is bullish on the U.S. stock market but not on the U.S. dollar can buy Standard and Poor's 500 index futures. In addition, hedging the margin deposited in dollars against currency risk would provide the Swiss with complete currency protection. Stock index options can likewise be used. A similar strategy applies to bond investments. For example, a U.S. investor who is bullish on interest rates in the United Kingdom can buy gilt futures on the LIFFE rather than bonds, and thereby simultaneously hedge against exchange risk. Other alternatives include buying bond warrants or partly liberated bonds.

Futures and options on foreign assets reduce currency exposure as long as an investor does not already own the assets in question. In addition, costs involved in taking such positions are less than those for actually buying foreign assets and hedging them with currency futures or options. On the other hand, if the assets are already part of a portfolio, more conventional methods of currency hedging are probably better, especially for assets that will remain in the portfolio for a long time.

In the same spirit, one should be aware of the currency impact on an investment strategy involving different types of instruments whose currency exposures are not identical. As an illustration, let's consider one of the strategies introduced in Chapter 8 on page 263. An American investor buys Australian natural resource companies and sells stock index futures to hedge the Australian stock market risk. The motivation for this strategy is the belief that natural resource stocks are undervalued relative to the Australian market. Such a position, which is long in stocks and short in futures, requires an Australian dollar net investment and is therefore exposed to the risk of the Australian dollar. A 10% depreciation would induce a currency loss in the stock position that would not be offset by a currency gain on the stock index futures. As a matter of fact, there will even be a small currency loss in the initial margin deposited for the futures contracts. (This aspect is neglected in the example.) This can be illustrated using the first scenario presented in Chapter 8 with the additional assumption that the Australian dollar drops from one U.S. dollar on September 1 to 0.90 U.S. dollar on October 1. Our investor would have made a gain of 45,000 U.S. dollars if the US$/A$ exchange rate had remained stable at one (see page 264). Instead, the 10% depreciation of the Australian dollar induced a loss of 59,500 U.S. dollars as shown in the following table.

	Futures market	*Stock market*
September 1 (US$/A$ = 1)	Sell 10 December All Ordinary futures at 1150	Buy natural resource stocks; cost = A $1,000,000, US $1,000,000
October 1 (US$/A$ = 0.9)	Market declines 10%, but natural resource stocks decline 6.9%	
	Buy 10 December All Ordinary futures at 1036	Sell natural resource stocks; proceeds = A $931,000, US $837,900
	Profit on futures = A $114,000, US $102,600	Loss on stocks = US $162,100
	Net loss on trade = US $59,500	

It would be wise to hedge the stock portfolio against currency risk if our investor fears a depreciation of the Australian dollar. Note that the stock beta is irrelevant to our currency hedge, where the hedge ratio should be close to one.

Several investment vehicles and strategies may be used either to take advantage of or to hedge against monetary factors. Many of these strategies have been discussed before, so that we already know that they usually involve a combination of investments in money, capital, and speculative markets. For example, a British investor expecting a weak U.S. dollar and falling U.S. interest rates could buy long-term U.S. bonds, or zero-coupons, to maximize the sensitivity of his or her portfolio to U.S. interest rate movements, and at the same time hedge against exchange risk with currency futures or options. A matrix of alternative investments in the U.S. dollar fixed-income markets is given in Exhibit 10.6. Each quadrant represents a specific scenario concerning U.S. interest rates and the U.S. dollar. Group I, for example, represents a set of strategies designed to capitalize on a strong U.S. dollar and falling dollar interest rates. The purpose in outlining strategies is to help an investor to take advantage of his or her specific forecasts with respect to interest rates and currencies. Of course, the actual performance of these strategies depends on how accurate the investor's forecasts are.

EXHIBIT 10.6

A Strategy Matrix of Alternative Investments in the U.S. Dollar Fixed-Income Markets

Securities / strategies are generally listed with the more traditional, or less risky, at the top of each group; the more highly leveraged, or risky, are toward the bottom of the list. In some instances, the same instruments / strategies appear in more than one quadrant. In such cases, they only appear with a code letter in that quadrant where they are especially appropriate. They appear without a code letter in the other quadrants.

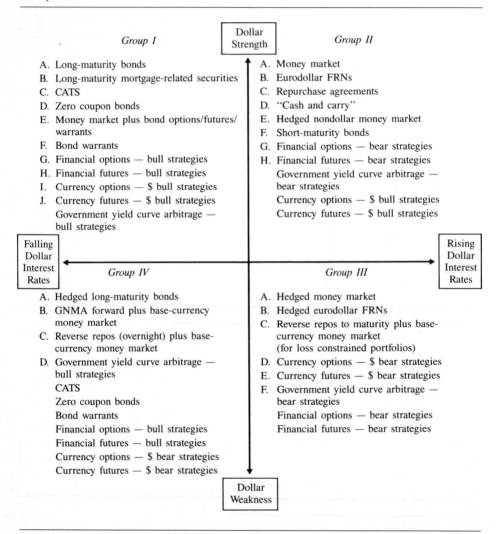

Dollar
Strength

Group I

A. Long-maturity bonds
B. Long-maturity mortgage-related securities
C. CATS
D. Zero coupon bonds
E. Money market plus bond options/futures/
   warrants
F. Bond warrants
G. Financial options — bull strategies
H. Financial futures — bull strategies
I. Currency options — $ bull strategies
J. Currency futures — $ bull strategies
   Government yield curve arbitrage —
   bull strategies

Group II

A. Money market
B. Eurodollar FRNs
C. Repurchase agreements
D. "Cash and carry"
E. Hedged nondollar money market
F. Short-maturity bonds
G. Financial options — bear strategies
H. Financial futures — bear strategies
   Government yield curve arbitrage —
   bear strategies
   Currency options — $ bull strategies
   Currency futures — $ bull strategies

Falling
Dollar
Interest
Rates

Rising
Dollar
Interest
Rates

Group IV

A. Hedged long-maturity bonds
B. GNMA forward plus base-currency
   money market
C. Reverse repos (overnight) plus base-
   currency money market
D. Government yield curve arbitrage —
   bull strategies
   CATS
   Zero coupon bonds
   Bond warrants
   Financial options — bull strategies
   Financial futures — bull strategies
   Currency options — $ bear strategies
   Currency futures — $ bear strategies

Group III

A. Hedged money market
B. Hedged eurodollar FRNs
C. Reverse repos to maturity plus base-
   currency money market
   (for loss constrained portfolios)
D. Currency options — $ bear strategies
E. Currency futures — $ bear strategies
F. Government yield curve arbitrage —
   bear strategies
   Financial options — bear strategies
   Financial futures — bear strategies

Dollar
Weakness

Source: J. Hanna and P. Niculescu, "The Currency and Interest Rate Strategy Matrix: An Investment Tool for Multicurrency Investors," Bond Market Research, Salomon Brothers Inc., September 1982. Reprinted with permission.

A similar strategy matrix can be designed for nondollar investments, even though the absence of speculative markets in some currencies sometimes limits the range of strategies an investor can choose.

SUMMARY

1. Currency futures, forward, and option contracts are primarily used to protect a portfolio against currency risks. Managers adapt their hedging strategies to their expectations of an asset's performance in local currency and of exchange rate movements.

2. The basic approach to the use of currency futures contracts is to hedge the foreign currency value of the foreign asset. One would sell short currencies in the amount of an asset's value. Ideally, one should hedge the future value of an investment, taking into account the expected price change and income. The covariance between the asset return and the currency movements should be considered. The interest rate differential is the forward basis, the percentage difference between the futures and the spot exchange rates. The correlation between changes in interest rate differentials and currency movements should also be taken into account in determining the optimal hedge ratio.

3. Hedging strategies for multi-currency portfolios usually involve the use of futures in the major currencies. The instability of the estimated hedge ratios reduces the effectiveness of hedging strategies.

4. Currency options are used for their asymmetric risk-return characteristic. They provide insurance against adverse currency movements, while retaining the profit potential in case of a favorable currency movement. There is a cost associated with this attractive insurance characteristic. More dynamic hedging strategies also can be implemented using currency options. They require option valuation models to estimate the hedge ratio.

5. Other methods can be used to manage the currency exposure of international portfolios. Leveraged instruments on foreign assets such as futures and options have little currency exposure, since the capital invested in foreign currency is very small compared to the value of the underlying asset. The impact of a currency movement on a combined position of several assets and contracts should be carefully studied.

QUESTIONS AND PROBLEMS

1. An American investor holds a portfolio of Japanese stocks worth ¥ 160 million. The spot exchange rate is ¥/$ = 158 and the three-month forward exchange rate is ¥/$ = 160. Our investor fears that the Japanese yen will depreciate in the next month, but wants to keep the Japanese stocks. What position can the investor take based on three-month forward exchange rate contracts? List all the factors that will make the hedge imperfect.

2. A Dutch investor holds a portfolio of Japanese stocks similar to that of our U.S. investor. The current three-month Dutch guilder forward exchange rate is DG/$ = 2.5. What position should the Dutch investor take to hedge the yen/guilder exchange risk?

3. A U.S. investor is attracted by the high yield on British bonds but is worried about a British pound depreciation. The current market data are as follows:

	United States	United Kingdom
Bond yield (percent)	7	12
Three-month interest rate (percent)	6	8
Spot exchange rate, $/£ = 2		

A bond dealer has repeatedly suggested that the investor invest in hedged foreign bonds. This strategy can be described as the purchase of foreign currency bonds (here, British pound bonds) with simultaneous hedging in the short-term forward or futures currency market. The currency hedge is rolled over when the forward or futures contract expires.

- What is the current three-month forward exchange rate ($/£)?
- Assuming a £1 million investment in British bonds, how would you determine the exact hedge ratio necessary to minimize the currency influence?
- When will this strategy be successful (compared to a direct investment in U.S. bonds)?

4. Futures and forward currency contracts are not readily available for most currencies. However, many currencies are closely linked. For example, the European Monetary System (EMS) described in Chapter 3 implies a close link between several European currencies.

An American investor has a portfolio of Belgian stocks that she wishes to hedge against currency risks. No futures contracts are traded on the Belgian franc, so she decides to use deutsche mark futures contracts traded in Chicago, since both currencies belong to the EMS. Here are the data:

Value of the portfolio	BF 100 million
Spot exchange rates	BF/$ = 50
	DM/$ = 2.5
Futures price (contract of DM 125,000)	$/DM = 0.41

How many deutsche mark contracts should our U.S. investor trade?

5. Let's go back to our first problem where a U.S. investor owns a portfolio of Japanese securities worth ¥ 160 million. He considers buying currency puts on yen instead of selling futures contracts. In Philadelphia, a yen put with a strike price of 0.62 U.S. cent and three-months maturity is worth 0.70 U.S. cent per 100 yen (0.007 cent per yen).

Assume that three months later, the portfolio is still worth ¥ 160 million and simulate various values of the spot yen/dollar exchange rate. Compare the results of the following two currency hedging strategies for your different values of the exchange rate three months later. In the first strategy, the investor sells ¥ 160 million forward, and in the second strategy he buys yen puts for ¥ 160 million (25.6 contracts on the Philadelphia Stock Exchange).

6. On October 1, a German investor decides to hedge a U.S. portfolio worth $10 million against exchange risk using deutsche mark call options. The spot exchange rate is DM/$ = 2.5, or $/DM = 0.40. The German investor can buy November deutsche marks with a strike price of 40 U.S. cents per deutsche mark at a premium of 1 cent per deutsche mark. The size of one contract is DM 62,500. The delta of the option is estimated at 0.5. How many deutsche mark calls should our investor buy to hedge the U.S. portfolio against the DM/$ currency risk?

A few days later the U.S. dollar has dropped to DM/$2.439, or $/DM = 0.41, and the dollar value of the portfolio has remained unchanged at $10 million. The November 40 deutsche mark call is now worth 1.6 cents per deutsche mark and has a delta estimated at 0.7. What is the result of the hedge? How should the hedge be adjusted?

7. Why is a purchase of a futures contract or an option on a foreign asset not exposed to much currency risk?

Take the following example for a U.S. investor:

	November	*December*
Financial Times (FTSE) Stock Exchange Index	1600	1700
December Futures on FTSE	1615	1700
December 1 650 FTSE Index Call	20	50
Dollar/Pound Spot Rate	2.00	1.80

As mentioned in Chapter 8, one FTSE futures contract has a multiplier of 25 pounds. The margin deposit is £1500 per contract. FTSE options have a contract size of 25 times the index.

What is the amount of currency loss if the U.S. investor had bought:

☐ the index in the form of stocks (e.g., £1600 worth of a FTSE index fund),

☐ a December futures on FTSE,

☐ a December 1650 FTSE call?

NOTES

1. See J. Madura and W. Reiff, "A Hedge Strategy for International Portfolio," *Journal of Portfolio Management*, Fall 1985.

2. For an empirical examination of the multi-currency betas of international portfolios, see M. Adler and D. Simon, "Exchange Rate Surprises in International Portfolios," *Journal of Portfolio Management*, Winter 1986.

3. See M. Eaker and D. Grant, "Cross-Hedging Foreign Currency Risk," *Journal of International Money and Finance*, March 1987. Also see C. Dale, "The Hedging Effectiveness of Currency Futures Markets," *Journal of Futures Markets*, Spring 1981 and T. Grammatikos and A. Saunders, "Stability and the Hedging Performance of Foreign Currency Futures," *Journal of Futures Markets*, Fall 1983.

4. A valuation model of currency option premiums and their hedge ratios was presented in Chapter 9. See M. Garman and S. Kolhagen, "Foreign Currency Option Values," *Journal of International Money and Finance*, December 1983; and J. O. Grabbe, "The Pricing of Call and Put Options on Foreign Exchange," *Journal of International Money and Finance*, December 1983.

5. For a detailed description of currency options strategies, see "Currency Options Strategy Manual" by the Chicago Mercantile Exchange, as well as various brochures prepared by the Philadelphia Stock Exchange, the London International Financial Futures Exchange, the European Options Exchange, etc.

6. See M. Adler and B. Dumas, "International Portfolio Choices and Corporate Finance: A Synthesis," *Journal of Finance*, June 1983.

BIBLIOGRAPHY

M. Adler and B. Dumas, "International Portfolio Choices and Corporate Finance: A Synthesis," *Journal of Finance*, June 1983.

M. Adler and D. Simon, "Exchange Rate Surprises in International Portfolios," *Journal of Portfolio Management*, Winter 1986.

J. Bodurtha and G. Courtadon, "Efficiency Tests of the Foreign Currency Option Market," *Journal of Finance*, March 1986.

C. Dale, "The Hedging Effectiveness of Currency Futures Markets," *Journal of Futures Markets*, Spring 1981.

M. Eaker and D. Grant, "Optimal Hedging of Uncertain and Long-Term Foreign Exchange Exposure," *Journal of Banking and Finance*, September 1985.

M. Eaker and D. Grant, "Cross-Hedging Foreign Currency Risks," *Journal of International Money and Finance*, March 1987.

M. Garman and S. Kolhagen, "Foreign Currency Option Values," *Journal of International Money and Finance*, December 1983.

J. O. Grabbe, "The Pricing of Call and Put Options on Foreign Exchange," *Journal of International Money and Finance*, December 1983.

T. Grammatikos and A. Saunders, "Stability and the Hedging Performance of Foreign Currency Futures," *Journal of Futures Markets*, Fall 1983.

J. Hanna and P. Niculescu, "The Currency and Interest Rate Strategy Matrix: An Investment Tool for Multicurrency Investors," Bond Market Research, Salomon Brothers, September 1982.

J. Madura and W. Reiff, "A Hedge Strategy for International Portfolio," *Journal of Portfolio Management*, Fall 1985.

A. Shapiro and S. Titman, "An Integrated Approach to Corporate Risk Management," *Midland Corporate Finance Journal*, Summer 1985.

C. Smith and R. Stulz, "The Determinants of Firms' Hedging Policies," *Journal of Financial and Quantitative Analysis*, December 1985.

B. Solnik, "Optimal Currency Hedge Ratios: The Influence of the Interest Rate Differential," in S. G. Rhee and R. P. Chang (eds), *Pacific-Basin Capital Market Research*, North Holland, Amsterdam, 1990.

R. Stultz, "Optimal Hedging Policy," *Journal of Financial and Quantitative Analysis*, June 1984.

Chapter 10: Appendix
Advanced Section on Optimal
Currency Hedging

In theory, the optimal hedging policy for an individual investor is the one that maximizes his or her expected utility. Policies would be individual-specific and a function of the parameters of the individual's utility function. But it is unclear why an investor should isolate exchange rate risk as a specific source of risk to be hedged. The mere definition of exchange risk in a general equilibrium framework is controversial, as discussed in Chapter 1 and by Adler and Dumas (1983).[6] Market imperfections and segmentation render the theoretical analysis an impossible task. A remark often made is that common economic factors may affect both return on the asset and the exchange rate. So why should an investor single out the currency translation risk and hedge it independently?

In practice, stock returns and currency movements are quite independent; an investor will want to specifically hedge currency translation risks when he or she fears a depreciation of the foreign currency. If a foreign asset is uncorrelated with short-term currency movements, a hedge ratio of one is a reasonable strategy. The foreign asset represents a given quantity of foreign currency, and the same amount of currency is sold short. This is a rather simple strategy based on the quantity of currency to be hedged. No cross hedging is involved. The analysis can be refined by calculating the minimum-variance hedge given by the minimization of the variance of

$$R_H - R = s(1 + R) - hR_F, \tag{10.A1}$$

where all variables have been defined in the text of Chapter 10. The first-order optimization condition can be written as in the appendix for Chapter 8. It implies that the optimal hedge ratio is equal to

$$h = \frac{\text{cov}\left[s(1 + R), R_F\right]}{\sigma_F^2} \tag{10.A2}$$

where σ_F^2 is the variance of R_F. This hedge ratio is also equal to the regression slope of the currency contribution, $R^* - R = s(1 + R)$, on the futures return, R_F.

At this point, it is useful to detail the components of R_F:

$$R_F = \frac{(F_t - F_0)}{S_0}.$$

We can write $F_t - F_0$ as

$$F_t - F_0 = F_t - S_t - (F_0 - S_0) + S_t - S_0.$$

Hence

$$R_0 = \frac{S_t}{S_0} \frac{F_t - S_t}{S_t} - \frac{F_0 - S_0}{S_0} + \frac{S_t - S_0}{S_0} \quad \text{and}$$

$$R_F = (1 + s)B_t - B_0 + s$$

where B_0 and B_t are the bases (interest rate differential) at times zero and t. This might be written as

$$R_F = s + B_t - B_0 + sB_t \tag{10.A3}$$

$$\frac{\text{Futures}}{\text{return}} = \frac{\text{Currency}}{\text{movement}} + \frac{\text{Change in}}{\text{interest rate}} + \frac{\text{Cross}}{\text{product}}$$
$$\text{in percent} \quad \text{differential}$$

Basically, the futures return is equal to the spot exchange rate variation plus the change in interest rate differential plus a smaller cross-product term. Clearly the covariance of the currency movement with the change in interest rate differential will affect the optimal hedge ratio in Eq. (10.A2). A rise in the U.S. interest rate that is unmatched by the British rate tends to strengthen the dollar relative to sterling. Given our notation this leads to a negative covariance and a smaller hedge ratio.

Another objective of a currency hedging policy is to remove totally the direct and indirect influences of a currency movement on the portfolio return. As mentioned in Chapter 1, a depreciation of sterling may lead to a rise in British interest rates in defence of the currency. In turn, this rise in local interest rates induces a drop in bond prices. In the end, both the sterling return and a currency translation yield a loss for the U.S. investor. The optimal hedge ratio is obtained by running a regression of the portfolio dollar return, R^*, on the futures return R_F:

$$R^* = a + hR_F \tag{10.A4}$$

where a is a constant term and all other variables have been defined above. One can verify that this optimal hedge ratio will differ from the previous one if the foreign currency return, R, is correlated with the futures return, R_F.

A diversified international portfolio can be hedged using only the futures contracts available in a few currencies, as discussed previously. The currency influence on the portfolio can be reduced by following the following procedure:

□ Select the major most-independent currencies with futures contracts available. For an American investor these may be the yen, deutsche mark and sterling. For a Swiss-based investor, these may be the yen, sterling, and U.S. dollar.

□ Calculate the hedge ratios jointly by running a multiple regression between the domestic currency returns on the portfolio (U.S. dollar return for a U.S. investor) and the futures returns in the three selected currencies.

$$R^* = a + h_1 R_{F1} + h_2 R_{F2} + h_3 R_{F3}.$$

□ Use the regression coefficients h_1, h_2, and h_3 as the hedge ratios in each currency. Because the spot currency movement is the major component of futures volatility, the hedge ratios obtained would be fairly close if we used currency movements in the regression instead of futures return.

Of course, this procedure requires historical data on the portfolio and will work well only if the estimated regression coefficients are stable over time. Eaker and Grant (1987) provide some evidence on the unstability of these coefficients.

11

Gold and Gold-Linked Investments

Gold has always played a special role in investments. It is a commodity traded worldwide, but, more importantly, it is regarded by many Europeans and Asians as the ultimate store of value. It is considered an international monetary asset that offers protection in case of a major disruption. Studies show that gold assets represent between 5 and 10% of a typical European or Middle Eastern portfolio, and Ibbotson, Siegel, and Love[1] found that gold bullion represents more than 5% of total investable world wealth. Furthermore, gold is regarded by central banks and most non-American investors as a monetary asset because it has been the core of domestic and international monetary systems for many centuries.

This chapter focuses on gold investment because of the traditional and quasi-mystical importance of gold in investment strategies, but also as an example of a real asset investment. Of course, precious stones, stamps, or paintings are also profitable long-term investments. But these usually require high transaction costs, and, moreover, each stone or painting is in a sense unique, which reduces its marketability. Domestic and international mutual funds have been created to invest in works of art, stamps, wines, and other goods, but most of these funds have failed. Although such investments may attract wealthy individuals, they are not appropriate for institutional investors, and are therefore excluded from this analysis.

Real estate (private housing or commercial or agricultural properties) is also an important category of investment. In most countries this is the preferred investment vehicle of pension funds and life insurance companies. Dutch pension funds are one of the few institutional investors that invest in foreign real estate. Their holding of foreign properties (mostly in the United States) is quite large. Japanese institutions seem to be moving in the same direction. But as a rule, foreign real estate is seldom considered by institutional investors. The reasons are obvious: First, it is difficult to monitor properties located abroad. Second, taxes, paperwork, and unforeseen risks make foreign real estate investment impractical on a large scale. To be sure, private deals can be arranged for special projects, but these are well beyond the scope of this book. For the same reason we do not address other forms of international private money management.

However, one should mention that there is a definite trend toward the development of negotiable forms of real property interests. In many countries, pooled funds have been created with the specific purpose of real estate investment. Mortgage-backed Eurobonds are rapidly growing in popularity. The time may not be too far off when foreign real estate will be a normal component of international investment strategies.

Gold offers a wide variety of investment vehicles that can be used in passive or active strategies. Gold-linked investments include gold bullion, coins, bonds, mining equity, futures, and options on gold and on mining equity or bonds. This will give us an opportunity to review the valuation of index-linked securities and their uses in active strategies.

THE MOTIVATION FOR INVESTMENT IN GOLD

The traditional role of gold as the ultimate hedge and store of value is well known. For centuries gold has been regarded by Europeans and Asians alike as the best-possible protection against inflation and social, political, or economic crises because it can easily be traded worldwide at any time and its real value increases during crises. Europeans and others who have suffered revolutions, invasions, and periods of hyperinflation need no correlation coefficients to be convinced of this attractive portfolio hedge characteristic. For example, gold kept its real value during the U.S. stock market crash from 1929 to 1932 and the London Stock Exchange collapse in equity and bonds from 1973 to 1975.

Furthermore, the central role gold has played in domestic and international monetary systems for thousands of years makes it in part a monetary asset with exceptional liquidity. Other real assets, such as diamonds or stamps, do not have this characteristic.

In general, gold allows one to diversify against the kinds of risks that affect all stock markets simultaneously. For example, in 1973 and 1974 bullion price tripled when stock markets worldwide dropped dramatically during the oil crisis; the New York Stock Exchange dropped approximately 50%. Conversely, the price of gold dropped from 1982 to 1983, when most stock markets rose during the economic recovery. Several studies have shown the existence of a small, and sometimes negative, correlation between gold and stock prices. As shown in Exhibit 11.1, gold had a negative correlation of -0.4 with the U.S. stock market for over more than twenty-five years (1948 to 1975). The conclusion can be drawn from this exhibit that gold price tends to go up when inflation accelerates

EXHIBIT 11.1
Correlation of Annual Rates of Inflation and U.S. Stock Returns with Gold Price Movements, 1948 to 1975

	Correlation coefficient	Arithmetic mean of yearly return (percent)	Yearly standard deviation (percent)
Gold	1.0	8.8	20.8
Inflation	0.60	3.8	4.2
S + P 500 Stocks	−0.40	12.8	18.3

Source: J. McDonald, B. Solnik, "Valuation and Strategy for Gold Stocks," *Journal of Portfolio Management*, Spring 1977. Reprinted with permission.

and stock prices drop. The same conclusion can be reached if one looks at the correlation of gold with non-American stock markets.[2]

This weak correlation is also found for other commodities used in investment strategies. A. Renshaw and E. Renshaw[3] computed the correlation of U.S. stock returns with price movements of gold bullion, silver bullion, and crude petroleum. They found correlation coefficients of −0.06 for gold, 0.06 for silver, and −0.17 for oil. Of course, a negative correlation is not a prerequisite for gold to be an attractive diversification vehicle. Even a small positive coefficient is sufficient to achieve diversification. To illustrate the diversification benefits of gold, Exhibit 11.2 compares the risk and performance of a portfolio solely invested in stocks (the Morgan Stanley Capital International world index) with a portfolio of 90% stocks and 10% gold. The risk (standard deviation) of the diversified portfolio is reduced; furthermore, the performance is increased. The comparison with a purely U.S. stock portfolio is even more telling.[4]

EXHIBIT 11.2
Risk and Performance of Simulated Portfolios
Monthly U.S. dollar returns, 1971 to 1989

Composition of portfolio	Risk (percent per year)	Return (percent per year)
100% Gold Bullion	26.4	14.2
100% U.S. Stocks (Standard and Poor's 500)	16.2	9.9
100% World Stocks	14.4	13.8
90% World Stocks and 10% Gold	13.6	14.0

These empirical findings emphasize the inflation protection and the diversification benefits provided by gold and gold-related assets. Purchase of gold-related assets usually reduces portfolio risk substantially: Gold-linked assets usually reduce the variability of returns on a diversified portfolio because they tend to appreciate when other securities depreciate. But the low statistical correlation between gold and other security prices is not an insurance that eliminates risk. In many years, gold and stock prices move in opposite directions, but in others they move in the same direction. This was the case in 1981, when U.S. gold, stock, and bond prices dropped together. Typically, this happens when real interest rates rise, increasing the opportunity cost of holding gold; this interest rate increase is also bad for bonds and stocks.

Sherman[5] conducted an extensive study of the performance of gold, stock, bond, and money markets in six countries. He concluded that gold prices outperformed other investments in periods of accelerating inflation, but underperformed them in periods of decelerating inflation (see Exhibit 11.3).

Because the variability of gold returns is very high, a small investment in gold provides good protection against inflation. That is why, in a global portfolio, gold is primarily used as an instrument for long-term risk protection. Secondarily, gold may also be used for profitable short-term speculation.

Although gold is a highly volatile investment with a large standard deviation, in return, its inclusion in a portfolio reduces the total risk of that portfolio.

A theoretical comment is in order here. In modern portfolio theory, a small or negative beta implies that the expected return on gold should be small. For example, a negative beta caused by a negative correlation between gold and the market portfolio implies that in the Capital Asset Pricing Model (CAPM) framework the expected return on gold should be less than the risk-free interest rate. Indeed, it can be claimed that we should expect, and certainly hope for, a modest long-term performance in gold and a greater return on the other assets in the portfolio; however, gold assets will greatly reduce the risk of the portfolio in case of adverse economic conditions. The question for a prudent portfolio manager, then, is whether or not these hedge benefits are worth the implicit premium he or she must pay in the form of a modest, expected long-term performance of a small part of the portfolio.

GOLD PRICE DETERMINANTS

The purpose of this book is not to provide the reader with recipes in financial analysis. The following material is intended only to indicate the kind of information and methods utilized by analysts and investment managers to analyse real-asset investments. Assets other than gold could serve as an example. However, gold has historically played a central role in international finance, and its analysis is somewhat simpler than that of other real assets.

Gold is a tangible international asset. Like other precious metals and stones, its supply is limited. Gold can be extracted at a cost but cannot be

EXHIBIT 11.3
Differential Rates of Return of Financial Assets Among Six Countries: 1977 to 1980; 1980 to 1983; and 1977 to 1983
Cumulative rate of return (percent per year)

Country	Gold less CPI	Gold less stocks	Gold less bonds	Gold less money markets	Stocks less CPI	Bonds less CPI	Money markets less CPI
Accelerating inflation, 1977–1980							
United States	34.3	33.1	46.0	35.9	1.2	−11.7	−1.6
Canada	40.9	23.8	48.1	40.3	17.1	−7.2	0.6
United Kingdom	19.7	10.7	20.9	20.3	9.0	−1.2	−0.6
West Germany	34.2	33.9	33.5	32.5	0.3	0.7	1.7
Switzerland	30.5	29.9	29.3	30.6	1.4	1.2	−0.1
Japan	26.8	23.0	24.7	26.2	3.8	2.1	0.6
Mean	31.1	25.7	33.8	31.0	5.5	−2.7	0.1
Decelerating inflation, 1980–1983							
United States	−14.9	−24.6	−16.6	−19.0	9.7	1.7	4.1
Canada	−15.4	−33.3	−19.1	−20.0	17.9	3.7	4.6
United Kingdom	−6.6	−28.5	−14.7	−10.3	16.1	8.1	3.7
West Germany	−1.2	−20.6	−4.3	−5.1	12.2	3.1	3.9
Switzerland	−4.6	−9.2	−5.1	−6.1	4.5	0.4	1.4
Japan	−12.9	−24.4	−17.9	−16.5	11.5	5.0	3.6
Mean	−9.3	−23.4	−13.0	−12.8	12.0	3.7	3.6
Total, 1977–1983							
United States	7.8	4.2	11.2	6.3	3.6	−3.4	1.5
Canada	10.4	0.9	11.3	7.7	9.5	−0.9	2.7
United Kingdom	8.0	−4.0	4.3	6.4	12.0	3.7	1.6
West Germany	14.2	7.0	11.5	11.6	7.2	2.7	2.6
Switzerland	10.5	6.9	9.0	9.9	3.6	1.5	0.6
Japan	7.6	−0.6	3.4	5.8	8.2	4.2	1.8
Mean	9.7	2.4	8.4	7.9	7.3	1.3	1.8

Source: E. J. Sherman, "Performance of Gold Versus Stocks, Bonds and Money Markets in Six Countries: 1968–1983," *International Gold Corporation*, March 1984.

CPI = Consumer Price Index.

produced artificially. The current estimate of the total past worldwide mining extraction is approximately 100,000 metric tons. Although gold is immune to the effects of weather, water, and oxygen, it suffers from human habits. The tradition of hiding gold treasures in the ground is consistent with the observation that gold is the ultimate physical store of value during major disruptions such as civil unrest, coup d'etat, and war. During World War II, most Europeans

EXHIBT 11.4
Supply and Demand for New Gold (in metric tons)

Supply to markets[d]	1972	1973	1974	1975	1976	1977	1978	1979	1980	1981	1982	1983	1984	1985	1986	1987	1988
Western Mine Production	1177	1111	996	946	964	962	972	959	952	973	1023	1088	1149	1213	1281	1373	1538
Net Sales of the Communist Bloc	213	275	220	149	412	401	410	199	90	280	202	92	205	210	402	303	258
Official Purchases (−) or Sales[a] (+)	(−151)	6	20	9	58b	269	362	544	(−230)	(−276)	(−85)	119	85	(−135)	(−181)	(70)	(270)
Total	1239	1392	1236	1104	1434	1632	1744	1702	812	977	1140	1299	1439	1288	1502	1606	1526
Private sector demand[d]																	
Carat Jewelry	999	508	216	516	936	1004	1004	728	126	596	715	598	819	898	874	908	1233
Other Industries[b]	241	263	214	187	216	228	254	265	217	219	207	207	228	215	231	229	203
Coins and Medallions	104	74	294	272	233	194	337	324	202	219	153	196	174	122	338	223	87
Investments[c]	−105	547	512	129	49	206	149	385	267	−57	65	298	218	53	59	246	3
Total	1239	1392	1236	1104	1434	1632	1744	1702	812	977	1140	1299	1439	1288	1502	1606	1526

Source: Consolidated Gold Fields, International Gold Corporation, Chamber of Mines of South Africa.

[a] Includes sales by the International Monetary Fund.
[b] Includes dentistry, electronics, and decorative industries.
[c] May include errors and omissions.
[d] Scrap excluded.

dug a hole in their garden or cellar to hide their gold holdings. Part of this hidden gold is never recovered if the owner dies. Most of the gold used in dentistry also disappears with the owner. Despite these losses, the stock of gold keeps slowly increasing with the amount extracted.

In a sense, the price of gold should be easy to forecast: The product is well defined. The supply sources are well identified and reserves can be reasonably estimated. The major demands are clearly identified: carat jewelry, industrial needs, coins, and investment. Historical supply and demand for gold is shown in Exhibit 11.4. This analysis is limited to supply and demand for gold in the Western world, since we have no indications for the Communist bloc. The variation in official reserves of national governments and the International Monetary Fund have been included in the supply: The bottom half of the table is simply the private demand. It appears that Western gold production has been quite steady, yielding approximately 1.000 metric ton (about 32 million troy ounces) per year. Production has slowly been rising through the 1980s. The dramatic increase in gold price from 1971 has allowed the exploitation of higher-cost mines. The South African production has remained remarkably stable, but other countries have emerged as major gold producers. As shown in Exhibit 11.5, South Africa produces slightly more than half of the gold produced in the non-Communist world. But various countries including Canada, the United States, Brazil, Columbia, the Philippines, Australia, and Papua New Guinea are also major producers; they have been the source of growth in production in the recent years.

Jewelry is the major source of gold demand. It seems quite sensitive to movements in gold prices. The dramatic gold price increases in 1974 and 1980 temporarily reduced the carat jewelry demand; for example, in 1980 it was eight times below that of the period from 1977 to 1978. However, the jewelry demand seems fairly stable except for occasional dramatic moves in reaction to gold prices. The demand for industrial needs is stable.

Supply and demand clearly determine the price of gold. It is therefore necessary to study the various components of supply and demand to forecast the price of gold. A different model may be required for each component. For example, western mine production is affected by technological considerations, South African extraction policy, and political situations in sensitive countries; Soviet gold sales depend on their need for hard currencies. Official sales may also be induced by monetary and balance-of-payments problems. The industrial demand depends on technological innovation and the discovery of cheaper substitutes. Jewelry demand is sensitive to short-term gold price movements as well as fashion; the investment motivation is often present in jewelry purchases. Investment demand for bullion and coins is a component of the total demand affecting gold price, but is also determined by expectations of future price movements. Gold provides no income, so the sole return to the owner is through price increase. In general, price expectations that are not directly linked to income flows are quite volatile, which explains the large volatility of gold prices.

EXHIBIT 11.5
Geographical Breakdown of Gold Mine Production in the Non-Communist World, 1988

Locality	Production (metric tons)
Africa	
South Africa	621
Other Countries	67
Total	688
Latin America	
Brazil	100
Columbia	33
Chile	23
Other Countries	70
Total	226
North America	
Canada	129
United States	205
Total	334
Far East	
Philippines	43
Other Countries	35
Total	78
Europe	
Total	19
Oceania	
Australia	152
Papua New Guinea	33
Other Countries	6
Total	191
Total	1538

Source: Consolidated Gold Fields, Annual Report, 1988.

As we can see, gold is a single, well-identified, extensively researched product, but its analysis and valuation is not a simple exercise. This difficulty may add another dimension to its mystical attraction.

THE VALUATION OF INDEX-LINKED SECURITIES

Some managers exploit the short-term price behavior of bullion. Its large volatility can mean substantial short-term profit for those who make accurate forecasts. But for this purpose, gold-related investments, not bullion, are the most appropriate vehicle. Also, managers may prefer, or be constrained, to hold only financial investments and not real assets such as gold ingots. For this reason, we will start by reviewing those gold-linked investments that are traded on capital markets. Gold bonds and gold mining equities are found on several national markets. The value of these securities is, in effect, linked to an index, namely the price of gold bullion. The indexation clause is explicit for index-linked bonds, but implicit for gold mining equity. Our main intention here is to explain how such index-linked securities should be valued.

Gold Bonds

There are many examples of index-linked securities in the world capital markets. Governments faced with large interest rate risk because of high inflation have often been forced to offer loans with coupons or principal indexed to either the price of a specific good or a global inflation index. Inflation index-linked gilts have recently become popular in the United Kingdom. The capital and coupons of these bonds are indexed to British retail prices. High-inflation countries, such as Brazil and Israel, have also issued inflation-indexed bonds, while corporations and governments have issued bonds indexed to a variety of specific prices. The Mexican Petrobonos is one such bond.

Gold bonds are attractive because they give an investor the choice of investing in either the index (gold ingot) or the bond. Among the few private issuers of gold bonds are Refinement International and Lac Minerals, Ltd. Refinement International, a U.S. corporation, issued 3.5% gold-indexed bonds for 1981 to 1996. Each bond is worth 10 ounces of gold, and the coupon is worth 0.35 ounce of gold. Lac Minerals Ltd., a Canadian corporation, issued 8% debentures for 1984 to 1989 with warrants. Each warrant entitles the holder to buy 0.5 troy ounce of gold from Lac Minerals Ltd., at a price of 230 U.S. dollars. More important are the public issues of gold bonds, and among them, those that most deserve mention are two French state loans: One is a 4.5% 1973 to 1999 bond usually referred to as the Pinay, after the French finance minister responsible for its issue. The other is a 7% 1973 to 1988 bond usually referred to as the Giscard. The Pinay is indexed to the Napoleon, the French gold coin, in a manner too complex to be described here. The Giscard, on the other hand, has a straightforward indexation clause that is fixed to the price of gold ingots in Paris and therefore suitable for illustrating how index-linked bonds are valued.[6]

The Giscard may be thought of as a bond that is reimbursed in full at maturity in the form of 95.3 grams of gold (or rather, its value at the time) and pays a coupon worth 6.67 grams of gold every year. Although payment is made in French francs, the amount is solely determined by the gold price during the month of payment. If the bond sold at (gold) par, it would amount to a bond yielding exactly 7% in real gold terms.

The valuation formula for the Giscard may be written as

$$P = \frac{CG_1}{1+r} + \frac{CG_2}{(1+r)^2} + \frac{CG_n}{(1+r)^n} + \frac{RG_n}{(1+r)^n} \tag{11.1}$$

where:

G_t is the expected price of gold at time t,
C is the gold content of the coupon (6.67 grams in our example),
R is the gold content of the redemption value (95.3 grams in our example),
r is the discount factor, or nominal yield-to-maturity, and
P is the price of the gold bond.

Strictly speaking, Eq. (11.1) holds only on the day of coupon payment. A more precise formula would take into account the exact number of days before the next coupon payment. Moreover, the formula computes bond value gross of taxes, and while there is no withholding tax on the bond, there are various income and capital taxes, depending on the type of investor.

The value of the bond depends on both the current gold price and the long-term expectations of its value. The simplest assumption to make is that the price of bullion follows a trend with a yearly price appreciation rate of $\alpha\%$. This, in fact, is not an unreasonable assumption in the long run, despite the high volatility of gold prices, although a more-complex price expectation structure could be built into the model.

$$G_t = G_0(1 + \alpha)^t \qquad (11.2)$$

Therefore

$$P = G_0 C \sum \frac{(1 + \alpha)^t}{(1 + r)^t} + \frac{G_0 R(1 + \alpha)^n}{(1 + r)^n}. \qquad (11.3)$$

Hence, the price of the bond P is a function of the ratio $1 + \alpha / 1 + r$. As a result, we may define the real (gold) return, p, on the bond as

$$\frac{1}{1 + p} = \frac{1 + \alpha}{1 + r} \quad \text{or} \qquad (11.4)$$

$$p \simeq r - \alpha.$$

This means that P is a function of the real rate of return p where r and p are the nominal and real yields-to-maturity, respectively, and α is the expected rate of increase in the price of gold. Intuitively, we know that with gold-indexed bonds, expectations of future gold prices play a role similar to that which the term structure of interest rates plays in valuing coupon bonds. The main technical difference is that there is no long-term futures market for gold, and thus, no direct way of determining the equivalent of long-term market interest rates, i.e., long-term expectations of gold prices. The best we can do is use Eq. (11.3) to derive an implicit measure for market expectations of long-term gold values. In a sense, the price of a Giscard is influenced by two factors: fluctuations in the nominal interest rate r and changes in the long-term expected gold price appreciation α. Here we focus only on the latter, more important, factor. If we had gold bonds for all maturities, we could derive the structure of forward gold prices. The exact value of the nominal discount rate r to be used is unclear. For a government bond such as the Giscard, most analysts use the yield-to-maturity on a straight government bond of the same maturity. At the end of 1983 the Giscard offered a real gold return of approximately 8%. This gross real return is quite attractive when compared to a direct investment in gold bullion with a zero return, even allowing for the fact that the bond is only paper gold and there is a minuscule chance that the French government will renege at redemption. In addition, because the French ingot price adjusts to any fluctuation in French currency, this bond is not directly exposed to currency risk. Net return on the Giscard depends on the income and capital gains tax status of the investor.

A gold bond follows short-term movements in gold prices with an elasticity, or *gold beta*, of approximately one. In this chapter we define gold beta as the percentage return on an investment following a 1% gold price appreciation, a traditional measure of return elasticity. Straight bond prices to not exactly follow short-term interest rate movements, but rather long-term interest rates. Similarly, a gold bond can soften gold spot price volatility thanks to the long-term price expectations built into the indexation clause.

To summarize, the Giscard does not offer leverage over gold. Rather, it is an index-linked bond contingent on the present and future prices of gold.[7]

Gold Mining Equity

The relationship between gold mining share prices and the price of gold is shown in Exhibit 11.6. This exhibit presents the price evolution of gold bullion (in dollars per ounce) and of the Financial Times Gold Mines index (in British pence) of all gold mining shares traded on the London Stock Exchange from 1972 to 1984. This graph uses a logarithmic scale to allow for direct comparison of percentage price changes between the two indexes. The correlation between the two curves is readily apparent, although the stock index amplifies movements in gold price. The yield on gold shares was very high (10 to 20%) over the period, given the mines payout policy, but is not taken into account in the graph. Therefore, the total performance of a gold mine portfolio would be much higher than shown on the graph. Note that the correlation between gold mine share prices and the price of gold is far from perfect. This is partly explained by the different currencies (American and British) used to calculate the two price series. More importantly, gold mine values are influenced by factors other than gold prices: Social and political factors have affected South African share prices, especially in the recent past. These factors have less of an effect on U.S. mines.

Gold mines are also paper securities, the value and coupon of which are linked to gold prices. These securities differ from index-linked bonds in that the indexation clause is not fixed by contract, but depends on mining economics. In fact, the mining industry is probably the simplest activity to describe in a valuation model.

EXHIBIT 11.6

Comparative Performance of Gold Bullion and Financial Times Gold Mines Index, 1972 to 1989

Logarithmic scale

Source: International Financial Markets, Lombard, Odier & Cier, 1985. Reprinted with permission.

The economics of mining can be described by a simple discounted profit model. The principal relationship in the model is the cost structure of the mine as measured by the ratio of costs to revenues. The cost to remove an ounce or a gram of gold from so-called storage and refine it depends on several factors: technology, wage rates, power rates, and the grade and depth of the mine. Revenues depend on the world price of gold, adjusted for any government subsidies or withholdings. And mine earnings, E, depend on the quantity of gold sold, Q, the gold price received, G, and the total cost per unit, C.

$$E = Q(G - C). \tag{11.5}$$

To value the mine, we assume for the time being a dividend policy with a fixed percentage of distributed earnings, d. That gives us a value P for the mine of

$$P = d\frac{Q_1(G_1 - C_1)}{1 + r} + d\frac{Q_2(G_2 - C_2)}{(1 + r)^2} + \cdots + d\frac{Q_n(G_n - C_n)}{(1 + r)^n} \tag{11.6}$$

$$P = d\sum \frac{Q_t(G_t - C_t)}{(1 + r)^t}$$

where r is the discount rate, and the earnings, $E_t = Q_t(G_t - C_t)$, vary over time.

Our next question is how the mine stock price reacts to a change in gold bullion price. In other words: What is its gold beta? A statistical answer to this question may be found by using past market data on price elasticity, β, as an estimate of the future elasticity. A gold beta may then be obtained by regressing stock returns on percentage changes in gold prices over a recent period:

$$R_t = \alpha + \beta\frac{dG}{G} \tag{11.7}$$

As a matter of fact, gold betas do not find their origin in modern portfolio theory, but directly in the technical aspects of mining activities. Different betas are the result of the differences in cost structure found among mines because of their differential influence on mine earnings.

Let us assume that production plans at a given mine have been made, wages negotiated, and the quantities to be produced specified for the coming quarter. The percentage change in earnings (dE/E) depends on the percentage change in the gold price (dG/G) and a multiplier, b, that we define for each mine as

$$\frac{dE}{E} = b\frac{dG}{G}.$$

The multiplier b is calculated using Eq. (11.5):

$$E = Q(G - C).$$

This is done as follows: Assume that quantities and costs are held constant over the period. That makes the percentage change in profit equal to the percentage change in gold price times the multiplier b. One can think of b as the elasticity of profit with respect to gold price;[8] in financial terms, the factor b is the *operating leverage*, the reciprocal of the mining company's profit margin, $1/(1 - C/G)$.

To illustrate how this affects earnings, we should compare the multiplier in a high-cost mine with that of a low-cost mine. A high-cost mine may have a ratio of total cost to gold price (C/G) of 0.8 per ounce; in other words, a profit margin of 20%. Here the multiplier b equals 5 (that is, 1 divided by 0.2). The multiplier measures the operating leverage of this company. In this case, a short-term 10% rise in the price of gold would boost earnings by 50% as long as both the quantity produced and costs remain constant over the period in question. By contrast, a low-cost mine may have a C/G ratio of only 0.2; that is, a profit margin of 80%, which translates to a multiplier of 1.25 (1 divided by 0.8). The lower multiplier would boost earnings by only 12.5% for a 10% rise in the price of gold.

In reality, both gold production and mining costs rise over time in response to gold price increases. Mines adjust production plans, unions respond to higher gold prices with higher wage demands, and utility companies raise the energy prices mines must pay. This process of rolling adjustment can only be approximated with a static model.

Stock brokers use such discounted cash flow analysis to value mining stocks, but uncertainty and extraction policy reaction to changes in gold prices are poorly taken into account. Brennan and Schwartz (1985) and Miller and Upton (1985)[9] have proposed valuation models consistent with modern finance theory. These models are presented in the appendix.

McDonald and Solnik[10] have shown that for all gold mines a strong relationship exists between the operating leverage multiplier, b, the gold beta estimated over a given time period, and the elasticity of stock returns to gold returns over the subsequent time period. The high correlation they found between greater common stock elasticity and higher cost-revenue ratios is consistent with the old-fashioned notion that the cost structure and average ore grade of a mine are the key determinants of market response to a change in gold price.

Recent estimates of average ore grade and operating leverage are given in Exhibit 11.7. The two variables are closely related because a lower ore grade is associated with a higher ratio of cost to revenue. We should also note that both the operating leverage and gold beta are not constant, but vary with the price of gold. Higher gold prices reduce both b and β.

EXHIBIT 11.7

Statistics on Gold Mines: Estimated Present Value Statistics

Mine	Cost / ounce produced (dollars)	Life (years)	Average mill rate (tons / year)	Ore Grade (grams / ton) maximum	minimum	Working profit (rands / ton)	Working cost (rands / ton)	Estimated gold price sensitivity[a]
Randfontein	147	28	8200	7.0	5.0	48.1	31.0	18
Western Areas	331	23	4354	5.1	4.8	11.5	64.5	46
Driefontein	124	48	5700	13.0	11.0	128.7	61.0	12
Western Deep Levels	161	32	4776	12.0	6.0	112.6	71.0	17
Vaal Reefs	218	26	9061	8.4	6.0	57.9	54.0	20
Southvaal	128	26	4708	11.3	6.0	117.1	57.0	14
St. Helena	217	19	2298	6.0	5.2	45.0	50.0	18
Buffelsfontein	219	21	3325	9.1	5.6	59.6	78.5	22
Free State Geduld	285	19	4457	6.6	5.3	31.1	71.0	27
Western Holdings	285	25	7200	4.4	3.0	22.6	45.5	20
President Brand	218	18	3154	6.9	6.3	46.2	59.0	20
President Steyn	218	16	3925	6.7	5.0	45.1	57.0	18
Deelkraal	340	25	1729	7.0	4.6	10.8	59.0	84
Kloof	121	22	2311	15.4	12.8	158.2	72.5	13
Elandsrand	245	32	2381	9.0	5.8	40.3	51.5	37
Doornfontein	259	19	1464	6.8	6.1	33.7	69.5	31
Hartebeestfontein	192	19	3050	10.1	6.6	75.3	75.0	16
Kinross	203	17	2364	6.2	5.3	45.9	50.0	17
Libanon	235	21	1680	6.2	4.1	30.1	54.0	20
Unisel	159	15	1384	7.5	7.1	68.9	41.0	14
Harmony	319	15	7993	4.1	3.8	12.0	51.0	34
Stilfontein	291	12	1760	6.6	5.7	28.5	76.0	18
Grootvlei	262	14	2321	3.9	2.6	17.1	43.0	25
Winkelhaak	163	20	2360	6.2	4.0	55.4	40.5	14
Blyvooruitzicht	220	9	2144	7.5	5.8	51.3	62.5	18
Venterspost	379	11	1613	4.2	3.4	2.7	61.0	48

Source: W. Greenwell and Co., December 1983.

[a] Gold price sensitivity is the percentage change in distributable earnings in the second financial year for a 10% increase in the gold price. Therefore, it is equal to 10 times the multiplier *b* that we have defined in the text.

To summarize, it appears that gold mines have predictably different stock price behaviors. Some of them are much more speculative than others. If a gold price increase is forecasted, it is better to invest in those mines that have a high gold beta or operating leverage multiplier. By investing in those mines, an investor runs the possibility of transforming a 10% gold price increase into a 30% or more profit. On the other hand, if gold prices drop instead of rise, the loss will be larger with speculative mines. Investing in gold mines may still be attractive in a stable environment as an alternative to bullion. Gold mines are a "productive" investment as opposed to the sterile physical storage of the ingots. But the counterargument here is that physical possession of the metal, as opposed to a paper security, is the only ultimate protection in the event of a major crisis. In all cases, valuation of gold mines as proposed above is a useful exercise in identifying over- or undervalued securities contingent on the bullion price.

Other Gold-Linked Investments

Many other gold-linked investments besides gold bonds and shares can be found. Gold coins are destined either for the numismatic collector, in the case of rare coins, or for the small investor, in the case of the common mints. Common gold coins such as the Mexican 50 Pesos, U.S. Double Eagle, Canadian Maple Leaf, South African Krugerrand, British New Sovereign, French Napoleon, and Swiss Vreneli have international market prices with active transactions. These modern coins trade for their metal content plus a small premium. Their small gold content (between five and forty grams of gold) as shown in Exhibit 11.8 makes them accessible to small individual investors. However, the transaction costs are high, and any scratch or damage makes the coin sell for only its gold content,

EXHIBIT 11.8
Premium Comparison of the Most Widely Traded Gold Coins

Coin	Fine gold content (grams)	Premium (percent over gold)
American Double Eagle	30,093	53.1
Austrian Coronae	30,488	2.0
Chervonez	7,742	6.7
Krugerrand	31,103	2.1
Maple Leaf	31,103	4.2
Mexican Peso	37,500	2.0
Napoleon	5,807	32.5
Sovereign, New	7,322	5.7
Vreneli	5,807	26.2

Source: Average Zurich market prices for March 13, 1986.

i.e., it loses its premium. Gold jewels and other physical goods are poor investments in terms of transaction costs and liquidity. However, they provide other pleasures besides the financial merits of gold.

Futures and options are a major vehicle for taking short-term positions in gold. One can find futures and options on gold bullion, as well as options on individual gold mining shares. (Futures and options exist for silver and other precious metals also.) It is interesting to study the various alternatives open to an investor who has come up with specific expectations of the future price of gold. This is illustrated on the following example.

AN EXAMPLE OF ACTIVE STRATEGY

Let's consider a simple example. G. O. Bug wants to invest $12,000 in gold. In December the spot price of gold is $400 per ounce. G. O. Bug is very confident that gold will appreciate by at least 10% before the end of January, and he is willing to assume fairly risky positions to maximize the return on his forecast. G. O. Bug is considering several alternatives:

Gold bullion. He could buy thirty ounces or roughly one kilogram.

Gold bonds.

Two gold mines. Mines A and B have the same stock price: $10 per share. A British broker has estimated the gold beta of both mines using a discounted cash flow model as well as historical regression analysis. Mine A is a rich mine with a gold beta equal to two, while mine B has much higher production costs with a gold beta equal to five. G. O. Bug could buy 1200 shares of one of the gold mines.

Gold futures. G. O. Bug would buy February futures, since he believes in a gold price appreciation by the end of January. These contracts trade at $413 per ounce with an initial margin of $1500 per contract of 100 ounces. Therefore, he could buy eight contracts (12,000/1,500).

Gold options. G. O. Bug considers two February call options with different strike prices. One contract covers 100 ounces. The February 410 call quotes at $8 per ounce, while the February 430 quotes at $4 per ounce. Therefore, he could buy fifteen contracts of the first option or thirty contracts of the second option.[11]

Fractional contracts and investments are considered in this example for the sake of simplicity. Margins are assumed to be posted in cash.

G. O. Bug quickly rules out investing directly in bullion or gold bonds because they do not offer enough leverage to capitalize on his expectations. Assuming that his expectations are realized by the end of February, the realized returns on his various alternatives are calculated in Exhibit 11.9. A direct investment in gold bullion would yield 10%, or $1,200 when the gold price moves to $440. The return on gold mining shares is somewhat uncertain, even if the

EXHIBIT 11.9
Performance of Various Gold Investments Following a 10% Gold Price Appreciation

Investment		Initial Value (dollars)		Final Value (dollars)		Performance	
Asset	Quantity	Market price	Value	Market price	Value	Profit (dollars)	Return (percent)
Bullion	30 ounces	400	12,000	440	13,200	1,200	10
Mine A	1200 shares	10	12,000	12	14,400	2,400	20
Mine B	1200 shares	10	12,000	15	18,000	6,000	50
Futures	8 contracts, 800 ounces	413	12,000 (margin)	440	33,600	21,600	180
February 410 Option	15 contracts, 1,500 ounces	8	12,000	30	45,000	33,000	275
February 430 Option	30 contracts, 3000 ounces	4	12,000	10	30,000	18,000	150

price of gold does move up 10% from $400 to $440. If the gold betas of the mines are reliable estimates of their gold price elasticity, the stock price of mine A should move up by 2 × 10 or 20% and that of mine B by 5 × 10 or 50%. (The stock price return is equal to β times the percentage movement in gold price.) Therefore, the stock prices should be worth $12 and $15. The expected profit on an investment in mine A is equal to $2400 while the profit would be $6000 on mine B.

The futures and option contracts are held until expiration, therefore, their final price is exactly known once the spot price of gold is known. The final February price of the February futures is $440 per ounce if the spot gold price is $440 at that time; so the investor makes a profit of $27 per ounce ($440 − $413). The total profit for eight contracts is 800 × $27 or $21,600. Furthermore, G. O. Bug recovers his initial margin investment of $12,000. The total value of his futures investment is equal to $33,600. This $21,600 profit, compared to an initial investment of $12,000, translates into a 180% rate of return. The calculation for the option is somewhat different. At expiration, the options are equal to their intrinsic value, the difference between the gold spot price and the strike price. If the gold price is $440, the expiration value of the February 410 option is $30 ($440 − $410), and that of the February 430 option, $10 ($440 − $430). Hence, the final value of the investment in the fifteen February 410 contracts is equal to 1500 × 30 or $45,000. This implies a $33,000 profit and a rate of return of 275%. The profit on a February 430 call is only $18,000 as shown in Exhibit 11.9.

Given G. O. Bug's expectations, the February 410 option offers the best alternative, with an expected return on the $12,000 equal to 275%. In practice, taxes and transaction costs should also be taken into account. Both the commissions and bid-ask spread are large relative to the option premiums, especially for out-of-the-money options. An investor should seriously consider these costs when engaging in active trading strategies.

His second choice would be to buy February 430 call options on 3000 ounces (12,000/4 = 3000 ounces, or thirty contracts of 100 ounces). And his third choice would be to buy February 410 options on 1500 ounces of gold (12,000/8 = 1500 ounces, or fifteen contracts of 100 ounces).

Of course, the outcomes would be quite different if G. O. Bug's expectations of a 10% gold price appreciation were not realized. Gold bonds and stocks are long-term income-producing assets, whereas options and futures are short-term leveraged investments. The risks are quite different if the forecast is not realized. To get a feeling for the risks involved, we calculated the rates of return for a range of simulated gold price variations in Exhibit 11.10. Only the three

EXHIBIT 11.10
Simulation of the Rate of Return on Three Speculative Investments

Gold price, end of February (dollars per ounce)

$320	$360	$380	$400	$420	$440	$480

Performance of investment, percent

	$320	$360	$380	$400	$420	$440	$480
Bullion	− 20	− 10	− 5	0	5	10	20
Feb. futures	−620	−353	−220	− 87	47	180	447
Feb. 410 option	−100	−100	−100	−100	25	275	775
Feb. 430 option	−100	−100	−100	−100	−100	150	1150

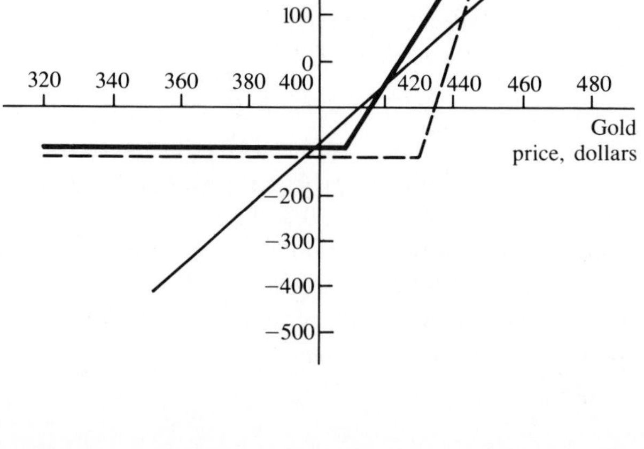

most-profitable investments are considered. All returns are calculated gross of transaction costs and taxes.

From the table, we see that options are poor investments compared to futures, where the price of gold moves very little. This is because, as mentioned above, the cost of the insurance premium is implicit in the option value. That is why, as shown in the graph of Exhibit 11.10, the futures contract has a higher return than the Feb 430 options, where the gold price at expiration is in the range of $400 to $440.

Above that range, the 430 option has a higher return, and below that range both options allow an investor to limit this loss. In general, the larger the gold price movement, the more attractive out-of-the-money options are, because they provide an investor with more leverage. A speculator must select the best contract for himself or herself depending on how much he or she expects the price of gold will change.

SUMMARY

1. Gold has always played a special role in international investment. It is regarded both as an international monetary asset and as the ultimate store of value. Gold keeps its real value in times of severe hardship, such as wars, revolution, and extreme monetary crises (stock market crashes, hyperinflation).

2. In the past, gold has provided good long-term protection against inflation and currency devaluation. In general, gold allows diversification against risks that affect all stock and bond markets simultaneously.

3. The market price of gold is determined by supply and demand. The supply to the free gold market is the sum of production by Western mines and sales by the Communist bloc, as well as Western central banks. The demand comes from jewelry and industrial needs, as well as investments.

4. Gold-linked investments exist in various forms: equity, bonds, coins, futures, options, and options on gold bonds and equity.

5. The valuation of gold-linked securities is a typical example of relative pricing. The techniques can be extended to the pricing of other types of mining activities or index-linked securities.

6. An example of an active strategy has been provided to illustrate the choice of a gold-related investment based on expectations of the future price of gold.

QUESTIONS AND PROBLEMS

1. Let's assume that you believe in the Capital Asset Pricing Model (CAPM). The beta of gold relative to the market portfolio is -0.3. The risk-free rate is 7%, and the market risk premium is 4%. Therefore, your current expectation of the market return is 11%, which is consistent with the long-term historical estimate of the market risk premium. What is the expected return on gold? Give an intuitive explanation for such a low expected return.

2. Bel Or Mine issues a five-year Eurobond with the following characteristics:

- □ Par value 100 gold ounces. Each bond is issued and repaid in dollars at the market value of 100 ounces of gold.
- □ Annual coupon payment of the dollar market value of three ounces of gold.
- □ Maturity of five years with no early redemption.

A few days after issue, the bond yield on straight dollar Eurobonds for issuers of the quality of Bel Or Mine is 10%. The price of gold is $400 per ounce. The gold-linked bond sells for $35,000. What can you say about the market expectation of gold prices?

3. Let's assume that you are a U.S. investor who wants to invest $10,000 in gold. The current price of gold is $400 and you expect it to go up by 10% in the very short term. You consider buying gold mines; you hesitate between Bel Or and Schoen Gold. Your broker gives you the following information:

	Bel Or	*Schoen Gold*
Cost/Ounce	147	340
Gold Beta	1.6	6

The gold beta is obtained by running a regression of the gold mine stock price changes on the gold bullion price changes. It indicates the stock market price sensitivity to gold. Which mine would you buy and why? What is your expected return, given your scenario?

4. To capitalize on your expectation of a 10% gold price appreciation, you consider buying futures or option contracts. Near-delivery futures contracts are quoted at $410 per ounce with a margin of $1000 per contract of 100 ounces. Call options on gold are quoted with the same delivery date. A call with an exercise price of $400 costs $20 per ounce.

- □ What is your expected return at maturity of both contracts (assuming a 10% rise in gold price)?
- □ Simulate the return of the two investments for various movements in the price of gold.
- □ Would you prefer in-, at-, or out-of-the-money options?

NOTES

1. R. Ibbotson, L. Siegel, and K. Love, "World Wealth: Market Value and Returns," *Journal of Portfolio Management*, Fall 1985.

2. See E. J. Sherman, "Performance of Gold Versus Stocks, Bonds and Money Markets in Six Countries: 1968–1983," *International Gold Corporation*, March 1984.

3. See A. Renshaw and E. Renshaw, "Does Gold Have a Role in Investment Portfolios?," *Journal of Portfolio Management*, Spring 1982.

4. Further evidence may be found in E. J. Sherman, "Gold: A Conservative, Prudent Diversifier," *Journal of Portfolio Management*, Spring 1982; K. Carter, J. Afflecte-Graves, and A. Money, "Are Gold Shares Better Than Gold for Diversification?," *Journal of Portfolio Management*, Fall 1982; J. Jaffe, "Gold and Gold Stocks as Investments for Institutional Portfolios," *Financial Analysts Journal*, March/April 1989; and J. Nichols, "The Gold-Plated Portfolio," *Investment Management Review*, December 1988.

5. See E. J. Sherman, "Performance of Gold Versus Stocks, Bonds and Money Markets in Six Countries: 1968–1983," *International Gold Corporation*, March 1984.

6. The indexation clause came into effect in 1978 because the French franc, like other currencies, was freed from being gold denominated. In the unlikely event that we revert to a gold-based international monetary system, the indexation clause might be removed. B. Jacquillat and R. Roll, "French Index-Linked Bonds for US Investors?" *Journal of Portfolio Management*, Spring 1979, provides an empirical analysis of the benefits of index-linked bonds.

7. E. Schwartz, in "The Pricing of Commodity-Linked Bonds," *Journal of Finance*, May 1982, provides a theoretical model for an index-linked bond with an option to repay the bond at face value or at an index-linked price. This leads to a more complex option valuation formula. Such a model was tested on a silver-linked bond issue by Sunshine Mining by G. A. Brauer and R. Ravichandran, "How Sweet Is Silver?," *Journal of Portfolio Management*, Summer 1986.

8. The value of b is obtained by taking, in Eq. (11.5), the derivative of E relative to G: $dE/dG = Q$. That means

$$\frac{dE}{E} = \frac{dG}{G}\frac{G}{G-C};$$

hence the value of b.

9. See M. Brennan and E. Schwartz, "Evaluating Natural Resource Investments," *Journal of Business*, 58(2) 1985; and M. Miller and C. W. Upton, "A Test of the Hotelling Valuation Principle," *Journal of Political Economy*, February 1985.

10. See J. McDonald and B. Solnik, "Valuation and Strategy for Gold Stocks," *Journal of Portfolio Management*, Spring 1977. McDonald and Solnik proposed a two-factor model description for gold mine stock returns, to account for the fact that mining companies are affected by general economic conditions. Also, note that some mines have other activities than gold, or other element, extraction, and that South African firms are subject to political risk, which affects their stock prices.

11. Another highly speculative gold-related investment is buying options on gold mining equity. The gold beta of a mine increases the elasticity of an option premium to movements in gold price. In a sense, it is like multiplying the leverage offered by an option by the elasticity of the gold mine. Again, we should remember that these relationships are not linear. They tend to change as the price of gold varies.

12. See M. Miller and C. W. Upton, "A Test of the Hotelling Valuation Principle," *Journal of Political Economy*, February 1985.

13. See R. Pindyck, "Uncertainty and Exhaustible Resource Markets," *Journal of Political Economy*, December 1980; and M. Sundaresan, "Equilibrium Valuation of Natural Resources," *Journal of Business*, 1985.

14. See M. Brennan and E. Schwartz, "Evaluating Natural Resource Investments," *Journal of Business*, 58(2) 1985.

BIBLIOGRAPHY

M. Brennan and E. Schwartz, "Evaluating Natural Resource Investments," *Journal of Business*, 58(2) 1985.

K. Carter, J. Afflecte-Graves, and A. Money, "Are Gold Shares Better Than Gold for Diversification?," *Journal of Portfolio Management*, Fall 1982.

E. Fama and K. French, "Business Cycles and the Behavior of Metal Prices," *Journal of Finance*, December 1988.

R. Gibons and E. Schwartz, "Valuation of Long-Term Oil-linked Assets," Working paper, UCLA, 1989.

R. Ibbotson, L. Siegel, and K. Love, "World Wealth: Market Value and Returns," *Journal of Portfolio Management*, Fall 1985.

B. Jacquillat and R. Roll, "French Index-Linked Bonds for US Investors?," *Journal of Portfolio Management*, Spring 1979.

J. Jaffe, "Gold and Gold Stocks as Investments for Institutional Portfolios," *Financial Analysts Journal*, March/April 1989.

M. Miller and C. W. Upton, "A Test of the Hotelling Valuation Principle," *Journal of Political Economy*, February 1985.

J. McDonald and B. Solnik, "Valuation and Strategy for Gold Stocks," *Journal of Portfolio Management*, Spring 1977.

J. Nichols, "The Gold-Plated Portfolio," *Investment Management Review*, December 1988.

R. Pindyck, "Uncertainty and Exhaustible Resource Markets," *Journal of Political Economy*, December 1980.

A. Renshaw and E. Renshaw, "Does Gold Have a Role in Investment Portfolios?," *Journal of Portfolio Management*, Spring 1982.

E. Schwartz, "The Pricing of Commodity-Linked Bonds," *Journal of Finance*, May 1982.

E. J. Sherman, "Gold: A Conservative, Prudent Diversifier," *Journal of Portfolio Management*, Spring 1982.

E. J. Sherman, "Performance of Gold Versus Stocks, Bonds and Money Markets in Six Countries: 1968–1983," *International Gold Corporation*, March 1984.

M. Sundaresan, "Equilibrium Valuation of Natural Resources," *Journal of Business*, 1985.

Chapter 11: Appendix
Advanced Section on Evaluating
Natural Resource Investments

The general valuation formula for a natural resource investment such as a mine or an oil field is given by Eq. (11.6), assuming all earnings paid as dividend:

$$P = \sum \frac{Q_t(G_t - C_t)}{(1+r)^t}.$$

In this appendix, we make the common assumption that all profits are distributed to the owner.

One major problem is that extraction costs, Q, are likely to be a function of the current extraction, Q_t, as well as the past extraction policy. The current costs will be higher if the mine already produced a lot and is left with low-grade ore, than if it produced at a slower pace without exhausting its rich ore. Of course, past and present extraction policies are a function of the output price, G, of gold, in our case. Microeconomic analysis can help us simplify Eq. (11.6) if we assume that producers attempt to maximize profits at each point in time. Miller and Upton (1985)[12] provided such an analysis in a simple discrete-time certainty framework. They assumed a finite horizon date, N, beyond which production could safely be presumed to have ceased, and known total reserves, R_0. They first considered the case where costs were only a function of current production, $C_t(Q_t)$. The first-order condition for profit maximization in every period is

$$\frac{(G_t - c_t)}{(1+r)^t} = \lambda \quad t = 0, \ldots, N$$

where c_t is the marginal cost of producing Q_t. Since the same condition applies at time 0, we have

$$(G_0 - c_0) = \lambda.$$

Hence

$$G_t - c_t = (G_0 - c_0)(1+r)^t. \qquad (11.A1)$$

Miller and Upton make the further simplifying assumption that the marginal costs of production are constant; then the valuation equation of the mine reduces to

$$P = (G_0 - c_0) \sum_{t=0}^{N} Q_t = (G_0 - c_0)R_0. \qquad (11.A2)$$

The value of the mine is equal to current earnings times the total reserves. In this case, the gold beta of the mine is exactly equal to its current operating leverage. They also worked out the more complex formula for situations in which costs are an increasing function of current production and cumulative post production.

One problem with this traditional microeconomic analysis is the existence of uncertainty. Pindyck (1980) considered the case of uncertainty assuming risk neutrality, while Sundaresan (1985)[13] also considered constant risk aversion. However, they did not consider the possibility of closing a mine and reopening it at a later time in response to current market conditions. Indeed, some gold mines were closed in the late 1960s when the low price of gold, around $40 an ounce, made it very costly to continue their operation. Many of these mines reopened in the mid-1970s, when the gold price surged to $200 an ounce.

Brennan and Schwartz (1985)[14] took a different approach to tackling this situation. They resorted to an arbitrage approach similar in spirit to the one developed for option pricing. This was based on constructing arbitrage portfolios on the mine equity, and futures contracts on the underlying commodity, gold. Using stochastic optimal control theory, they derived a set of differential equations that could be solved numerically. While the mathematics are tough, the implications and potential uses of the model are attractive.

12

Strategy, Organization, and Control

An organization that is planning to invest internationally first needs the information on institutions and techniques provided in the beginning of this book. Then it needs to structure properly its entire international investment decision process from research to management and control. Among the many international investment organizations in the world today, there are a great variety of approaches to structuring the international investment process. Different approaches reflect different investment philosophies and strategies.

This chapter addresses some of the practical aspects of international investment, from various investment philosophies to the nitty-gritty of portfolio accounting and custody.

INVESTMENT PHILOSOPHY AND STRATEGY

An organization must make certain major choices in structuring its international decision process based on several factors:

- □ its view of the world, regarding price behavior;
- □ its strengths, in terms of research and management;
- □ the available data, communication, and computer technology; and
- □ its marketing strategy.

These important choices are discussed below in terms of investment philosophy and strategy.

Active or Passive

The passive approach A fund managed according to a passive approach reproduces a market capitalization–weighted index of all securities markets. The Morgan Stanley Capital International or the Financial Times international indices are generally used as a model for equity funds, and the Lombard Odier or the Salomon Brothers international bond index is usually favored for international bond portfolios. The passive approach is an international extension of modern portfolio theory, which claims that market portfolios should be efficient. In the United States the domestic index-fund approach is supported by extensive empirical evidence of the efficiency of the stock market. Since most stocks follow domestic market behavior to a large degree, any well-diversified domestic portfolio tends to track the domestic market index. A similar domestic index-fund approach has developed in the United Kingdom and, more recently, in Japan and in other European countries. However, foreign markets tend to be very independent of each other. This independence, when combined with substantial currency movements, means that different international asset allocations will yield very different performances. Furthermore, little empirical evidence of the international efficiency of world market portfolios exists so far. Academic research has demonstrated varying degrees of efficiency of individual foreign stock markets (see Chapter 1 references), but no study has yet established that the world market portfolio is indeed efficient in a risk-reward framework and that active asset allocation strategies (markets and currencies) cannot consistently outperform the passive approach.

The wide dispersion of performance among international portfolios is illustrated in Exhibits 12.1 and 12.2. Exhibit 12.1 shows the distribution of the non-U.S. equity performance of a large number of U.S. pension fund portfolios as tracked by Intersec in terms of the annualized rates of return, in U.S. dollars, for the one-year and four-year periods ending December 1988. Besides the distribution of performance, this exhibit also indicates the return on the EAFE index, as well as the median and the two quartiles of the distribution. The median is the rate of return such that exactly 50% of the portfolios have a performance above or below this value. The upper quartile, Q_1, is the rate of return such that exactly 25% of the portfolios have a performance above this value. The lower quartile, Q_3, is the rate of return such that 25% of the portfolios have a performance below this value. In the one-year graph the performance of funds ranged from 5 to 40% with a wide dispersion. The median performance of a non-U.S. equity portfolio was 17.4% well below that of the EAFE index (28.5%). In the four-year graph the dispersion of annualized rates of return is less but still quite wide, and the portfolios underperformed the EAFE on the average by more than 9%. Exhibit 12.2 gives similar information on global world equity accounts, but in a different format and for a different period. This exhibit shows the distribution of annualized rates of return for a universe of equity portfolios invested worldwide as tracked by Frank Russell International. The exhibit shows the distribution range from the lowest to the highest performance, the median, and the upper and the lower quartile, as well as the Morgan Stanley Capital International world equity index. Again, the dispersion of performance is quite wide, and the average portfolio underperformed the world index over the long term.

EXHIBIT 12.1
Frequency Distribution of Total U.S. Pension Fund Returns in U.S. Dollars
Non-U.S. equity universe, one- and four-year periods ending December 1988.

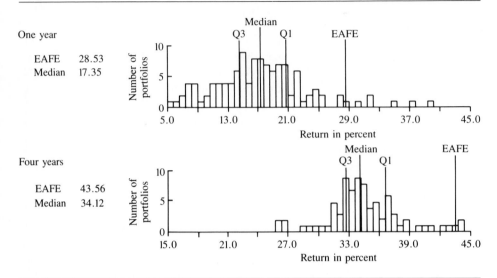

Source: Intersec Research Corporation, Stamford, CT, London, Tokyo, performance measurement as of December 1988. Reprinted with permission.

This underperformance mostly comes from the fact that money managers systematically underweighted Japan, the best-performing market, compared to its market weight in international indices. It may have been a wise management decision *ex ante*, but it certainly strengthened the case for passive international management. Large pension funds have extensively moved to indexing their domestic assets. Indexing is a passive strategy that simply attempts to replicate the market index that is assigned as an objective. In 1989, U.S. public pension funds had indexed over 40% of their domestic equity investments. U.S. corporate pension funds and UK pension funds had indexed around 25% of their domestic equity investments. The trend toward international indexing is strongly felt among institutional investors. A large number of pension funds worldwide have moved to passive international investment strategies.

The question that remains is the choice of the proper international market index. In Chapter 4 we indicated that extensive cross-holding of shares by Japanese companies significantly inflated the reported market capitalization for Japan. When two companies hold shares in the other one, one cannot simply add their stock market capitalization; their share cross-holding has to be removed from the addition. McDonald[1] reports that the share of Japan in the world market capitalization at the start of 1989 would be reduced from 44 to 39% if Japanese cross-holdings are taken into account. Some managers have suggested

EXHIBIT 12.2
Active Management Results
World equity accounts, periods ending December 1985

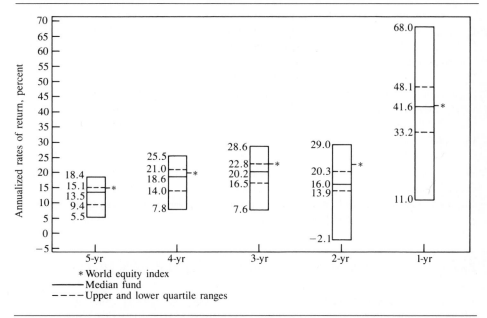

Source: Frank Russell Co. Reprinted with permission.

using GDP country weights, instead of market capitalization country weights, to structure the international index funds. The idea is interesting since it gives each country a weight proportional to its economic strength. But implementing it is not easy and fairly costly in a passive portfolio that needs to be rebalanced each time a new GDP figure is published or revised in any country. Also, the question of currency hedging is an open theoretical question as discussed in Chapter 1. It is not clear whether the foreign passive fund should be unhedged, or fully or partly hedged. In a simplistic, perfect version of the world, theory suggests that the optimal portfolio of risky assets is the world market portfolio hedged against currency risk. But these assumptions are unrealistic: It has been shown that the contribution of currency risk to the total risk of a fund is nil (or minimal) when foreign assets are only a small proportion (say, 5 or 10%) of the total assets (see Jorion[2]).

The inclusion of bonds and cash investments in a variety of currencies makes the concept of a world market portfolio very hard to measure and implement. As mentioned in Chapter 1, the world market portfolio would not be optimal, even in efficient markets, because of differences in currency, consumption preferences, transaction costs, differential tax treatments, and transfer risk exposures. Different investor groups should follow different core strategies that reflect their situation and comparative advantage in terms of costs, taxes, and risks.

An analysis of the relative costs and risks of foreign investments would lead to an underweighting of foreign assets relative to the world market portfolio. Typically, an investment organization decides on the percentage of funds it is willing to commit abroad and adopts a passive management of that foreign core. What the optimal amount of foreign assets is is an empirical question in the absence of a complete theory of world market equilibrium. In a passive framework, investors look for the optimal asset allocation assuming zero forecasting ability. Historical risk and return studies as described in Chapter 2 can assist investors in determining such an asset allocation.

The basic argument supporting the passive index approach is that the alternative, an active strategy, requires above-average ability at forecasting markets or currencies or both. Forecasting is never easy and, moreover, entails higher commissions and costs. With a passive strategy, the fund can achieve the full benefits of international risk diversification without incurring these high costs.

The active approach Managers using an active approach attempt to time markets and currency switching between them so as to take advantage of low intermarket correlation. This approach requires high-quality investment management skills and sometimes lacks a systematic structure. Passive managers stress international risk reduction, rather than the higher-performance higher-risk strategy favored by active managers. Uncontrolled, an active strategy can lead to increased portfolio risk if the manager makes the mistake of focusing on only a couple of markets or currencies.

The risk diversification argument is usually at the heart of the marketing pitch made by both active and passive international money managers. Besides citing expost risk measures, such as standard deviations and correlation coefficients, as supporting evidence, institutions must develop a systematic framework for incorporating risk into their international asset allocation decision process. In the quickly changing international environment, active money managers have a special need to evaluate and to control the risk of their accounts as rapidly as possible. This approach is implemented in a practical example below.

In an active strategy, investors place bets on the various factors that affect securities behavior. Of course, the strategy itself depends on the investor's view of the world. In the international arbitrage pricing theory framework introduced in Chapter 5, one must forecast movements in the various domestic and international factors that have been identified. In the multi-country model, one must forecast returns on the various national market factors. Each factor is associated with a national market index and compounds the national market and currency influences for a foreign investor (see Chapter 5). Securities are selected according to their sensitivity to these factors. The multi-country approach will be used in the rest of this chapter.

An active strategy is usually broken down into three parts: asset allocation, security selection, and market timing. The manager using an active asset allocation strategy is primarily concerned with determining the proportion of various asset classes in each currency, for example, Japanese equity or sterling bonds, needed to optimize the portfolio's expected return-risk trade-off. The proportions generally differ from those of a passive or world market portfolio and must be frequently adjusted to accommodate changes in market expectations or risk estimates. Practically speaking, this can be done by investing in index funds for every major asset class. An important ramification of this method is that the manager must pay careful attention to market forecasts (stocks, bonds, and currencies) rather than forecasts of individual securities.

In each asset class, the manager may want to engage in security selection to try to beat the market. Other managers resort to market timing to temporarily increase or reduce their exposure in one or more markets or currencies. But these are short-term trading tactics, as opposed to long-run strategies for allocating assets.

Top-Down or Bottom Up

Domestically, portfolio managers use either a top-down or a bottom-up approach to the investment process. The same is true internationally.

Top-down approach The manager using a top-down approach first allocates his or her assets and then selects individual securities to satisfy that allocation. The most important decision in this approach is the choice of markets and currencies. In other words, the global money manager must choose from among several markets (stocks, bonds, or cash) as well as a variety of currencies. Once these choices have been made, the manager selects the best securties available.

Bottom-up approach The bottom-up approach is most often used in international equity portfolios. The manager using this approach studies the fundamentals of many individual stocks from which he or she selects the best securities (irrespective of their national origin or currency denomination) to build a portfolio. For example, a manager may be bullish on car manufacturers and buy shares in all of them (GM, Toyota, Volkswagen, Peugeot, etc.); or the manager may buy shares in only the best electronics firm in the world, regardless of its national origin. The product of this approach is a portfolio with a market and currency allocation that is more or less the random result of the securities selected. Implicit in this approach is that the manager is more concerned with risk exposure in various sectors than with either market or currency risk exposure.

Many organizations claim to combine a top-down with a bottom-up approach. But this seems unlikely: To be consistent, the entire investment decision process should be structured along a single approach. For example, a research department using the top-down approach focuses on country and currency analysis. Typically, the financial analysts in the department are specialized by country. On the other hand, financial analysts using the bottom-up approach are specialized by worldwide industry. Accommodating these contrasting professional requirements is not easy.

The empirical evidence presented in previous chapters showed that all securities within a single market tend to move together, but national markets and currencies do not. This underscores the fact that the major factor contributing to portfolio performance is the choice of markets and currencies, not individual securities. Indeed, a variety of international performance measurement services have shown that the performance of international money managers is attributable mainly to asset allocation, not to superior security selection. This, in turn, suggests that an international investment organization should be organized along primarily top-down lines, and its analysts should be specialized by country, and possibly by a few international sectors, such as oil stocks.

Some institutions have started to offer products that solely capitalize on the asset allocation expertise. The manager decides on the country asset allocation and implements it by using a national index fund for each country. Other institutions have developed an international "tactical asset allocation." This approach also uses country index funds, but the asset allocating decision is only based on publicly available data such as the consencus estimate of earning forecasts published by financial analysts in all countries.[3]

Global or Specialized

European managers have traditionally been global money managers. Typically, a Swiss bank will manage all the assets of a customer and determine both the asset allocation and the selection of each security for the portfolio. By contrast, American institutional managers tend to specialize in particular investment areas such as Japanese stocks, Eurobonds, or energy stocks. These specialized managers often handle specific funds that a customer can buy into to diversify away his or her portfolio risk. The allocation decision is then made by the costomer based on advice he or she gets from one or several managers. Thus it is not unusual to find investors with the bulk of their international portfolio in a passive, well-diversified fund and the remainder invested in a few active funds in specialized areas.

The trend toward specialized international management is derived from the fact that no manager is a superior expert on all markets, though some are superior on one or a few markets. Because asset allocation is potentially the most profitable decision, a combination of global and specialized management is required. Global management is the only reasonable solution for the small investor, whereas large investors may afford both global and specialized management.

Currency

Some managers treat currencies only as residual variables; their currency breakdown is determined by the countries, industries, and securities they select for the portfolio. They generally consider currency risk a necessary evil and argue that currency movements are impossible to predict and wash out in the long run, anyway, since it is the real economic variables that ultimately determine a portfolio's performance.

Some managers fully hedge their foreign portfolios or decide on a permanent hedge ratio based on an historical estimate. This strategy is based on the theory outlined in Chapter 1 or on the belief that foreign currency risk premia are small or unpredictable and hence that one is not compensated to carry foreign exchange risk.[4]

Other managers take a proactive approach to currency forecasting. They try to minimize the contribution currency makes to total risk and cash in on opportunities created by currency movements. These managers prefer the currency-asset allocation method.

At the extreme end of the spectrum, we find a new brand of international money manager who is very active in currency management. These managers make currency selection an important part of their asset allocation and often resort to currency options and forward or futures contracts for selective hedging and speculation.

Naturally, the approach an investment manager takes toward currencies leads to very different portfolio strategies.

Quantitative or Subjective

Quantification of the investment process is very helpful in international investment management because of the large number of parameters and decision variables it involves. Quantification can be applied to various models or aids used in the investment process, including:

- □ econometric or technical forecasting models of markets and currencies;
- □ international asset allocation optimizers;
- □ dividend-discount models, betas, durations, or option valuation models (for quantitative assessment of individual securities);
- □ risk management models; and
- □ performance and risk analysis.

An example of a quantified system is outlined below.

EXHIBIT 12.3
Investment Philosophies of 112 International Money Managers of U.S. Pension Funds

Investment philosophy	Managers claiming the philosophy (percent)
Active	82
Passive	18
Top Down	34
Top Down and Bottom Up	53
Bottom Up	13
Active Asset Allocation Process	39
Currency Emphasis	32
Quantitative Overlay	39
Value Orientation	26
Contrarian	4

Source: Intersec Research Corporation, Stamford, CT, 1989, London, Tokyo. Reprinted with permission.

Other managers rely primarily on subjective judgment. In either case, a lot of information is required before decisions can be made. The difference between the two approaches is that managers who favor the subjective approach argue that the international environment is too complex to permit formal quantification. They say that models based on past data are not helpful because constant changes in the international environment distort them.

A breakdown of international institutional managers according to investment philosophy and strategy is shown in Exhibit 12.3. A vast majority of investment managers claim some degree of active management (94%). Although the top-down approach dominates the bottom-up approach, a majority of managers claim to do both. The dominance of a top-down approach with a priority on country analysis is evidenced in Exhibit 12.4. Frank Russell found that the average international manager puts 50% of his or her resources into country analysis, only about 15% into industry analysis, and 35% into company analysis.[5]

STRUCTURING AND QUANTIFYING THE ASSET ALLOCATION PROCESS

Apart from the obvious technical and practical problems inherent in investing abroad, the key issue in international diversification is how to structure the asset allocation process. Essential to this decision process are a variety of uncertain forecasts concerning exchange rates, interest rates, and stock market patterns. The task is further complicated by the fact that many of these variables are, to varying degrees, interdependent in the international context. For example, all the major stock markets are linked, but some are more closely linked than others, depending on the integration of the underlying economies. Similarly, a change in the interest rate of one currency will affect the exchange rates and

EXHIBIT 12.4
Investment Philosophy: Relative Emphasis Universe of Thirty International Investment Firms

	Low	Medium	High
Country analysis	7	9	14
Industry analysis	15	9	6
Company analysis	5	16	9

Source: Frank Russell Co. Reprinted with permission.

interest rates of other currencies, but not to the same degree. Domestic asset allocation is simplified by the fact that an investor chooses from only a limited variety of assets: namely, cash, bonds, common stocks, and possibly commodities. In the international context, however, these choices are multiplied by the number of countries and currencies available, which themselves can present certain practical problems. For example, an investor may be bullish on the Japanese stock market but not on the yen. The complexity of the international scene, which is involved in so many interactions, makes quantification all the more useful and calls for computer technology. Ideally, an asset allocation system should enable a portfolio manager to react quickly and efficiently to any change in the international environment.

This section describes a quantified system for portfolio management based on a top-down approach that is currently used by several international money management firms.[6] Because it is internally consistent, it avoids the pitfalls often found in the bottom-up approach that lead to suboptimal decisions. The purpose of this system is to ensure the most efficient use of existing expertise within an organization. It relies on the multi-country view of the world described in Chapter 5. The system must therefore be structured along the lines of the major common factors (here, national market influences) affecting a security's price behavior. A different model of the world capital market (such as an international arbitrage pricing theory) would lead to a different system.

Our portfolio management system has four major stages: market analysis, asset allocation optimization, individual security selection, and performance and risk control. The novelty of the system lies not in its components but rather in the way it integrates the four stages, with the aid of computers, to benefit money managers. The idea is not to generate more reliable forecasts, but to use currently available forecasts better, which requires capitalizing most efficiently on the existing expertise within an organization. A diagram of this system is shown in Exhibit 12.5.

Research and Market Analysis

To cope with the complexity and rapid changes of the international environment, a manager must use an interactive computer system. Ideally, everyone involved in the investment decision process, i.e., analysts, investment committee members, and managers should have terminals or microcomputers linked by interactive programs to a mainframe computer.

To monitor markets a large international database with on-line connections to major outside databank services is necessary. The database should contain both price histories and information on economic statistics, markets, and individual securities. Ideally, the data should cover several previous years and be updated frequently, preferably daily. Only by having access to the most current data can managers update their correlation matrix properly, giving greater weight to more recent observations. A properly updated correlation matrix, in turn, helps managers to sort the interdependencies among the various markets (stocks, interest rates, exchange rates, etc.) that affect the portfolios under management.

A major responsibility of the research department in an investment organization is to provide forecasts on currencies, interest rates, gold and commodity prices, and national stock indexes. The forecasts should then be translated by a computer into estimates of total return in particular base currencies.

Asset Allocation Optimization

Asset allocation has a major influence on fund performance. Of course, astute security selection on a given market can enhance the return on that segment of the account, but not as much as astute currency or market allocation can.

The objective of any investment policy is to achieve a superior performance for a given risk. This may be achieved through subjective discussion among the members of an investment policy committee or by using formal optimization models. An investment policy should aim to achieve an efficient asset allocation matrix by country (or currency) and type of investment (stocks, bonds, money markets). Toward this end, a mean-variance quadratic program is often used to merge the forecasts and risk estimates generated by an investment organization. Such an optimization model is described in the appendix. Providing it is optimal, the resulting asset allocation will outperform a passive strategy only to the extent that the organization's forecasts reflect superior expertise in one or more markets such as stocks, bonds, or foreign exchange. Another thing to remember is that the allocation must conform to the objectives and constraints of the various accounts managed by an organization. Some accounts permit only

EXHIBIT 12.5
An Integrated Investment Process

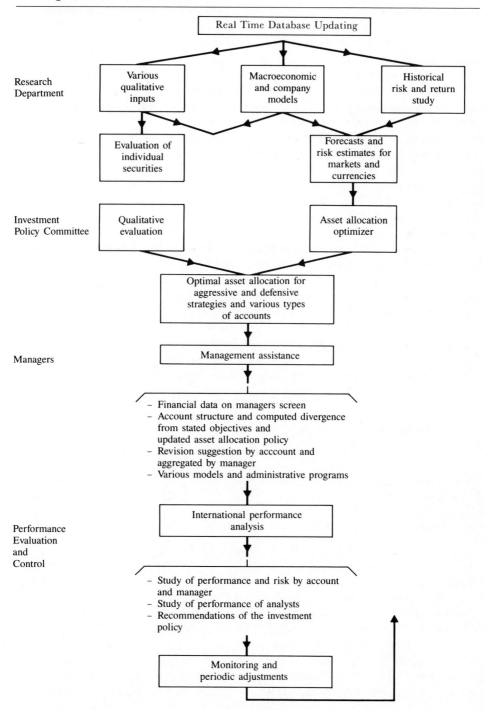

Real Time Database Updating

Research Department

Various qualitative inputs

Macroeconomic and company models

Historical risk and return study

Evaluation of individual securities

Forecasts and risk estimates for markets and currencies

Investment Policy Committee

Qualitative evaluation

Asset allocation optimizer

Optimal asset allocation for aggressive and defensive strategies and various types of accounts

Managers

Management assistance

- Financial data on managers screen
- Account structure and computed divergence from stated objectives and updated asset allocation policy
- Revision suggestion by acccount and aggregated by manager
- Various models and administrative programs

International performance analysis

Performance Evaluation and Control

- Study of performance and risk by account and manager
- Study of performance of analysts
- Recommendations of the investment policy

Monitoring and periodic adjustments

equity investment, others impose restrictions on selling short, and still others do not permit investment in gold. Plainly, constraints such as these will affect the potential return on an account, just as the choice of risk level or any other limitation will affect it.

In theory, one should care about real returns, not nominal returns. In other words, one should consider the returns calculated in the currency of the investor and adjusted by the appropriate inflation rate. Because the volatility of inflation rates is very small compared to that of most asset returns or currency movements, the use of real or nominal returns would not make much difference in the results of the optimization procedure.[7]

The computer programs should be interactive so that an investment committee can simulate several scenarios and thereby determine the most profitable investment policy. They should also enable the investment committee to check the sensitivity of the optimal asset allocation against a variety of projected forecasts. This helps to focus discussion at the policy-making level on the practical recommendations of the managers. Once the committee has chosen a policy, the resulting investment policy matrices should appear on each manager's terminal. The money managers can then use this optimization package to introduce their own scenarios. A sample output from an interactive program is shown in Exhibit 12.6.

The institution whose matrix is depicted in Exhibit 12.6 considers ten countries and three asset types plus gold. Basically, the asset allocation matrix is made up of thirty-one cells to be determined. Maximum constraints have been put on each asset type (10% for cash, 20% for bonds, and 10% for gold) and no

EXHIBIT 12.6
Asset Allocation Matrix
Balanced Strategy in U.S. dollars, May 29, 1981

	Total	Cash	Bonds	Equities	Gold
United States	0.0	0.0	0.0	0.0	
Switzerland	9.2	0.0	0.0	9.2	
West Germany	18.5	0.0	6.5	12.0	
Netherlands	12.1	2.1	5.0	5.0	
United Kingdom	11.5	2.9	8.5	0.0	
Japan	36.2	5.0	0.0	31.2	
France	0.0	0.0	0.0	0.0	
Australia	7.3	0.0	0.0	7.3	
Hong Kong	0.0	0.0	0.0	0.0	
Singapore	2.8	0.0	0.0	2.8	
Gold	2.5				2.5
Total	100.	10.0	20.0	67.5	2.5

Expected return = 29.0% Risk estimate = 12.9%.

EXHIBIT 12.7
Efficient Frontier

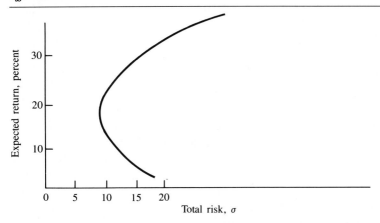

short selling is allowed. The optimization model as described in the appendix allows the derivation of the optimal asset allocation for each risk level, given the forecasted returns, the correlation matrix, and the investment constraints.

Calculating the entire efficient frontier allows the portfolio manager to estimate expected return on the optimal international asset allocation for all risk levels (see Exhibit 12.7).

Ultimately, the quality of inputs is what counts. Bad forecasts will not generate superior performance, no matter what optimization method is used. However, any forecasting ability will best be exploited through such an approach.

Portfolio Construction

Active stock and bond selection in each market is a natural complement to active market selection. With the aid of computers, a research department should maintain an active list of individual securities in each market. This regularly updated list should provide a manager with an analyst's recommendation, possibly in the form of an expected return in local currency, as well as major risk characteristics of the security, including betas with respect to several factors, actuarial yields, and, for bonds, a measure for duration. The manager can then use this active securities list to construct the portfolio according to the asset allocation policy right on his or her terminal.

Managers of a large number of medium-sized accounts find that rebalancing those accounts to reflect even modest alterations in the organization's (or their own) investment policy is extremely time consuming and unduly repetitive. Reacting to a drastic policy change takes that much longer. To cope with this problem, a manager should first value each portfolio in the asset allocation matrix format. This will generate aggregated asset allocations for each of the following categories:

- all managed accounts;
- all accounts of each manager, and
- homogeneous classes of accounts of each manager.

Next, each manager should modify the new investment policy matrix so that it reflects client guidelines for his or her major classes of accounts. The extent of this modification will depend on the type of client, base currency, and size of the account. Any deviations of the current asset allocation from the new policy matrix will show up on the manager's screen in a format similar to that of Exhibit 12.6. Drawing on the active securities list, the computer will make sell and buy recommendations for stocks and bonds that would enable the account to satisfy the new asset allocation guideline. The manager can either validate the proposed transactions on the screen or make his or her own. The market orders and attendant paperwork required for implementing the validated transactions are generated by the computer automatically.

More quantitatively oriented managers would probably make extensive use of the several models described in Chapters 5 and 7. One could adjust the sensitivity of the portfolio to specific market factors in each cell of the asset allocation matrix: For example, a manager very bullish on interest rates in West Germany could select deutsche mark bonds with long duration to increase the sensitivity to a drop in deutsche mark bond yields.

At this level, fine tuning of the risk management strategy should also come into play. Futures and options can be used to react to sudden threats of a large market movement in some currency or asset classes.

Performance and Risk Control

The final step in the investment process is to monitor the performance and risk of individual portfolios. A common problem is that many money managers are concerned with international risk diversification but do little in their allocation process to achieve it. This problem is all the more serious for managers with active strategies, which tend to concentrate on a few currencies and markets and are therefore vulnerable to the high risk associated with those currencies and markets.

Performance control should be driven by an organization's daily accounting system, which should note measurements available on a daily, weekly, or monthly basis, if desired. The objective is to be able to answer the following questions about a portfolio, and in so doing, assess the effectiveness of its manager:

- What is the total return on the fund over a specific period?
- What is the breakdown of the return in terms of capital gains, currency fluctuations, and income?

- To what extent is the performance explained by asset allocation, market timing, currency selection, or individual stock selection?

- How does the overall return compare to that of certain standards? For example, does it outperform the EAFE index in terms of return, given its level of risk?

- Is there evidence of unusual expertise in a particular market (e.g., Japanese stocks or British bonds)?

- Has the risk diversification objective been achieved?

- How aggressive is the manager's strategy?

The characteristics and use of an account review of an international performance analysis (IPA) system are discussed next. It should be stressed that the performance of a research department should be studied to pinpoint the areas of expertise. This can be done by constructing paper portfolios based on analyst recommendations for each country and comparing the subsequent returns to those on the corresponding national indexes.

INTERNATIONAL PERFORMANCE ANALYSIS

Objectives and Difficulties

Objectives The first thing to remember in international performance analysis[8] is that accounting valuation should not be confused with performance measurement. Multi-currency accounting systems keep track of transactions, including forward commitments, on a daily basis, providing a valuation of the account based on current market prices from around the world and computed in one or more reference currencies (often in U.S. dollars). Every item, including stocks, bonds, and, of course, cash, is included in an accounting valuation. International performance analysis systems measure the return on either a portfolio or a portfolio segment, usually on a monthly or quarterly basis. Some IPA systems also compare performance against certain standards. To date, few institutions have developed comprehensive in-house IPA systems to evaluate and assist management. In-house IPA systems are driven largely by daily accounting systems and allow quick monitoring of the performance and risk of all major accounts. Outside services have begun to measure the performance of managers, mostly on behalf of trustees whose funds are under management. The oldest established services are provided by Intersec, Frank Russell International, and Wood McKenzie.

Total rates of return are usually computed on a quarterly (or sometimes monthly) basis and compared to one or more standards. The standard can be either a passive index such as the Morgan Stanley Capital International world or EAFE index, or the U.S. Standard and Poor's index, or the mean return of a universe of managed funds. Calculating total return is easy once the manager provides the advisor with a total valuation for the start and the end of a period, and the major cash flows that occurred during the period. In fact, it is just like calculating the return on a purely domestic fund. The interesting part lies in breaking the performance down into its various components such as yield, capital gain or loss in local currency, and currency contribution.

The performance of a manager in each market is estimated by calculating the rate of return for every segment of the portfolio that is associated with a national stock or bond market (e.g., Japanese stocks) and comparing it to the return on the corresponding national index. Any disparity between the two reflects the manager's stock selection ability. If the performance is measured relative to an internationally weighted index, this disparity can be further broken down into the following: (1) the portion resulting from a difference in market weighting between the portfolio and the international index, and (2) the portion resulting from the manager's security selection and timing ability in each market. To perform this analysis, IPA services obtain the quarterly valuation for each portfolio segment as well as the cash flows affecting each segment.

Unfortunately, serious technical and conceptual problems arise due to the quality of the data used as input to the analysis. These problems are present, to some extent, in a domestic performance analysis, but they are magnified in an international setting.

Calculating a rate of return There are several methods of calculating the rate of return on a portfolio. The most common are the time-weighted rate of return (TWR), the internal rate of return (IRR), and the money-weighted rate of return (MWR).[9] The rate of return over a period on a portfolio segment or on a total portfolio is easy to calculate if there are no cash inflows or outflows. Then the rate of period r is simply equal to the change in value over the period $(V_1 - V_0)$ divided by the initial value V_0:

$$r = \frac{V_1 - V_0}{V_0} \quad \text{or}$$

$$1 + r = \frac{V_1}{V_0}.$$

However, let's now assume that a cash withdrawal, C_t, took place on day t during the period. Consider the following example:

☐ value at start of the year is $V_0 = 100$;
☐ cash withdrawal[10] on day t is $C_t = 50$, $t = 30$ days; and
☐ final value at year end is $V_1 = 60$.

The change in value over the year is unquestionably equal to $V_1 + C_t - V_0$ $= 10$. However, methods differ on how to calculate the rate of return. Dividing the change in value by the initial capital value, V_0, would be a mistake, since a much smaller capital was invested during most of the year. A common approach is to calculate the money-weighted rate of return (MWR), which is the division of the change in value by the average capital invested during the period:

$$\text{MWR} = \frac{V_1 + C_t - V_0}{V_0 - \frac{1}{2}C_t} = \frac{60 + 50 - 100}{100 - 25} = \frac{10}{75} = 13.33\%.$$

This approach does not take into account the exact timing of cash flows: It assumes that they take place in the middle of the period so that their average contribution is half their value. A more accurate method is to divide not by $V_0 - \frac{1}{2}C_t$, but by a term that takes into account the length of time the funds have been invested. For a yearly rate of return, we have

$$\text{MWR*} = \frac{V_1 + C_t - V_0}{V_0 - \frac{365 - t}{365}C_t} = \frac{10}{100 - \frac{335}{365}50} = 18.48\%.$$

If several cash flows take place, each is weighted according to the portion of the period for which the funds have been left in the portfolio segment.

This linear method of calculating a rate of return is questionable. Financiers are used to calculating the rate of return on an investment with multiple cash flows using discounting. The internal rate of return (IRR) is the discount rate that equals the start-of-period value to the sum of the discounted cash flows including the end-of-period value. In our example, the internal rate of return is the value of r in the following equation:

$$V_0 = \frac{C_t}{(1-r)^{t/365}} + \frac{V_1}{(1+r)}.$$

In this example, the internal rate of return is equal to 18.90%. However, the calculation of an IRR is a cumbersome task; the MWR is generally accepted as a measure of the rate of return on a portfolio.

By contrast, the time weighted rate of return (TWR) is the performance per dollar invested and is calculated independently of the cash flows to or from the portfolio segment. In other words, it measures the performance that would have been realized had the same capital been under management over the period. This method is necessary for comparing performance among managers. The TWR is obtained by calculating the rate of return between each cash flow and chain linking those rates over the total period under study. As mentioned above, the rate of return over a period without cash flows suffers no controversy, and the TWR simply compounds the rates of return per unit of base currency.

The calculation of a TWR requires the valuation of a portfolio segment each time a cash flow takes place.

The calculation requires knowledge of the value of the portfolio segment, V_t, just before a cash flow takes place. The rate of return for the first subperiod is given by r_t:

$$1 + r_t = \frac{V_t}{V_0}.$$

The rate of return for the second subperiod is given by r_{t+1}:

$$1 + r_{t+1} = \frac{V_1}{V_t - C_t}.$$

The total time-weighted rate of return, r, is given by

$$(1 + r) = (1 + r_t)(1 + r_{t+1}) = \left(\frac{V_t}{V_0}\right)\left(\frac{V_1}{V_t - C_t}\right).$$

In the example, the portfolio was worth 95 at the time cash was withdrawn, so the TWR is equal to 26.66% as shown below:

$$1 + r_t = \frac{95}{100} = 0.95\% \qquad r_t = -5.00\%,$$

$$1 + r_{t+1} = \frac{60}{45} = 1.33\% \qquad r_{t+1} = 33.33\%, \text{ and}$$

$$1 + r = 1.27 \qquad\qquad r = 26.66\%.$$

Clearly, the various methods of calculating a rate of return yield very different results: from 13.33% to 26.66%. However, everyone agrees that the TWR is the method to use to measure and compare the performance of money managers.

Application to IPA In the international context, the problems associated with using quarterly summary figures are compounded by the multi-currency and multi-market nature of performance measurement. All IPA services currently base their analyses on monthly or quarterly money-weighted rates of return for both the entire portfolio and each national component. These figures are usually calculated either by dividing the capital gain on a portfolio component net of cash flows by the average investment, or by computing a discounted rate of return. When monthly MWRs are used, they are chain linked into quarterly returns to provide a time-weighted average. This crude substitute for a genuine quarterly TWR is a necessary evil in the absence of precise daily transaction data. Unfortunately, the approximation introduces serious potential biases, especially if one is interested in the performance of the manager in specific markets. A short hypothetical example should illustrate this point.

Let us consider a small $1 million fund that is restricted to a 10% investment limitation in Japan. The trustee wants to evaluate the skill of the

EXHIBIT 12.8
TWR and MWR of a Hypothetical Japanese Portfolio

	Day			TWR *(percent)*	MWR *(percent)*
	1	*15*	*30*		
Index	100	130	91	−9	−9
Portfolio	100	130			
		100	70	−9	0

manager in this market. Assuming no currency problem (i.e., assuming a fixed ¥/$ rate), we will consider the following scenario.

The manager invests $100,000 in the Japanese stock index, thereby tracking it exactly. After two weeks, the index rises from 100 to 130, and the manager transfers $30,000 to a falling market (such as the UK market) to keep within the 10% limitation on Japanese investment. Over the next two weeks, the Japanese index loses 30% of its value (falling to 91), so that by the end of the month the Japanese portfolio is down to $70,000, and the TWR on that subportfolio is −9%: that is, the performance of the Japanese index, which was perfectly tracked and fell from 100 to 91. The money-weighted rate of return computed by the IPA service will be 0% (a net profit equal to 0), wrongly implying that the manager outperformed the Japanese market and has great skills in Japanese stock selection. In fact, he precisely tracked the Japanese stock index and no more.

The calculations for the portfolio TWR and MWR as shown in Exhibit 12.8 are as follows:

$$1 + \text{TWR} = \frac{130}{100} \times \frac{70}{100} = 0.91 \qquad \text{TWR} = -9\% \text{ and}$$

$$\text{MWR} = \frac{70 + 30 - 100}{100 - \frac{1}{2}(30)} = 0.$$

This 9% difference will not average out in the chain-linked quarterly rate of return.

Although the MWR is useful for measuring a fund's total return, it does not accurately measure its performance relative to a preselected index. In the domestic context serious distortions can be avoided by valuing a portfolio in total every time a large cash flow occurs. In a detailed international analysis of the performance of each national segment of an account, shifting funds between markets creates the same cash flow problem. Since these internal cash flows are frequent, the total portfolio should be valued frequently. The larger the cash flows relative to the average investment in a given market, the larger the potential bias. Thus, statistical errors can obscure real overperformance or underperformance in a national market, especially in small markets. Since international funds are often diversified over ten or more different bond and stock markets, this statistical error will affect the performance measurement of any reasonably active manager. Moreover, there is no reason to believe that these measurement errors will average out over several months, especially in recently created funds that are still receiving injections of cash (as are many international pension funds). The only way to remedy this bias is to use precise daily data to compute the TWR. But accounting for portfolio transactions on a daily basis is no easy task when there are so many currencies, types of investments (stocks, bonds, cash, precious metals, forward and future contracts, options, etc.), and differences in national trading procedures to reconcile.

Using monthly or quarterly returns to compute operational risk measures is not realistic, either. At least four years of quarterly data are required to obtain significant estimates of a fund's volatility; and this assumes stationary currency and market returns over that period, as well as a constant risk objective on the part of the manager. These assumptions are risky (especially for currencies) in light of the marked instability that many financial markets have displayed over time. Furthermore, averages over four years do not help the manager to evaluate and monitor his or her current risk exposure. Also, as with any performance measurement system that attempts to condense a vast amount of information into a few summary numbers, certain technical problems arise, for instance, in separating currency gains from local currency returns (the two compound each other). Again, the use of daily transaction data allow one to obtain up-to-date risk estimates.

The importance of exact computations cannot be overstressed, even to nonmathematicians. Astute stock selection is supposed to be the most significant contribution made by a manager. This is computed as a residual, subtracting the currency and market effect from the overall performance of the subportfolio. Unfortunately, this residual is also the repository for a variety of errors arising from poor data, incorrect calculations and approximations, and transaction and management fees.[11]

A conceptual problem lies in choosing a standard for comparison. Performance must be measured relative to some norm. If the objective set by the trustee is to surpass the well-known Morgan Stanley Capital International world or EAFE stock index, or to invest solely in Japan, then the standard for comparison is obvious. But what if the objectives are several, or the fund comprises a variety of instruments, including bonds, time deposits, and gold? There is no such thing as a truly global index, nor is it clear what the proper weightings would be for such an index. Moreover, what if the objective is to create a portfolio having a minimum (or even a negative) correlation to U.S. assets or inflation? This objective might be chosen in order to maximize the diversification benefits of a foreign portfolio to the total fund. To what standard should we measure a fund's performance in that instance? The answer, once again, is unclear.

A method often used by outside services is to compare performance to that of a universe of funds. The only drawback to this technique is that, to date, there are still only a few internationally invested pension funds and the guidelines imposed by their trustees are often quite different.

Designing an IPA System

A portfolio is broken down into various segments according to type of asset (e.g., stocks, bonds, cash, convertible bonds, gold) and currency. Each homogeneous segment (say Japanese stocks) is valued separately in its local currency. Thus Japanese stocks are valued in yen, and German bonds in deutsche marks.

A mathematical model for measuring return The basic unit of measurement is the rate of return on each segment before any cash movement between segments.[12] If we call P_j^t the value of one segment, j, in local currency, the rate of return in local currency for period t is given by

$$r_j = \frac{P_j^t - P_j^{t-1} + D_j^t}{P_j^{t-1}} = \frac{P_j^t - P_j^{t-1}}{P_j^{t-1}} + \frac{D_j^t}{P_j^{t-1}} = p_j + d_j \qquad (12.1)$$

where

$\quad D_j^t \quad$ is the amount of dividends paid during the period (or accrued interest plus income received),

$\quad p_j \quad$ is the capital gain (price appreciation) in percent, and

$\quad d_j \quad$ is the yield.

In most countries, as well as on the Eurobond market, accrued interest, A^t, is computed and quoted separately from the price of a bond, P^t. An investor must pay both the price and accrued interest to the seller. Therefore, the total value of the bond is $V^t = P^t + A^t$. A notable exception is the long-term British gilt (over five years), which is quoted flat, that is, with a market price that includes the coupon.

The rate of return on the bond segment is given by

$$r_j = \frac{V^t - V^{t-1} + D^t}{V^{t-1}} = \frac{P^t - P^{t-1}}{P^{t-1} + A^{t-1}} + \frac{A^t - A^{t-1} + D^t}{P^{t-1} + A^{t-1}} = p_j + d_j. \qquad (12.2)$$

Note that accrued interest should be taken into account for nonnegotiable interest-bearing instruments (e.g., Euro-dollar deposits) but not for securities that are negotiated on a flat or discounted basis (e.g., British gilts, treasury bills, common stocks, etc.).

Over a longer period, these unit rates of return can be chain linked to get a time-weighted rate of return for each segment. This return in local currency is

EXHIBIT 12.9
Geographical Breakdown and Return Statistics on Equity and Gold Investments

Portfolio Composition				Total return in local currency	Total return on equity index
July, 8 1982	*Average over period*	*September 30, 1982*	*Market*		
11.53	8.62	5.62	West Germany	6.37	5.58
1.36	1.38	1.50	Canada	13.53	17.39
20.85	19.87	16.73	United States	18.00	11.32
1.37	1.01	0.90	United Kindom	2.07	11.05
3.40	3.49	3.52	Japan	13.44	0.72
2.75	2.73	2.76	Netherlands	9.52	1.27
7.52	3.98	7.16	Other Countries	—	—
51.22	58.92	61.81	Gold and Gold-Related	26.05	23.61

then compared to the return, I_j, on the appropriate market index as shown in Exhibit 12.9.[13] This allows us to identify superior performance on each national stock market. A similar table exists for bonds and cash investments.

The base-currency rate of return is easily derived by translating all prices into the base currency o at exchange rate S_j:

$$r_{jo} = \frac{P_j^t S_j^t + D_j^t S_j^t - P_j^{t-1} S_j^{t-1}}{P_j^{t-1} S_j^{t-1}}.$$ (12.3)

After some algebraic reshuffling this may be written as

$$r_{jo} = p_j + d_j + s_j(1 + p_j + d_j) \qquad \text{or}$$

$$r_{jo} = p_j + d_j + c_j \qquad (12.4)$$

$$\left(\begin{array}{l} \text{Total return} \\ \text{in base-currency} = \end{array} \begin{array}{l} \text{Capital} \\ \text{gain} \\ \text{component} \end{array} + \begin{array}{l} \text{Yield} \\ \text{component} \end{array} + \begin{array}{l} \text{Currency} \\ \text{component} \end{array} \right)$$

where c_j denotes the influence of exchange rate fluctuations on the estimated return in the base currency. Note that the exchange rate component, c_j, is equal to zero if the exchange rate, S_j, does not move, but differs from s_j because of the cross terms.

The compounding of currency and market movements on a foreign security is illustrated in Exhibit 12.10. The value of a foreign investment is represented as a rectangle, where the vertical axis represents the exchange rate and the horizontal axis represents the value of the investment in local currency. As an

EXHIBIT 12.10
Market and Currency Gains

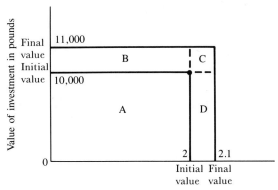

illustration, consider a U.S. investor holding £10,000 of British assets with an exchange rate of $/£ = 2. The dollar value of the assets is represented by area A, or $20,000. Later, the British assets have gone up by 10% to £11,000, and the pound has appreciated by 5% to $/£ = 2.10. The total dollar value is now $23,100, or a gain of 15.5%. The dollar gain, if the currency had not moved is represented by the area B (10% of initial value). Because of the currency movement, this gain is transformed to a total gain of 15.5% equal to the sum of areas B, C, and D. Area C plus D is the exchange rate component to the total return. Note that it can be seen as a pure exchange rate movement (area D) and a cross-currency market term (area C).

Performance analysis Over period t, the total return on account r is computed in the base currency as follows:

$$r = \sum_j w_j r_{jo} = \sum_j w_j (p_j + d_j + c_j) \qquad (12.5)$$

where w_j represents the percentage of segment j in the total portfolio at the start of the period. The various sources of return may be regrouped into three components:

$$r = \sum_j w_j p_j + \sum_j w_j d_j + \sum_j w_j c_j \qquad (12.6)$$

$$\left(\begin{array}{ccc} \text{Capital} & \text{Yield} & \text{Currency} \\ \text{gain} & + \text{ component} & + \text{ component} \\ \text{components} \end{array} \right)$$

As an illustration, the last column of Exhibit 12.11 breaks down the total return of an account (which is 12.95% in Swiss francs) into capital gains in the local currency (11.33%), yield (0.67%) and exchange rate gains (0.95%). The

EXHIBIT 12.11
Performance Analysis

			Returns (percent)
Total return			12.95
Capital gains (losses)			11.33
Fixed income		0.84	
Equity and gold		10.49	
Market return	9.24		
Individual stocks selection	1.25		
Currency movements			0.95
Fixed income		0.23	
Equity and gold		0.72	
Yield			0.67
Fixed income		0.41	
Equity and gold		0.27	

middle column breaks these numbers down further into the contribution of fixed and nonfixed income securities.

The relative performance of a manager may be measured by making two comparisons. First, a manager's security selection ability is determined by isolating the local market return of his or her account. Let's call I_j the return, in local currency, of the market index corresponding to segment j (e.g., the Tokyo Stock Exchange index). The rate of return on segment j (Japanese stocks) may be broken down into the following components:

$$r_{jo} = I_j + \left(p_j - I_j \right) + d_j + c_j \tag{12.7}$$

the total portfolio return may be written as

$$r = \sum w_j I_j + \sum w_j \left(p_j - I_j \right) + \sum w_j d_j + \sum w_j c_j \tag{12.8}$$

$$\left(\begin{array}{cccc} \text{Market} & \text{Security} & & \\ \text{return} + & \text{selection} + & \text{Yield} + & \text{Currency} \\ \text{component} & \text{contribution} & \text{component} & \text{component} \end{array} \right).$$

The first term on the right-hand side measures the performance the manager would have achieved had he or she invested in a local market index instead of individual securities. This contribution is calculated net of currency movements, which are picked up by the last term in the formula. The second term measures the contribution made by the manager's individual security selection. To illustrate this type of analysis, Exhibit 12.11 shows a breakdown of the performance of an equity investment. The 10.49% capital gain in equity breaks down into a 9.24% market index return and a 1.25% individual stock selection contribution. For this particular portfolio, the impact of exchange rates on total return (which was 12.95% for the quarter) was quite weak (only 0.95%). Most of the return, in fact, is explained by capital gains in the local markets (11.33%). In terms of security selection, the manager did well overall, since the portfolio outperformed some markets substantially (1.25% on average). (More detailed results for each market are shown in Exhibit 12.9.)

Relative performance The final step is to study the performance of the portfolio relative to that of a standard. This comparison is usually made with respect to the return I^* on an international index such as the Morgan Stanley Capital International EAFE or world index. The objective is to assess the portfolio manager's ability as measured by the difference in return, $r - I^*$.

To do this, additional notations are required. Let's call I_{jo} the return on market index j, translated into base currency o. We have

$$I_{jo} = I_j + E_j$$

where E_j is the currency component of the index return in base currency, i.e., $E_j = s_j(1 + I_j)$. Let's call w_j^* the weight of market j in the international index chosen as a standard. In base currency, the return on this international index equals

$$I^* = \sum w_j^* I_{jo}.$$

Eq. (12.8) may be rewritten and transformed into Eq. (12.9) by simultaneously adding and subtracting $\sum w_j^* I_{jo}$:

$$r = \sum w_j^* I_{jo} + \sum (w_j - w_j^*) I_j + \sum (w_j c_j - w_j^* E_j) + \sum w_j d_j + \sum w_j (p_j - I_j)$$

(12.9)

$$\begin{pmatrix} \text{International} & & \text{Market} & & \text{Currency} & & \text{Yield} & & \text{Security} \\ \text{index} & + & \text{allocation} & + & \text{allocation} & + \text{component} + & \text{selection} \\ \text{return, } I^* & & \text{contribution} & & \text{contribution} & & & & \text{contribution} \end{pmatrix}$$

This breakdown allows us to estimate the contribution to total performance of any deviation from the standard asset allocation $w_j - w_j^*$.

The word *contribution* in this context indicates performance relative to a selected index, while the word *component* refers to a breakdown of the portfolio's total return. Eq. (12.9) states that the relative performance of a manager, $r - I^*$, is the result of the two factors (after allowing for the yield on the portfolio) described below.

1. An asset allocation different from that of the index. This factor is a source of positive performance for the manager who overweights the best-performing markets ($w_j > w_j^*$) and underweights the poorest-performing markets. This factor can be further broken down into market and currency contributions.[14] So it is possible for a manager to have chosen his or her markets very effectively (resulting in a positive market allocation

contribution) but be penalized by adverse currency movements (resulting in a negative currency allocation contribution).

2. Superior security selection.

This breakdown of relative performance is the simplest of many possibilities. IPA services use a variety of similar approaches and often employ graphics in presenting their results.

Asset allocation varies over time so that, over a given performance period, there is a contribution made by timing (the variation in weights w_j). Moreover, the contribution made by market timing can be further broken down and measured for each market (e.g., British equity) by simply adjusting the risk level (beta) of each segment.

Finally, the manager's performance can be compared to that of a large universe of funds with similar objectives. As we already discussed, this is not an easy task because the guidelines imposed on international managers are diverse. Portfolio performance should therefore be measured both relative to the median return on a universal fund and relative to a complete distribution of similar funds. In addition, each return component or performance contribution should be compared to that of competing managers. Graphic displays of performance and its various components relative to a large universe of funds are provided by IPA services such as Frank Russell International, Intersec, and Wood McKenzie. An example of such a display is given in Exhibit 12.12.

A final word of caution is in order. The simple mathematical formulas shown above break down when there are movements between portfolio segments during a period. Adjusting for these cash movements (i.e., changes in w_j) is not easy. As a matter of fact, a multi-period extension of Eq. (12.8) or Eq. (12.9) with changing weights would prevent us from deriving simple breakdowns of performance such that each component could easily be identified. Only approximations can be used. Four quarterly performance breakdowns do not add up or compound easily into a yearly performance breakdown, even when time-weighted returns are used.

Risk The final step in performance analysis is to analyze the risk borne by the manager. The total risk of an account is measured by the standard deviation of its rate of return. As we mentioned previously, return should be measured frequently (at least monthly) to get a reliable estimate of the standard deviation. Quarterly valuation does not give an up-to-date risk estimate in a rapidly changing environment, since at least four years of data (sixteen quarters) are required for a decent risk measure. Over several years, the risk estimate is likely to be very unstable.

Exhibit 12.13 compares risk return on the portfolio in our previous example with that of several preselected indexes, where risk estimates (standard deviation) are computed from daily returns. To allow for meaningful risk and return comparisons, all returns and risk estimates are presented on a monthly basis.

EXHIBIT 12.12
Analysis of Contribution of Performance: Non–North American Equity Return in U.S. dollars
Periods ending September 1983

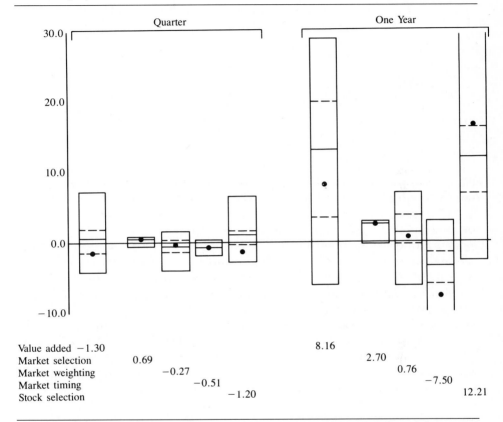

	Quarter	One Year
Value added	−1.30	8.16
Market selection	0.69	2.70
Market weighting	−0.27	0.76
Market timing	−0.51	−7.50
Stock selection	−1.20	12.21

Source: Inersec Research Corporation. Stamford, CT., London, Tokyo. Reprinted with permission.

We see that this portfolio had a higher return than the EAFE index (4.46% per month versus 1.05%), but had more risk (4.50% per month versus 3.02%). It also outperformed the U.S. Standard and Poor's and the Swiss Bank Corporation Swiss stock indexes. However, its exposure to exchange risk was quite large (2.30% per month). IPA services display risk-return performance comparisons for the universe of managers they evaluate. An example for world equity portfolios is reproduced in Exhibit 12.14.

The total risk of a portfolio is not the only relevant measure of risk. Investors who are interested primarily in diversification typically spread their assets among several funds. Pension funds, for example, invest abroad mainly to diversify their domestic holdings. Calculating the correlation of a portfolio to

EXHIBIT 12.13
Risk Analysis

Risk-return statistics in Swiss francs over the period

	Total return (percent per month)	Risk (percent per month)	Correlation with account
Account	4.46	4.50[a]	1
S + P 500 Index	4.24	6.50	0.43
EAFE Index	1.05	3.02	0.68
SBC Switzerland Index	0.48	5.61	0.36

SBC = Swiss Bank Corporation.
[a] Risk in Local Currency: 4.08; exchange risk: 2.30.

other preselected indexes reveals whether or not the benefits of diversification have been achieved. A low correlation means that there are great diversification benefits, while a correlation close to one indicates that the portfolio closely followed the performance of the index, even over the short run. Some services compute betas rather than correlation coefficients to derive the same type of information. (A beta coefficient is equal to the correlation coefficient times the ratio of the standard deviation of the portfolio over that of the market index.)

Risk estimates are often highly unstable over time because they are derived from a mixture of many types of assets and sources of uncertainty. That is why an analysis of both past and present risk exposures is necessary. Currency markets are particularly prone to periods of calm followed by periods of extreme volatility. Portfolios that are low risk during one period can experience a larger standard deviation, or beta, the next period. In fact, funds invested solely in foreign currency short-term deposits often behave this way.

Risk-adjusted performance In a domestic setting, performance measurement services often attempt to rank managers on their risk-adjusted performance. It seems attractive to derive a single number taking into account both performance and risk. This is often done by calculating a *reward* (mean excess return over the risk-free rate) *to variability* (standard deviation of return). This measure, introduced by Sharpe,[15] is both simple and intuitive. However, it can only be used for the investor's global portfolio. A portfolio whose objective is to be invested in foreign assets to diversify risk of the domestic assets cannot be evaluated separately from the total portfolio. The standard deviation of the foreign portfolio will get partly diversified away in the global portfolio, so it is not a relevant measure of the total risk of the foreign portfolio. Other methods take the ratio of mean excess return to the market risk (β). These are often called the Treynor, or Jensen, measures.[16] The application of these methods poses serious problems, as outlined by Roll,[17] in a domestic context. The

EXHIBIT 12.14

Risk–Return Performance Comparisons

Thirty-six world equity portfolios over four years, January 1, 1982 to December 31, 1985

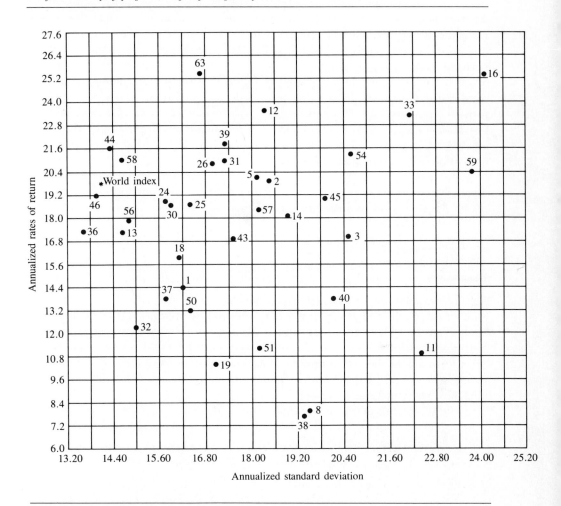

Source: Frank Russell Co. Reprinted with permission.

problems are even worse in an international context, where we lack an asset pricing theory that precisely defines what is meant by market risk. For instance, why should an investor care about the beta relative to his or her home market portfolio?

If risk is a complex, multi-dimensional notion, no single reward to risk ratio can be used and we are left with a more qualitative discussion of the risk-return trade-off.

In-house performance measurement is useful in determining the strengths and weaknesses of an organization. This is even more important in an international than in a domestic setting because of the number of factors influencing return and risk. An IPA system can also be used by a client to select managers. However, it is extremely difficult to separate performance due to luck from that due to expertise. Past performance is often not a good indicator of future performance, whereas switching from one manager to the next is a costly process. For example, the Japanese portfolios of most foreign managers outperformed the Japanese stock index by a wide margin in the early 1980s. They focused on industrial companies, which outperformed the overall index, and held few bank stocks. But these same portfolios drastically underperformed the index in 1984 when bank stocks went up by more than 100%, while stock prices in industrial sectors only had a modest rise.

One must be careful with respect to the statistical significance of performance comparisons to prevent inefficient churning of the portfolio and management changes based on insignificant information.

PRACTICAL CONSIDERATIONS

Databases

An international money manager must have access to financial information from all over the world. Fortunately, foreign brokers now provide up-to-date financial analysis on most foreign stocks traded globally. American, Japanese, and some European brokers even provide forecasted earnings and investment advice directly to customers on computer time-sharing systems. To be sure, language differences are still a problem, even though many investment research houses publish reports in English as well as their native languages.

Market prices are also available worldwide on computerized information systems. Three types of international information systems are available:

1. Real-time news systems, such as Telerate and Reuters, provide real-time news and prices on selected markets and securities.

2. Price systems, such as Exshare and Telekurs, provide exhaustive price coverage of all capital and money markets in the world. These services focus on prices rather than analysis, although some (like Quotron) provide both services. They also provide information on capital adjustments, dividends, and exdates.

3. Portfolio management packages provide both price quotations and databases to assist financial research. These services, such as IDC and Datastream, feature easy-to-use software that can be run on desk-top computers.

Basically, a money manager can get real-time information from anywhere in the world as long as he or she can bear the heavy cost of subscribing to one or more of these international databases.

Accounting

An international portfolio accounting system is by definition complex. To begin with, it must incorporate a multi-currency system that both adjusts for the differences between national markets and allows any currency to serve as a reference. Transactions should be accounted for on the trade date, not on the settlement date. In addition, adjustments should be made for the trading procedures of different countries, for example, the account period on the U.K. stock market or the règlement mensuel on the French stock market (see Chapter 4). The system should also be able to accurately account for accrued interest on bonds. As shown in Chapter 6, countries have different methods for calculating interest. Another problem is foreign withholding tax, which should be reclaimed either in full or in part by the investor.

The databases mentioned above can and should be used for both revaluing the portfolio daily and for helping to generate a flow of fund reports on each currency in the account.

Custody

Only a few institutions currently provide international securities custody.[18] The Securities and Exchange Commission closely regulates custodians used by U.S. investors. A truly international custodial service requires subcustodians in each home market, as well as Euroclear or Cedel for the Eurobond market. Several countries have already developed central clearing and deposit systems for their domestic stocks and bonds, and these should be used whenever possible. Two examples of these systems are SICOVAM in France and SIGA in Switzerland. There are plans to develop an international equity custodial service similar to that of the Eurobond market.

In spite of the services and systems that are currently available, numerous practical problems arise in international custody. Accurate information from across the world should be gathered rapidly. Automated trade notification is necessary. Computer-to-computer links with the subcustodians, clearing services, and the manager should be set up. Income collection should be swift and correctly reported. Tax recovery should be automated and carefully checked with each government. Finally, a cash management system in many currencies should be implemented.

SUMMARY

1. Major choices in terms of investment philosophy and strategy have to be made by an organization structuring its international investment process. These choices are based on a view of the world and, more importantly, the behavior of security prices. A major question is how active an international strategy should be. In an active strategy a manager can decide on (1) international asset allocation by type of asset and currency, (2) security selection, and (3) market timing. An active manager can also selectively hedge certain types of risks, such as currency risk. Another important question is whether the major emphasis should be on market analysis (top-down approach) or on security analysis (bottom-up approach). These and other choices dictate how the organization should be structured.

2. Structuring and quantifying the investment process is a difficult task because of the large number of parameters involved. The major decision is asset allocation. In the domestic context, asset allocation requires the choice between cash, bonds, common stocks, and, possibly, other assets. In the international context, these choices are multiplied by the number of countries (i.e., currencies). A disciplined and efficient approach calls for a quantified integrated system. The objective is to make optimal use of all expertise and control risk.

3. International performance analysis is important to understanding how a performance has been achieved. A good performance analysis relies on the availability of data and the problems are magnified in the international context. A major problem is that cash flows between the various portfolio segments are frequent and calculation of the performance of each segment (e.g., Japanese equity) requires the valuation of segments on each cash flow date. Ideally, an international performance measurement system should be linked to the daily accounting system.

4. In active management, a superior performance can result from any of the major-investment decisions: asset allocation (market and currency choices), market timing, security selection on each market. The total performance should therefore be broken down and attributed to the various management decisions.

5. Risk reduction is an important motivation for international diversification and the realized performance should be evaluated in light of the risk assumed. In terms of risk, the contribution of the foreign portfolio to the total risk of the global portfolio should be considered. In the absence of a clear model of international risk pricing, no simple measure of risk-adjusted performance can be used.

QUESTIONS AND PROBLEMS

1. An American pension fund wants to invest $1 million in foreign equity. Its board of trustees hesitates between investing in a commingled index fund tracking the EAFE index and giving the money to an active manager. The board learns that this active manager turns the portfolios over about twice a year. Given the small size of the account, the transaction costs are likely to be at the highest point of the range reported in Chapter 4. The active manager charges 0.75% in annual management fee, and the indexer charges 0.25%. By how much should the active manager outperform the index to cover the extra costs in the form of fees and transaction costs on the annual turnover?

2. Is the total risk (standard deviation) of a foreign portfolio the relevant measure of risk?

As an illustration, consider a U.S. pension fund with the following performance:

	Percentage total portfolio (percent)	Total dollar return (percent)	Standard deviation of return (percent)	Correlation with U.S. stock index
U.S. Equity	90	10	15	0.99
Foreign Equity	10	11	20	−0.10

Is the risk-return performance of the foreign portfolio attractive?

3. Mr. Smith is an investor of foreign nationality who has an account with a small Luxembourg bank. He does not pay taxes on his account. He gave a complete management mandate to the bank and wants to judge the performance of the manager. He is using the U.S. dollar as his reference currency.

1. He is looking at the two most-recent valuation monthly reports which are given in Exhibit 12.15 and wonders how to compute the performance. He reads in the financial press that the Morgan Stanley Capital International world index has risen by 2% this month (in U.S. dollars). Basically, he would like to answer the following questions:

□ What is the total return on his portfolio?

□ What are the sources of this return, i.e., how much is caused by capital appreciation, yield, and currency movements?

□ How good is the manager in selecting securities on the various markets?

You must give him precise, quantified information that will help him to answer these questions. (First compute the return for each segment of the portfolio and its components, i.e., price, yield, currency; then combine these returns to answer the last two queries.)

2. Mr. Smith is aware that cash flows as well as movements between the various segments of his portfolio may obscure his analysis. He tries to compute the performance during the next month where the manager has been more active.

He wants to make sure he understands how a valuation report is constructed before doing his analysis (he does not trust his banker). He gets the following information to prepare his own version of the valuation report:

Cash flow. Mr. Smith added $10,000 to his account.

Transactions. The manager sold the 500 Exxon. The total proceeds of the sale, net of commissions, were $20,000. He bought 400 Pernod-Ricard on the Paris Bourse for a total cost of $30,860.

Income received. A semiannual coupon was paid on the EIB bond for a total receipt of $575. Three-hundred fifty-seven dollars were received from AMAX dividends.

Market prices on February 28.

AMAX	24	Yen 0.0047 dollars	
Hitachi	880	French franc 0.105 dollars	
TDK	6000	U.S. stock index	103
Club Mediterannee	850	Japan stock index	97
Pernod-Ricard	720	France stock index	110
Government 6% 92	92	Yen bond index	101
(accrued interest, 1.55%)		World index	104
EIB 8.5% 93	98		
(accrued interest, 0.62%)			

Mr. Smith has no indication of the exact day of the transactions, and it would be too complicated to break down the month into subperiods, anyway. He therefore decides to make the assumption that every transaction or cash flow occurred just before the end of the month. To help him, you should

□ establish a new valuation report,

□ discuss the methodology for adjusting for cash movements, and

□ analyze the performance of the manager.

EXHIBIT 12.15
Account Valuation Report

Explanation of Account Valuation Report

The valuation report is set up following a standard method.

□ The first column gives either the number of securities for common stocks or the nominal invested for fixed income.

□ The second column describes the security and its quotation currency.

□ The third column gives the market price in local currency. For bonds, this is given in percentage of the nominal (par) value.

□ The accrued interest is given in the fourth column as the percentage of the nominal (par) value. Usually a bond with a coupon of, say 8%, will bear an interest of 8/360% per day. This is cumulated in the accrued interest column until the coupon is paid (semiannual, here).

□ The fifth column gives the capital amount in reference currency (here, U.S. dollars). It is the market price (third column) multiplied by the second column values multiplied by the exchange rate.

□ The sixth column gives the amount of accrued interest in reference currency. It is the accrued interest in percentage (column four) multiplied by the second column values multiplied by the exchange rates.

□ The last two columns give subtotals in capital and percentage.

(Continued)

Account Valuation for Mr. Smith, December 31, 1990 *(Continued)*

Description of Security	Number of securities or nominal	Market price (local currency)	Accrued interests (percent)	Capital amount (dollars)	Accrued interests (dollars)	Subtotal (dollars)	Subtotal (percent)
Equity							
United States							
AMAX (dollars)	1,000	24.50		24,500			
Exxon (dollars)	500	37.25		18,625		43,125	29.8
Japan							
Hitachi (yen)	10,000	800		34,320			
TDK (yen)	1,000	6,500		27,885		62,205	43.0
France							
Club Mediterannee (French francs)	200	770		18,326		18,326	12.7
Bonds							
Yen							
Government 6% 92 (yen)	2,000,000	91%	0.52	7,807	45		
EIB 8.5% 93 (yen)	3,000,000	98.5%	3.47	12,677	447	20,976	14.5
Cash							
U.S. Dollars	0			0	0	0	0
Total				144,140	492	144,632	100

Exchange rates:
Yen = 0.00429 dollar
French franc = 0.119 dollar

Market Indexes
U.S. stocks = 100
Japan stocks = 100
France stocks = 100
yen bonds = 100
World index = 100

387

Account Valuation for Mr. Smith, January 30, 1991

Description of security	Number of securities or nominal	Market price (local currency)	Accrued interests (percent)	Capital amount (dollars)	Accrued interests (dollars)	Subtotal (dollars)	Subtotal (percent)
Equity							
United States							
AMAX (dollars)	1,000	23.5		23,500			
Exxon (dollars)	500	38.0		19,000		42,500	28.8
Japan							
Hitachi (yen)	10,000	820		36,900			
TDK (yen)	1,000	6,100		27,450		64,350	43.5
France							
Club Mediterannee (French franc)	200	870		19,140		19,140	12.9
Bonds							
Yen							
Government 6% 92 (yen)	2,000,000	90%	1.04	8,100	94		
EIB 8.5% 93 (yen)	3,000,000	96.9%	4.16	13,081	562	21,837	14.8
Cash							
U.S. Dollars	0			0	0	0	0
Total				147,171	656	147,827	100

Exchange rates:
Yen = 0.0045 dollars
French franc = 0.110 dollar

Market indexes:
U.S. stocks = 102.5
Japan stocks = 98
France stocks = 108
Yen bonds = 99
World index = 102

NOTES

1. See J. McDonald, "The Mochiai Effect: Japanese Corporate Cross-holdings," *Journal of Portfolio Management*, Fall 1989.

2. See P. Jorion, "Asset Allocation with Hedged and Unhedged Foreign Stocks and Bonds," *Journal of Portfolio Management*, Summer 1989.

3. See R. Arnott and R. Henricksson, "A Disciplined Approach to Global Asset Allocation," *Financial Analysts Journal*, March/April 1989.

4. See A. Perold and E. Schulman, "The Free Lunch in Currency Hedging: Implications for Investment Policies and Performance Standards," *Financial Analysts Journal*, May/June 1988.

5. D. Botkin, "Strategy Setting and Expectations," in M. Tapley (ed), *International Portfolio Management*, Euromoney Publications, 1986.

6. See T. Lombard and B. Solnik, "Computing Complexities of Foreign Investment," *Pensions and Investment Age*, October 29, 1984. See also the July 1985 issue of *Institutional Investor*.

7. For a discussion of this point, see Chapter 1 or M. Adler and B. Dumas, "International Portfolio Choice and Corporation Finance: A Synthesis," *Journal of Finance*, June 1983.

8. A good analysis of international performance measurement is presented in C. Nowakowski, "International Performance Measurement: Problems and Solutions," *Columbia Journal of World Business*, May 1982. See also J. Gillies, "Performance Measurement. The Practical Aspects," *Benefits International*, November 1982, and G. Brinson and N. Fachler, "Measuring non-US Equity Portfolio Performance," *Journal of Portfolio Management*, Spring 1985.

9. These methods are discussed in Bank Administration Institute, *Measuring the Investment Performance of Pension Funds*, Parkridge IL, 1968. The problems posed by the application of these methods are well discussed in M. Tapley, "Accounting and Performance Measurement," in *International Portfolio Management*, Euromoney Publications, 1986.

10. Note that a cash addition would be represented here by a negative value of C_t.

11. The data collection problems and the bases created in IPA have been well described in J. MacQueen, "International Measurement," *Quantec*, October 1981.

12. The adjustment for cash movements to and from an account or between segments is not described here. Valuation of the account should be made on the date of each cash movement as mentioned above. Daily calculations ensure that no information is lost.

13. The author is grateful to Lombard Odier for providing this example, where the Swiss franc was the base currency. This example is further detailed in T. Lombard and B. Solnik, "International Performance Measurement," Lombard Odier & Cie, June 1983.

14. Remember that c_j and E_j are close to s_j, the exchange rate variation, so that the currency allocation contribution term is approximately the same as $\Sigma(w_j - w_j^*)s_j$.

15. See W. F. Sharpe, "Mutual Fund Performance," *Journal of Business*, January 1966.

16. See J. Treynor, "How to Rate Management Investment Funds," *Harvard Business Review*, January/February 1965; M. C. Jensen, "The Performance of Mutual Funds in the Period 1945–1964," *Journal of Finance*, May 1968. A good reivew of the various measures of investment performance is given in H. Levy and M. Sarnat, *Portfolio and Investment Selection: Theory and Practice*, Englewood Cliffs, NJ: Prentice Hall, 1984.

17. See R. Roll, "Ambiguity When Performance Is Measured by the Securities Market Line," *Journal of Finance*, September 1978.

18. A description of international custody problems is given in C. G. Grimsley, "Global Custody," in M. Tapley (ed), *International Portfolio Management*, Euromoney Publications, 1986.

19. See P. Jorion, "International Portfolio Diversification with Estimation Risk," *Journal of Business*, July 1985.

BIBLIOGRAPHY

M. Adler and B. Dumas, "International Portfolio Choice and Corporation Finance: A Synthesis," *Journal of Finance*, June 1983.

R. Arnott and R. Henricksson, "A Disciplined Approach to Global Asset Allocation," *Financial Analysts Journal*, March/April 1989.

Bank Administration Institute, *Measuring the Investment Performance of Pension Funds*, Parkridge, IL, 1968.

D. Botkin, "Strategy Setting and Expectations," in M. Tapley (ed), *International Portfolio Management*, Euromoney Publications, 1986.

G. Brinson and N. Fachler, "Measuring non-US Equity Portfolio Performance," *Journal of Portfolio Management*, Spring 1985.

J. Gillies, "Performance Measurement. The Practical Aspects," *Benefits International*, November 1982.

C. G. Grimsley, "Global Custody," in M. Tapley (ed), *International Portfolio Management*, Euromoney Publications, 1986.

M. C. Jensen, "The Performance of Mutual Funds in the Period 1945–1964," *Journal of Finance*, May 1968.

P. Jorion, "Asset Allocation with Hedged and Unhedged Foreign Stocks and Bonds," *Journal of Portfolio Management*, Summer 1989.

H. Levy and M. Sarnat, *Portfolio and Investment Selection: Theory and Practice*, Englewood Cliffs, NJ: Prentice Hall, 1984.

T. Lombard and B. Solnik, "Computing Complexities of Foreign Investment," *Pensions and Investment Age*, October 29, 1984.

T. Lombard and B. Solnik, "International Performance Measurement," Lombard Odier & Cie, June 1983.

J. Mac Queen, "International Measurement," *Quantec*, October 1981.

J. McDonald, "The Mochiai Effect: Japanese Corporate Cross-holdings," *Journal of Portfolio Management*, Fall 1989.

C. Nowakowski, "International Performance Measurement: Problems and Solutions," *Columbia Journal of World Business*, May 1982.

A. Perold and E. Schulman, "The Free Lunch in Currency Hedging: Implications for Investment Policies and Performance Standards," *Financial Analysts Journal*, May/June 1988.

R. Roll, "Ambiguity When Performance Is Measured by the Securities Market Line," *Journal of Finance*, September 1978.

W. F. Sharpe, "Mutual Fund Performance," *Journal of Business*, January 1966.

M. Tapley, "Accounting and Performance Measurement," in *International Portfolio Management*, Euromoney Publications, 1986.

J. Treynor, "How to Rate Management Investment Funds," *Harvard Business Review*, January/February 1965.

Chapter 12: Appendix
Advanced Section on Optimal Asset Allocation

In this appendix we describe the asset allocation optimizer that is derived from mean-variance optimization theory.

NOTATIONS

The asset allocation is presented in a matrix by country (i.e., currency) and asset type as shown in Exhibit 12.6. One cell of this matrix is referred to as an *asset class*. The proportion of the account invested in the asset i of country (currency) j is denoted X_{ij}. For example, 10% (X_{ij}) could be invested in Japanese (j) stocks (i). The various proportions, X_{ij}s add up to 100%. The asset class (e.g., Japanese stocks) is referred to as A_{ij}. Some institutions may use an asset allocation matrix in which small markets are grouped by region. A typical country breakdown could be domestic, North America, Japan, other Far East, Europe.

Futures contracts are implicitly allowed in this matrix. As mentioned in Chapters 1 and 3, a currency futures contract is equivalent to a short-term borrowing-lending swap in two currencies. For example, an American investor wanting to sell sterling forward can simply borrow sterling short term, transfer it into U.S. dollars, and invest it in dollar short-term deposits. Accordingly, selling a currency forward shows up as a negative proportion X_{ij} for the foreign currency cash investment and an offsetting positive proportion for the domestic cash investment. A similar reasoning applies to other futures contracts on stock indexes or bonds.

The base currency used for the account has been chosen and all rates of returns are calculated in this base currency, denoted o.

The forecasted rate of return on an asset class is denoted E_{ij}. This is obtained by compounding the forecasted return in local currency by the expected currency movement. For example, if the Japanese stock market is forecasted to provide a return of 10% in yen (capital gain plus yield), and if the yen is expected to appreciate by 5% relative to the base currency, the U.S. dollar, the total forecasted return for a U.S. investor is:

$$E_{ij} = (1 + 10\%)(1 + 5\%) - 1 = 15.5\%.$$

The return on a bond asset class can be derived from a forecast of changes in market yield by taking into account the average duration of the market. The expected return on the total account is simply written as E.

The covariance between returns on two asset classes A_{ij} and A_{kl} is denoted $\sigma_{ij,kl}$. (The covariance between two assets is equal to the correlation of returns multiplied by the standard deviations of the two assets.) The variance of the total account is simply written as σ^2.

The objective of an optimal asset allocation is to maximize the expected return, E, while minimizing the risk level, σ^2. Operationally, this can be achieved by minimizing the risk level for a given level of expected return.

However, investment constraints are often imposed on the asset allocation. These take numerous forms, but are usually expressed as linear combinations of the investment proportions X_{ij}. The most typical constraints are

- No short sales are allowed on some assets such as stocks and bonds ($X_{ij} \geq 0$).
- A maximum limit is put on asset class, currency, or asset type. A typical constraint could be no more than 10% in French franc assets ($\sum_j X_{ij} \leq \max_j$, where j refers to French francs), or no more than 20% in cash ($\sum_i X_{ij} \leq \max_i$, where i refers to cash investments).
- Currency short selling cannot exceed the amount of currency-exposed assets held in the portfolio.

Mathematically the optimization problem can be written as

$$\min_X \sum_{ijkl} X_{ij} X_{kl} \sigma_{ij,kl}$$

subject to

$$\sum_{ij} X_{ij} E_{ij} = E$$

and linear constraints on X_{ij}.

The optimal asset allocation can be obtained using standard quadratic programming packages.

The estimation of the covariance matrix is an important perequisite. The covariance estimates are somewhat unstable over time, so the statistical procedure used to estimate the covariance matrix makes a difference.[19]

Transaction costs can also be incorporated into the optimizations.

The example presented in the text has been generated by a multi-currency comprehensive package written by the author.

Index